PEDAGOGIES OF GLOBALIZATION

The Rise of the Educational Security State

Sociocultural, Political, and Historical Studies in Education
Joel Spring, Editor

For more information about books in this series, please contact LEA at www.erlbaum.com

PEDAGOGIES OF GLOBALIZATION

The Rise of the Educational Security State

Joel Spring
Queens College
City University of New York

LEA LAWRENCE ERLBAUM ASSOCIATES, PUBLISHERS

2006 Mahwah, New Jersey London

Lawrence Erlbaum Associates, Inc., Publishers
10 Industrial Avenue
Mahwah, New Jersey 07430

Cover design by Tomai Maridou

Library of Congress Cataloging-in-Publication Data

Spring, Joel H.
Pedagogies of Globalization : the rise of the educational security state / Joel Spring.
p. cm. — (Sociocultural, political, and historical studies in education)
Includes bibliographical references and index.
ISBN 0-8058-5556-4 (cloth)
ISBN 0-8058-5557-2 (pbk.)
1. Education and globalization—Cross-cultural studies. 2. Education and state—Cross-cultural studies. I. Title. II. Series.

LC71.S67 2006
338.4'337—dc22   2005053475
                                                          CIP

Printed in the United States of America
10   9   8   7   6   5   4   3   2   1

Contents

6   Wars of Liberation and Formal Schooling: India, Africa,   **152**
    the Middle East, Indonesia, and Korea

7   The Educational Security State: China, Japan,   **190**
    the United States, and the European Union

Preface

In the 21st century national schools systems have similar grades and promotion plans, instructional methods, curriculum organization, and linkages between secondary and higher education. There are local variations but the most striking feature is the sameness of educational systems. How did this happen? How was education globalized? My purpose is to explain the globalization of the common characteristics of national school systems and the consequences for human life and the future improvement of social and economic organizations.

A central thesis of the book is that nations combined economic and educational planning into economic security states. Industrial consumerism is dominant economic paradigm used in the integration of education and economic planning. In chapter 1, I explain the elements of the educational security state and the industrial-consumer paradigm in relationship to classical forms of education such as Confucianism, Islam, and Christianity, and their concerns with creating a just and ethical society. Also, I discuss the role of the "other" in the globalization of educational structures as international military and economic rivalries spark competition between educational systems. By the 19th century, classical forms of education began to fade with the development of the educational security state and its pedagogical rival progressive education. As an example of the conflict between progressive education and educational security state, I discuss the transition in the Soviet Union from the progressive educational practices following the Bolshevik revolution to the eventual Stalinization of Soviet education.

Chapter 2 is devoted to the transition from the Confucian village school to Western forms of education as exemplified by the lives of Ho Chi Minh and Mao Zedong. They were both political and educational revolutionaries whose legacies continue to play an important role in global politics. In chapter 3, I discuss the effect of the cultural and economic rivalry between the Soviet Union and the United States and its impact on schooling in both countries. Chapter 4 focuses on the rise of the educational security state in China, the Soviet Union, and the United States as these countries focus their educational efforts on military and economic development. The evolution of progressive education is explored in chapter 5 as it appeared in revolutionary movements in South America, Cuba, Nicaragua, and El Salvador. Liberation theology, literacy crusades, and the works of Paulo Freire gave a new life to progressive traditions.

The transition from traditional to Westernized forms of Islamic education is explained in chapter 6 against the background of European imperialism, Arab nationalism, and wars of liberation. There remains an uneasy tension between Western educational ideals and Islamic religious values. Also in chapter 6, I discuss, in the context of wars of liberation, socialist education in the Democratic People's Republic of Korea. Chapter 7 analyzes current developments in educational security states, such as China, Japan, the United States, the new Russia and the European Union. And finally, the concluding chapter focuses on the consequences of English as the global language and the global spread of the industrial-consumer paradigm.

The Globalization of Schooling and Pedagogy: The Bolshevik Revolution, John Dewey and Progressive Education, and China

The globalization of common educational practices involves an interplay between classical, industrial-consumer, progressive, and indigenous pedagogies,[1] global and local languages and cultures, and the nation-state and civil society. In this chapter, I introduce the basic concepts used in this book and illustrate them by discussing the Bolshevik Revolution and progressive education and John Dewey's impact on China.

As an example of the interplay of global ideas, American antiwar students marched in the 1960s and 1970s carrying Mao Zedong's *Little Red Book* and chanted,

> Ho! Ho! Ho Chi Minh!
>
> The NLF [National Liberation Front] is goin' to win!

Mao Zedong and Ho Chi Minh, both born in the 1890s, abandoned classical Confucian education to embrace the modernizing effects of Western education in order to, ironically, resist Western imperialism. Both became revolutionary leaders. Mao brought the Chinese Communist Party to power in 1949, and Ho, after many years of armed conflict with France and the United States, ensured the triumph of communism in Vietnam. In demands for more progressive forms of education, European and American students in the 1960s and 1970s invoked the names of these two revolutionary leaders while resisting the power of the nation-state and seeking alternatives to an industrial-consumer society.

This is just one illustration of how ideas about pedagogy and school organization move and change in the global flow of ideas.[2] Historically, this cross-fertilization of ideas about education was the result of Islamic and Christian proselytizers, Western and Japanese colonialists, and, in the 20th century, the ideologists of the competing forces of the Cold War. By the early 20th century, Japan, England, France, Spain, Holland, Portugal, Russia, and the United States had transplanted or influenced the development of schools and pedagogy in the Americas, Africa, India, Indonesia, the territories of the Russian Empire extending to the Pacific Ocean, Vietnam, Malaysia, treaty ports in China, Australia, New Zealand, and Pacific islands. Islamic madrasas and Qur'anic schools had spread from the Arab world through the Indian Subcontinent, Malaysia, Indonesia, the Philippines, eastern and southern Russian territories, the Ottoman Empire, and Sub-Saharan Africa. At the beginning of the 21st century, the European Union (EU) was at the most advanced stage of integrating schooling into the needs of an industrial-consumer economy as nongovernment organizations advocated progressive pedagogies to protect human rights and the environment.

EDUCATIONAL TRADITIONS

Historically, the great educational traditions focused on the ethical relations of humans and the problem of creating a just society. Scholars of Confucianism, Hinduism, Islam, Christianity, and Buddhism interpreted and debated sacred texts and scholarly teachings. These traditional educational forms changed swiftly with industrialism and the development of military technology. Nations around the world began to organize national systems of education to supply workers for factories and to promote scientific and mathematical learning for industrial and military development. The study of the sacred and classical text gave way to the study of how to best fit humans into the machinery of an industrial-consumer society and how to ensure continued economic development. Testing skills for the modern economy replaced the testing of knowledge on how to live the good or moral life. Assessment or exam-driven instruction was imposed in schools to ensure that the student did not escape a life of serving a global economy.

With the advent of industrial-consumer societies, nation-states used ethical instruction in public schools as a means of controlling the population. In the West, Christian morality became the basis for secular moral instruction in public schools. In Islamic countries, the teachings of Mohammed became secularized in public schools to provide social control. In Japan, the pioneer of Eastern industrialism and militarism, public education incorporated traditional values into moral education courses to ensure that Western industrialism was balanced by Eastern values. Across the globe, the values in sacred and classical texts were incorporated into the school curriculum and plans for forming student behavior to guarantee obedient industrial workers and soldiers.

There arose concerns about the protection of local languages and cultures as the industrial-consumer model of education moved swiftly around the world. Would there be a single global language of commerce? Could local languages be maintained? Did the industrial-consumer model contain cultural values that would supplant local cultures? What about indigenous groups that wanted to maintain traditional cultures? Would they succumb to the power of global economic development?

Different forms of progressive education became the major dissenting traditions to schooling that served industry and the nation state. The search for the best way to organize human society reappeared in the scientific ethics of educational progressivism. Rejecting the idea that education should simply prepare people to fit into an industrial-consumer society, educational progressivism in the late 19th and 20th centuries advocated empowering people to improve society by exploring and experimenting with new ways of living, and creating new economic and political systems. In various forms, progressive education gained global attention from the United States to China.

In the late 20th and 21st centuries, progressive education expanded its reach as differing cultural groups resisted the homogenizing tendencies of industrialism. In South America, Paulo Freire advocated the use of dialogical methods to empower people to free themselves from the ideological control of the nation-state and industrialism and to gain control of their own lives. Faced with the expansion of multinational corporations and the deplorable actions of some nation-states, a global civil society developed, with the largest groups being nongovernment organizations advocating human rights and environmental protection. In the 21st century progressive education found a home in this civil society.

THE EDUCATIONAL SECURITY STATE
AND THE INDUSTRIAL-CONSUMER PARADIGM

In an educational security state, the government attempts to mold and control the learning of children and youth for economic and military purposes, and the government incorporates educational planning into national economic and military planning. The educational security state places science and math along with the teaching of economic and religious ideologies at the center of the school curriculum because of their importance for industrialization, militarization, national patriotism, and cultural cohesion.

Schools in the Soviet Union emphasized science and technology as part of their effort to industrialize and to win the Cold War. In the 1950s, political and educational leaders in the United States wanted schools to graduate more students in science, engineering, and mathematics in order to keep up with the Soviet Union. In Japan, China, and North Korea, education in science and engineering was considered necessary for industrial growth and to stop imperialism.

The educational security state supports a consumer model of industrialism. The goal of the an industrial-consumer society is to constantly produce more products for consumption and measure economic improvement by economic growth of products and services. There exists a vast literature on the historical development of the industrial-consumer paradigm with a general agreement that consumerism was a unique development in industrial organization.[3] This industrial model was developed in the United States in the late 19th century when some economists and public leaders feared that industrialism would result in greater leisure time for the worker. Fearing that more leisure time would corrupt workers, these scholars and public officials argued that the goal of industrialism should be the constant production and consumption of new products promoted by the psychological techniques of the new advertising profession. Rather than reducing work time, new technologies would seduce workers into working harder for the consumption of new products. It was this industrial-consumer model that was integrated into the educational security state.[4]

In the industrial-consumer paradigm, personal fulfillment is achieved through the purchase of products. Of course, actual satisfaction cannot take place because consumers might want to stop buying new products. Planned obsolescence, particularly by changing designs of products and adding new features as exemplified by automobiles, would continue to spur people to work harder to buy new products. Brand names and brand loyalty became an important aspect of consumer desires and often served to define social status and create new personal images. A recent example is the planned marketing of high-priced sport cars and sedans to well-paid, middle-aged U.S. women. In an article with the descriptive title "What Women Want: More Horses" about two professional women in their 50s who decide one day to buy new Mercedes—one a sports car and the other, a sedan—*New York Times* reporter Alex Williams comments, "For each their car was a statement as much as a means of transportation. For too many years, they said, they had let the roles of wife and mother define their purchases: minivans and stodgy family sedans."[5] One of the women explained, "I'm just celebrating my life." The other trumpeted, "I don't have the disease to please anymore. I'm pleasing me."[6] Reporter Williams found car salesmen targeting this cohort of middle-aged professional women, whom the salesmen believe want to seize the freedom once reserved for men by buying a sexy and indulgent car as a means of creating their own new personal image.

THE EDUCATIONAL SECURITY STATE: RELIGION AND MILITARISM

Except for China, the educational security state sometimes has strong ties to religion or, in the case of the former Soviet Union, atheism. Wars of religion marked the late 20th and early 21st centuries. Whereas the United States in the 1950s was adding the words "Under God" to the Pledge of Allegiance said by its school children, the Soviet Union was beefing up school courses on atheism. Pakistan and Arab nations integrated Islamic teachings into their political and educational institutions. India's attempt to remain a secular state was compromised by the rise of Hindu nationalism. Exemplifying connections between Christianity and the state were television clips of British actor Peter Ustinov shortly after his death in 2004, describing his first day in a British school where he encountered a picture on the classroom wall of Jesus Christ holding the hand of a Boy Scout and pointing to a map of the British Empire.

The educational security state is part of what is called the *national security state*. National security states enlist all elements of the nation for military preparedness, including schools, media, and other instruments of ideological control. In the second half of the 20th century, the Cold War between so-called "capitalist" and "communist" national security states shaped the future direction of global society. In both ideological systems, schools and other sources of propaganda were enlisted in the war effort. Later in the book, my discussion of the educational debates of the Cold War will be on the national security states of the Union of Soviet Socialist Republics, the People's Republic of China, the Democratic People's Republic of Korea, Vietnam, and the United States. As I demonstrate, there are important similarities and differences in the evolution of educational systems in these countries.

The educational security state resulted from global economic competition that brought together the military demands of the nation-state with educational plans for economic growth and development. In earlier books, I explored some of the issues that led to the creation of the educational security state. I have analyzed global educational ideas spread by Western and Japanese imperialism, the World Bank, the Organization for Economic Cooperation and Development, and the United Nations; debates about the right to an education between Confucian, Islamic, Hindu, and Western societies; and how global nongovernment organizations have pressed for human rights and environmental education.[7] In this book, I focus on previously unexamined facets of the globalization of schooling and pedagogy and the growing interconnectedness and uniformity of national education systems, and the rise of the educational security state.

THE GLOBALIZATION OF SCHOOL ORGANIZATION AND PEDAGOGY

The globalization of a bureaucratic, age-graded school organization, where progress is marked by promotions between grades and graduation certificates, is the result of a combination of Western imperialism in Asia, Africa, and the Americas; the adoption of a Euroamerican education model by Asian countries, particularly Japan and China; the activities of international organizations, such as the World Bank and the United Nations; and the adaptation of traditional Islamic schools to the Euroamerican education ladder.

The similarity of debates about school organization and pedagogy is a striking feature of the steady evolution to a global society. Global trends support school organizations based on an Euroamerican educational ladder with students progressing in age-graded classes from elementary to secondary schools. With the globalization of school organization, schools around the world have age-graded classes studying a set curriculum in a variety of subjects ranging from reading to science. Progress between age-graded classes requires student mastery of the subjects in the previous grade with mastery being demonstrated by grades or an examination. Of course, there are variations in this bureaucratic pattern with some national school systems dividing students into vocational and academic tracks, and with differences in the separation of the age-graded classes between elementary and secondary school.

One of the themes of this book is the difference between formal and progressive pedagogies. In this section, I provide a broad definition of these terms. However, there are different types of formal and progressive instruction. Throughout this book I explore these differences, such as the formalistic pedagogical approaches following the Stalinization of Soviet education and progressive educational approaches resulting from attempts to adapt Marxism to indigenous cultures. As a generalization, I am defining *formal* as pedagogical theories that support direct instruction; authoritarian classroom discipline; promotion between classes based on grades and testing; clearly defined subjects that are taught separately; and recitation and drill. By *progressive*, I mean pedagogical theories stressing learning by doing; instruction based on student interests and activities; informal self-regulated classroom organization; group work; and an integrated curriculum in which a single learning activity teaches a combination of subjects such as reading, science, history, math, and geography. Formalistic forms of education are often used to prepare students to accept and fit into existing economic and social systems. Progressive forms of education are considered a means for preparing students to actively influence the direction of economic, political, and social systems.

There have been attempts to break out of the global educational paradigm of the Euroamerican educational ladder. For instance, after the Russian Revolution, education theorist V. N. Shul'gin argued that the traditional formalistic school structure was inappropriate for a communist society. He envisioned the school, like the state, eventually withering away. There is, he stated, "a parallel between what Marx had described in *The Civil War in France* and the Soviet cultural revolution. Just as an armed populace could replace a standing army, so the professional work of Soviet teachers could be dissolved into the processes of communal life."[8] Along similar progressive lines, during the late 1960s and the 1970s, Ivan Illich coined the term *deschooling* in a campaign to abolish the age-graded school organization, which, he argued, had the negative effects of separating learning from the life of the community and determining a student's economic and social advancement. Illich believed that the formalistic Western model of school organization was created to maintain existing economic and political structures and undermine the ability of people to work independently.[9] The very existence of deschooling movements posing an alternative to the Western form of school organization and range of pedagogical styles highlights the almost universal acceptance of formalistic models.

THE "OTHER" AND THE EDUCATIONAL SECURITY STATE

Fear of the "other" has shaped the educational security state. The "other" has often prompted fears of military and economic defeat. Fear of the "other" created global competition between the educational ideas of socialist, communist, and capitalist nations, and between Christian, Islamic, and Hindu societies. It has contributed to the globalizing of educational ideas. For instance, in response to the 1917 Russian Revolution, American school leaders and public officials in the 1920s rolled out a campaign for "100% Americanism," which was to be achieved through increased patriotic school exercises, censorship of textbooks, and purges of teachers with so-called subversive ideas. Interesting in terms of the global flow of ideas is that, during the same period, Soviet educators were implementing American progressive educational ideas as part of their own educational reform movement. In China, John Dewey was introducing progressive education ideas that had a major impact on Chinese educational theory. During the Cold War of the 1940s and 1950s, whereas some Americans wondered if the perceived superiority of Soviet school system would cause the United States to fall behind in developing military technology (a concern that seemed validated by the Soviet Union's launch of the first manned space capsule in the late 1950s), others were labeling progressive education as communist and accusing it of weakening educational standards, U.S. politicians forced schools to emulate what they perceived to be the advantages of the Soviet system. Soviet schools had abandoned progressive education in the 1930s when the schools underwent Stalinization, which required exams, order, discipline, and nationalism. Colonialism and religious rivalries spawned educational security states in India, Pakistan, and the Middle East. In the Middle East, the withdrawal of colonial powers resulted in garrison states with their leaders calling for highly nationalistic and Islamic forms of education.

The remainder of this chapter analyzes the role of the other in shaping global education in the early 20th century. The focus is on those countries that became major players in the Cold War and global capitalism, namely the Soviet Union, the United States, China, Japan, Vietnam, and Korea. Although Vietnam and Korea were not world powers, the military struggles occurring in those countries in the 1950s through the 1970s were major factors in the Cold War. This chapter begins with an analysis of the impact the Soviet Union and the United States had on each others educational systems. I then examine the evolution of educational systems in China, Vietnam, Japan, and North Korea in the early 20th century as a consequence of fear and resentment of the other.

PRELUDE TO THE EDUCATIONAL COLD WAR: THE UNION OF SOVIET SOCIALIST REPUBLICS AND THE UNITED STATES OF AMERICA

Tensions between the United States and the Soviet Union initiated a global interplay of educational ideas. Leaders in both countries were influenced by educational changes in their opponent's countries. This global interplay of educational ideas increased after the triumph of Chinese communism. Mao Zedong gave new meaning to socialist education that, in turn, influenced educational movements in other countries including the United States. In North Korea, which also received aid from the Soviet Union, Kim Il Sung, Premier of the People's Republic of North Korea, became a leading exponent of a new socialist education. Both Mao Zedong and Kim Il Sung reacted strongly to previous imperialistic conquests of Western nations and Japan. And in the late 1950s, Fidel Castro's rise to power in Cuba provided another model of socialist education that influenced global discussions.

Although this section of the chapter focuses on the interplay of educational ideas between the Soviet Union and United States, the reader should keep in mind that this is just one part of the dynamic of the global flow of educational ideas. They were the military giants among the educational security states emerging from World War II. Their struggles shaped the direction of their educational systems and global society. Although allies during World War II, both powers after the war were suspicious of each others intentions. Prior to the war, school systems in both countries propagandized against the political, economic, and social systems of the other country.

Contrasting images of the other drove ideological instruction in each country's school system. In the United States, the Soviet Union was portrayed as a godless nation enslaving its population to an unworkable economic system. In the Soviet Union, the United States was portrayed as a nation where greedy capitalists exploited the masses causing them to live in a state of wage-slavery and alienation by the industrial system. In the United States, most ideologies that questioned representative government or capitalism were treated as subversive. In the Soviet Union, ideas that questioned the vanguard role of the Communist Party and Marxism–Leninism were branded as bourgeois and subversive.

In the United States, fears of the "other" were heightened by acts of political terrorism such as the anarchist slaying of President William McKinley in 1901, which resulted in laws restricting political activities. Using rhetoric that would eventually include communism, President McKinley's successor President Theodore Roosevelt demanded laws limiting anarchist activities.[10] He told Congress in 1901, "The anarchist is the enemy of humanity, the enemy of all mankind, and his is a deeper degree of criminality than any other."[11] After the 1917 Bolshevik revolution, local, state, and the federal governments worked with organizations such as the American Legion to ensure that public schools propagandized against so-called subversive movements.[12] In 1921, the U.S. Commissioner of Education John Tigert declared his "determination to crush out of the schools communism, bolshevism, socialism, and all persons who did not recognized the sanctity of private property and 'the right of genius to its just rewards'."[13]

Feeling threatened by the United States and other capitalist nations, Soviet leaders used their school system to propagandize against the other and educate the "New Socialist Man." The Soviet Academy of Sciences (later named the Communist Academy) was founded in 1918 as an association for the study and teaching of socialism and communism. In 1926, the All-Union Congress of Soviets defined the functions of the academy as:

(a) elaboration of problems of Marxism and Leninism; (b) combating of bourgeois and petty-bourgeois distortions of Marxism–Leninism; and c) rigid advocacy of the standpoint of dialectical materialism both in the social and the natural sciences, and repudiation of the survivals of idealism.[14]

The interplay between Soviet and U.S. educational systems is highlighted by the global flow of progressive educational ideas to the Soviet Union; Stalinist reaction to progressivism; the illogical branding of progressivism as communist by U.S. conservatives in the 1950s; and the contention in the 1950s that U.S. schools needed to adopt Soviet-Stalinist school standards to win the Cold War.

THE GLOBAL FLOW OF PROGRESSIVE EDUCATION

After the 1917 Revolution, Soviet leaders confronted a vast illiterate population and a general lack of understanding of communist ideology. As revolutionary leader Valdimir Lenin warned, "An illiterate person stands outside of politics; he must first be taught his ABC's."[15] Soviet educators utilized the ideas of American and Russian progressive education, and Karl Marx's idea of polytechnical education. John Dewey was the major global figure and icon of progressive education. Besides influencing early Soviet education, as mentioned previously, John Dewey left his stamp on Chinese education in the early 1920s when he was declared the "Second Confucius."[16] The experimental phase of Soviet education lasted until 1931 when, under the pressures of Stalinization, schools adopted a uniform curriculum and disciplined academic regulations.

The educational problems facing the Soviet Union were staggering. After the 1917 revolution it was estimated that only one third of the population had an elementary education. Most of the educated population was concentrated in urban centers. There were few schools in the outlying areas. Nigel Grant describes,

> In 1914, Tadzhikistan had ten elementary schools, thirteen teachers, and a literacy rate of one half of one percent; Turkmenia had fifty-eight schools, literacy reaching the level of 0.7 percent ... Uzbekistan ... two percent were literate ... in Georgia ... only twenty percent were literate.[17]

Despite Joseph Stalin declaring a 1930 campaign for universal education, the eligible cohort group enrolled in elementary and secondary school remained low, only increasing from 13.4% in 1929–1930 to 31.4% in 1938–1939.[18]

In planning a mass literacy program, Communist Party leaders accepted the basic school structure and imperialist educational policies created by the previous Czarist administration. Chinese communist leaders simply accepted the Euroamerican educational ladder of elementary schools, middle schools, and secondary schools. Soviet leaders inherited the imperialist education policies of Czarist Russia, which included "Russification." Russification involved extending the usage of the Russian language and the influence of Russian culture throughout the Russian empire which extended to the Pacific Ocean and included a vast number of different cultures and languages. The goal of Russification was to make Russian the common language of the empire. The success of this policy was limited by the few number of schools and teachers in rural areas. Most rural schools were simple one-room schoolhouses serving multiple grades. Nina Khrushchev, the wife of Soviet Premier Nikita Khrushchev, was born in 1900 in an Ukrainian village and she recalls, the "people spoke Ukrainian in the villages, but the administration in the village, the *gmina*, and above was Russian. In school children were taught in Russian, although they did not speak Russian at home. From history it is known that the government of the Kingdom pursued a policy of Russification of the population."[19]

The debate over language paralleled those occurring in other countries such as the United States after the American Revolution when Noah Webster advocated the teaching of a common American form of English.[20] Prior to the Russian Revolution, Lenin argued that minorities should use their own languages in school and that Russian should not be compulsory because modernization "would create a natural need for learning Russian."[21] Others argued for the use of minority languages in the classroom but requiring the teaching of Russian. Alexander Bogdanov wanted a world language to be taught that would contribute to the internationalization of the revolution. He actually suggested the teaching of English as the world language.[22] The resolution of the language debate was to allow for the use of minority languages in classrooms with Russian being the official language of the U.S.S.R. Article 121 of the Soviet Constitution specified "Instruction in schools in native language."[23]

Lenin believed it was necessary for schools to create a working-class consciousness in the population of the Soviet Empire. In the framework of Lenin's theories, the Communist Party, as the vanguard of the proletariat, should control the schools to ensure proper ideological instruction. The assumption, and reality, was that the majority of the Russian population did not understand and accept communist principles. The schools were to implant this new political ideology.

An important part of this ideological schooling was atheism, which became a standard subject in Soviet schools. Many in the 21st century have forgotten the importance of atheism in radical movements in the late 19th and early 20th centuries.[24] In Russia, the Russian Orthodox Church was considered by communists as an instrument of Czarist control. For instance, Nikita Khrushchev recalled the dilemma he faced as an atheist in burying his first wife in a Russian Orthodox cemetery. Born into a poor family in a small Ukrainian village in 1894, Khrushchev was working by 14 as a farm laborer and cleaning boilers in mines. In 1918, he joined the

Communist Party. His son, Sergei Khrushchev, writes that shortly after joining the Party he was faced with problem of his first wife's burial. "The Russian Revolution, after the example of the Great French Revolution," Sergei states, "completely rejected religion and called it the opiate of the people. But now he [Nikita] was expected to carry the coffin ... through the gate of the cemetery, which happened to be across from a church. Father decided to bypass the church by ... passing [the coffin] from hand to hand over the cemetery fence."[25]

Early Soviet educators were attracted to U.S. progressive education because the basic ideas seemed to fulfill Marx's concept of polytechnical education and support the idea that theory must be informed by practice. In *Capital*, Marx argued that a crippling effect of industrialization made it difficult for workers to adapt to technological changes. Marx advocated polytechnical education for a "fully developed individual, fit for a variety of labors, ready to face any change of production, and to whom the different social functions he performs are but so many modes of giving free scope to his own natural and acquired powers."[26] He predicted that "there can be no doubt that when the working class comes into power, as inevitably it must, technical instruction, both theoretical and practical, will take its proper place in the working-class schools."[27]

Polytechnical education was recognized in the 1917 Soviet Constitution, which called for "free, compulsory general and polytechnical education (familiarizing in theory and practice with the main branches of production) education for all children of both sexes up to 16 years of age; close linking of instruction with children's socially productive work."[28] Polytechnical education was to be realized through a unified labor school which provided a 5-year course for students between 8 and 13 and a 4-year course for the 13- to 17-year old group. The Statute on Unified Labor School described the first stage of teaching as resting "on processes of a more or less handicraft nature, suitable to the weak strength of the children and to their natural bents at that age."[29] In the second stage, modern industrial and agricultural labor was to be studied. All this was to be integrated into a wide range of activities and studies from photography to sculpturing and languages to chemistry. In 1931, just before the Stalinization of Soviet Schools that occurred that year, the Council of the Peoples Commissars of the Russian Soviet Federation of Soviet Republics defined polytechnical education as "(a) the combination of education with productive labor; (b) the acquaintance in theory and in practice with fundamental forms of social production; [and] the scientific knowledge of the fundamental productive processes."[30]

In the 1920s, the People's Commissariat of Education created a decentralized and experimental educational system. The unified labor school dispensed with formalistic education such as grades, examinations, and homework. Informal relations existed between teachers and students. The People's Commissariat of Education encouraged active learning through class discussion and aesthetic education along with an integrated curriculum in which reading, writing, arithmetic, history, geography, literature, chemistry, and other subjects were studied together. The Commissariat also recommended the use of the Dalton plan developed by U.S. progressive educator Helen Parkhurst in 1918. In the Dalton plan, students signed monthly contracts in which all subjects were to be studied in the context of a single theme. Students fulfilled their contracts working at their own pace.[31]

American progressive educational ideas received further support in 1929 when the People's Commissariat of Education ordered all schools to adopt the project method as the system of instruction.[32] The project method was first proposed in 1918 by American progressive educator William Heard Kilpatrick, who was a friend and colleague of John Dewey at Teachers College, Columbia University.[33] It eventually became a standard instructional method in many public schools in the United States.

The reasoning behind the project method was similar to that of the unified labor school. Active learning showed the relationship between learning and socially useful occupations. In the project method, a student (or more ideally a group of students) selects a particular task, such as construction or investigation of a social or natural phenomenon. In completing the project, students learned academic skills such as arithmetic and reading along with general knowledge related to the subject of the project. In his book on the project method, Kilpatrick used the example of a girl making a dress. The act of making a dress was a project if the girl was motivated by a social purpose and if she planned and made the dress. According to Kilpatrick a purposeful act prepared students to be responsible towards others. "A man who habitually so regulates his life with reference to worthy social aims [through the project method]," Kilpatrick wrote, "meets at once the demands for practical efficiency and of moral responsibility."[34]

The emphasis on collective responsibility probably appealed to early Soviet educators. Kilpatrick defined moral character as a "disposition to determine one's conduct and attitudes with reference to the welfare of the group."[35] A group project, according to Kilpatrick, provided an ideal opportunity for students to experience group acceptance or rejection. Group approval was key to the project method. Kilpatrick stressed, "there are few satisfactions so gratifying and few annoyances so distressing as the approval and disapproval of our comrade.... When the teacher merely coerces and the other pupils side with their comrade ... conformity may be but outward. But when all concerned take part in deciding what is just ... conformity is not merely outward."[36]

THE STALINIZATION OF SOVIET EDUCATION

In 1931, the Commissar of Education Andrei Bubnov condemned the project method at the meeting of the All-Russian Conference of Heads of Regional Departments of Education. He asserted that teachers were inadequately prepared to use the project method and activity-based instruction. He demanded that schools provide systematic instruction in mathematics, chemistry, and physics. The Central Committee of the Communist Party declared, "It is necessary to wage a decisive struggle against thoughtless scheming with methods ... especially against the so-called project method."[37] In 1932, the Central Committee condemned the Dalton plan.

The result was the centralization of control over schools and the institution of a formalistic education involving direct instruction, examinations, and strict classroom discipline. By the late 1930s, polytechnical education was largely abandoned for academic study. In 1937, the teaching of labor as an independent subject was abolished in all elementary and secondary schools; all school workshops were closed and converted into scientific laboratories; and it was decreed that "all hours freed from teaching of labor to be given to the teaching of the Russian language, literature, mathematics and the Constitution of the U.S.S.R."[38]

The progressive concept of group attachments was transformed into forced collectivization. Unpopular in the 1920s, the famous Soviet educator Anton Makarenko rose to prominence in the 1930s. He was sometimes referred to as the Benjamin Spock of the Soviet Union because of the wide distribution of his book on child rearing, *A Book for Parents*. In this book, Makarenko urged a combination of disciplining children for collective living and teaching patriotic allegiance to the Soviet Union. On the opening page of *A Book for Parents* he declared, "The books and deeds of the Revolution—these are the teachers of the new man. Every thought, every movement, every breath of our life vibrates with the glory of the new citizen of the world. Is it possible not to sense that vibration, is it possible not to know how we should educate our children?"[39]

During the 1920s, Makarenko established communities for orphaned and delinquent children using a military-type organization with uniforms, brigades, bugle calls, salutes, and industrial shops organized along military lines. Everyone was assigned work that was considered good for the community. He rejected ideas of self-discipline and self-organization popular among progressive educators. In *The Road to Life*, Makarenko criticized educators for "deciding that 'conscious discipline' is no good when it is the result of adult influence. This, they [progressive educators] maintained, is ... mere drill ... they reasoned that any form of organization for children is unnecessary and harmful, excepting 'self-organization,' which is essential."[40]

Using conscious discipline to achieve collective thinking and organization became the hallmark Makarenko's educational philosophy and Soviet schools. Using an industrial model, he wrote, "it was clear to me that many of the details of human personality and behavior could be made from dies, simply stamped out en masse, although of course the dies themselves had to be of the finest description, demanding scrupulous care and precision."[41] The type of "dies" to mold Soviet children were for him self-evident. "We all know perfectly well," he asserted, "what sort of human being we should aim at turning out. Every class-conscious person knows this too. Every Party member knows it well."[42]

In *A Book for Parents*, Makarenko wrote, "Remember the words of the great gardener Comrade Stalin: 'People should be reared with care and attention as a gardener rears his chosen fruit-tree'."[43] Makarenko used Stalin's image of the cultivation of trees to contrast educational methods that allowed the child to follow their own interests as contrasted with directing a child's interests. He argued that just as humans learned to improve on nature through cultivation: "Soviet educationalists are also no longer 'servants of nature,' but her masters. Our education is a similar corrective. And only on these lines is education possible."[44]

The abandonment of progressive education and decentralized control was typified by Moscow's Model School No. 25 attended by Stalin's daughter Svetlana. Centralization and tighter controls resulted in standardization of curriculum, texts, teaching methods, and teacher manuals. Model schools were exactly what the name suggests; they were models for other schools throughout the nation. The Russian Republic and the Moscow Department of Education both held contests for the best model school. Model School No. 25, also known as Stalin's School, won prizes from both governments.[45]

Disciplined collectivization was the hallmark of Stalin's School. On the first day of school students gathered outside in military formation by class. Teachers and student militia supervised the cloakroom and movement between classes and floors. There was a staircase regulating student movement between classes. Classes marched to the lunchroom. A bulletin board announced the day's lessons, homework, and reprimands. Students all had standard notebooks with strict rules about margins and penmanship. Erasing was not allowed in the notebooks and violation of rules governing notebooks would lead, according to one teacher, to sloppy work and "sloppiness goes hand in hand with illiteracy."[46] The school was praised by Markovich Rives of the People's Commissariat of Education Central Pedagogical Laboratory and Moscow's Pedagogical Institute for its "unceasing concern for the petty details of school organization and pupils' life."[47]

The school's Rules of Order stated that there should be "conscious discipline, political development, civic responsibility, and cultural behavior."[48]

Students were frequently reminded that they were representatives of Soviet power and each school year began with an evening session, "What It Means to Be a Soviet Pupil."[49] Similar to many other national school systems, including U.S. schools, the curriculum was heavily laden with patriotic and political education. A goal was "producing warriors for communism."[50] Textbooks, school banners, and activities all promoted the value of communism, the glory of the Soviet Union, and the responsibilities of the people to the national collective.

An important issue that would plague U.S. and other school systems was the question of testing and standardization. Testing and standardization is a key method for controlling any school system. In 1933, the People's Commissariat of Education issued a draft order calling for written or oral promotion exams for all disciplines in all grades. There were immediate objections from educators that testing was burdensome and complicated. There was a particular concern about testing for promotion of first and second graders. The final resolution was to exempt first and second graders but require promotion exams beginning in the third grade. Along with standardization of the curriculum, pedagogy, and texts, rules for pupil conduct were standardized for all schools. In 1935, the People's Commissariat of Education issued an order requiring that all students maintain elaborate and standardized daybooks tracking their daily assignments and performance in each subject. In 1943, the People's Commissariat of Education standardized Rules of Order and required identification cards for all schools.[51]

Atheist education in Soviet schools was particularly abhorrent to Christian and Islamic nations and it prompted religious movements against communist ideologies. In 1918, the Soviet Union decreed the separation of churches from the government and schools, and providing for religious freedom including the right to profess no religion. Lenin referred to religion as "one of the most vile things existing in the world."[52] The atheist teachings of Soviet schools would also cause bitterness among many citizens who still believed in the teachings of the Russian Orthodox Church. Imagine the resentment among the religious of the following example from the *Young Pioneer Leader's Handbook:* "It was decided that every Pioneer would set up an atheist's corner at home.... Grandma's icons were hanging in one corner, and on the opposite wall her grandson Seryozha hung a sheet of paper with anti-religious pictures, poems an sayings by scientists and writers. It was headed: 'I am godless.'"[53]

As representatives of atheism and political change, Soviet educators encountered massive resistance in rural areas. Kulaks, farm owners who hired peasant labor to work their lands, considered school people instruments of a government that was taking away their farms and enforcing a policy of agricultural collectivization. Devout Russian Orthodox were threatened by the atheistic teachings of schools. And there was also a general anti-intellectual resentment particularly towards teachers from urban areas. The plight of rural teachers was depicted in a 1931 Soviet film *Alone*. The movie opens with the main character, Elena Kuz'mina, completing her pedagogical studies in Leningrad and looking forward to wonderful life as a city teacher. Her dreams are shattered when she is ordered to teach in a small village located between Kazakhstan and Siberia. She is greeted with hostility by the local elites and wealthier villagers who refuse to allow poorer children tending sheep herds to attend school. Elena demands that the poorer children be allowed to attend school and threatens the traditional authority structure of the village. The village elite cause Elena to be thrown out of a sleigh in a remote snowy field where she is left to die. She is "left alone by her 'class enemies'" and then rescued by "her 'class allies,' the poor children."[54]

Alone depicted real conditions facing rural teachers. In 1928 and 1929, 150 teachers were murdered and another 200 were physically assaulted.[55] Historian E. Thomas Ewing provided many examples of hostility towards teachers as representatives of Soviet government power:

> In a village near Tambov, Petrukhina taught children to sing revolutionary songs, refused to close the school on religious holidays, and participated actively in agricultural campaigns ... anti-Soviet peasants retaliated by making threats of violence including throwing bricks through Petrukhina's window.... Early in 1931, Ekatrina Sinitsyna and her husband Trofim Sinitsyn, both teachers, were shot in their home, while their seven-year-old son survived.... According to subsequent reports, the Sinitsyns had assumed an active role during collectivization, while Belov [the murderer] became an outspoken advocate of breaking up the collective farms.[56]

Eventually, the Stalinization of Soviet education in the 1930s would impact the future communist countries of China, Vietnam, and North Korea along with the United States. Also, the Westernization of education in China and the rise and fall of Japanese imperialism would add other dimensions to the globalization of educational ideas. The Westernization of Chinese education and Japanese imperialism paralleled, in time, the Russian Revolution and Japanese expansionism.

THE IMPACT OF THE SOVIET UNION ON U.S. EDUCATION

American leaders reacted to the Russian revolution with the demand that public schools work actively to stamp out the spread of communist ideas. Spearheaded by the American Legion, an organization founded during World War I with the specific purpose of combating the power of the Soviet Union, national leaders demanded that schools emphasize anticommunist rhetoric and patriotic exercises. Loyalty oaths were demanded of teachers and local school boards were urged to look out for "subversive" educators. The 1921 American Legion convention passed a resolution calling for state laws to cancel certificates of teachers "found guilty of disloyalty to the government."[57] In addition, Legion members were asked to volunteer to local school boards the names of subversive teachers. In 1919, the Legion's National Americanism Commission warned, "We have those who believe that the red, white and blue presided over by the eagle shall be replaced by the red flag with the black vulture of disloyalty and international unrest perched upon its staff. Through the schools and through the churches the radicals are now seeking to put across their policies."[58] During the 1930s, the American Legion continued to advocate the firing of "disloyal" teachers. To that end, it supported requiring loyalty oaths of all teachers. The Legion considered any opposition to loyalty oaths to be the work of "subversive" elements in American society. In 1933, the National Americanism Commission reported that eight states had passed legislation requiring loyalty oaths of teachers. Other reports showed that by 1935, 20 states required loyalty oaths of teachers.[59] After World War II, the American Legion joined many other patriotic organizations in attempts to weed subversion from schools. Suspected teachers and administrators were fired, and patriotic groups purged textbooks of anything that sounded like liberalism or communism.

Eventually, in the 1950s, the American Legion would be one among many organizations labeling progressive education and educators as communist. Contributing to the charges was the association of progressive education with the 1930s social reconstructionist movement. Social reconstruction was born in a speech, "Dare Progressive Education Be Progressive?" given by George Counts at the 1932 annual meeting of the Progressive Education Association. A version of the speech was later distributed under the title "Dare the Schools Build a New Social Order?" In his speech, Counts attacked the organization of capitalism as being "cruel and inhuman" and "wasteful and inefficient." He argued that concepts of competition and rugged individualism were outmoded with the development of science and technology and he called for a new economic system that would free people from poverty.[60] In Counts's vision, teachers would lead children down the path of social reconstruction by openly admitting that all teaching was indoctrination. Counts recognized that teachers would need to choose between indoctrinating children into a conservative or a progressive economic philosophy and that doing so would require teachers to "combine education with political statesmanship." In *The Progressive Educator and the Depression: The Radical Years*, C. A. Bowers quoted Counts's statement: "I am not over sanguine, but a society lacking leadership as ours does, might even accept the guidance of teachers." Counts went on to exhort teachers to reach for power: "If democracy is to survive, it must seek a new economic foundation ... natural resources and all important forms of capital will have to be collectively owned."[61] In other words, American teachers were to engage in revolutionary politics similar to Soviet teachers placed in small rural villages.

Conservatives were quick to label social reconstructionism as communist. For instance, Augustin Rudd blamed the supposed deterioration of public schools and their infiltration by subversives on progressive education. In 1940, Rudd was made chairperson of the newly organized Guardians of American Education. The organization's goal was to defeat "left-wing ... educational leadership ... [which is trying to replace] our American way of life ... [with] a 'new social order' based on the principles of collectivism and socialism."[62] Particularly distressing to Rudd were statements in the social reconstructionist journal *The Social Frontier* calling for economic planning and presenting society as a collective organization. Rudd objected to a lead editorial: "For the American people the age of individualism in economy is closing and the age of collectivism is opening. Here is the central and dominating reality in the present epoch...." To Rudd and other members of patriotic organizations, social reconstructionism was a subversive plot to undermine U.S. capitalism. Rudd was particularly upset by an April 1935 issue of the *Social Frontier* which proclaimed: "The end of free enterprise as a principle of economic and social organization adequate to this country is at hand."[63]

Rudd and other conservatives, similar to Soviet educators who rejected progressive education, demanded a return to classroom discipline, individual work and competition for grades, and direct instruction. A comparative timeline between the United States and the Soviet Union would show a parallel in the 1920s between progressive education combined with formal instruction and anticommunist education in U.S. schools, and experimental progressive education and anti-United States and capitalist teachings in Soviet Schools. In the 1930s, American schools could be characterized as continuing with progressive education while experiencing increasing attacks from conservatives demanding an emphasis on anticommunist and antifascist instruction. During the same period, Soviet Schools rejected progressive education and continued with anti-United States and capitalist education. And, finally in the 1940s and 1950s, as I discuss in later chapters, U.S. schools rejected progressive education in favor of a Stalinist model. In this manner, the other played an important role in shaping education in both countries.

CONFUCIANISM AND THE "OTHER" IN CHINESE, VIETNAMESE, AND JAPANESE EDUCATION

During the same years that progressive education was debated in the Soviet Union and the United States, Chinese educators were welcoming John Dewey and undergoing the Westernization of their schools. Fearing Western, and later Japanese imperialism, some Chinese leaders turned to educational reform as means of building a modern army. "We should know," the Ministry of Education of the newly formed Republic of China declared in 1912, "that our people are not foolish or lazy. The only reason we have not as yet been able to attain the same level as other more advanced countries is that our education is lacking."[64] Who were these other advanced countries? They were the countries that defeated China beginning with the 1840 Opium War, when British warships traveled up China's rivers to protect their right to sell opium to the Chinese population. In the words of the Preamble to the 1982 Constitution of the People's Republic of China, "Feudal China was gradually reduced after 1840 to a semi-colonial and semi-feudal country."[65] As late as 1984, Chinese leaders were still feeling angry at the English victory. Deng Xiaoping, 1976 successor to Mao Zedong, told a visiting Japanese delegation, "For more than a century after the Opium War, China was subjected to aggression and humiliation."[66]

In 1884, China declared war against France because of France's growing influence over Vietnam; China's tributary vassal state. In 1885, China lost the war resulting in expansion of France's colonial empire. In one of those unexpected historical twists, French colonization of Vietnam would eventually contribute to political turmoil and school reform in the 1960s and 1970s in the United States. In 1895, China lost Korea, another tributary vassal state, to Japan, which ensured its control over Korea after the 1904–1905 Russian–Japanese War. The loss of Korea set the stage for the post-World War II Korean War, another war that affected U.S. school policies, and the rise to power of North Korean leader Kim Il Sung, a major contributor to concepts of socialist education.

Defeat caused Chinese leaders to look abroad for ways of improving their educational system as a stimulant for industrial development that it was believed, would lead to improved military technology. One possible model was Japan, which had blended Western forms of education with traditional ethics. Many Chinese scholars studied in Japan and returned with hopes of modernizing Chinese education. The other models were European and American school systems; the original models for reform of the Japanese school system.

What educational modernization meant for these nations was abandoning or modifying traditional Confucian education. This was true not only in

China and Japan, but also in Vietnam and Korea. Traditional Confucian education emphasized ethical and moral instruction through the study of classical texts. Confucius (circa 551–479 B.C.E.) believed people were born morally equal but differed later in life as a result of education. The goal of Confucian education was preparation of a moral person and society. Because it was believed morality should be the cornerstone of good government, then the best government officials should then be Confucian scholars. This reasoning led to an elaborate set of civil service exams based on Confucian ethics. Passing these exams became the path to government positions. Confucian scholars held high government posts and were greatly honored by society.

Ho Chi Minh's father provides an example of Confucian scholarship and participation in the examination system. Born in 1863 in the small Vietnamese village of Ha Thy Hy, Ho Chi Minh's father Nguyen Sinh Sac studied as a child with a local Confucian scholar Vuong Thuc Mau. A Confucian teacher Hoang Duong living in a nearby village supposedly noted Sac's love of learning and invited him at the age of 15 to live in his home to continue his studies. Hoang Duong or Master Duong was descended from a long line of Confucian scholars. His father had taken the civil service exams three times before receiving the grade of *tu tai* or "cultivated talent," which was the lowest level of achievement. Master Duong, like many local Confucian scholars, supplemented his farming income through his teaching.[67]

Nguyen Sinh Sac devoted himself to preparing for the civil service exam. He married Master Duong's daughter Hoang Thi Loan who worked their rice field while her husband studied. They had three children with Nguyen Sinh Cung (later known as Ho Chi Minh) being born on May 19, 1890. Ho Chi Minh spent his early life watching his father struggle through the examination system. In 1891, his father took the civil service exams in the provincial capital of Vinh and failed to gain candidacy for the level of "cultivated talent." Taking the exams again in 1894, he passed at the level just above "cultivated talent" as *cu neban* or "recommended man." As a result, his village honored him by giving him a small plot of land; the usual reward by a community for successful passing of the civil service exam.

Refusing an official position in the imperial bureaucracy, Ho Chi Minh's father continued his studies while teaching classics in his village. His wife continued to work in the family rice field to support her husband-scholar. William Duiker, Ho Chi Minh's biographer, quotes the Vietnamese saying, "*vong anh di truoc,* or 'the carriage of the husband goes before, that of his wife after.'"[68]

In 1895, Sac traveled to Hué where he failed to pass the highest exams in the Confucian system, the imperial examinations (*thi boi*). He remained in Hué to study at the Imperial Academy and was joined by his wife and two sons. His wife worked to support his study at the Imperial Academy. Sac eventually passed the imperial examinations earning the degree of *pho bang* or doctorate, second class. In honor of his passing the imperial examination, his village planned a ceremonial entry into the village and a banquet. In true Confucian tradition, Ho's father declined the ceremony and requested that the banquet's food be distributed to the poor. Because of his examination success, his home village was declared "a civilized spot, a literary location" and the village used public land to erect a three room house as his residence. Again, Sac refused an official government position and opened a small school for classical learning.[69] Ho Chi Minh's father exemplifies the life of a Confucian scholar; the honored place given Confucian scholars in Vietnam, China, Japan, and Korea; and the important social and political role of the examination system.

Japan became an symbol of modernity for those raised in Confucian traditions. In Japan integration of Western and Eastern educational traditions was referred to as *Japanese Spirit, Western Skills* and *Western Science, Eastern Morals,* and in China as *Western Function, Chinese Essence.*[70] As part of the effort to confront European and American military and industrial power, in 1855 Sakuma Shozan, a leading Japanese advocate of Westernization, urged the study of foreign languages: "In order to master the barbarians ... there is no better first step than to be familiar with barbarian tongues."[71] The tone of Shozan's statement indicates the disdain many Japanese and Chinese felt towards Western culture in contrast to their desire to learn about Western technology and science. Japanese imperialist ambitions were suggested in Sakuma's comment, "Learning a barbarian language is not only a step toward knowing the barbarians, but also the groundwork for mastering them."[72] The Charter Oath issued by the newly created Japanese Education Department in 1868 reflected a global view in organizing a new educational system: "Knowledge shall be sought from throughout the world."[73] Adopting a Western style school structure, Japan's 1872 Fundamental Code of Education mandated the building of 54,760 primary schools, middle-school districts, and university districts.[74] The organizational plan in 1885 divided primary school into lower (ages 5–9) and upper or vocational (ages 10–13), with all students being required to attend 4 years of lower primary school. Graduates of lower primary schools were divided into vocational and upper primary. Graduates of the upper primary school could attend middle school (ages 14–16), then a college preparatory school and a university.[75] Of great importance in maintaining moral traditions, the Japanese schools combined moral instruction with the study of math and science. This pattern was replicated in Chinese schools.

The Chinese government adopted the model of lower and upper primary schools after many years of debate about the value of Westernization versus Confucianism and because of the influence of Chinese scholars who studied in Japan,. The 1904 curriculum for primary schools required study of Confucian Classics, Moral Training, and Chinese literature along with the study of Arithmetic, History, Geography, Physical Education, and Science.[76] This curriculum was a major departure from concentrating on classical Confucian literature. In 1905, the examination system was abolished.

In 1912, the Empress-Dowager Longyu, acting for the 6-year-old Emperor Puyi, abdicated the throne and a Chinese Republic was declared. The new minister of education Cai Yuanpei issued an edict eliminating Confucian Classics from the primary school curriculum, banning of all textbooks not in agreement with republican ideals, and the compulsory teaching of handicrafts. The new curriculum for the lower primary school included moral training, Chinese, Arithmetic, Physical Education, Handicrafts, Drawing, Singing, and Sewing (sewing for girls). In the upper primary school, the additions to the curriculum were English and Agriculture.[77] Graduation from primary school could lead to middle school and the university or to vocational training.[78] The addition of handicrafts to the Chinese school curriculum set it apart from the Japanese schools. Similar to the manual training movement in Europe and the United States, Chinese educators argued that "dexterity in manual skills was intimately linked with intellectual, moral, and physical education."[79]

American progressive education received a lasting following in China after John Dewey's 2-year lecture tour beginning in 1919. In another book, I describe a contemporary school in the People's Republic of China where children are surrounded by quotations from Dewey.[80] Originally, Dewey planned a short visit, but his former Chinese students, who had studied with him in the United States, pleaded for him to remain and they arranged an extensive series of lectures. During Dewey's visit, he was frequently compared to Confucius. A symbolic relationship was discovered when Dewey announced to his Chinese host that his 60th birthday would be on October 20, the same date as Confucius's birthday.[81] It was during this lecture trip that one university gave Dewey a citation naming him the "Second Confucius." However, when the communists gained power, Dewey's writings were heavily criticized for lacking a class analysis.[82]

Dewey's former Chinese students returned home with Western ideas about how society should be organized. The United States was an attractive place to study, as Chinese became wary of Japanese imperialism. Also in 1908, the U.S. Congress agreed to return funds owed to the United States to China for support of Chinese students to study in the United States. In 1910, Tsinghua, a 2-year preparatory school, was founded in Peking. Its graduates received automatic grants to study in the United States. Between 1921 and 1924, it was estimated that the United States was hosting the largest number of Chinese students studying abroad.[83] In the 1920s, as I explain later, both the United States and the Soviet Union were trying to attract Chinese scholars in order to influence China's political development.

Many of the students returning to China had studied at Columbia University and had contact with Dewey. In 1905, *The Chinese Students' Monthly* began publication in New York City. In 1920, the *Monthly* reported that the largest number of Chinese students were attending Columbia University. The first two doctorates granted by Columbia's Teachers Colleges in 1914 and 1917 were to men who, on returning to China, became leading exponents of Dewey's philosophy. The first, P. W. Kuo, founded the Nanking Teachers' College, while the second, Chiang Meng-lin, became Chancellor of Peking University. In 1919, the Peking Teacher's College began publishing a journal named after Dewey's book *Democracy and Education*. By the time Dewey left China in 1921, he had given 78 different series of lectures. At the time of his departure, 100,000 copies of his Peking lectures—a 500-page book—were in circulation and three of his lectures were reprinted as classroom texts.[84]

Four months before Dewey's arrival in China, his sponsors founded the Society for the Promotion of New Education. This organization promoted Dewey's writings and worked for the more general reform of education. In part, they were responsible for the government's School Reform Decree of 1922 adopting the U.S. school model of 6 years of elementary school, 3 years of junior high school, and 3 years of high school. Both John Dewey and Teachers College Professor Paul Monroe participated in the initial meetings that led to the 1922 decree.

Dewey's ideas were used to justify the work of the Society for the Promotion of New Education or, as their activities were called, the New Education Movement. Oddly, since Dewey could be interpreted as emphasizing the importance of community and group as the social underpinnings of democracy, the New Education Movement supported individualism and individual development as necessary for a republican government. The stress on individuality was a direct criticism of the Confucian emphasis on the ethical responsibility to maintain the harmony of the group. The New Education Movement also criticized the existence of the scholar-citizen class that was a product of the Confucian examination system. Members also rejected the idea that education should simply serve the government and argued that it should prepare students for a democratic society. John Dewey noted that the New Education Movement did retain the fundamental Confucian "belief in the primacy of ideas, of knowledge, and in the influence of education to spread these ideas."[85]

The work of the New Education Movement was seriously hampered by the realities of Chinese life. As noted on the pages of *The New Education*, the monthly publication of the Society for the Promotion of New Education, 2% of the population was literate and only a small fraction of a percent attended secondary schools. The editor of the journal, Chiang Meng-lin, proposed a literacy campaign with secondary school students working with 15 people and an alliance of merchants and students to operate schools. Each group of newly literate people would, in turn, educate others. This grand scheme was never adopted, but it highlighted the educational problems facing China. Like the postrevolutionary Russia, communist leaders after their 1949 victory confronted a largely illiterate population with few educational institutions serving rural areas.[86]

After returning to New York City in 1922, Dewey commented on what he perceived to be the failure of the New Education Movement:

> The difficulties in the way of a practical extension and regeneration of Chinese education are all but insuperable. Discussion often ends in an impasse: no political reform of China without education; but no development of schools as long as military men and corrupt officials divert funds and oppose schools from motives of self-interest. Here are the materials of a tragedy of the first magnitude.[87]

Dewey left a complex legacy in China. As I mentioned previously, Dewey's educational ideas are still popular. In the early 1920s Mao Zedong ~~operated a book store that sold Dewey's work which he would later condemn~~ for lacking a class analysis. In the 1920s, Dewey's ideas were associated with republican liberalism. The adoption of the U.S. school model would later be criticized by pro-communist educational writer Julia Kwong, who noted, "The educational system inherited by the communists in 1949 was organized along the American pattern, with six years of elementary school, three years of junior high school, three years of senior high school, and three to five years of university."[88] She went on to criticize the acceptance of the U.S. model because it primarily resulted in certifying one's place in society or, in other words, certifying one's class position. Kwong noted that there was a major disparity between the organization of the socialist economy and the educational system: "The economy had become largely socialist with the transformation of the property relations of production, but the educational system retained its pre-liberation capitalist form, disputing the simplistic assumption that the ideological superstructure is necessarily a mirror image of the economic base."[89] A 1951 article in the official Chinese newspaper *People's Daily* warned, "The school system of old China was an imitation of the system of capitalist states and reflected the reactionary ideology of landlords, bureaucrats, and the compradore class of semi-colonial, semi-feudal society.... The laboring people had no position in the culture and education of old China."[90]

It is easy to make parallels between Dewey and Mao Zedong's pedagogies that stress linking theory and practice, and immersing students in the real social relations of society. Many comparisons are made between Dewey's pragmatism and Confucian ethics. Dewey, like Confucius, argued that morality was a product of social interactions and that it needed to be constantly improved and adapted to changing social situations. "Learning By Doing" and "Education Through Experience" are Deweyan slogans that attest to this pragmatic approach to morality. In addition, Dewey emphasized the importance of human interaction as the source of knowledge. Similar to the Confucian tradition, Dewey advocated the study of morality as a means of increasing our understanding of how to improve social conditions. U.S. philosophers David Hall and Roger Ames believed that Deweyan pragmatism can close the gap between Western and Far Eastern concepts of society. They argued that the Western reliance on an abstract set of "natural rights" has little meaning in a tradition governed by "rites" or the search for the best means of achieving social harmony. Referring to Dewey's emphasis on the community as the source of knowledge and human progress, Hall and Ames contended, "John Dewey's vision of a democratic society demonstrates surprising affinities with the traditional Chinese understanding of social organization.... Confucianism and pragmatism share a number of important philosophical assumptions, and may thus serve as resources for intercultural conversations."[91]

In later chapters, I compare Mao Zedong's educational theories with those of John Dewey and other American progressives. Also, Mao, like Dewey, shared ideas with Confucianism, particularly the belief that humans had equal moral capacities and should share equal social duties. This belief in equality was the foundation of China's traditional, but unrealized, commitment to universal education. In addition, Confucian stress on self-reflection and self-criticism was mirrored in Mao's educational philosophy, which included an obligation to speak out against corrupt governments and social injustice.

CONCLUSION

This chapter illustrates the global flow of educational ideas and the role of fear of the "other" in causing educational change. Western educational models were adopted in Russia and Asia. After the 1917 revolution, Soviet leaders welcomed U.S. progressive ideas whereas U.S. educators worried about communist influences. Fear of advancing Western imperialism caused Asian countries to Westernize their schools systems and to open their doors to American progressive education. The interconnectedness of these educational events brought nations closer to the time when they all would be engaged in similar debates about school models and pedagogy.

In the next chapter, I trace the educational biographies of Ho Chi Minh and Mao Zedong. They exemplify how educational transformations in one part of the world can result in causing change in other parts of the globe. They represent the important transition from Confucian to Western style education. Also, along with Kim Il Sung, they developed socialist pedagogies that would influence progressive education around the globe. Mao Zedong's pedagogy influenced the work of Brazil's Paulo Freire who, in turn, would influence national liberation movements in the late 20th and early 21st centuries. The Cold War and the globalized economy speeded up the flow of educational ideas and increased fears of the other.

Chapter 2

The Education
of Revolutionaries:
Ho Chi Minh and Mao Zedong

Mao Zedong and Ho Chi Minh grew up in an environment of Confucian scholarship that was rapidly giving way to Western ideas about education. The attendance of both men at Western-style schools brought them into contact with revolutionary ideas. Born in 1893, three years after Ho's birth, Mao grew up in a small village in the Hunan province of China. These were the years when Chinese and Vietnamese scholars were returning from Japan with glowing reports about Western education. Initially, Mao and Ho received a Confucian education. Ho received his introduction to the Confucian classics while traveling and living with his father during his father's efforts to pass the imperial examinations. Unlike Ho Chi Minh, Mao's father was not a scholar, but a peasant who hoped to apprentice his son to a rice merchant. Similar to Ho's father, Mao received his Confucian education in a village school. Although I can't find a record of what Ho read during his Confucian education, most classical education used similar methods and curriculum. Probably the Confucian education of these revolutionaries was similar. At the age of 6, Mao was sent to a village school that used rote instruction to learn Confucian classics. The first schoolbook he used, *Three Character Classic*, opened with the familiar Confucian concept of moral equality:

> Men at their birth are by nature radically good,
>
> In this, all approximate, but in practice widely diverge.[1]

Also, he read the four great classics of Confucianism–*Analects*, *The Great Learning*, *The Doctrine of the Mean*, and the writings of Mencius.[2]

Philip Short, Mao's biographer, contends that Mao learned three key ideas from his early Confucian education that would be reflected in his later thought. These ideas were:

1. The notion that every human being, and every society, must have a moral compass; if not Confucianism, then something else which fulfills the role.
2. The primacy of right-thinking, which Confucius called "virtue": only if a person's thoughts were right—not merely correct, but morally right—would his actions be right.
3. The importance of self-cultivation.[3]

Both Ho and Mao grew up in societies seething with anger towards Westerners and later, after Japan's invasion of their countries, towards the Japanese. This anger was tempered by a desire to learn about Western methods of education. Most authorities believed that the use of Western modes of education would provide the scientific and technological human power necessary to defeat Western colonialism. At first, Japan was considered a model for the adaptation of Western Education, but as Japanese imperialism increased many scholars headed to Europe.

THE EDUCATION OF HO CHI MINH AND MAO ZEDONG

Ho Chi Minh's world was filled with animosity towards the French colonialists. Regarding Mao's birthplace, Griffith John, an English missionary, wrote in 1895, "it is one of the few places left in the whole world which no foreigner may presume to enter. It is perhaps the most intensely anti-foreign city in the whole of China, a feeling kept up by the literati [Confucian] with the full sympathy of the officials."[4] At an early age, Mao was exposed to the idea that China could only be saved by adopting Western industrialism while reading Zheng Guanying's *Words of Warning to an Affluent Age*. This book described Western technological developments and urged the introduction of Western-style education.[5]

In contrast to Japan and China, French colonialism introduced a more controlling and limited form of Western education in Vietnam that was experienced by Ho Chi Minh. During the summer of 1905, Ho Chi Minh began studying the French language. Similar to attitudes expressed in Japan, there was a sentiment among some Vietnamese that learning the language of the imperialists was essential to their defeat. Ho Chi Minh's French tutor told him, "If you want to defeat the French, you must understand them. To understand the French, you must understand the French language."[6] In the fall of 1905, Ho Chi Minh's father enrolled him in a

Franco-Vietnamese preparatory school. These schools were established by French authorities to woo students away from traditional Confucian schools and to prepare them as bureaucrats for the French colonial administration. In 1907, Ho Chi Minh passed the entrance examination to the highest level Franco-Vietnamese School, the National Academy in Hué. The school focused on French culture and language and offered courses in history, geography, literature, and science. This curriculum contrasted sharply with father's classical Confucian education and represents a major generational change in education.

In May 1908, Ho Chi Minh was dismissed from the National Academy because of participation in demonstrations against French rule. He left Hué and traveled to Phan Thiet where he taught in the Duc Thanh school. The Duc Thanh school was founded by Vietnamese who hoped to prepare citizens to resist French colonialism. The Duc Thanh school was modeled after the Hanoi Free School founded in 1907. The Hanoi Free School, like the Duc Thanh school, was a private school dedicated to teaching "modern" ideas. The school was modeled on an academy established in Japan by Fukuzawa Yukicihi. Similar to Chinese scholars, many Vietnamese studied in Japan. One important Vietnamese scholar in Japan was Phan Boi Chau, whose writings were used by the Hanoi Free School, causing it to be closed by French authorities.[7]

The educational writings and education work of Phan Boi Chau influenced Ho Chi Minh, Vietnamese nationalism, and the educational movement initiated by the Hanoi Free School. Phan Boi Chau was impressed by the educational reforms in Japan and the growing strength of the Japanese military and its potential ability to resist European and U.S. expansionism. In 1904, he established a school in Japan to educate Vietnamese for national independence from French rule. When Ho Chi Minh asked Chau how Japan had achieved its technological strength, Chau replied that they had learned from the West. Chau's response supposedly sparked Ho Chi Minh's original desire to learn the French language.[8]

At the Duc Thanh school, Ho Chi Minh adapted what he had learned at the National Academy to the cause of independence. He taught ideas about equality and liberty based on the works of French philosophers Voltaire, Montesquieu, and Rousseau. Also, he had students recite poems from an anthology written for the Hanoi Free School. One poem reflects the intense anger towards Westerners that permeated the school's instruction.

Oh, Heaven! Can't you see our
suffering?
The nation is in chains, languishing in grief,
Foreigners have doomed it to hunger,
They've robbed it of everything it had.[9]

In 1911, Ho Chi Minh left the Duc Thanh school, heading south to Saigon where he found work as a kitchen helper on a French ocean liner. Later in life, he commented, "When I was about thirteen years old, for the first time I heard the French words 'liberté', 'éqalité', and 'fraternité'. At the time, I thought all white people were French. Since a Frenchman had written those words, I wanted to become acquainted with French civilization to see what meaning lay in those words."[10]

As Ho, at the age of 21, was heading to Saigon in 1911, Mao, at the age of 18, was traveling to Changsha to attend a Western-style middle school after completing work at a newly founded upper elementary school near his village. Like Ho's experience at the National Academy, Mao was quickly involved in the political activities of student societies that were directing their efforts at replacing the emperor with a more representative form of government. A symbolic revolutionary gesture made by faculty and students was to cut off their queues or pigtails which were required as a sign of supplication to the imperial government. After cutting off his own queue, Mao later claimed, "my friend and I ... assaulted them [other students] in secret and forcibly removed their queues, a total of more than ten falling victim to our shears."[11] As the revolution against the imperial government gained momentum in 1911, Mao and other students decided to enlist in the revolutionary army.

Mao recalled that after the 1912 abdication of the Emperor, "Modern schools sprang up like bamboo shoots after a summer rain."[12] After leaving the army, Mao looked for a school to attend and decided in 1913 on a Western-style teaching preparation program at the Human Fourth Provincial Normal School. Similar to Ho's school experience, he read French enlightenment philosophers and stories of the revolutionary exploits of George Washington. Under the influence of teacher Yuan Jiliu, or Yuan the Big Beard, as Mao fondly called him, he read German philosopher Friedrich Paulson's *System der Ethick*. Mao's original copy was preserved and it contains 12,000 words of Mao's marginal notes. His notes reflected, according to his biographer Philip Short, a concern with the role of a strong state, individual will, and the conflict between Chinese and Western ideas. These were all important intellectual issues in the tension between Confucianism and Western thinking.

Mao decided that a focus on Chinese learning must proceed to a study of Western ideas. In 1915, Mao wrote, "One ought to concentrate on the comparison of China and the West and choose from aboard what is useful at home.... General knowledge of Chinese studies is most crucial for our people."[13] At the Normal School, Mao didn't like natural science and life-drawing courses and he struggled with learning foreign languages, particularly English. His difficulties with English dissuaded him from later traveling to France because he wondered about his ability to learn

French. Otherwise, his path might have crossed Ho's. One of his study plans indicates his student life:

1. In the early morning I study English
2. From eight in the morning to three in the afternoon I attend class
3. From four in the afternoon until dinner, I study Chinese literature
4. From the time the lights are lit until they are extinguished, I do homework for all classes;
5. After lights are extinguished I exercise for one hour.[14]

While Mao was attending the Hunan Normal School, Ho was continuing his education traveling around the world, including a stay in New York City in 1913 where he made contact with the Black civil rights movement. Later he would link the struggles of the colonized with the plight of African Americans in the United States. In 1917, Ho Chi Minh settled in France. At the time more than 50,000 Vietnamese resided in France as a result of a policy that transported workers to France from colonized areas in Africa and Asia. These workers, often forced to immigrate, filled the jobs left vacated by local French workers serving in the army during World War I. In France Ho studied Lenin and became an ardent communist.

Mao's exposure to Marx and Lenin occurred after his 1918 graduation. Mao first encountered the idea of socialism in a 1912 article, but other material on communism and socialism was scarce in China. Even in 1918, none of Marx's works were available in Chinese translation and a complete translation of the *Communist Manifesto* did not appear until 1920. In 1918, the first Chinese article on Bolshevism appeared in the Chinese publication *New Youth* that was read by Mao. Mao's encounter with Bolshevik ideas further increased his concerns with Confucianism. The year before graduation, he and a group of students founded an evening school that required students to bow three times to a portrait of Confucius. But he was critical of this practice and wrote, "Our country's three bonds must go," referring to Confucian bonds between the leader and the scholar, father and son, and husband and wife. At the same time, he declared the "four evil demons of the world" to be "the churches, the capitalists, monarchy and the state."[15]

After graduation, Mao joined a group of friends in the New People's Study Society, which symbolically began living in the buildings of an abandoned Confucian academy on the top of a mountain. At the end of the summer of 1918, the group decided to visit Beijing where they came into contact with a broad stream of Western radicalism. Sightseeing along the way, Mao made a symbolic trip to Confucius' grave. In Beijing, Mao was most attracted to Anarchist writings because of their criticism of authority. Under the leadership of Chancellor Cai Yuanpei, Beijing University was a major center of anarchist ideas. In 1919, Mao explained why his initial contact with anarchism and Marxism left him favoring anarchist writings, particularly those advocating communities organized around the principle of mutual aid. The quote indicates the Mao's primitive knowledge of Marxism at this time.

> There is one extremely violent party, which uses the method, "Do unto others as they do unto you," to struggle desperately to the end.... The leader of this party is a man named Marx.... There is another party more moderate than that of Marx ... they want to unite the whole globe into a single country, unite the human race in a single family, and attain together in peace, happiness and friendship ... and of prosperity. The leader of this party is a man named Kropotkin, who was born in Russia.[16]

During his stay in Beijing, Mao wrote a number of wide-ranging articles calling for liberation of women, workers, and citizens.

On returning to Changsha, Mao continued with the New People's Study Society and experimented with establishing anarchist-communal villages. In 1920, he founded the Self-Study University of Changsha and the Cultural Bookstore. Indicating the interest being taken in John Dewey's Chinese lecture series, more books were sold through the bookstore by anarchist Prince Kropotkin and John Dewey than by Marx.

During this time, Mao began calling for a revolution against the old order. Thinking about the power of slogans and ideology, he stated an "ism" needed to be adopted that would galvanize the people: "Without an ism, the atmosphere cannot be created. I think our study society should not merely be a gathering of people bound by sentiment; it must become a group of people bound together by an ism. An ism is like a banner; only when it is raised will the people have something to hope for and know in which direction to go."[17]

Prompted by the need for an "ism," a meeting was called of the New People's Study Group. Their task was to select an "ism" from a list that included communism, liberalism, socialism, and anarchism. It was certainly strange that Mao's allegiance to a communist ideology was the product of a vote taken by a study group in 1921. On New Year's day of 1921, eighteen members of the New People's Study Group met in the Cultural Bookstore to decided on which "ism" to follow. They debated for 2 days: 12 voted for Bolshevism. The Socialist Youth League, composed mainly of students and members of the new People's Study Group, was founded on January 13th. Mao wrote a friend stating his rejection of anarchism for Marx's "materialist concept of history."[18] From Shanghai , the Socialist Youth League received a copy of the Manifesto of the newly founded Chinese Communist Party which proclaimed, "The Communist Party is to guide the revolutionary proletariat to fight against capitalists.... Power will be placed in the hands of workers and peasants, just as the Russian Communist Party did in 1917."[19]

In 1919, Ho Chi Minh published his first article in France while Mao was making his early discovery of Marxism. The article was on French education policy in Vietnam. Ho asserted that the policy was a form of indoctrination used to control the population and, as part of this control, education was limited to a small percentage of the population. Unlike British colonial rule that emphasized education as a way of winning allegiance to English culture, French rule was based on restricting educational opportunities.[20] In a 1920 speech to the 18th National Congress of the French Socialist Party, Ho Chi Minh charged France with intellectual oppression of the Vietnamese people: "We are forced to utter ignorance and obscurity because we have no right to study. In Indochina the colonialists find all ways and means to force us to smoke opium and drink alcohol to poison and beset us."[21] He blamed part of the intellectual oppression on the French administration's maintenance of "1,500 alcohol and opium houses for a thousand villages, while there were only ten schools for the same number of localities."[22]

In 1920, Ho Chi Minh read Lenin's "Theses on the National and Colonial Question," in which Lenin argued that the struggle against capitalism required communists to support national liberation movements in colonized countries. Later, Ho Chi Minh wrote about the experience of reading Lenin: "Leninism is not only a miraculous 'book of the wise,' a compass for us Vietnamese revolutionaries and people: it is also the radiant sun illuminating our path to final victory, to Socialism and Communism."[23]

In his biography of Ho Chi Minh, William Duiker pointed out the compatibility between Confucian traditions and socialist and communist rhetoric. He argued that revolutionaries coming from Confucian backgrounds like Ho Chi Minh and Mao Zedong felt comfortable with an ideology that stressed cooperation and working for the social good, as opposed to a capitalist society stressing economic competition. This may explain the popularity of progressive education in the 1920s in the Soviet Union and in China. Duiker wrote, "In the Confucian mind, Western industrialism was too easily translated into greed and an unseemly desire for self-aggrandizement. By contrast, socialism stressed community effort, simplicity of lifestyle, equalization of wealth and opportunity, all of which had strong overtones in the Confucian tradition."[24]

In 1920, Ho Chi Minh participated in the founding of French Communist Party; this was before the January 1, 1921 vote of Mao's New People's Study Group. Those attending the Eighteenth National Congress of the French Socialist Party were divided over joining Lenin's Communist International (Comintern). Those wanting to join the Comintern bolted from the Socialist Party and created the French Communist Party. For Ho Chi Minh, the choice was obvious. Lenin had demonstrated the dependency of capitalist countries on the exploitation of colonized countries. The plight of the proletariat in industrialized countries was linked to the enslavement of nonindustrialized workers in colonies. This was a theme Ho Chi Minh elaborated on throughout his life. At the 1924 Moscow meeting of the Comintern, he presented convincing statistics on the importance of colonialism to the development and strength of capitalist countries. The following statistical table (Table 2.1) is of historical interest because of the convincing evidence he presented to the Comintern for supporting wars of liberation.

Ho Chi Minh summarized the statistics in Table 2.1: "The whole area of the colonies is five times greater than that of the mother countries, and the whole population of the mother countries amounts to less than three-fifths of that of the colonies."[25] From the perspective of Asian anti-imperialists, including Indians, the most unjust colonizers were Great Britain, France, and Holland whose homelands' sizes and populations were tiny compared to the size and populations of their colonies. For Great Britain, the land area of the colonies was more than 231 times that of Great Britain and the colonial population more than eight times that of the mother country. For France, the colonial lands were more than 19 times larger and the colonial

TABLE 2.1
**Statistical Information Presented By Ho Chi Minh
to the 1924 Comintern Meeting**

Countries	Mother Countries		Colonies	
	Area (Sq. Km.)	Population	Area (Sq. Km.)	Population
Great Britain	151,000	45,000,000	34,910,000	403,600,000
France	536,000	39,000,000	10,250,000	556,000,000
United States	9,420,000	100,000,000	1,850,000	12,000,000
Spain	504,500	20,700,000	3,716,000	853,000
Italy	286,600	38,500,000	1,460,000	1,623,000
Japan	418,000	57,070,000	288,000	21,249,000
Belgium	29,000	7,642,000	2,400,000	8,500,000
Portugal	92,000	5,545,000	2,062,000	8,738,000
Holland	32,500	6,700,000	2,046,000	48,030,000

Note. Adapted from Ho Chi Minh, "Report on the National and Colonial Questions at the Fifth Congress of the Communist International," in *Ho Chi Minh on Revolution: Selected Writings, 1920-66* edited by Bernard B. Fall (New York: Signet Books, 1968), p. 63.

population was one and a half times larger than the mother country. For Holland, which controlled Indonesia, the lands under colonial control were more than 62 times larger and their populations were seven times larger than the mother country. Ho concluded that colonialism was the driving force of Western capitalism.

RACE, CLASS, AND GENDER: THE CIVIL RIGHTS MOVEMENT IN THE UNITED STATES, THIRD WORLD LIBERATION MOVEMENTS, AND WOMEN'S RIGHTS

By the end of the 20th century, radical thought encompassed not only social class as a mode of analysis, but also race and gender. The mantra of critical theory became race, class, and gender. Marx assumed social class was the central component of social analysis. In this section, I want to emphasize, I am not asserting that Ho and Mao were the sole sources for the incorporation of race and gender into Marxist theory, or that they were the major influences on the many Westerners in the 1960s and 1970s who saw as related issues women's liberation, racism, and third world liberation movements. Certainly, gender equality and racism were discussed in Western nations since at least the 18th century and they were important concerns in the Soviet Union. However in the 1960s and 1970s, the struggles in Vietnam and other former colonized countries, the linking of racism to colonialism, and Mao's struggles for women's liberation, resulted in Ho Chi Minh, Mao Zedong, and national liberation movements becoming symbols in the Western world for antiracism and antisexism.

Ho recognized through his personal experiences in Europe and the United States, that racism was a major issue in struggles of liberation from colonial powers. For Ho, racism became as important as Marxist's concept of social class. Ho was joined by others struggling against colonialism in charging the West with racism. Bhimrao Ramji Ambedkar, a leader in the Indian independence movement against Great Britain, was also affected by U.S. race relations while studying in the United States and this experience directly influenced his writing of the Indian constitution after World War II.

As Ho was integrating racism into Marxist thought, Mao was concerned about traditional Chinese male practices towards women. Of course, equality for women was an important result of the Bolshevik revolution. But Mao made it a central issue because of the extreme conditions under which women lived in China. It is important to note that Mao did not travel outside of China during his early years. In fact, Mao devoted himself to giving a Chinese quality to Marxist ideology and, as part of that effort, stressed the importance of gender equality. In this section, I first discuss Ho's concerns with racism and then turn Mao's thoughts on gender in China.

Ho was impressed with the issue of racism in the United States during his early visit after leaving Saigon in 1911. He stayed in New York City, working as a laborer and attended meetings of the Universal Negro Improvement Trust in Harlem, an organization founded by Marcus Garvey. Later, Ho told a peace activist's group visiting Hanoi that he had been disturbed by the condition of U.S. Black people and "had contributed generously to the movement."[26] Ho was not the only foreigner disturbed about race relations in the United States. In a later chapter I detail the close connection between school desegregation in the United States and foreign relations during the 1940s into the 1960s. In *Cold War Civil Rights*, Mary Dudziak contends, "As presidents and secretaries of state from 1946 to the mid-1960s worried about the impact of race discrimination on U.S. prestige abroad, civil rights reform came to be seen as crucial to U.S. foreign relations."[27] By the late, 1960s, U.S. radicals also linked civil rights and racism to colonial wars of liberation.[28]

Affected by his contact with racial prejudice in the United States, Ho Chi Minh wrote to articles in 1924 on "Lynching" and "The Klu Klux Klan." In "Lynching," which he subtitled "A Little-Known Aspect of American Civilization," he lamented, "after sixty-five years of so-called emancipation, American Negroes still endure atrocious moral and material sufferings, of which the most cruel and horrible is the custom of lynching."[29] He provided a graphic history of lynching from the time it was named after Judge Lynch during the American Revolutionary War to the 1920s. He concluded, "Among the collection of crimes of American 'civilization,' lynching has a place of honor."[30] In "The Klu Klux Klan," Ho Chi Minh traced the Klan's history and optimistically predicted its early demise because Black migration to the industrial North was causing a labor shortage that required Southern planters to act more humanely in order to retain future generations of Black workers.[31] In other writings on colonialism, Ho discussed racism. After recounting the horrors of the French forcing colonial subjects to serve in its army and factories, he commented, "As soon as the guns had had their fill of black or yellow cannon fodder, the loving declarations of our leaders were magically silenced, and Negroes and Annamese [Vietnamese] became people of 'a dirty race'."[32]

Ho argued that racism permeated the Communist Party. He accused the French and English Communist Parties of racism for ignoring wars of liberation. He pointed out Stalin's criticism that some communists "dared not align the white people of the colonies with their colored counterparts."[33] He asserted, "According to Lenin, the victory of the revolution in Western Europe depended on its close contact with the liberation movement against imperialism in enslaved colonies."[34]

While Ho Chi Minh was making the connections between racism, the American civil rights movement, and national liberation movements,

Bhimrao Ramji Ambedkar was participating in India's revolt against British colonialism. He drew parallels between America's treatment of African Americans and the plight of Untouchables in Hindu society. Similar to Ho Chi Minh, Ambedkar attended a school administered by colonial authorities. Born in 1891, one year after Ho Chi Minh, Ambedkar faced a life as an outcast because of his Untouchable status. Fortunately for his family, the British military, in its efforts to build a colonial army, allowed Ambedkar's father to advance from village servant to army officer and eventually headmaster of a military school. Despite his father's position in the colonial government, Ambedkar was treated by the rest of Indian society as an Untouchable. In school, he was forced to sit in a corner and his teachers, fearing pollution, refused to touch him. Once, he was asked by a teacher to solve a problem on the chalkboard. The students stored their lunch containers behind the board. Fearing that his presence would pollute their food, the other students hurriedly moved their lunches away before Ambedkar could reach and touch the chalkboard.[35] After struggling with discrimination in high school and college, he eventually became the first Untouchable to graduate from the Elphinstine College in Bombay in 1908. From there he went to New York and London to earn advanced degrees.

Later, while studying for a PhD in Economics from Columbia University in New York City, he compared the plight of Untouchables to the racism felt by African Americans. He sympathized with the work of Booker T. Washington and the struggle for equal rights for women. Reflecting on the meaning of Washington's life for Ambedkar and other Indians involved in the struggle against the caste system, Ambedkar's Indian biographer, Dhanajay Keer wrote, that,

> Ambedkar's mind must have been deeply impressed with ... the life of Booker T. Washington whose death occurred in 1915. He was a great reformer and educator of the Negro race in America and was founder and President of the Tuskegee Institute which disseminated among the Negroes the doctrine of *education ... and thus broke the shackles of bondage which had crushed the Negroes for ages physically, mentally and spiritually* [my emphasis].[36]

Also, while in the United States, Ambedkar became acquainted with the 14th Amendment of the U.S. Constitution, which guaranteed equal protection of the law. Certainly, the equal protection clause was in stark contrast to the unequal application of Indian laws based on gender and caste.[37]

In New York, he wrote letters home advocating equal education for women. Ambedkar placed his faith in education as a means of providing equality and reforming society. In 1911, he wrote to a friend in India, "We ... can mould the destiny of the children; and if we but follow this principle, be sure that we shall soon see better days and our progress will be greatly accelerated if male education is pursued side by side with the female education the fruits of which you can very well see verified in your own daughter."[38]

Influenced by the American civil rights movement, equal educational opportunity became a theme throughout his writings and eventually was made part of the Indian Constitution. In 1919, he wrote to the *Times of India* that independence and home rule were as much a birthright of the Untouchables as it was of the Brahmins. He argued that the first duty of the "advanced classes" was to educate Untouchables to ensure social equality.[39] The theme of education to achieve social equality continued in his newspaper *Mook Nayak* (Leader of the Dumb), which was first published on January 31, 1920. India, he wrote in the first issue, was the home of social inequality. He portrayed Hindu society as a multileveled tower with no ladders connecting each level. People were doomed to die in the level in which they were born. The aim of the Brahmins, he argued, was to ensure their place at the top of the tower by denying education and power to those below. The depressed state of non-Brahmins, Ambedkar claimed, was a result of their lack of education and unequal political rights.[40]

Ambedkar demanded affirmative action in education to ensure that Untouchables had equal access to educational opportunities. In this context, affirmative action meant a conscious attempt by the government to provide special help to those previously denied an education. Regarding equal educational opportunities, Ambedkar argued, "Education is something which ought to be brought within the reach of every one.... If all communities are to be brought to the level of equality, then the only remedy is to adopt the principle of inequality and to give favored treatment to those who are below the level."[41]

Ambedkar's biographer compared this educational struggle to the work of Booker T. Washington in the United States. It is not clear whether Ambedkar actually made this comparison. However, in the mind of at least one Indian, Dhanajay Keer, the situation was comparable. In his words,

> When the leaders of enslaved humanity rise to lift up their race, those who resort to the political side of the movement arouse hatred of slavery and fan the slaves' passion against their oppressors; but the leaders, who are of reformative zeal, bend inward and preach the doctrine of education of the head, heart and hand. Booker T. Washington ... laid more stress on the practical education and economic development than on the right of vote.[42]

Ambedkar and Mahatma Gandhi can be credited with having major influence over provisions in the 1949 Constitution outlawing untouchability and discrimination based on caste. The actual wording of the Indian Constitution's Fundamental Rights section reflected a study of the United

States's Constitution.[43] Consequently, Ambedkar's U.S. schooling and exposure to U.S. racism played an important role in the liberation movement against England and in attempts to end discrimination in Hindu society. In 1956, Ambedkar finally abandoned Hinduism and converted to Buddhism.

Both Ho Chi Minh and Ambedkar demonstrate the direct impact of colonial schooling and contact with American racism in shaping their world views and the integration of race into wars of liberation. Mao was to become a world leader in advocating the importance of gender equality. Mao made gender equality central to revolutionary process in Asia.

Two years prior to the famous "ism" vote of the New Student's Study Group, Mao publically took on the cause of women's rights. In 1919, he addressed a crowd from the perspective of women, "Gentlemen, we are women!... We are also human beings ... [yet] we are not even allowed to go outside the front gate. The shameless men, the villainous men, make us into their playthings."[44]

Mao made gender an explicit part of revolutionary theory with his involvement in trying to create a communist-led peasant movement. In 1927, Mao wrote a "Report on an Investigation of the Peasant Movement in Hunan" in which changing the status of women was an important part of the revolutionary effort. After listing the three major sources of authority—political, clan, and religious—Mao wrote, "As for women, in addition to being dominated by these three systems of authority, they are also dominated by the men (the authority of the husband)."[45] He contended that overthrowing the power of the landlord would weaken the power of the husband. Also, peasant women tended to have more power than most wealthy Chinese women, according to Mao, because of the importance of their manual labor in supporting the family. "With the rise of the peasant movement," Mao claimed, "the women in many places have now begun to organize rural women's associations; the opportunity has come for them to lift up their heads, and the authority of the husband is getting shakier every day."[46]

Mao was an advocate of women's sexual liberation. He approved of women engaging in premarital and extramarital affairs and even "triangular and multilateral relationships."[47] Mao's biographer, Philip Short, claimed that Mao's popular espousal of sexual liberation occurred many years before it became a popular movement in the West; though sexual liberation movements were espoused by Western utopian and radical movements. Mao urged women to become more sexually liberated.

Mao criticized the authoritarian quality of traditional marriages. He wanted women to have the power to freely enter and leave marriages. This raised the issue of whether changing the economic structure, such as integrating women into the industrial workforce, or changing cultural institutions, such as marriage, was key to social change. Traditional Marxist thought gave economic arrangements the power to determine social relations. Mao, on the other hand, considered both approaches to be important. In part, this reflects Mao's tendency to carry on the Confucian tradition of believing that ideas were a factor in determining history in contrast to Marxist arguments that the determining factor was material conditions. Do ideas determine the material relations of society or are ideas determined by material relations? Mao's acceptance of the importance of ideas in determining material conditions is an important part of the "Chinese essence" he gave to Marxism.

Reflecting Mao's position on gender equality, the first law enacted after the 1949 establishment of the People's Republic of China gave men and women equal rights in marriage.[48] And, regarding economic conditions, Mao urged in 1955 that, "it is of the utmost importance to arouse the broad masses of women to join in productive activity." And, most importantly, "Men and women must receive equal pay for equal work in production. Genuine equality between the sexes can only be realized in the process of the socialist transformation of society as a whole."[49]

Again, I want to emphasize that Ho, Mao, and Ambedkar are not the sole source of global concerns with racism and sexism. However, the adoption by some Westerners of Ho, Mao, and other national liberation struggles as symbols of the fight against racism and sexism represents the global flow of ideas and symbols. By the end of the 20th century, many economic and political radicals replaced social class as the sole basis of social analysis with the new radical triumvirate of class, race, and gender.

NIGHT SCHOOLS AND THE COMMUNIST UNIVERSITIES OF THE PEOPLES (TOILERS) OF THE EAST AND CHINA

After receiving his teacher's certificate, Mao became an instructor of Marxists ideas with a "Chinese Essence" to peasants, scholars, and industrial workers. In this capacity, Mao played a major role in ensuring the spread of Western political and economic ideas. In contrast, Ho remained for many years a foreign student in France and eventually in Moscow attending the Communist University of the Peoples of the East which existed between 1921 and 1937. Eventually, Ho became a political teacher on return to Asia as a member of the Comintern. In their capacities as instructors on world revolution, Mao and Ho contributed to the global sharing of common ideas.

As a teacher, Mao adapted Marxist–Leninist thought to Chinese cultural traditions and economic conditions. Also playing an instructional role on communism was Hendricus Sneevliet, the first member of the Comintern sent to China by Lenin in 1921. The addition of "Chinese essence" to Marxism reflected the continuing antiforeigner feeling in China and a belief in the superior qualities of Chinese civilization. Even foreign communists were resented. Sneevliet's arrival caused Zhang Guotao, a Chinese communist organizer, to comment, "This foreign devil was aggressive and hard to deal with.... He left the impression ... that he had acquired the habits and attitudes of the Dutchmen who lived as colonial masters in the East Indies ... in the eyes of those of us who maintained our self-respect and *who were seeking our own liberation, he seemed endowed with the social superiority complex of the white man* [my emphasis]."[50] In 1917, Mao had commented, "In my opinion Western thought is not necessarily all correct.... Very many parts of it should be transformed at the same time as Eastern thought."[51]

Reflecting the Confucian commitment to education as the vehicle for social change, Mao channeled his teaching talents into the Self-Study University he founded in 1920 with an initial government grant of 2,000 U.S. dollars. Confucius could have written the school's objective of preparing students "for reforming society." Marx might have written the school's other objective of bringing "together the intellectual class and the working class."[52] The school was an academic commune that practiced, according to Mao, the principles of communist living. When the school opened, Mao introduced what were considered at the time extreme ideas on physical fitness. On hot days, he encouraged students to study in a state of undress and engage in a range of physical exercises. And, of course, the school taught the principles of communism as the means of reforming society. In 1922, Mao organized a network of workers' night schools. He wrote a text for the schools that was used to teach both literacy and communist ideas. Party members served as teachers and the most successful, the Miners' and Railwaymen's Club, had 7,000 members using its library, schoolroom, and recreation center. In 1925, Mao participated in the peasant night-school movement.[53]

While Mao was launching his night-school program in literacy and communist ideology, the Communist University of the Peoples of the East was expanding its student recruitment from its original targeted populations in Eastern Soviet countries to other Asian nations and colonies. In the context of the previous discussion of Chinese education, although some Chinese students were attending the Communist University of the Peoples of the East and Mao's night schools, many were also traveling to the United States to study. In both cases, the Soviet and U.S. governments were spending money to attract students as part of an effort to export their particular ideologies.

"What is the mission of the University of the Peoples of the East in relation to the colonial and dependent countries?," Stalin rhetorically asked in 1925 in a speech to the university's students. "Its mission," he asserted, "is to take into account all the specific features of the revolutionary development of these countries ... and to make them [students from these countries] into real revolutionaries, armed with the theory of Leninism, equipped with practical experience of Leninism and capable of carrying out the immediate tasks of the liberation movement in the colonies."[54] In 1925, the University of the Toilers of China was opened and, in 1928, was renamed the Sun Yat-Sen University. In 1926, Deng Xiaoping, Mao's successor left France for Moscow, where he attended Sun Yat-Sen University. Similar to Ho Chi Minh, Deng Xiaoping was attracted to Marxist–Leninist thought while living in France.[55]

The Communist University of Toilers of the East used student-centered instruction to teach a Westernized curriculum and Marxist ideology. Reflecting Lenin's desire to include struggles against imperialism in the work of the Comintern, the Soviet government provided free room and board, clothing, and a stipend for students. At the school they studied science and mathematics along with communist ideology and organizing techniques. This curriculum appealed to Asian students because it offered the scientific and technological tools to defeat Western imperialism and an ideology that supported wars of liberation. Students leaving the school, such as Ho Chi Minh, became communist organizers in their native countries while supporting protection of national cultures and languages, and spreading concepts of Western industrialization and science.

Ho Chi Minh noted that the 1,022 students at the university could be divided into 547 peasants, 265 workers, and 210 proletarian intellectuals. He observed, "If account is taken of the fact that Eastern countries are almost exclusively agricultural, the high percentage of students of peasant origin can readily be understood. In India, Japan, and especially in China, it is the intellectuals faithful to the working class who lead the latter in struggle: this explains the relatively large number of intellectuals among the students."[56] In addition, he stressed, "The relatively low number of worker students is due to the fact that industry and commerce in Eastern countries—naturally excepting Japan—are still undeveloped."[57]

Nationalism and protection of indigenous languages were important issues for liberation movements, Ho Chi Minh, and the Comintern. European and Japanese colonialists tried to make their languages universal. This was particularly true of England, France, and Japan; countries that believed their languages and cultures were superior to those of the rest of the world. Also, Czarist Russia engaged in Russification of its vast empire. For colonized peoples, imperialism encompassed language and culture.

Stalin, who headed the Communist University of Toilers of the East, explained Lenin and the Comintern's position on national languages and culture to the school's student body in 1925. Inherent in the idea of a world revolution was the possibility of a resulting world proletarian culture and lan-

guage. Similar to imperialism, communism raised the possibility of the eradi-
cation of national languages and cultures. However, Stalin dismissed the idea
"of the creation of a single universal language and the dying away of all other
languages in the period of socialism. I have little faith in this theory of a single, all-embracing language."[58] He highlighted the potential tension between communism and national cultures in answering questions received in a
letter from Buryat (southern Siberia) comrades. The letter asked,

> We earnestly request you to explain the following, for us, very serious and dif-
> ficult questions. The ultimate aim of the Communist Party is to achieve a sin-
> gle universal culture. How is one to conceive the transition to a single
> universal culture through the national cultures which are developing within
> the limits of our autonomous republics? How is the assimilation of the specific
> features of the individual national cultures (language, etc.) to take place?[59]

Stalin's answer distinguished between bourgeois and proletarian cultures. A socialist revolution produces a proletarian culture which, he argued, "assumes different forms and modes of expression among the
different peoples.... Proletarian culture does not abolish national culture, it
gives it content. On the other hand, national culture does not abolish proletarian culture, it gives it form."[60] Therefore, nationalist proletarian cultures
can be supported by a socialist world order.

The Communist Universities of the Peoples (Toilers) of the East and
China played an important role in the globalization of culture and education. Many of its graduates, like Ho, traveled to other countries as representatives of the Comintern. The school provided a common education for a
group of ideological missionaries. Similar to religious missionaries, these
ideological missionaries under the sponsorship of the Comintern returned
home to organize and teach a communist revolutionary ideology including
the importance of studying Western science and industrialism. These ideological missionaries, such as Ho Chi Minh and Deng Xiaoping, became
teachers to an entire nation.

JAPAN AS THE "OTHER"

Japan's military and industrial strength plus its imperialistic impulses worried other nations not only in Asia, but also in the West. Japan became an
important "other" that was used by national leaders to rate their own countries. Japan's power played an important role in the thinking of Mao
Zedong. He recalls after reading a pamphlet in 1907 at the age of 14 on Japan's takeover of Korea and Taiwan and which predicted that China would
loose power in Burma and Vietnam: "I felt depressed about the future of my
country and began to realize it was the duty of all people to help save it."[61]
Anger towards Japan continued after World War II as exemplified by North

Korean communist leader Kim Il Sung telling school graduates in 1947, "Comrades, under Japanese imperialist rule the desire for learning ... was left unfulfilled and our people's talents remained hidden. Even those who had the good fortune to receive a slave education were condemned to a miserable and pitiable fate and position."[62]

Japan became an object of both admiration and loathing as it pioneered the nineteenth century Westernization of Asian education and economic systems and then engaged in an extended period of imperialism leading to World War II. As already mentioned, scholars, including political radicals from China and Vietnam, flocked to Japan to study and in the 1930s became Japan's enemies. In 1931, Japan forced the Chinese to withdraw from Manchuria and established the puppet government of Manchukuo. In 1933, Japan invaded China. Already in control of Korea and Taiwan, the country was ready to launch its imperialist thrust into Indochina, the Philippines, and other parts of southeast Asia.

Soviet leaders worried about Japanese imperialism taking over Soviet lands in the East. Through the Comintern, the Soviet Union urged a united front against Japanese power. The call for a united front plus the Japanese takeover of Manchuria cemented Mao's already existing anti-Japanese feelings. In 1937, Mao participated in the opening of the Anti-Japanese Military and Political University or Red Army University as part of the resistance movement against Japanese invaders. At the opening of the university, Mao mixed communist revolutionary rhetoric with calls to defeat Japanese imperialism: "You have now the spirit to overcome difficulties and unite with the masses. If you can use your talents to develop from this basis, it is entirely possible to defeat Japan and drive the Japanese out of China."[63] Celebrating Stalin's birthday in 1939, Mao answered the rhetorical question of why Chinese should observe the day of Stalin's birth: "Because he is the leader of the great Soviet Union, of the great Communist International, and of the liberation movement of mankind, and *because he helps China to fight Japan* [my emphasis]."[64]

In 1937, Mao delivered his now famous lecture "On Practice" at the Anti-Japanese Military and Political University. The lecture is subtitled, "On The Relation Between Knowledge and Practice—Between Knowing and Doing."[65] The lecture provides a summary of his thoughts on the role of ideas and education in changing society. By placing an emphasis on the role of ideas in changing society, while also stressing the dialectical relationship between ideas and material conditions, Mao gave a "Chinese essence" to Marxism. The Preamble to the 1982 Constitution of the People's Republic of China recognizes Mao's distinctive contribution to Marxism in its declaration, "Under the leadership of the Communist Party of China and the guidance of Marxism–Leninism and Mao Zedong Thought, the Chinese people ... will ... follow the socialist road."[66] From the perspective of current leaders, China is guided not only by the ideas of Marx and Lenin but also by Mao's contributions to communist ideology. Much of Mao's thinking would later appear in the educational works of Paulo Freire and his discussions of the dialogical process.[67]

"Extraordinary" only modestly describes the circumstances of Mao's lecture "On Practice." The Anti-Japanese Military and Political University was founded shortly after Mao and Red Army completed the historic Long March from 1934 to 1935, which was marked by military engagements, food shortages, extreme physical conditions, and many other hardships. The army settled in a desolate area of northern China near the Mongolian border. The University was situated in a natural cave with students sitting on rocks or the bare ground taking notes. Imagine members of the Red Army listening to philosophical lectures while waiting to engage the Japanese in battle.

"On Practice" was part Confucian and part Marx. Traditional Confucianism placed a great deal of emphasis on self-reflection about personal conduct that promoted harmony and justice in a collective society. Examining and changing ideas as a result of social practice was important in Confucianism for developing ethical behavior. From a Marxist standpoint, what was missing from Confucianism was how material conditions, particularly social class, determined ideas. Confucianism accepted a hierarchical society with moral leaders directing the actions of the masses. If you add the effect of class position and material conditions on intellectual reflection, then Confucian-style reflection involved the personal examination of possible bias caused by one's social class or material advantages. Self-reflection required a testing of ideas to see if they resulted in greater social and economic equality. In other words, a combination of Confucian and Marxism required a consideration of how material conditions determined ideas and, in turn, how ideas affected material conditions; this process resulted in a dialectical process between inner thoughts and the outside world.

This dialectical process was a fundamental part of Mao's thinking about education and the support of the Cultural Revolution of the 1960s. For Mao, revolution required more than simply changing economic arrangements, it also required changing the cultural influences on thinking. In the opening lines of "On Practice," Mao described his purpose: "To make clear the dialectical-materialist process of knowledge arising from the practice of changing reality—the gradually deepening process of knowledge."[68]

As examples of the dialectic process, Mao used evolving levels of understanding of the nature of capitalism and imperialism. These levels of understanding closely parallels Paulo Freire's levels of consciousness that a person passed through as they gained a clearer understanding of their objective reality.[69] In his analysis of the evolution of thinking about imperialism, Mao argued that, "The first stage was one of superficial, perceptual knowledge, as shown in the indiscriminate antiforeign struggles." Put into practice, simple antiforeign actions did little to curb imperialism. This led to the second stage when "the Chinese people arrived at rational knowledge, when they saw the ... oppression and exploitation of China's broad masses by imperialism in alliance with China's compradors and feudal class."[70]

Based on the example of imperialism and other stages of knowledge, Mao outlined the steps in formulation of knowledge involving an interaction between thought and material conditions. I have summarized these ideas in the following outline.

1. The first step in the process of knowledge is contact with the things of the external world or, in other words, social practice; this belongs to the stage of perception.
2. The second step is a synthesis of the data of social practice by making a rearrangement or reconstruction.
   a. This is the stage of conception and judgment.
   b. If the data of perception is rich enough than one can develop valid concepts and correct reasoning.
3. The third stage is changing the world through the application of concepts and reasoning derived from reflection on social practice; this is revolutionary practice.
4. The fourth stage is reflecting on whether or not anticipated results occur as a result of attempting to change the world through the application of concepts and reasoning derived from the first stage of perception.
5. The fifth stage again attempts to change the world by applying concepts and reasoning resulting from reflection on the social results of the application of the knowledge derived in third stage.
6. According to Mao, this interactive process between thought and action never ends as humans continually seek revolutionary knowledge.[71]

Mao summarized his theory: "To discover truth through practice, and through practice to verify and develop truth; to start from perceptual knowledge and actively develop it into rational knowledge; and then, starting from rational knowledge, actively to direct revolutionary practice so as to remold the subjective and objective world will require practice, knowledge, more practice, more knowledge."[72] This cyclical process, according to Mao, would continue to infinity.

So here was Mao formulating a theory of knowledge that would affect educational and political practices against the background of the deprivations of the Long March and an impending war against Japanese imperialism. Later, during the 1960s' Cultural Revolution, Mao commanded intellectuals to correct their thinking through practice by working in factories and on farms. In "On Practice," Mao asserted that, "not only must a true revolutionary leader be adept at correcting his ideas, theories, plans, or programs when they are found to be erroneous ... but he must also ... be adept at making himself and all his fellow revolutionaries advance and revise their subjective ideas accordingly."[73] In this framework, all revolutionaries become teachers helping each other to achieve knowledge.

Ho Chi Minh was agreeing to the anti-Japanese policies of the Comintern as Mao was joining with the Soviet Union to fight Japanese imperialism,. As discussed previously, Ho Chi Minh was influenced by Vietnamese anti-imperialist Phan Boi Chau who studied and operated a school in Japan. By the 1930s, Ho Chi Minh was warning the Comintern about the "Japanese fascist scheme" for Asia.[74] In 1941, he announced the formation of the Viet Minh Front and, utilizing the slogan "national liberation," cried out, "our people suffer under a double yoke: they serve not only as buffaloes and horses to the French invaders but also as slaves to the Japanese plunderers. Alas! What sin have our people committed to be doomed to such a wretched plight!"[75] He turned to the example of China and he urged, "Let us follow the heroic example of the Chinese people.... Raise aloft the insurrectionary banner and guide the pole throughout the country to overthrow the Japanese and the French."[76]

Similar to Mao, Kim Il Sung's socialist pedagogy developed during his experience fighting a guerrilla war against Japan in Manchuria. On April 25, 1932, Kim Il Sung claims to have organized the first anti-Japanese guerrilla group in Manchuria; North Korea now celebrates this day as the founding date of the Korean People's Army. In 1933, he began fighting with groups of Chinese communists against a common Japanese enemy. In 1935, the Seventh Congress of the Comintern called for a united front against all imperialist forces including Japan. The same year, the Chinese Communist Party issued a declaration uniting all the anti-Japanese guerrilla fighters. In 1941, Il Sung was forced to retreat to the Soviet Union where Kim Jong Il, his first son and successor to power in North Korea, was born. In 1945, after the United States and the Soviet Union liberated Korea from Japan, Kim Il Sung returned and was declared a hero of the Korean revolution by Soviet occupation troops. The same year, he became head of the North Korean Branch of the Korean Communist Party.[77]

The struggle against Japan was echoed throughout Il Sung's writings on socialist pedagogy. In his 1947 congratulatory remarks to the first school graduates under the new communist government, he asserted that education under Japanese rule had deprived Koreans of knowledge of their own language and history, and scientific and technical competence. "You suffered," he told the graduates, "from the harmful education of Japanese imperialism in the past, but after liberation received democratic education for two years. You are a new generation of Korean youths who have learned our spoken and written language, history, science, and technology, the path Korea should follow, and the law of historical development [Marxism]."[78] At the 1947 opening of the Kim Il Sung University, he urged students: "First, you should strive to eliminate the survivals of Japanese imperialism from your way of thinking." Second, he called on them to develop a political awareness of the country's mission. And third, "you should study hard and make every endeavor to master science and technique and to equip yourselves with Marxism–Leninism.... You have to produce trains, cars and ships on your own and also create a splendid literature and art."[79]

CONCLUSION: THE GLOBAL TRANSFER OF EDUCATION

Ho and Mao's educational biographies demonstrate the global flow and adaptation of ideas. Consider the following sequence of events:

1. Worried about Western imperialism, Japanese leaders want to utilize Western military technology;
2. To utilize Western military technology, Japanese leaders adapt Western schooling, particularly in science, math, and foreign languages to Japanese culture;
3. As a symbol of resistance to Western imperialism, Japan attracts scholars from other Asian nations;
4. Interest in Confucian education declines as U.S. progressive education is applauded;
5. The Bolshevik revolution spreads ideas about socialist education and anti-imperialism;
6. Fear of Japanese imperialism unites the Soviet Union with anti-Japanese Asian nations;
7. Mao adds a Chinese essence to socialist pedagogy and curriculum while still emphasizing Western concerns with math and science;
8. Eventually Mao's educational ideas spread around the world as an educational Cold War develops between communist and capitalist nations.

Although the list just presented tells only part of the story of the global transference of educational ideas, it does highlight the importance of the "other." By the 20th century, the nature and content of schooling was linked to military and economic strength. Fear of the other often led to educational changes that were suppose to counter the other's power. These changes involved attempts to adopt the other's educational system and methods or to adapt the other's ideas to an indigenous culture.

Out of this process developed important global trends in education. First, education for industrial and scientific work became a focus of most school systems. Secondly, a split occurred between pedagogies labeled as progressive or socialist and pedagogies emphasizing assimilation into the existing workforce and political culture. The two major super-powers, the Soviet Union and the United States, abandoned progressive pedagogy for more formalistic or Stalinist methods of preparing workers to serve national economic goals. Progressive and socialist pedagogies remained attractive to those seeking social change. These educational methods emphasized critical thinking by linking thought and action, and learning through experience. As I suggested, there is a direct connection between Mao's socialist pedagogy and that of Paulo Freire whose ideas played a critical role in radical education movements in the late 20th and early 21st centuries.

In the next chapter, I explore the impact on global education trends of the development of educational security states after World War II. Post-World War II national agendas called for the integration of education into the military needs of the national security state. During this period, Kim Il Sung and Mao Zedong made significant contributions to socialist pedagogical theory. Ho Chi Minh became a symbol for the global struggle against racism and for third world wars of liberation. After the 1953 death of Stalin, the Soviet Union focused its military preparation on the development of missiles for space exploration and carrying nuclear weapons, which affected its education system. In the United States, the Cold War, the civil rights movement, and the Korean and Vietnam wars, caused rapid educational changes that integrated schools into global military and economic concerns. National educational agendas were increasingly affected by the results of Western and Japanese colonialism, and communist revolutions.

Chapter 3

Schooling and Cultural Wars: Stakhanovite Workers and the American Way

After World War II, the Cold War between the Soviet Union and the United States enlisted schools, media, and other instruments of ideological control to the cause of military preparedness. Both nations launched a global educational offensive to persuade others of the justness of their cause. Educational systems were integrated into Cold War planning. Both nations tried to persuade other countries to join their side. As the Cold War unfolded, communism triumphed in China and colonial empires crumbled. Wars of liberation fed the flames of the Cold War. Confronting the revolutionary activities of Ho Chi Minh and Kim Il Sung, the United States was drawn into wars in Korea and Vietnam.

In this chapter, I focus on the interchange of educational ideas between the Soviet Union and the United States during the 1940s and 1950s as the two superpowers integrated their educational security states. I analyze the instruments for ideological management that were developed in the Soviet Union and the United States. In the Soviet Union, where leaders acknowledged the use of propaganda, socialist realism dictated the content of the arts, which in combination with school work, was to create the new "socialist man and woman." Less willing to acknowledge the use of propaganda, American leaders talked about public relations and influencing public opinion during their campaign against Soviet ideological influence. Americans used the arts, public monuments and memories, and schools to influence national and international public opinion.

STAKHANOVITE WORKERS, LEI FENG,
AND SOCIALIST REALISM

During the 1930s and 1940s, Soviet citizens looked at posters portraying the smiling faces of the new socialist man and woman with thickly developed muscles bulging under their worker's shirts and trousers, whereas U.S. citizens looked at billboards displaying a happy White family riding in an automobile under the banner "American Way." In both countries, schools were joined by the arts and public celebrations to consciously create and reinforce a belief in nation and national culture. Traditionally, government-operated schools engaged in culture and nation building. These efforts were often reinforced by novels, paintings, plays, music, and other forms of art. In the 19th century, these different sources of culture and nation building usually acted independently of each other. Seldom were there efforts to coordinate these various disseminators of ideas and images. This changed in the 20th century as the Soviet leaders under the banner of "socialist realism" educated the new socialist man and woman to be dedicated communist superworkers, and United States's leaders used public relations methods to counter the influence of communist ideas by creating an image of the "American way of life."

Capturing the public imagination with heroes and myths played an important part in efforts to mold public opinion. By influencing the public imagination, it was hoped that control would be exerted over how people interpreted their experiences. To illustrate the parallel use of these methods, I compare the Soviet glorification of the Stakhanovite worker with the American Way campaign. In the Soviet Union, mythologizing the Soviet worker through socialist realism was considered the key to developing united support for communism and the building of a strong industrialized state. In the United States, the American Way campaign tried to win citizen loyalty to images of democracy and capitalism by associating them with the happiness and economic success of White middle-class families.

Socialist realism embodied Lenin's belief that art should be for the people, and contain ideological and social class themes, particularly "educating workers in the spirit of communism."[1] Maxim Gorky, after being appointed Chairman of the Union of Soviet Writers in 1932, translated Lenin's ideas into a socialist realist philosophy that gave art the role of contributing to a glorious future for the Soviet Union. In the words of art historian Matthew Brown, "Most famously, he [Gorky] asserted that the artist should be both 'midwife and gravedigger', that he should 'bury everything harmful to people, harmful even when they like it.' In other words, the artist was called upon not only to create a new art, but to exterminate the pernicious elements of the old."[2]

Born in 1868, Gorky grew up in the bleak world of extreme poverty in Czarist Russia. As a hobo, he drifted through villages and cities hustling odd jobs. Self-educated, he would later consider his real teachers to be the pros-titutes, thieves, small shopkeepers, stevedores, peasants, police, industrial workers, and students that he encountered living in a world of violence, de-pravity, and sometimes hope. Published in 1923, his autobiographical sketch *My Universities* explained why he believed that through the social re-lations of the masses one could understand real sources of knowledge. In *My Universities*, he recounts a conversation with a policeman who just admit-ted being responsible for arresting Gorky's friend on the charge of illegally printing anti-Czarist pamphlets. The policeman complained that institu-tions, particular religion, spent too much money and time helping the poor and weak. "It's the strong people that ought to be helped," the policeman explained, "the healthy ones—so they won't have to waste their strength."[3] Gorky reflected that he had heard these ideas many times and that, "Read-ing Nietzsche, some 7 years later, I vividly recalled the philosophy of the Kazan policeman. And I may remark in passing: *I have seldom found ideas in books which I had not already encountered in actual life* [my emphasis]."[4]

As Chairman of the Union of Soviet Writers, Gorky articulated the pur-pose of socialist realism in building the Soviet State. In 1934, to the dele-gates of the First All-Union Congress of Soviet Writers, Gorky explained the difference between communist and capitalist art. Originally, Gorky ar-gued, art originated in people's work but was later divorced from these ori-gins. This separation made it possible for capitalist art to be devoted to the "constant development of external and material living comforts and devel-opment of luxury."[5] Besides enhancing the material comfort of capitalists, Gorky asserted, bourgeois art extended capitalist morality over the world. In the same manner, capitalist schools, he contended, were in "the business of training only obedient servants of capitalism, who believed in its perma-nence and lawfulness."[6] In addition, literacy was used to divide the working class and to teach a belief in the irreconcilable differences between races and nations as a justification for colonial policy. The result was that capital-ist art, education, and literacy programs provided expensive goods for the rich, obedient servants for capital, and supporters of racist colonial policies.

The meaning Gorky gave to equality of educational opportunity re-flected his overall concern about the use of ideas to suppress the working class. From his standpoint, equality of educational opportunity should not simply be determined by the single criterion that everyone has an equal chance to be educated, but also by whether or not the content of instruc-tion empowers the learner. He used a similar argument regarding equal-ity of access to art. Real equality of access to art depended on the type of art that was available; art should be something that workers could appreciate and understand. Regarding equality of educational opportunity, Gorky argued, "In our country the target has been set of providing equal educa-tional opportunities to all; all members of our society are to be equally acquainted with the successes and achievements of labor, in a striving to transform human labor into the art of controlling the forces of nature."[7] From this perspective, students receiving an education for service to capitalist masters did not have real equality in educational opportunity. They were not given an education that provided them with equality of control over the labor process or equal understanding of the economic processes of societies. The result of this distorted concept of equality of opportunity was to deny people what Gorky called "world understanding." In his words, "Begun in antiquity and continuing down to the present time, this criminal exclusion and expulsion of millions of people from the business of world-understanding have led to hundreds of millions of people, disunited by ideas of race, nation and religion, to remain in a state of abysmal ignorance and horrifying intellectual blindness, in the darkness of superstitions and prejudices of every kind."[8]

The masses were denied a "world understanding" by the separation of art and education from peoples' work. Plato, Gorky told the delegates, "founded a world-understanding divorced from labor processes and the conditions of phenomena of everyday life."[9] Later, religious leaders took over the business of providing a world-understanding and used a metaphysical explanation that continued to divorce ideas from concrete social relations. In the 20th century, this reasoning was used to support a fallacious concept of freedom of art. "Art's freedom and creative thought's self-will," he stated, "were defended with fury and verbosity, the possibility of literature existing and developing outside of classes, and its independence of social politics was insisted on."[10]

For art and education, Gorky argued, to provide an equal world understanding to all people, it must be based on social reality; the real labor of the people. Consequently, the Communist Party must take an authoritarian role, according to Gorky, to ensure that art and education serves the interests of the working class. "Party members who work in literature," Gorky told the members of the Congress, "must be not only teachers of the ideology that organizes workers of all lands for the final battle for freedom; in all its behavior Party leadership must be a morally authoritative force. This force must above all inculcate in writers a consciousness of their collective responsibility for everything taking place in their midst."[11]

The goal of social realist art, according to Gorky, was to promote socialist labor. This meant that art should glorify the contribution of individual workers to the socialist cause. Gorky described these individual workers as "our heroes of labor, the flower of the working mass … whose lofty and wise aim it is to emancipate toilers all over the world from the power of capitalism with its distortion of man."[12] By encouraging people to be heroes of labor, Gorky asserted,

Socialist realism proclaims that life is action, creativity, whose aim is the unfettered development of man's most valuable individual abilities for his victory over the forces of Nature, for his health and longevity, for the great happiness of living on earth, which he, in conformity with the constant growth of his requirements, wishes to cultivate as a magnificent habitation of mankind united in one family.[13]

Through all forms of art, mass media, and schooling, socialist realism mythologized the worker as the real hero of the Soviet state. Posters, movies, books, and art were all used to eulogize the contributions of the working class. For Gorky, the celebration of workers was similar to the contributions of traditional folklore and myth in motivating the masses to action. "At one time in antiquity," Gorky argued, "the oral history of the workers was the only means of organizing their collective experience, the only incarnation of their thoughts in images and simulator of their collective energy."[14] The oral history of antiquity, Gorky contended, created myths about gods and heroes that guided the actions of humans. These myths, Gorky asserted, operated on individual and collective imaginations. Therefore, the creation and dissemination of myths through the arts was a means of controlling citizens' imaginations and, as a result, directing their energies into activities that supported the Soviet state as the representative of the working class.

There are several important things to note about Gorky's arguments before turning to the actual use of socialist realism to mythologize workers. First is Gorky's criticism of the idea of freedom of art or "art for art's sake." In the 1950s, U.S. leaders supported abstract art as an example of how U.S. society supported artistic freedom and art for art's sake as opposed to the authoritarian control exerted by the Communist Party in promoting socialist realism. In part, the ideological struggle between capitalism and communism in the 1950s was symbolized by the differences between abstract and socialist realist art. Second, Gorky and others provided an argument that allowed socialist realism to glorify leaders like Lenin and Stalin. Gorky made a distinction between leaderism and leadership. Leaderism, he defined, as attempt by individuals to have power over others. Leadership, on the other hand, organizes human behavior for "achieving the best practical results with the least expenditure of energy."[15] Lenin and Stalin provided leadership and, therefore, along with workers, they should be extolled by socialist art and education.

Using myths embedded in people's imaginations to control mass behavior was, as I explain later, very close to the methods used by U.S. advertising, public relations, and others wanting to shape public opinion in the United States. The major difference was that Soviets mythologized the worker whereas in the United States, an effort was made to mythologize the "American way of life." In socialist realism, the most important myths were those associated with hero-workers and leaders. The hero-workers myth was based on Aleksei Stakhanov, a 30-year-old miner working at the Central Irmino Mine in the Donets Basin. On August 31, 1935, according to legend, Stakhanov dug out 102 tons of coal in a 6-hour shift or 14 times his daily quota. The newspaper Pravda hailed this as a world record and Stakhanov as a hero of the working class. Soviet leadership used this achievement to launch the Stakhanovite movement. Workers were honored with the title of "Stakhanovite" for exceeding quotas. In 1935, the All-Union Conference of Stakhanovites in industry and transportation met in the Kremlin. At the meeting, Stakhanovites recounted their heroic efforts to surpass their quotas. At the meeting, Stalin declared that under socialism, "Life has become better, and happier too."[16] Stalin's words were set to music and became the anthem for the Stakhanovite movement.

In the context of Gorky's reasoning, one could envisage a Soviet worker's imagination being filled with the heroic deeds of Stakhanov as the worker hummed the song, "Life has become better, and happier too." Besides hard work, Stakhanovites were to display qualities of cleanliness, neatness, and a desire to learn. Educating Stakhanovites became a goal of Soviet schools. Images of Stakhanovite workers driving cars and consuming goods appeared on posters. A public image was generated that the good life could be achieved by being a Stakhanovite. Images of consumer happy Stakhanovites were often contrasted with the harsh life of pre-Soviet times to prove that "Life has become better and happier too."[17]

Stakhanovite images appeared in educational material. In Stalin's favorite *A Book for Parents*, A.S. Makarenko tells the story of hard-working librarian Vera Ignatyevna who is unable to convey to her children the ethic and joy of hard work. Vera, as head of a factory library, loves her work and devotes many hours to ensuring that the factory's workers are well supplied with uplifting reading material. One evening, she is informed by Stakhanovite worker Andrei Klimovich Stoyanov that she will be given a prize for her cultural work. Makarenko's description illustrates the use of socialist realism to create the myth of the heroic Soviet worker.

> He was a milling-machine operator and rather a special one at that, for the other operators never mentioned his name except in double form:
>
> "Stoyanov-Himself."
>
> "Even-Stoyanov."
>
> "Only-Stoyanov."
>
> "Oh!-Stoyanov."
>
> "Stoyanov's-the-man."

Stoyanov's team had overfulfilled its quota by 170–190 percent.... Stoyanov's team had planted a whole flower-bed round their machines; there were even jokes that the team would soon be renamed "The Andrei Stoyanov Milling-Machine Nursery-Garden."[18]

At Vera's award ceremony, Andrei Stoyanov explained the importance of her work as a devoted factory librarian: "Round such people as Vera Ignatyevna a new socialist culture was growing and spreading."[19] While listening to his comments, her imagination embraces the mythology of the Soviet hero worker. She "realized with that she was indeed performing a great task, that her love of books was by no means a secret personal feeling, but something great and useful and important. She came face to face with something she had not noticed before—the social significance of her job."[20]

But Vera's life is plagued by the contradiction between her model working life and raising two selfish and lazy children who treat her like a servant. Stakhanovite Andrei accuses Vera, who is a single mother, of raising children who will be enemies of the working class. He disciplines her children and teaches them the "joy" of fulfilling household duties. Vera then realizes the connection between her library work and raising children. "In the library there was duty," she reflects, "the joy of labor, and love for her job. In the family there was the joy of labor, and love, and there was also duty. Duty ... it was almost impossible to distinguish where duty ended and delight in work, the joy of labour, began. Here duty and joy were blended in such gentle harmony."[21]

According to Gorky's theories, Vera's imagination was permeated with images of heroic overachievers willing and effortlessly fulfilling their duties at work, school, and political activities. These images motivated Vera to heroic efforts in maintaining the library and ensuring the cultural growth of the factory workers, and in raising children who were not class enemies, but shared the same imaginative qualities as their mother. In this imaginative world, joy was a by-product of overachievement for Soviet society. Makarenko wrote, "Joy! What a strange, old-fashioned word.... The word for happy poets, for lovers, the word for the family nest. Who before the revolution would have thought of applying this word to business, to labour, to office work?"[22]

Socialist realist paintings portrayed happy workers and beloved leaders. A 1937 painting by Olga Yanovskaya, *Stakhanovites in a Box at the Bolshoi Theater,* illustrated the rewards given to overachieving workers. In the painting, old and young Stakhanovite workers fill a theater box intently watching a ballet. An important aspect of the painting was that it was workers in the box seats and not wealthy capitalists.[23] The importance of Communist Party control of factory life was portrayed in Ilya Lukomski's *The Factory Party*

Committee, 1937, which showed a group of Party members sitting around a table with their attention focused on a speech given by a standing worker; the viewer learned that Party leaders listened seriously to workers.[24] Gorky's distinction between leaderism and leadership justified the paintings, photographs, busts, and statues of Marx, Lenin, and Stalin that adorned public spaces. According art historian Matthew Bown, the most celebrated of these "leadership" forms of art was Vasili Efanov's *An Unforgettable Meeting, 1936–1937* which showed Stalin clasping the hand of a female delegate to a Kremlin conference while a surrounding group claps and cheers.[25] One commentator declared, "To see Stalin, to shake his hand, is the supreme reward for the creme de la creme of the people of the Soviet country."[26] The idolatry of Stalin ended after his death in 1953 but socialist realism survived in the what was called the "Severe Style." Brown wrote, "The Severe Style did not represent a revolt against the communist ethic, but a revision of it which closely reflected Khrushchev's [Stalin's successor] own reforms, designed to give communism a caring face, such as his [Khrushchev's] crash programme in residential building."[27]

In the 1950s in China, after the successful takeover by the Communist Party, the mythical figure became a People's Liberation Army soldier named Lei Feng who led a self-sacrificing life cleaning his comrades' bedding and clothes, helping army cooks, and serving the public, "under the motto, 'It's glorious to be a nameless hero'."[28] His selfless loyalty to Mao Zedong and the Communist Party was expressed in a well-publicized diary that contained exemplary passages, as quoted by Mao's biographer Philip Short:

> I felt particularly happy this morning when I got up, because last night I had dreamed of our great leader, Chairman Mao. And it so happens that today is the Party's 40th anniversary. Today I have to much to tell the Party, so much gratitude to the Party.... I am like a toddler, and the Party is like my mother who helps me, leads me, and teaches me to walk.... My beloved Party, my loving mother, I am always your loyal son.[29]

In chapter 4, I discuss in more detail communist China's efforts to influence public opinion. In the case of Lei Feng, there was a dramatic difference between him and Stakhanovite workers who were action figures building as new socialist state. Lei Feng seemed like a figure straight out of Confucianism who obediently served a moral leader and father. In either case, imagining Stakhanov or Lei Feng were to evoke emotional warmth and joy; a feeling of goodness caused by thinking of working hard for the state or showing willing obedience to the socialist cause.

THE AMERICAN WAY OF LIFE

In the United States, images of a prosperous "American way of life" were used to influence public opinion. Advertising executives, public relations experts, and political philosophers like Walter Lippmann in his 1922 book *Public Opinion,* advocated psychological techniques for shaping mass opinion.[30] Some Americans in the 1920s, including Lippmann, public relations pioneer Edward Bernays, and Stanley Resor, head of J. Walter Thompson, the world's largest advertising firm until the latter part of the 20th century, believed that the masses primarily act on irrational impulses.[31] During this period, there was a growing distrust of public behavior in the political arena and marketplace. Democratic and capitalist theories often assumed a rational voter or consumer. Stanley Resor and other advertising pioneers rejected the notion that the buyer made rational decisions in a free market. Advertising utilized irrational emotions to persuade people to buy products. Resor believed that "Advertising, after all, is educational work, mass education."[32] Resor attributed his advertising methods to the influence of William Graham Sumner, whose lectures he heard while attending Yale. Sumner's analysis of human motivation made consumer a function of the irrational desires of hunger, vanity, fear, and sexuality. J. Walter Thompson pioneered the advertising use of sex and social fears to sell products.

Established as the propaganda arm of the United States during World War I, Committee for Public Information was, according to its Chair George Creel, the "greatest adventure in advertising" in its use of speakers, posters, schools, and movies to whip up fervor in support of the war. Using the methods of the advertising industry, the Committee for Public Information appealed to emotions rather than reason. The Committee blanketed the country with posters using menacing German soldiers to sell Liberty Bonds and U.S. soldiers rushing back to camp with the warning "He Must Not Overstay His Leave." One grotesque poster, "This is Kultur," showed German soldiers cutting off the hands of a victim while in the background another German soldier was strangling a woman.[33]

Adolph Hitler was an admirer of the Committee for Public Information's work. Reflecting on the German war experience, Hitler praised U.S. propaganda methods for portraying a monstrous German enemy whose image was reinforced by the fears of the battlefield. German propaganda failed, Hitler argued, because it showed the enemy as a cartoon figure which did not receive a reinforcing stimulus on the battlefield.[34] In *Mein Kampf,* written in the 1920s, Hitler called propaganda "political advertising" and asserted, "The art of propaganda lies in understanding the emotional ideas of the great masses and finding, through a psychologically correct form, the way to the attention and thence to the heart of the broad masses."[35] Assuming that the masses had a limited intelligence, Hitler argued that propaganda should not use reason and should avoid complicated arguments: "the receptivity of the great masses is very limited, their intelligence is small, but their power of forgetting is enormous."[36]

Slogans, Hitler argued, was the key to propagandizing the irrational and of limited intelligence of the masses. "All effective propaganda," Hitler claimed, "must be limited to a very few points and must harp on these in slogans until the last member of the public understands what you want him to understand by your slogan."[37] Hitler's disdain for the masses and the necessity of utilizing their "primitive sentiments" as opposed to their reason was expressed in the following passage:

> But the most brilliant propagandist technique will yield no success unless one fundamental principle is borne in mind constantly and with unflagging attention. It must confine itself to a few points and repeat them over and over. Here, as so often in this world, persistence is the first and most important requirement for success.[38]

Hitler also argued that propaganda must be prolonged and consistent: "All advertising, whether in the field of business or politics, achieves success through the continuity and sustained uniformity of its application."[39]

Another fan of the Committee for Public Information was American political philosopher Walter Lippman. In *Public Opinion* (1921), Lippman wrote about the Committee: "The administration was trying, and while the war continued it very largely succeeded, I believe, in creating something that might almost be called one public opinion all over America."[40] Interspersing his book with examples of wartime censorship and propaganda methods, Lippman cynically concluded, "the manufacture of consent is capable of great refinements ... and the opportunities for manipulation [are] open to anyone who understands the process."[41]

The idea of a rational and knowledgeable voter, Lippman argued, was a product of a time when the United States was primarily composed of small and simple communities where voters could understand the issues. In the more complex 20th century society, the voter was reduced to voting "yes" or "no" without fully understanding the issues involved. Very often, Lippman contended, voting was based on pictures or symbols in the voter's imagination rather than on rational decisions. Symbols were, according to Lippman, one means of controlling voter behavior: "The symbol [Americanism] in itself signifies literally no one thing in particular, but it can be associated with almost anything. And because of that it can become the common bond of common feelings, even though those feelings were originally attached to disparate ideas."[42]

Like Maxim Gorky, Lippman believed mass behavior could be manipulated by influencing the public imagination. In Lippman's words, "For the most part we do not first see, and then define. We define first and then see.... We imagine things before we experience them. And these preconceptions ... govern deeply the whole process of perception."[43] Imagination, from Lippmann's perspective, could be manipulated through pictures, words, and symbols that, of course, were also utilized by Gorky and Soviet leaders to implant Stakhanovite myths in Soviet minds. Imagination acted as a filter to real-life experiences. Therefore, according to Lippman, the control of public opinion could be accomplished by preparing the human imagination to interpret events in a distinct manner.

Founder of the public relations profession, Edward Bernays referred to "the wires which control the public mind"[44] Like the advertising industry and Lippman, Bernays believed that public relations campaigns should be directed towards a person's desires and emotions rather than reason. Symbols could be used to evoke positive emotions. The wires controlling the emotions or public opinion were, from the perspective of public relations, connected to schools, mass media, clubs, community organizations, civic speakers, and other disseminators of information. Public opinion could be controlled by the information and symbols sent through these wires. The result, according to Bernays, would be the "regimenting the public mind."[45]

Controlling the wires leading to the public mind underpinned the response of U.S. industry to threat of the other; the other being socialism and communism. Under the shadow of the other, Lewis H. Brown, president of the Johns-Manville Corporation, claimed in 1937 that teachers knew more about Karl Marx than the inner workings of local factories. As a leader of the American Way campaign, Brown contended, "We must with moving pictures and other educational material carry into the schools of the generation of tomorrow an interesting story of the part that science and industry have played in creating a more abundant life for those who are fortunate to live in this great country of ours."[46]

Paralleling in time Soviet uses of Stakhanovites images, the U.S. National Association of Manufacturers (NAM) launched the American Way public relations campaign in 1936. During the depression years of the 1930s, U.S. industry worried that the economic downturn would result in greater acceptance by the American public of communist and socialist ideologies. NAM officials assumed that public opinion was not based on rational discourse. A 1936 internal NAM memo stated, "Public sentiment is everything—with it nothing can fail; without it nothing can succeed.... Right now Joe Doakes—the average man—is a highly confused individual."[47] The memo went on to argue that Joe Doakes should be convinced of the advantages of a competitive economy.

The two major goals of the American Way campaign were to create filters in the public mind so that on hearing or seeing the word "American" or "democracy," there was an immediate association with the consumption of goods produced by a capitalist economy. Thus, "the American way of life" meant economic prosperity, high wages, and the ability to consume large amounts of products. The American Way campaign included disseminating images and information through billboards, advertising, schools, mass media, and civic organizations. An early American Way advertisement captured the meaning of the campaign:

WHAT IS YOUR AMERICA ALL ABOUT?

Our American plan of living is simple.

Its ideal—that works—is the greatest good for the greatest number.

You ... are part owner of the United States, Inc....

Our American plan of living is pleasant.

Our American plan of living is the world's envy.

No nation, or group lives as well as we do.[48]

In 1937, the National Industrial Council, the newly formed public relations arm of the NAM, created a public relations diagram, which looked like Bernays' wires to the public mind. The diagram showed a local public relations committee composed of manufacturers, merchants, civic clubs, churches, bar associations, and educators. "Wires" led from the publicity director to schools, newspapers, radio, civic speakers, clubs, open house meetings for workers in factories, and theaters. The NAM suggested that publicity directors introduce pro-business ideas into schools through the medium of printed materials for school libraries and classrooms, by sparking an interest in studying local industries, and using movies and slides.

In 1937, the NAM placed billboards in every U.S. community; more than 2,500 declared either "World's Highest Standard of Living—There's no way like the American Way" or "World's Highest Wages—There's no way like the American Way."[49] Billboards relied on emotional slogans and symbols to sell Americanism by proclaiming: "World's Highest Standard of Living" and showing a happy White family of four riding in a car. Through the car's front windshield could be seen a smiling clean-shaven father wearing a suit and tie seating next to his grinning wife. In the rear seat were equally happy children. Hanging out the window was a white dog. Next to the car was the slogan, "There's no way like the American Way." Billboards proclaiming "World's Highest Wages" showed an aproned White mother standing in a doorway looking out at her clean-shaven husband dressed in a suit, tie, and hat tossing their blond-haired daughter into the sky.[50] There were no effort to provide a rational explanation as to why the "American Way" provided the "World's Highest Standard of Living" and the "World's Highest Wages." Believing that emotions rather than reason controlled public opinion, the 1939 NAM public relations committee declared as its task to "link free enterprise in the public consciousness with free speech, free press and free religion as integral parts of democracy."[51]

SCHOOLING STAKHANOVITES AND CONSUMERS

In the Soviet Union and the United States, schools tried to implant images of the Stakhanovite superworker and the happy consumer of the American way. In literature, student activities, and courses in communist morality, Soviet students were barraged with images of workers who overachieved for the glory of the Soviet state. In fact, the overachieving student was a Stakhanovite worker in the making. Writing about the development of work attitudes, Felicity O'Dell states, "The Soviet school child is taught in different ways, explicitly and implicitly, throughout his or her school career that the main way in peacetime to demonstrate one's patriotism and to serve the Soviet union is through work."[52]

A basic Soviet textbook, *The Foundations of Communist Morality*, instructed students that work was the source of happiness and life's meaning.[53] *The Foundations of Communist Morality* claimed that socialism created a new relationship between the individual and labor, with labor being a means of loving society. Soviet schools practiced *subbotniki*, where citizens worked for society without pay; something Americans called "community service." In schools, children were educated for *subbotniki* by performing extra chores such as cleaning around the outside of the school building or working in the school garden.

School lessons emphasized the importance of work for the happiness and the well-being of the Soviet citizen. Students donated their paintings to decorate local factories and they built gardens around industrial plants. Reading lessons conveyed the importance of socialist work. A Soviet teacher's journal explained that reading material "constantly draws the children's attention to the fact that socially useful work and its results define a person's role in the life of society and that our state is a workers' state."[54] The teacher impressed "on her pupils the awareness that labour for the good of the Motherland is the very basis of morality and that only his work makes a person both necessary to others and happy in himself."[55]

Of course, what was important was Stakhanovite work efforts. In factories, work teams were to try to outproduce others. For their efforts, they were to receive monetary and honorary rewards such as those given to Makarenko's librarian and to the workers in the painting *Stakhanovites in a Box at the Bolshoi Theater*. Socialist competition was based on cooperation and not individual competition. Groups of workers tried to outperform other groups. In the end, socialist competition was for the benefit of everyone. In schools, students were prepared for socialist competition by competing students by row or classroom for the best marks. In youth groups, such as the Young Pioneers, awards were given for the best group behavior. As O'Dell pointed out, these lessons were reinforced outside of school by mass media, children's magazines, and clubs.[56]

In the United States, the NAM took the American Way campaign directly into schools by flooding classrooms with printed material and movies. The NAM distributed to schools a series of booklets titled *You and Industry*, which were designed to connect reader's positive emotions to the U.S. industrial system. In 1937, the NAM began distributing to 70,000 schools a news weekly, *Young America*, which contained articles such as "The Business of America's People is Selling," "Building Better Americans," and "Your Local Bank."[57] A 10-minute film, *America Marching On*, was distributed to schools with the message, "America marching upward and onward to higher standards of living, greater income for her people, and more leisure to enjoy the good things of life as the greatest industrial system the world has ever seen began to develop."[58]

By the 1940s, the American Way was transmuted into "civic consumerism." "Civic consumerism" was Kelly Schrum's description of the editorial message for teenagers in *Seventeen* magazine in the late 1940s and early 1950s.[59] "Civic consumerism," Scrum defined as "combining one's democratic role as active citizen with one's duty as a responsible and active consumer."[60] During the late 1940s and 1950s, she argued, "Voting and democracy, as well as pride in America and the right to buy goods, were common themes through this period, a reflection of both lingering war rhetoric and the beginning of the Cold War."[61]

As I discuss in *Educating the Consumer-Citizen: A History of the Marriage of Schools, Advertising, and Media*, anti-communist fears of the 1950s resulted in purges of mass media, teachers, and textbooks. Fears of the other spurred the dissemination of ideological messages supporting the American way of life. In schools, reading textbooks portrayed happy White middle-class suburbanites while ignoring the existence of city dwellers, poor people, and minority groups. Advertising played to an irrational public as new consumer items were trumpeted as a source of happiness. Movies, radio, and television steered clear of any neutral or positive material about socialism or communism while selling the American way of life.[62]

Schools, advertising, commercial media, and public relations campaigns were to create a spontaneous association between consumption and the

American way of life. Whereas Soviet citizens imagined themselves as heroic workers, Americans dreamt of consumer objects. A 1959 *Saturday Evening Post* magazine cover showed a young couple sitting under a tree gazing into a night sky illuminated by a full moon. Floating among a host of stars was their dream world consisting of a house, a swimming pool, two cars, pets, two children, a power drill, a refrigerator, a washer and dryer, a stove, a toaster, an electric coffee pot, a waffle maker, an iron, a television, a sound system, and a vacuum cleaner. The cover's artist, Constantin Alajalov, had originally planned to have the couple staring at castles floating in the air.[63]

UNDER GLASS:
STALIN AND THE DECLARATION OF INDEPENDENCE

In 1947, Jefferson's draft of the Declaration of Independence was sent in a glass display case along with other documents around the country on the Freedom Train in what one historian called, "The most elaborate ideological undertaking of the early postwar years."[64] Similar to the glass displays on the Freedom Train, Soviet citizens's were able to view Stalin's corpse under glass. After his death in 1953, he was placed, after being embalmed, in a glass-covered coffin next to Lenin's displayed body in a mausoleum in Moscow's Red Square near St Basil's Cathedral and the Kremlin. Although there is no exact count of the people who viewed Lenin and Stalin under glass, the number might have been the same or larger than the 3.5 million viewers of 127 glass-covered documents in the Freedom Train, which traveled 37,000 miles visiting 322 cities between 1947 and 1949.[65]

These types of public displays of history, as Maxim Gorky recognized, were traditionally methods for regulating public behavior by mythologizing the past. Statues and monuments have always served as an important means for invading the public mind with heroic fantasies. Gorky pointed out, "In our own days folklore has raised Lenin to the level of the mythical heroes of antiquity and made him the equal of Prometheus."[66] Historian John Bodnar argued that maintaining various forms of public memories through memorials and public displays involved "serious matters in the present such as the nature of power and the question of loyalty to both official and vernacular cultures."[67] Most leaders were always in doubt about the extent and enduring quality of their power. Governments engaged in memorializing the past to gain allegiance to present power arrangements. Bodnar asserted, "Public memory speaks primarily about the structure of power in society because that power is always in question in a world of polarities and contradictions and because cultural understanding is always grounded in the material structure of society itself."[68]

It is difficult to draw a clear distinction between public imagination and public memory because they were often interdependent. Socialist realism and the American Way campaign were intended to capture the public imagination, whereas placing Lenin, Stalin, and the Declaration of Independence under glass-maintained public memories. In these examples, influencing public imagination and memory was to ensure the continuation of the power of the state, and loyalty to an economic and political ideology.

Both Lenin and Stalin were enshrined in public memories to ensure the power of the Soviet state. When Lenin died in 1924, there were real concerns about the survival of the Soviet Union because of economic turmoil and sometimes open rebellion against the Communist Party. Ensuring Lenin's continued place in public memory was important for the continued power of the Party and its future leaders. Future Soviet leaders could draw on public memories of Lenin to justify their actions. Placing Lenin's embalmed corpse—he was embalmed by a Professor Vorobyev who installed an electric pump in the body to maintain constant humidity—in Red Square was a far more graphic means of maintaining his public memory than a mere statue though many were erected around the country.[69]

The connection between public memory and political power was highlighted by the placement, and later removal, of Stalin's body from Lenin's Mausoleum. After Stalin's death in 1953, an assistant of the then-dead Professor Vorobyev was called on to embalm the body. Three years later, Stalin's successor, Nikita Khrushchev, condemned Stalin's policies and his murderous activities while in power. To maintain his own power, Khrushchev felt it necessary to erase Stalin from the public's memory. In 1961 at the Twenty-Second Party Congress, in supposedly preplanned speeches, a Party loyalist, Dora Abramovna, criticized Stalin's placement in Lenin's mausoleum. This was followed by Khrushchev reading a decree for removal of Stalin's remains. Abramovna and Khrushchev's statements demonstrated the relationship between public memories and power. In fact, Abramovna illustrated the political power of memory and imagination by saying, "My heart is always full of Lenin. Comrades, I could survive the most difficult moments only because I carried Lenin in my heart, and always consulted him on what to do." With regard to erasing public memories, she concluded, "Yesterday I consulted him. He was standing there before me as if he were alive, and he said: 'It is unpleasant to be next to Stalin, who did so much harm to the party'."[70]

Khrushchev used more official language in erasing Stalin from public memory:

> The further retention in the mausoleum of the sarcophagus with the bier of J. V. Stalin shall be recognized as inappropriate since the serious violations by Stalin of Lenin's precepts, abuse of power, mass repressions against honorable Soviet people, and other activities in the period of the personality cult make it impossible to leave the bier with his body in the mausoleum of V. I. Lenin.[71]

In my lifetime, I witnessed a similar death in public memory of a communist official. In a trip to Bulgaria in 1987, I attended the annual commemoration of the Soviet liberation of Bulgaria during World War II. The ceremony was held in front of Bulgarian communist leader Georgi Dimitrov's mausoleum. Dimitrov was also embalmed and placed under glass for public viewing. While I was there, numerous guards dressed in elaborate uniforms with plumes and feathers marched in front of the mausoleum while others stood inside at the corners of the glassed coffin. I saw a recent photograph of a now-graffiti covered mausoleum without guards and with people climbing on its exterior making it a symbol of a discarded past.

The political value of public memories is in their distortion. As Marc Bloch commented, "By a curious paradox through the very fact of their respect for the past, people came to reconstruct it as they considered it ought to have been."[72] In the United States, this reconstruction of the past according to how "it ought to have been" is exemplified by theme parks, such as Colonial Williamsburg and Disneyland. Disneyland, as I discuss in another book, idealizes the past within the context of Cold War concerns of the 1950s.[73]

In contrast, Colonial Williamsburg was an actual reconstruction of a historic site for the purpose of preserving its public memory. Between 1927 and 1928, John D. Rockefeller, Jr., the financier of the restoration, acquired the site and remaining buildings of the original capital of colonial Virginia. In 1934, President Franklin Roosevelt marked the progress in restoring the site by personally opening the Duke of Gloucester Street in Colonial Williamsburg. The theme park quickly attracted tourists with the number of visitors rising from 4,047 in 1932 to 210,824 in 1941.[74] By 2004, more than 100 million people had visited Williamsburg.[75]

John D. Rockefeller, Jr.'s mission statement for Williamsburg plays on the image of America as the land of freedom and equality with the qualification that this image might not be reality. Rockefeller proclaimed, "Here we interpret the origins of the idea of America, conceived decades before the American Revolution. The Colonial Williamsburg story, 'Becoming Americans,' tells how diverse peoples, having different and sometimes conflicting ambitions, evolved into a society that valued liberty and equality. Americans cherish these values as a birthright, *even when their promise remains unfulfilled* [my emphasis]."[76]

GOOD VERSUS EVIL: AMERICA'S CULTURAL MANAGEMENT AND THE EDUCATIONAL SECURITY STATE

Whereas Soviet leaders openly supported the authority of the Communist Party in managing culture, education, and news media under the banner of socialist realism and fighting capitalist propaganda, U.S. leaders were reluctant to recognize government's role in managing ideas. For instance, when the U.S. Office of War Information (OWI) was opened in 1942, its director Archibald MacLeish made a distinction between propaganda and the OWI's work. Propaganda, he argued, involved the distortion of information by mostly totalitarian governments. In contrast, his office practiced a "strategy of truth." At the 1942 annual luncheon of the Associated Press, MacLeish called on journalists and news executives to cooperate in defending against enemy propaganda by engaging in a "strategy of truth ... [that was] appropriate to our cause and our purpose ... which opposes the frauds and the deceits by which our enemies have confused and conquered other peoples ... [and provides] the simple and clarifying truths by which a nation such as ours must guide itself."[77] In other words, MacLeish believed that the government could win the ideological struggle by simply telling the truth. Under the slogan "strategy of truth," the U.S. government tried to integrate its control of mass media. The Executive Order establishing OWI specifically gave as its purpose, "to coordinate the dissemination of war information by all federal agencies and to formulate and carry out by means of the press, radio and motion pictures, programs to facilitate an understanding in the United States and abroad ... of the policies, activities, and aims of the government."[78]

Of course, the problem was how much of the "truth" should be told and what was really true. For instance, during World War II, OWI representatives sent messages back to the Washington, D. C. office that contained positive information about the struggle of Mao's Red Army against the Japanese and the opposing Chinese Nationalist Army. The Chinese Nationalist Army was forcing peasants to fight by tying them together with ropes and marching them to battle fields with many dying of starvation along the way. Because the U.S. government supported the Nationalists over the Communists, the OWI maintained its "strategy of truth" by issuing no information that might weaken public support of the Nationalists. Also, the OWI avoided releasing any information that might be considered critical of Great Britain's colonial empire. In 1942, the OWI agreed to maintain a common front with British policies regarding India.[79]

An ironic effect of the OWI's strategy of truth was to convince America's future enemy Ho Chi Minh that the United States would be an ally in the struggle against French colonialism. In 1943, Ho spent a great deal of time reading the OWI's library in China prior to returning to Vietnam to fight against the Japanese. According to Ho's biographer William Duiker, Ho's reading probably made him aware of President Franklin Roosevelt's antipathy towards European colonialism and his dislike of France's role in Indochina, as expressed in Roosevelt's statement: "France has milked it for one hundred years. The people of Indochina are entitled to something better than that."[80]

To what degree Ho was influenced by the OWI's strategy of truth would be impossible to measure. However, Ho opened his 1945 Declaration of Independence of the Democratic Republic of Vietnam with a direct reference to the American Declaration of Independence. According to Duiker, "Although Ho Chi Minh was well aware that the United States was a capitalist society, he had always expressed admiration for its commitment to democratic principles and may have felt that Roosevelt himself might lead the United Sates on the path of greater economic equality and social justice."[81]

Of course, Soviet leaders had another perspective on America's campaign of truth and the existence of a free press that surfaced in symposium papers written in 1947 about the United Nation's proposal for a Universal Declaration of Human Rights. Boris Tchechko, the Soviet representative to the symposium, noted that individual liberties, particularly "liberty of conscience, publication, association, and ultimately, the formation of political parties" were not necessary rights in the Soviet Union.[82] The reason, according Tchechko, was that these liberties were no longer necessary in a socialist state. In a classless society, there was no need for individual liberty, in fact, individual liberty could result in revolt against the classless society and a regression to capitalism. "Maxim Gorky" Tchechko wrote, "defines individualism as a fruitless attempt by man to protect himself from the violence and oppression of the capitalist State."[83] Tchechko wrote, that intellectual freedom exists because "intellectuals have equal rights and freedom in a Soviet country, on exactly the same footing as the working classes and the peasants."[84] In other words, intellectuals had the freedom to believe in communism and there was no reason for intellectuals to present opposing political ideas because there were no conflicting social classes. And because the Communist Party represented the interests of the working class, it had the right to control to control Soviet culture, including education, movies, radio, and newspapers. Freedom to express views contrary to the interests of the working class, as embodied in the dictatorship of the Communist Party, was simply the freedom to express fallacious ideas that were counter revolutionary and against the interests of the people. Therefore, like the OWI, the Communist Party could claim that it was involved in a "strategy of truth" where truth was defined by the dictatorship of the proletariat.

However, America's strategy of truth was incorporated into the 1947 National Security Act, which created the U.S. government's Office of the Secretary of Defense, the Joint Chiefs of Staff [of the military], the National Security Council, and, most importantly for the management of ideas, the Central Intelligence Agency (CIA).[85] After passage of the National Security Act, Cold War tensions increased with Mao Zedong's 1949 proclamation founding the People's Republic of China and Kim Il Sung's 1950 attempt to unify Korea that resulted in U.S. involvement in a Korean civil war. The international causes of the Cold War, from the perspective of American leaders, was outlined in a 1950 secret document from the National Security Conference (NSC) to President Truman. Known as "NSC–68," the recommendations were approved by President Truman, and NSC–68 is now considered a key document in the founding of the U.S. national security state. NSC–68 described a world divided by the military strength and ideologies of two superpowers—the United States and the Soviet Union:

> Within the past thirty-five years the world has experienced two global wars of tremendous violence. It has witnessed two revolutions—the Russian and the Chinese—of extreme scope and intensity. It has also seen the collapse of five empires—the Ottoman, the Austro-Hungarian, the German, Italian, and Japanese—and the drastic decline of two imperial systems, the British and French.... Two complex sets of factors have now basically altered ... [the] historical distribution of power. First, the defeat of Germany and Japan and the decline of British and French Empires have interacted with the development of the United States and the Soviet Union in such a way that *power has increasingly gravitated to these two centers*. Second, the Soviet Union, unlike previous aspirants to hegemony, is animated by *a new fanatic faith, antithetical to our own, and seeks to impose its absolute authority over the rest of the world* [my emphasis].[86]

NSC–68 and statements by President Truman and other government officials were filled with slogans about freedom, slavery, good, evil, "our way of life," and America's divine mission.[87] Also, the concept of the other played a major role in reference to "un-American actions and ideas." As historian Michael Hogan writes, "the national security ideology framed the Cold War discourse in a system of *symbolic representation by reference to the un-American 'other'*."[88] NSC–68 was a good example of this ideological approach to the Cold War. Offhand, one might think that members of the National Security Council would have engaged in a serious critique of Lenin and Stalin's ideas about the Communist Party as being representative of the working class or discussed anti-imperialism and wars of liberation, world revolution, and centralized economic planning. Instead the report in the section titled, "The Underlying Conflict in the Realm of Ideas and Values between the U.S. Purpose and the Kremlin Design," opens with the simplistic notion that it was a conflict between slavery and freedom: "The Kremlin regards the United States as the only major threat to the conflict between the idea of slavery under the grim oligarchy of the Kremlin.... The idea of freedom, moreover, is peculiarly and intolerably subversive of the idea of slavery. But the converse is not true. The implacable purpose of the slave state to eliminate the challenge of freedom has placed the two great powers at opposite poles."[89]

The concept of the other also played a role in the NSC–68's use of the term "free world." As used in the document, "free world" meant any country opposed to the actions of the Soviet Union; China and Korea were erroneously treated in the document as mere extensions of the power of the Soviet Union. In other words, there was the "free world" and the other. The meaning of "free" in "free world" was ambiguous because some of the "free world" nations were dictatorships and monarchies. NSC–68 gives the United States the leadership role of the "free world": "Our position as the center of power in the free world places a heavy responsibility upon the United States for leadership. We must organize and enlist the energies and resources of the free world in a positive program for peace which will frustrate the Kremlin design for world domination."[90]

For the authors of NSC–68, Bruce Kuklick contended, the struggle between the United States and the Soviet Union was "one between the good and the depraved, between true religion and satanism."[91] Kuklick's remarks were written from the perspective of an historian of U.S. ideas and they appeared as one of several commentaries on NSC–68 gathered by Harvard Professor Ernest May in the early 1990s. As author of *The Rise of American Philosophy* and other histories of America ideas, Kuklick traced NSC–68's moral vision back to the Puritan image of the colonies being the world's moral leader. As he pointed out, NSC–68 rejected military victory for a victory of ideas, as represented by the United States, that would, in the words of NSC–68, "light the path to peace and order" by projecting its "moral and material strength."[92] Commenting on this language, Kuklick argued, "The synthesis of righteousness, pride in *patria*, and sense of the evil in other polities, as well as the belief in the spiritual potency of American ideas, places NSC–68 in a long line of similar documents ranging from John Winthrop's 'Model of Christian Charity (1630),' a sermon given by the leader of the Puritan Massachusetts Bay Colony and the Declaration of Independence to 'George Bush's less eloquent rationales for war against Iraq in 1991.'"[93] Kuklick stated that some people might reject his argument because it is too narrow considering the breadth of American ideas. His response was, "Yet in fact a small elite with a long record of holding power and *a monopoly on communication* has dominated American public life for over three centuries…. From Winthrop to the Founding Fathers to Lincoln to Wilson to … Bush, those authors have found comfort and truth in the narrative world of Reformed Protestantism."[94] For many Christians, atheism was a Satanic doctrine, consequently it was easy for many Christians to think of communists as being in league with the Prince of Darkness. This Protestant tradition was illustrated in a 1951 speech by then Senator, and later President, Lyndon Johnson, "We shall, we must, with the guidance of God, here embark upon this course to redeem humanity … [with the] righteous strength, which centuries of freedom under God have given us, we cannot fail."[95]

NSC–68 contained proposals for overt and covert international programs for managing information and psychological warfare to be conducted by the CIA and other government agencies. Regarding overt activities, NSC–68 proposed, "Development of programs designed to build and maintain confidence among other peoples in our strength and resolution, and to wage overt psychological warfare calculated to encourage mass defections from Soviet allegiance and to frustrate the Kremlin design in other ways."[96] For covert actions: "Intensification of affirmative and timely measures and operations by covert means in the fields of economic warfare and political and *psychological warfare* with a view to fomenting and supporting unrest and revolt in selected strategic satellite countries [my emphasis]."[97] And, of course, there was a call for "development of internal security ... and intensification of intelligence activities."[98] Shortly after the 1950 announcement that the United States would attempt to stop Kim Il Sung's efforts to unify Korea, the U.S. Army created the Office of the Chief of Psychological Warfare.[99]

Psychological warfare was defended using the World War II language of the "strategy of truth." In the 1950s, President Eisenhower declared at a press conference, "Our aim in the Cold War is not conquering of territory or subjugation by force. Our aim is more subtle, more pervasive, more complete. We are trying to get the world, by peaceful means, to believe the truth.... The means we shall employ to spread this truth are often called 'psychological'.... 'Psychological warfare' is the struggle for the minds and wills of men."[100]

THE "OTHER" IN AMERICA'S GLOBAL EDUCATIONAL OFFENSIVE

America's educational security state engaged in global education using psychological warfare to convince the world's people of the justice of its cause. There was little interest in the actual ideological underpinnings of the different national communist parties and the struggle against imperialism. Ron Robin, an historian of America's psychological warfare practices, asserted that those involved in overt and covert psychological warfare dismissed ideology as an important factor in human relations accept as a "manifestation of emotional dysfunction that one could unmask by means of Freudian apparati, such as repression, displacement, and projection."[101] It was assumed that all communists acted according to the dictates of the Soviet Union making Mao Zedong, Kim Il Sung, and Ho Chi Minh into mere puppets of Soviet power. American agents demonstrated little understanding of Chinese, Korean, or Vietnamese history. For instance, U.S. officials believed Soviet leaders supported Korean unification in order to distract the West from the establishment of communist governments in Turkey and Greece. It seemed impossible for them to imagine that Mao Zedong and Kim Il Sung could act independently. Robin wrote, "This Eurocentricity defined by default, the meaning of the Korean War. Despite the distinctly Asian contours of the conflict, America's decision makers interpreted Korean hostilities as a sideshow of an eventual European showdown."[102] American leaders placed little emphasis on the importance of cultural diversity as demonstrated by the fact that American behavioral scientists tested the effect that leaflets might have on Koreans by dumping leaflets associated with a brand of coffee from planes on small towns in Washington state and measuring their impact.[103]

Discounting of the importance of ideology, America's global educational offensive relied on advertising and public relations methods. The head of the Office of the Chief of Psychological Warfare advocated using "the best advertising techniques."[104] Methods used in the American Way campaign were replicated during American resistance to Kim Il Sung's reunification efforts. The American Way billboards relied on appeals to personal comfort and prosperity by associating pictures of happy middle-class families with slogans about the American way of life. By simply changing the pictures and retaining the slogans, the billboards could have been ads for cigarettes or cars that associated these products with the American way of life. American Way billboards were free of complicated ideas about ideology.

In Korea, the same methods were used. During the war, the Army's Office of the Chief of Psychological Warfare was responsible for the aerial bombardment of 2 million leaflets a day on Kim Il Sung's troops and supporting members of China's Peoples Liberation Army. The leaflets were dropped in cluster bombs that released from 22,000 to 45,000 leaflets at 1,000 feet above ground.[105] The leaflets were primarily designed by academics and members of private U.S. think tanks hired by the army and they relied on two types of appeals. The first type of leaflet attempted to convince troops to surrender because of the physical and psychological hardships they were facing during the war. The second type tried to convince troops they were acting as puppets of the Soviet government.

Examples of these two types of pamphlets were reproduced in Ron Robin's study of American psychological warfare. A leaflet appealing to basic physical and psychological needs contained two side-by-side illustrations. On one side, a lonely-looking soldier dressed in thick winter clothing was shown squatting in bushes. On the other side, an equally lonely looking woman clutches an infant while another child snuggles close to her. The caption stated, "it is communists who force you to spend such a miserable Lunar New Year."[106] Another surrender leaflet contained three photos illustrating the warmth and comfort of U.S. prisoner of war camps. In one photo, prisoners were shown leisurely eating, and in another photo a smiling U.S. nurse was helping a hospitalized prisoner drink from a cup. The third photo showed prisoners enjoying a boxing match. An official looking "Safe Conduct Pass" promised that: "food, warm clothing and cigarettes are provided for all. And you will be given the opportunity for health-restoring recreation." Robin reproduced 1991 Gulf War leaflets that used similar methods. Dropped on Iraqi troops, the top part depicted an Iraqi soldier thinking about the horrors of warfare and the bottom part showed the same soldier surround by his family. The caption read, "Fellow Iraqi soldier. It hurts us that you may return to Iraq dead or maimed."[107] Advertising and public relations methods continued into the 21st century. In March 2004, the U.S.-led Iraqi Coalition Provisional Authority forces gave a $5.6 million contract to a British public relations firm, Bell Pottinger, to create television and radio commercials to sell the idea of democracy. It was announced that the commercials would carry a "message of participation in the democratic process, and the hope for the future that democracy brings to Iraq."[108] Harry C. Boyte, senior fellow at the Hubert H. Humphrey Institute of Public Affairs commented, "Learning about democracy through advertising could make it seem like a product that should be blamed or abandoned if things do not go well."[109]

Another set of leaflets dropped on Korea reflected the Eurocentric attitude of American leaders by showing Soviet advisors dangling Mao and other Chinese leaders on puppet strings. The leaflet contained a Chinese and Korean text. The Chinese text read: "So-called Soviet advisors are Russian special agents sent to control China. Under the domination of Chinese communist Soviet puppets, China has no independence. Stay safe and keep fit for fighting against the communist Soviet puppets." The Korean text explained, "This is a UN message to the CCF [Chinese Communist Forces]. Place it for them to see."[110] Another three paneled leaflet, showed a poor Korean farmer giving his produce to Kim Il Sung in one panel, and in the next panel a bowing Kim Il Sung giving the produce to a fat Soviet official sitting in a chair. The final panel showed the Korean farmer looking at an empty food bowl while a Soviet leader gluttonously chewed on a piece of meat.[111]

During the same years as leaflets were being dumped on Korea, the United States Information Agency was trying to put a positive spin on school segregation and racism in the United States by the international distribution of a pamphlet, *The Negro in American Life*. The pamphlet admitted problems in U.S. race relations, but claimed that rapid advances were being made to end racism. At the time, legal segregation of schools and public facilities still existed in the South. As proof of racial progress, the pamphlet contained a photo of a racially integrated New York City public school classroom with the caption, "In New York, a Negro teacher teaches pupils of both races."[112] Another photograph showed a group of Black students in front of a newly constructed rural school with the caption, "Education and progress for the Negro people move together. Thousands of new rural schools, like the one above provide free education in the South."[113]

THE AMERICAN WAY AND SCHOOL DESEGREGATION

Walking down Chicago's Michigan Avenue in 1961, I was given a pamphlet which illustrated the contradiction between America's anti-communist crusade, the concept of the American way of life, and the Soviet Union's international image. At the time, U.S. schools were in turmoil as political and educational leaders tried to implement, and sometimes resisted, the U.S. Supreme Court's 1954 decision that racial segregation must end in public schools. The pamphlets were being passed out by a political refugee from Lithuania wearing a sandwich board covered with anti-communist slogans. The pamphlet contained a map of the American South with a blackened area where, according to the text, the civil rights movement was attempting to establish a separate African-American nation. The pamphlet asserted that school desegregation and the overall civil rights movement was part of an international communist conspiracy controlled by Moscow and financed by a cabal of Jewish financiers.

The pamphlet's portrayal of school desegregation exemplifies the contradiction in U.S. propaganda between the reality of racial segregation and claims that America was the world leader in the fight for freedom and democracy. Yes, the Communist Party of the Soviet Union and international communist leaders like Ho Chi Minh were advocating the end of global racism and they did criticize racial policies in the United States. Did this mean that the fight against racism and segregated schools was a communist plot? What about strange anti-Semitic suggestion that Jewish financiers supported the Soviet government? Why would international capitalists support communism? Was protection of racial segregation and the denial of voting rights part of the American way of life? Wayne Clark noted in his PhD dissertation, "An Analysis of the Relationship Between Anti-Communism and Segregationist Thought in the Deep South, 1948–1964": "Realizing the vulnerability of racial segregation as a social system, southerners most intent on pressing white supremacy consistently promoted the notion that only *alien forces* bent on social upheaval would challenge the racial status quo. Large segments of the population in the Deep South, including educated whites, accepted this explanation as the primary force behind resistance to white supremacy."[114]

"The twin efforts of the anticolonial and civil rights movements," Thomas Borstelmann points out in *The Cold War and the Color Line: American*

Race Relations in the Global Arena, "presented the U.S. government with a dilemma. How could it defend equality and the rule of law while not alienating its allies across the Atlantic and local authorities south of the Mason-Dixon line?"[115] As I already discussed, Ho Chi Minh and Bhimrao Ramji Ambedkar were inspired by the American civil rights movement. In their minds, and in the minds of others, American racism was an important aspect of the general racist policies of colonialism. When the U.S. State Department sponsored African-American Jay Redding on a 1952 speaking tour of India in an attempt to show Indians that Blacks held prestigious positions in the United States, he reported being asked embarrassing questions such as "Isn't it true that the Haitian Ambassador to the U.S. must live in a ghetto in Washington?" "Aren't Negroes prohibited public education in America?"[116] Borstelmann wrote,

> The Cold War developed after World War II as a new bipolar U.S.–Russian competition that encompassed the globe, and strident American anti-communists presented critics with the image of a totalitarian Soviet Union that bore some resemblance to white-controlled Dixie ... [such as] inequality before the law; involuntary labor (peonage and prison labor in the South); kangaroo courts and summary executions; arbitrary imprisonment; the denial of human rights through the use of inhumane prison conditions and even torture.[117]

The Korean War demonstrated the contradiction between the global images that the U.S. government was disseminating and the reality of race relations. As the 2 million daily leaflets promised the hospitality of American prisoner of war camps, American generals were referring to Chinese and Koreans as "gooks" and losing several important battles because they assumed that Chinese and Koreans were inferior fighters. Prisoners who were persuaded by the leaflets to surrender were probably surprised when at the prisoner of war camp at Koje-do, according to Borstelmann, "U.S. guards expressed their disdain for Chinese and North Korean prisoners in explicitly racial language. Those prisoners witnessed considerable conflict, sometimes armed, between white and black or Latino Americans guarding them."[118] Adding to the confusion about America's global image was Radio Moscow's comparing America's actions in Korea to "the oppression of the colored people in the U.S."[119]

American schools were entangled in the contradictory international images of America, the anti-communist crusade, and the civil rights movement as teachers, textbooks, and school desegregation were swept up in the confusion of global politics; a situation that was easily criticized to the world community by the Soviet Union. For instance, a 1963 cartoon in the Soviet publication *Krokodil* showed a fat American sheriff in a cowboy hat backed up by a uniform policeman stopping the entry of an African-American student into a university. Protestors stood behind the policeman waving signs saying: "Nigger Go Away," "Lynch Him," "We Want Segregation," and "Put the Colored on Their Knees."[120]

The world image of the United States was very much in mind of the U.S. Justice Department when it filed an amicus brief with the U.S. Supreme Court regarding school segregation cases that led to the 1954 *Brown* decision that declared school segregation unconstitutional. The brief referred to school segregation in Washington, D.C. as an embarrassment: "Foreign officials and visitors naturally judge this country and our people by their experiences and observations in the nation's capital; and the treatment of colored persons here is taken as the measure of our attitude toward minorities generally." Outside of the Washington, D.C. area, the brief stated, "the existence of discrimination against minority groups in the United States has an adverse effect upon our relations with other countries." The brief went on to quote a State Department report that, "during the past six years, the damage to our foreign relations attributable to [race discrimination] has become progressively greater. The United States is under constant attack in the foreign press, over the foreign radio.... Soviet spokesmen regularly exploit this situation in propaganda against the United States." The brief concluded. "If you wish to inspire the people of the world whose freedom is in jeopardy, if we wish to restore hope to those who have already lost their civil liberties, if we wish to fulfill the promise that is ours, we must correct the remaining imperfections in the practice of democracy."[121]

The U.S. Supreme Court's 1954 *Brown* decision ended legal school segregation but it did not end the negative reports in the international press. It was the threat to America's international image that finally forced President Dwight Eisenhower to enforce the *Brown* decision. Originally, President Eisenhower avoided supporting the decision. He claimed, "that if I should express, publicly, either approval or disapproval of a Supreme Court decision in one case, I would be obliged to do so in many, if not all, cases."[122] When civil rights groups in 1955 demanded federal troops be sent to Mississippi to do something about the race-related murder of a 14-year-old black named Emmett Till, Eisenhower refused and claimed that the communist party was behind the demand. Eisenhower freely interjected the image of a communist conspiracy in the civil rights movement. At one point, he asserted, similar to the pamphlet I got from the Lithuanian refugee in 1961, "The Communist Party of the United States, doing its best to twist this movement for its own purposes, was urging its members to infiltrate the NAACP ... and had launched a program to drive a wedge between the administration and its friends in the South in the election year of 1956."[123]

In 1957, Eisenhower was forced to take action because of the furor in the international press over Arkansas's Governor Orval Faubus blocking the integration of the Central High School in Little Rock and declaring it off-limits to "colored" students. The incident triggered mob violence and required the sending in of federal troops. Eisenhower later reflected that before September 1957, a line from the musical South Pacific in which a Frenchman mistakenly called the heroine's home town "Small Rock" was meaningless to foreign audiences. After the school segregation riots, Eisenhower wrote, "The name Little Rock Arkansas, would become known around the world. But the world's disapproval should not have been for a city, only for a man and a handful of its population.... Overseas, the mouthpieces of Soviet propaganda in Russia and Europe were blaring out that 'anti-Negro violence' in Little Rock was being 'committed with the clear connivance of the United States government'."[124]

In a television and radio speech on September 24, 1957, Eisenhower justified sending troops into Little Rock by referring to the Cold War and America's world image. His actions, he declared, demonstrated "to the world that we are a nation in which laws, not men are supreme." He warned that incidents like Little Rock were threatening the security of the world: "At a time when we face grave situations abroad because of the hatred that communism bears toward a system of government based on human rights, it would be difficult to exaggerate the harm that is being done to the prestige and influence, and indeed to the safety, of our nation and the world." He continued, "Our enemies are gloating over this incident and using it everywhere to misrepresent our whole nation." Eisenhower concluded the speech with the hope that after Arkansas's citizens stopped interfering with school integration and federal troops were removed, "a blot upon the fair name and high honor of our nation in the world will be removed. Thus will be restored the image of America and of all its parts as one nation, indivisible, with liberty and justice for all."[125]

How much did Cold War worries about America's foreign image contribute to school desegregation and success for other parts of the civil rights agenda? Since the 19th century, many Americans, with limited success, had struggled to eliminate laws requiring racial segregation in schools and public places, and laws limiting voting rights. However, it was in the Cold War years of the 1950s and 1960s that segregation laws were rescinded and voting rights were protected. During this period, the anti-communist crusade resulted in major American involvement in Vietnam to defeat Ho Chi Minh's national war of liberation against colonialism and racism. Obviously, American leaders could not justify American racism when claiming to fight for freedom and equality abroad. The Cold War, including the Korean and Vietnamese Wars, forced American leaders to attend to the demands of the civil rights movement.

COMMUNISM IN SCHOOLS AND MASS MEDIA

American reliance on public relations and advertising reduced public conceptions of communism to images of insidious Satanic forces using many paths to invade the minds of teachers and students, and to sneak messages into textbooks. The follow-up story to the anti-communist pamphlet I received on the streets of Chicago in 1961 illustrates the image of Communism as an invisible force taking over human wills. After taking the pamphlet, I asked my instructor of an American Social History Seminar (I was a college student at the time), if I could invite the Lithuanian refugee distributing the pamphlets to speak on anti-communism to the Seminar. The instructor thought it would be interesting, but the Lithuanian declined because of his difficulty speaking English and said he would send two friends. When his two friends arrived at the Seminar, they immediately announced that they were members of the Minute Men organization that was made up of a loose federation of groups. None of the groups had more than four members, they explained, because of the ability of the communists and the U.S. Federal Bureau of Investigation (FBI) to infiltrate large organizations. Why the fear of the FBI? Because the U.S. Federal government, they claimed, had been infiltrated by communists. The two men then told of a recent visit to Moscow where they saw a single guard wearing a revolver controlling large numbers of prisoners. They asked the guard how he could control so many people. The suspicious guard refused to answer the question. Later, the two men claimed, they talked to a scientist friend who told them that the prisoners were made docile through the addition of fluorides to their drinking water and that communists were using similar methods in the United States by sponsoring the addition of fluorides to drinking water under the cover of claims that the chemical reduced dental decay. For these two Minute Men Communist enslavement of Americans was rapidly taking place through chemical control of minds.

Often, schools and media were treated as victims of an invisible infection by communist forces. In discussing this phenomenon, I don't want to repeat material I've covered in other books dealing with the management of ideas in U.S. society, namely *The Sorting Machine: National Educational Policy Sine 1945* and *Images of American Life: A History of Ideological Management in Schools, Movies, Radio and Television*.[126] As I explain in these books, anti-communists looked for communist influence in teaching methods, textbook contents, and teachers' speech and activities. Typically, anti-communist groups used local and national media to broadcast claims of communist subversion. These groups included the American Legion, National Council of Education, American Coalition of Patriotic Societies, Defenders of American Education, Anti-Communist League of America, Christian National Crusade, and the Daughters of the American Revolution.[127]

For instance, the charge that progressive education methods were communist-inspired appeared in national headlines with the 1950 forced resignation of Superintendent Willard Goslin from the Pasadena, California school district. Ironically, Goslin was accused of introducing communist ideas by inviting William Kilpatrick to lead a teacher training workshop; this was the same Kilpatrick whose project method came under attack by Stalinists in the Soviet Union in the 1930s. From a global perspective, the whole incident was full of contradictions with Soviet school leaders having rejected Kilpatrick's teaching methods and Pasadena residents associating the project method with communism. Pasadena's citizens were influenced by pamphlets from the National Council of Education founded in 1948 by Allen Zoll. The pamphlets' titles were *The Commies are After Your Kids* and *Progressive Education Increases Juvenile Delinquency*. Pasadena residents criticized Kilpatrick's methods as "part of a campaign to *sell* our children on the collapse of *our way of life* and substitution of *collectivism* [my emphasis]."[128] In this statement, ideological warfare was associated with the advertising idea of *"sell[ing]."* The effect of the American Way campaign appeared in the image of *"our way of life."* And, of course, *"collectivism"* was posited as the opposite of "American individualism."

Textbook censorship, which, in chapter 1, I noted was a practice spearheaded in the 1920s by the American Legion, was characterized after World War II by Lucille Crain's quarterly publication, *Educational Reviewer*, started in 1949. Crain targeted a high-school textbook, Frank Magruder's *American Government*, as presenting an interpretation of democracy "straight from Rousseau, through Marx, to totalitarianism."[129] Crain's criticism was broadcasted and reported by leading radio commentators and newspapers, such as Fulton Lewis, Jr., and the *Chicago Tribune*.

The anti-communist crusade resulted, not surprisingly, in a significant decrease in discussions of controversial topics in American classrooms. Any discussion of communism might lead to a charge of subversion. The fervent anti-communist Director of the National Council for the Social Studies from 1943 to 1974, Merrill Hartshorn, was criticized for suggesting that schools teach about communism to defeat it. "Some people," according to Hartshorn, "interpreted that as teaching communism. But I was just saying that we should teach *about* communism. We can't deal with something we don't understand."[130] As I discovered, teaching about communism meant presenting a negative portrayal of life in the Soviet Union. As a student teacher in 1965, I team-taught an American Problems course with William Dunwiddie who had been selected by *Look Magazine* as one of the top 10

American teachers and who worked closely with the National Council for the Social Studies. One day I was given the task of lecturing to students on some aspect of the Soviet Union. I decided to explain Lenin's justification for the Communist Party, as representative of the working class, being the sole political party in the Soviet Union. Personally, I never accepted the argument that the Communist Party played a vanguard role for the proletariat. However, I thought it was important for understanding the political organization of the Soviet Union. Shortly into my talk, Dunwiddie jumped up and asked me to sit down while he completed the class. He then launched into a talk about the exploitation and enslavement of women under the communist system despite promises of gender equality. Obviously, teaching about communism did not mean explaining ideas or conditions that prompted people to join the international communist movement; it simply meant teaching that communism was enslaving and evil.

The movie and television industry were forced to purge writers and censor scripts. Unlike the Soviet Union, where the government directly controlled the content of media, censorship in the United States resulted from government pressure and commercial interests. Radio and television were at the mercy of their sponsors and program content usually steered clear of controversial issues. Obviously, no U.S. advertiser wanted to be associated with a radio or television program that provided a favorable view of communism. The movie industry felt the heavy hand of government in the Congressional investigation into communism in Hollywood conducted in 1947 by the House Un-American Activities Committee.[131] The industry responded by producing movies, such as *The Red Curtain, The Red Menace, The Red Danube,* and *I Married a Communist.*[132] Advertisers and nongovernment groups played the major role in anti-communist efforts against the television industry. In 1948, the American Legion began issuing a newsletter titled, *Summary of Trends and Developments in Radio and Television,* which suggested that any sign of subversion in a radio or television program warranted organizing "a letter writing group of six to ten relatives or friends...." The newsletter urged, "Don't let the sponsors pass the buck back to you by demanding 'proof' of Communist fronting by some character about who you have complained. You don't have to prove anything ..."[133] A 1950 book with the descriptive title, *Red Channels: The Report of Communist Influence in Radio and Television* warned that the "Communist Party USA now rely[s] more on radio and TV than on the press and motion pictures as 'belts' to transmit pro-Sovietism to the American public."[134]

The 1962 movie *Manchurian Candidate* provides a good example of Hollywood's imagery of communism as an insidious and evil disease infecting human brains. In the movie, American Raymond Shaw, is brainwashed in a Korean prisoner of war camp. Raymond's mother is secretly a communist agent masquerading as an anti-communist. As part of his brainwashing, Raymond is programmed to kill the presidential candidate whose running mate is Raymond's stepfather. Eventually, with the help of his army friends, Raymond is cured of the brainwashing and kills his mother and stepfather. He then commits suicide and, in the words of Ron Robin, "thereby destroying the last American link in the communist conspiracy to overtake America."[135]

ABSTRACT ART VERSUS SOCIALIST REALISM

The U.S. government's covert support of abstract art against social realist art highlights how educational security states enlist the world of art in their global educational efforts. In its covert operations, the U.S. government promoted abstract painting as a truly American art representing the possibilities of artistic freedom as opposed to the socialist realism imposed by the Soviet government on artists. This covert support of abstract art was different from the overt censorship and the inclusion of images of communism as Satanic enslavement in schools and mass media. In contrast, U.S. government support of abstract art was done in secret and it was congruent the NSC–68's recommendation for "Intensification of affirmative and timely measures and operations by covert means in the fields of economic warfare and political and *psychological warfare* ..."[136]

In the early days of the Cold War, according to Frances Saunders' *The Cultural Cold War: The CIA and the World of Arts and Letters*, the U.S. government's Central Intelligence Agency (CIA) became actively involved in supporting writers, painters, and musicians as part of a covert cultural offensive against the Soviet Union.[137] One of the first efforts was to bring together American and German intellectuals through the 1948 publication of the monthly magazine, *Der Monet*, which was initially funded by secret funds from the Marshall Plan and later by the CIA. A collection of articles from the magazine was published as the anti-communist book, *The God That Failed* and distributed by the U.S. government to people throughout Europe. Also, the Office of the Chief of Psychological Warfare promoted important anti-communist books, such as Arthur Koestler's *Darkness at Noon* and Ignazio Silone's *Bread and Wine*.[138]

In 1950, the CIA sponsored the founding of the Congress for Cultural Freedom and soon afterward the American Committee for Cultural Freedom. The Congress for Cultural Freedom issued a Freedom Manifesto that was in stark contrast to Maxim Gorky's definition of socialist realism. The Freedom Manifesto stated, "We hold it to be self-evident that intellectual freedom is one of the inalienable rights of man.... Such freedom is defined first and foremost by his right to hold and express his own opinions, and particularly opinions which differ from those of his rulers. Deprived of the right to say 'no', man becomes a slave."[139] Gorky might have responded to the Manifesto that social class and material conditions defined the meaning of freedom in art. Under capitalism, artists were "free" to produce art that served the rich or commercial interests as opposed to socialist freedom which served the worker. A senior CIA official explained,

> The purpose ... was to unite intellectuals against what was being offered in the Soviet Union. The idea that world would succumb to a kind of Fascist or Stalinist concept of art and literature and music [was] a horrifying prospect. We wanted to unite all people who were artists, who were writers, who were musicians, and all the people who follow those people, to demonstrate that the West and the United States was devoted to freedom of expression.[140]

So the world's peoples were treated to a struggle between the two superpowers over the control of art. Although both Soviet and U.S. leaders championed different versions of artistic freedom; the reality was that both governments were trying to determine the type of art that would capture the public's imagination. The first General Secretary of the Congress for Cultural Freedom, Nicolas Nabakov, explained the state of affairs, "There were no modern precedents, no models in the western world. No one before had tried to mobilize intellectuals and artists on a world wide scale in order to fight an ideological war against oppressors of the mind."[141]

These differences over the meaning of artistic freedom were central to the ideological warfare between socialist realist and abstract art.[142] The Congress for Cultural Freedom and the CIA promoted abstract art as representing true freedom of artistic expression. Abstract art represented the ability of the artist to do art for art's sake supposedly free of political pressure and content. The American Congress for Cultural Freedom included in its membership famous abstract artists, like Robert Motherwell, Jackson Pollock, and Alexander Calder. Also, artists Mark Rothko and Adolph Gottlieb helped found the openly anti-communist Federation of Modern Painters and Sculptors.[143] In addition, the CIA, through its covert organizations, worked closely with the Museum of Modern Art (MOMA) in New York City. The Congress for Cultural Freedom sponsored exhibits of MOMA's collection of abstract art throughout Europe.

Jackson Pollock, who gained fame for spattering and throwing paint on canvases, was representative of the CIA's idea of the free American artist. He was described by fellow artist Budd Hopkins as "the great American painter. If you conceive of such a person, first of all, he had to be a real American, not a transplanted European. And he should have the big macho American virtues—he should be rough-and-tumble American ... and if he is a cowboy, so much the better [Pollock was born in Wyoming.]."[144]

Pollock's rise in the art world was assured when conservative publisher Henry Luce was convinced by representatives of MOMA to put Pollock on the August 1949 cover of *Life* magazine; an honor seldom given to painters. The Congress for Cultural Freedom ensured that his paintings, along with those of other abstract artists, were displayed throughout Europe.[145] Pollock was the model of artistic freedom: an artist willing to break the boundaries of conventional art by simply throwing paint on a canvas and make a great deal of money.

CONCLUSION:
FROM CONTROLLING BRAINS TO BRAINPOWER

Support for socialist realist and abstract art were examples of overt and covert methods used by educational security states to influence public opinion. Both the Soviet Union and the United States's governments treated human behavior as a function of imagination. Authorities, like Gorky, American public relations experts, and those working in the U.S. Army's Office of the Chief of Psychological, treated human imagination as an important interpreter of messages from the outside world received by the human brain. The Cold War became a struggle to control thinking by implanting in citizens images of Stakhanovites, servile Lei Fengs, the American way of life, national heroes, mythologized pasts, good and evil, colonialism and racism, and freedom and slavery. The war of images helped the U.S. civil rights movement and speeded up the process of school desegregation as the United States tried erase its international racist image and replace it with one of equality and freedom. The Soviet Union battled against images of being a slave state by projecting an image of friend of the working class and fighter against racism and colonialism.

The Cold War was also about the development of "brainpower," as I discuss in the next chapter, along with attempts to control behavior. Nineteenth century changes in Japanese education initiated an era when the development of brainpower was a central theme in the world flow of education ideas. The study of science, mathematics, and engineering were fundamental to developing human brainpower for industrial and military development. Japanese and Chinese advocates of modernization, and anti-colonialists like Ho Chi Minh, believed educational reform should emphasize Western-style science, mathematics, and engineering courses. Marxist ideology stressed the importance of scientific understanding of the world. United States leaders believed that science was the key to military leadership of the world. However, as I discuss in the next chapter, educational security states' scientific endeavors were often guided by imaginations dominated by images embedded by political forces. The crosscurrents of global conflict turned schools into developers and controllers of brainpower.

Chapter 4

Schooling Brainpower:
China, the Soviet Union,
and the United States

"Red and expert" was the phrase favored by Chinese communists to describe the educational security state's combining of ideological control of consciousness with the utilization of human brainpower to advance economic and military projects. Human emotions, imagination, sensual perceptions, reason, and analytical abilities were brought under the controlling power of educational security states. The goal was a fusion of individual minds with the plans of state leaders. Human emotions were to be attached to patriotic symbols of nations; imaginations were to be filled with fantasies of overproducing Stakhanovite workers, of overconsuming patriots of the American Way, and the self-sacrifices of Lei Feng; and reason and analytical abilities were to be utilized to advance military technology and industrial development. In China, "red and expert" was used to describe the educational efforts to enlist the total human mind into the states' plans; in the United States, the effort was captured in title and content of the 1958 National Defense Education Act; and in the Soviet Union it was symbolized by the 1957 launching of the first satellite, Sputnik I.

During the late 1940s and 1950s, leaders in China, the Soviet Union, and the United States organized schools to serve the human power needs of industrial and economic development, which included educating more engineers, scientists, and technicians. All three countries feared the military might of the other. All three countries were faced with rebuilding their economies. The economies of China and the Soviet Union were ravaged by years of war. American leaders worried about depression and massive unemployment with the demobilization of World War II fighting forces while they planned rebuilding a war-devastated Europe as a buffer against the spread of Communism.

In this chapter, I first analyze educational changes in the People's Republic of China to illustrate attempts to make human thought and emotions subservient to the needs of the nation. Also, Chinese education was further impacted by the global flow of education ideas as the Soviet Union participated in restructuring its school system. Stalin's death in 1953 changed the relationship between the two countries while changing the basic direction of Soviet military policy and, consequently, education policies. I examine how the military and education policies of Nikita Khrushchev eventually caused U.S. leaders to look to Soviet schools as model institutions. As a result, U.S. leaders pressed for greater integration of education into economic and military planning.

RED AND EXPERT

In the late 1950s, "red and expert" became a popular Chinese slogan. It should be noted that Mao, along with the leaders of other nations, seemed to agree with Hitler's contention in Mein Kampf that slogans were the best means of unifying the masses to achieve a goal. Mao was a master of slogans, such as "red and expert," "the great leap forward," and "let a hundred flowers bloom." The slogan "red and expert" embodied the combination of political education and technical training needed to employ a mainly rural and illiterate population in building an industrialized communist state. Also, the anti-foreign attitudes of Mao Zedong and other Chinese leaders resulted in a nationalistic interpretation of Marxist–Leninist ideas by changing the early 20th century saying *"Western Function, Chinese Essence"* into *"Marxism–Leninism, Chinese Essence"* or, as stated in the Preamble to the 1982 Constitution of the People's Republic of China, *"Marxism–Leninism and Mao Zedong Thought."* The actual wording of the 1982 Preamble indicates that China had developed its own form of communism: "Under the leadership of the Communist Party of China and the guidance of Marxism–Leninism and Mao Zedong Thought, the Chinese people ... will ... follow the socialist road."[1] Mao had always been resistant to simply incorporating without any changes Western ideas into Chinese culture. In 1930, Mao warned, "We must study Marxist 'books,' but they must be integrated with our actual situation."[2] Mao's famous 1940 publication, *On the New Democracy*, warned that: "So-called 'wholesale Westernization' is a mistaken viewpoint. China has suffered a great deal in the past from formalist absorption of foreign things. Likewise, in applying Marxism to China, Chinese communists must fully and properly unite the universal truth of Marxism with the specific practice of the Chinese revolution."[3] Nationalistic sentiments were heightened by a sense of shame caused by subjugation to Western and Japanese imperialism. In 1949, ten days before the official creation of the People's Republic of China, Mao waved the nationalistic flag declaring: "the Chinese people, comprising one quarter of humanity [a more accurate estimate discussed below gave China one-fifth of the world's population in 1949], have now stood up ... we have closed ranks and defeated both domestic and foreign aggressors.... Ours will no longer be a nation subject to insult and humiliation."[4]

Overcoming a less than 20% literacy rate for one fifth of the world's population was a staggering task for a nation decimated by war. The expansion of the school system involved large numbers of students as indicated in Table 4.1.

These school enrollment figures take on more meaning when placed in the context of China and the world's total populations, and the population and enrollment figures in the United States. In 1950, China's population was estimated by the United Nations Population Division to be 556.7 million and estimates of the world's population in 1950 ranged from 2.4 to 2.55 million people. The estimated school population (ages 5–19) in 1950 was 165 million, which meant that only about 15% (25.5 million) of the school-age population was in school. In the United States in 1949–1950, the estimated total population was 150 million—less than the school age population of China—with a total primary and secondary school enrollment of about 25 million. The school-age population of the United States (5–17)[5] was about 30 million meaning that roughly 83% of school-age children were in school as compared to 15% in China. For China to reach the percentage of school-age children in U.S. schools would have meant increasing China's school population by about 112 million students or more than quadrupling the size of the Chinese school system.[6]

TABLE 4.1
School Enrollment in China 1949–1958

School Year	Primary	Secondary	University
1949–1950	24,391,000	1,039,000	117,000
1951–1952	43,154,000	1,568,000	137,000
1953–1954	51,664,000	2,933,000	212,000
1955–1956	53,126,000	3,900,000	288,000
1957–1958	64,279,000	6,281,000	441,000

Note. Adapted from *Ten Great Years* (Peking: Foreign Languages Press, 1960), p. 192 as reprinted in Julia Kwong, *Chinese Education in Transition: Prelude to the Cultural Revolution* (Montreal: McGill–Queen's University Press, 1979), p. 69.

Plans for tackling China's education problems within the framework of what would later be called "red and expert," were adopted in 1949 as part of the "Common Program of the Chinese People's Political Consultative Conference." Declaring the People's Republic of China a "people's democratic dictatorship led by the working class, based on the alliance of workers and peasants," the Common Program contained nine articles devoted to cultural and educational policies. Article 41 emphasized the dual goals of ideological instruction (red) and training for economic development (expert): "The main tasks of the cultural and educational work of the people's government shall be the raising of the cultural level of the people, training personnel for national construction work, liquidating of feudal, compradore, fascist ideology and developing of the ideology of serving the people."[7] From Mao's perspective, it was also necessary to provide for the political reeducation in Marxist–Leninist Mao Zedong thought of already educated groups. Article 47 proclaimed the necessity of universal education along with political reeducation.

> In order to meet the widespread needs of revolutionary work and national construction work, universal education shall be carried out, middle and higher education shall be strengthened, technical education shall be stressed, the education of workers during their spare time and education of cadres who are at their posts shall be strengthened, and *revolutionary political education shall be accorded to young intellectuals and old-style intellectuals in a planned and systematic manner* [my emphasis].[8]

Two articles called for the development of emotional attachments to the state and the use of the arts—socialist realism—to develop political consciousness.

Article 42   Love for the fatherland and the people, love of labour, love of science and the taking care of public property shall be promoted as the public spirit of all citizens of the People's Republic of China.

Article 45   Literature and arts shall be promoted to serve the people, to heighten the political consciousness of the people, and to encourage the labor enthusiasm of the people. Outstanding works of literature and arts shall be encouraged and awarded. The people's drama and cinema shall be developed.[9]

Although Articles 42 and 45 proposed the use of emotions ("love") and imagination ("literature and arts") as part of ideological education, Article 43 emphasized training in science as a means of harnessing brainpower to economic and military development: "Efforts shall be made to develop the natural sciences to place them at the service of industrial, agricultural and national defense construction. Scientific discoveries and inventions shall be encouraged and awarded and scientific knowledge shall be popularized."[10] Three of the other articles dealt with the use of "scientific historical viewpoint" in studying history, politics, economics and culture; promotion of sports; and the importance of newspapers.

Highly unusual for a national plan, Article 46 prescribed a teaching method, "theory and practice," that reflected Mao's criticism of Confucianism ideas and his theory of knowledge and practice. Article 46 stated, "The method of education of the people's Republic of China is the unity of theory and practice. The people's government shall reform the old educational system, subject matter and teaching method systematically according to plan."[11]

First, Mao and others criticized Confucian society for the elite status given to the intelligentsia and their lack of contact with the working world. In this context, theory and practice meant eliminating the elite status of the scholars and having them work in factories and alongside peasants. Working side-by-side with the common laborer, intellectuals would be able to reflect on the meaning of their ideas in the context of the material conditions of society. This concern about the intellectual's alienation from the means of production was embodied in Article 47's call to provide "revolutionary political education ... to young and old-style intellectuals." During the 1960s' Cultural Revolution, in keeping with the unity of theory and practice and worries about the status of intellectuals, university scholars and school teachers were forced to work side-by-side with workers and peasants.

Second, the "unity of theory and practice" could be considered the common thread in most progressive education methods. Certainly, John Dewey would have agreed on the importance of testing theory through practice. Of course, unity of theory and practice was a basic tenet of Marxist thought. As I discussed in chapter 2, Mao sold more books by Dewey than by Marx in the 1920s from his Cultural Bookstore and his 1937 lecture "On Practice" laid out the basic conditions for learning, including the application of thought to material conditions and reflection on the results as part of a five-stage process of learning.

Third, "unity of theory and practice" also referred to the fusing of human consciousness with economic and military needs. In 1958, Mao explained, "Red and expert, politics and business are the unification of two pairs of opposites.... There is no doubt that politics and economy, and politics and technology should be united.... Ideological and political work is the guarantee for the accomplishment of our economic and technological work.... *Ideology and politics are the commanders, the soul. A slight relaxation in our ideological and political work will lead our economic and technological work astray* [my emphasis]."[12]

And lastly, according to Mao, "unity of theory and practice" was necessary for a complete education. To know only theory, a person was partially educated and unable to meaningfully participate in national economic development: "To have no practical knowledge is to be pseudo-red, empty-headedly political. Politics and technology must be combined together. In agriculture, this means carrying out experiments; in industries, understanding advanced models, trying out new techniques, and producing new goods."[13]

Despite Mao's own feelings about education there continued throughout his lifetime a tension between what Theodore Hsi-en Chen refers to as Mao's revolutionary model and the academic model. Chen's academic model is the same as the formal model of education I refer to in chapter 1. A summary and restatement of many of Mao's criticisms of the academic model, includes the charge of elitism because the model only serves the few; that it inherently contains a capitalist ideology; there is a preoccupation with intellectual work; students are artificially evaluated as to their worth by examinations and grades; the model promotes competition and selfish ambition; and it isolates the student from "social, economic, and political struggles of contemporary society."[14] In contrast, Mao's revolutionary model, which falls into the progressive education tradition, includes a belief that teaching should relate knowledge to the material conditions of life; that theory must be learned through practice and tested through practice; that education should include manual labor; that study from books is less useful than learning through action and practice; and that the study of ideology requires constant reflection on the consequences of ideology put into practice.[15] Chen concluded about the competition between the two models that there were "periodical shifts in the relative influence of one model or the other. The revolutionaries gained the upper hand after 1958, but in the period 1960 to 1964 the academicians endeavored to revive and strengthen academic education, only to be defeated and to make way for the full triumph [during the Cultural Revolution] of the revolutionaries."[16]

In 1951, the Council of the Central People's Government reorganized the educational system by shortening the elementary school to 5 years (ages 7–11), a junior middle school (ages 12–14), and a senior middle school (ages 15–17). More importantly, given China's massive educational problems, elementary schools were to provide make-up classes and vocational training courses for elementary students unable to continue their schooling. Workers and peasants' were given the opportunity to attend short course elementary schools of 2 to 3 years. Spare-time elementary schools allowed workers and peasants to attend at their convenience without any strict attendance requirements. Literacy schools were established. Short-course and spare-time middle schools were established to serve older workers. Teacher training was addressed through expansion of normal schools that admitted graduates of junior middle schools.[17] As reported in Table 4.1, school enrollment more than doubled by 1953, but more than half the school-age population remained out of school.

In the arena of cultural affairs, the Vice Premier and Chairman of the Committee of Cultural and Educational Affairs of the State Administration Council, Kuo Mo-jo, reported a massive publication program and that in "the field of motion picture enterprises, our fundamental policy lies in the gradual obliteration of obnoxious imperialistic films ... whereas formerly 75 percent of the motion picture audience used to see American pictures, the ration has gone down to 28.3 percent."[18] In keeping with the tenets of socialist realism, Kuo hoped to strengthen "the educational influence of the people's motion pictures and ... [enable] the motion picture to reach out to workers, peasants, and soldiers."[19] In addition, "improvement" in journalism was ensuring, according to Kuo, "the strengthening of press activities designed to serve the interests of economic reconstruction and the implementation of the criticism and self-criticism campaign [political education] through the medium of the newspaper."[20]

In summary, the 1949 Common Program of the Chinese People's Political Consultative Conference laid out the basic ways for schooling citizens to fulfill the military, industrial, and agricultural plans in the educational security state. Human emotions were to be harnessed to ensure loyalty and devotion to the state. Literature and other arts were to focus human imaginations on images that encouraged the "labor enthusiasm of the people;" "heightened political consciousness;" and on living according to the myth of Lei Feng's self-sacrificing fidelity and work for the People's Liberation Army, the People's Republic of China, and Mao Zedong.

FREEDOM AND THE EDUCATIONAL SECURITY STATE: SOVIETIZATION AND LET HUNDRED FLOWERS BLOOM

In the early days of communist control, China modeled its nascent security state after the Soviet Union. In 1950, Mao and Stalin agreed, after much wrangling and displays of distrust, to a Treaty of Friendship, Alliance and Mutual Assistance. Shortly after signing the agreement, Soviet experts and money began to flow into China. The result was a strong influence of Soviet educators on the development of Chinese schools, including the translation and use of Soviet textbooks and the replacement of instruction in the English language with Russian. Rather than strengthening the potential progressive direction of Mao's theories, Soviet experts brought with them a Stalinist model of school organization, including student rules of conduct similar to those introduced in Russian schools in the 1930s. The rules of conduct created a formalistic and authoritarian classroom organization. During the Cultural Revolution of the 1960s, Mao would lead a revolt against these types of hierarchical school rules with calls for students to question and denounce teachers' authority. In contrast, the Soviet-like 1955 rules were designed to enforce the authority of the teacher and school. The "Rules of Conduct for Primary School Students" contained the following regulations governing student behavior:

6. Be orderly and quiet and assume a correct posture during the class. When desiring to leave the classroom, ask the teacher's permission first.
7. During the class, work diligently and listen attentively to the teacher's instruction and the questions and answers by your classmates. Do not talk except when necessary; do not do anything else besides your classwork.
8. During the class when you want to give an answer or to ask a question, raise your hand first. Stand up and speak when the teacher allows you to; sit down when the teacher tells you so.
11. Respect the principal and the teachers. Salute your teacher when the class begins and again at the end of the class. When you meet the principal or the teacher outside the school you also salute them.[21]

Similar rules governed the lives of middle school students, such as: "6. During the class, assume a correct posture; listen to the lecture attentively; do not talk unless when necessary; do not do anything else besides your class work. When desiring to leave the classroom, ask the teacher's permission first."[22] Both sets of rules demanded obedience to school regulations, teachers, and principals.

Studying the Soviet model of economic and educational development was mandated for Chinese higher education. In 1953, Minister of Education Ma Hsu-lun issued "The Policy and Tasks of Higher Education" calling for "the study of advanced Soviet experiences and pedagogical reform by positive but appropriate measures in order to improve the quality of pedagogical work."[23] The policy paper addressed Mao's concern with reeducating professors in communist theory: "Keep up the ideological reform of teachers in institutions of higher education." Minister Ma specified the study of "Stalin's *Economic Problems of Socialism in the U.S.S.R.*, Stalin's *On Marxism and Problems of Philology*, Mao Zedong's *On Practice, On Contradiction*, and other treatises."[24]

This ideological reform of intellectuals and the restrictions placed on freedom of thought were criticized by Mao when, in 1957, he launched the Hundred Flowers campaign with the slogan, "Let a hundred flowers bloom, a hundred schools of thought contend."[25] Formally, the Hundred Flowers campaign was presented to the public on February 27, 1957 in a 4-hour speech by Mao titled, "On Correct Handling of Contradictions Among the People" in which he noted that "several million intellectuals who worked for the old society have come to serve the new society ... [and that] they must continue to remold themselves gradually shed[ding] their bourgeois world outlook."[26] On the other hand, Mao noted the importance of freedom of thought for the advancement of politics and science: "Take for example, Marxism. Marxism was [once] considered a poisonous weed.... The astronomy of Copernicus ... the physics of Galileo, Darwin's theory of evolution were all, at the start, rejected."[27] With his usual colorful language, Mao summarized the dilemma of intellectual freedom, "If you want only [fragrant flowers] and not weeds, it can't be done ... to ban all weeds and stop them growing, is that possible? The reality is that it is not. They will still grow.... It is difficult to distinguish fragrant flowers from poisonous weeds."[28]

The Hundred Flowers campaign required a clear definition of the meaning of freedom in a strong national security state like China that, among other things, insisted on socialist realism in art and the subordination of science to politics. As I discussed in chapter 3, the Soviet representative to discussions on the United Nations Universal Declaration of Human Rights, Boris Tchechko, had argued that in the Soviet Union intellectuals experienced freedom to express ideas that served the working class and that fallacious ideas contrary to the interests of the working class were counterrevolutionary and undermined the interests of the working class. Because Soviet intellectuals lived in a working-class society, it would only be expected that they would express ideas from the perspective of peasants and the working class.

In China, the detailed response to the difficult question of intellectual freedom in a worker and peasant dictatorship was given by Lu Ting-yi, Director of the Propaganda Department of the Central Committee of the Chinese Communist Party, in a 1956 speech colorfully titled, "Let All Flowers Bloom Together, Let Diverse Schools of Thought Contend."[29] Using the metaphor of the flower, Lu explained, "In literary and art work, if there is 'only one flower in bloom,' no matter how good the flower may be, it would not lead to prosperity."[30] And, referring to a period in Chinese history when the phrase "letting all schools contend in airing views" was popular, Lu warned, "The history of our country has proved that if there were no encouragement of independent thinking and if there were no free discussion, then academic development would stagnate."[31] But, Lu reminded the audience, "We see also that in a class society, literature and arts and scientific works have after all to be used as a weapon in class struggle."[32]

After stating the importance of independent thought, Lu, speaking as Director of the Propaganda Department, went on the justify the censorship of "yellow novels," which he claimed preached obscenity and lawlessness, such as "let us play mah-jongg and to hell with all State affairs" and "the moon over the United States is rounder than the moon over China." He declared the importance of literature and arts serving the class struggle. He also reiterated previous criticisms of notions of "literature and arts for the sake of literature and arts" and "science for the sake of science" as a "rightist unilateral view."[33]

Similar to his Soviet comrade Tchechko, Lu made a distinction between freedom he was advocating and freedom in a bourgeois democracy: "The freedom advocated by the bourgeoisie is nothing more than freedom for the minority which the laboring people have little or no chance to share."[34] Similar to Tchechko, Lu advocated, "that the counter-revolutionaries should be denied freedom. We hold that we must practice dictatorship over counter-revolutionaries."[35] The freedom Lu supported was "freedom within the camp of the people."[36] Thus, freedom of thought or "letting all flowers bloom together and all schools contend in airing their views" would be allowed as long as it did not question or undermine the dictatorship of the people. In his official capacity as Director of Propaganda, Lu concluded,

> inside the camp of the people, the ideological struggle must be rightly distinguished from the struggle against the counter-revolutionaries. Inside the camp of the people, there is not only the freedom to publicize materialism but also the freedom to publicize idealism. As long as the parties concerned are not counter-revolutionaries, they are free to publicize both materialism and idealism, and both parties are free to enter into controversy.... In short, while we advocate the drawing of a distinction between ourselves and the enemy in the political field, we also advocate that we must have certain freedom in the camp of the people.[37]

In practice, freedom within the "camp of the people" was also limited. Mao made a distinction between "blooming and contending" that strengthened Party leadership as opposed to causing disorganization and confusion. Many intellectuals had a hard time distinguishing between bourgeois and peoples' freedom, and between strengthening and causing social disorganization. Many were accused of being counterrevolutionaries resulting in 520,000 intellectuals being forced to work in factories and farms to develop a working class consciousness.[38]

In summary, the Sovietization of the Chinese school system added an authoritarian and formalistic direction to the preparation of a population to be "red and expert." Added to this was the backlash to the Hundred Flowers campaign that, ironically, increased ideological control by defining freedom of thought; people were now free to express thoughts that were in the "camp of the people," which increased Mao's control over the people. The Cultural Revolution of the 1960s would challenge the formalistic qualities of the school system. But, before that occurred, Mao announced the Great Leap Forward, which was one more step in the integration of schooling into economic planing.

SPUTNIK AND THE EDUCATIONAL SECURITY STATE

On October 4, 1957, Soviet Union missile experts successfully launched the first space satellite Sputnik I. To the rest of the world, the Soviet Union seemed to be the most advanced scientific and technological nation. Sputnik I turned what had been an ideological competition into a competition for scientific and educational superiority. The question was now: Which political and economic system would be the best in advancing scientific progress? Mao commented at the time that the United States "hadn't launched a potato."[39] For Mao, the Soviet achievement proved the superiority of a communist over a capitalist system. The accomplishment motivated Mao to announce a plan for a "Great Leap Forward" that more fully integrated the educational system into national planning. American leaders concluded that Sputnik was the product of a superior Soviet school system which emphasized science and math. In *Brainpower for the Cold War: The Sputnik Crisis and National Defense Education Act of 1958*, Barbara Clowse reported that Senator Henry Jackson of Washington called the launch a "'devastating blow' to the United States and called on President Eisenhower to proclaim 'a week of shame and danger'."[40] At a White House meeting held 11 days after the Sputnik launch, the Science Advisory Committee of the Office of Defense Mobilization persuaded President Eisenhower that he must increase the supply of scientific "manpower," otherwise the Soviet Union would permanently surpass the United States in technological developments.[41]

Concerns increased about America's scientific and educational status with the November 3, 1957 launch of Sputnik II weighing six times more than Sputnik I and carrying a dog wired for medical monitoring. Five days later, President Eisenhower told his cabinet to pay close attention to a report on the Soviet education system to be released by the Department of Health, Education, and Welfare (HEW) because of "the great strides made in the educational field in the USSR."[42] Later, the author of the report claimed that HEW officials tried to suppress the report. As a result, Arkansas Senator J. William Fulbright criticized HEW officials for "deprecating Russian ability and accomplishments."[43]

There was a growing belief among U.S. leaders and the general public that Soviet schools were superior to U.S. schools in the teaching of science and mathematics. The March 3, 1958 issue of *Life* magazine reported a survey conducted by the Opinion Research Corporation of Princeton, New Jersey, which found that one third of the American public believed that Soviet schools were superior in teaching science and mathematics. America's education and science deficit seemed to be confirmed by the May 15, 1958 launch of Sputnik III carrying a payload larger than the first two Sputniks. In May, 1958, the U.S. Commissioner of Education Lawrence Derthick led a team of educators on a tour of Russia. After the trip, the Commissioner gave several speeches containing the ominous statement, "The Soviet union is like one vast, sprawling college campus on the eve of a football game with its great rival. That rival is the United States. The game is economic and cultural conquest of the world." He also expressed his amazement at Soviet commitment to education "as a means of national advancement."[44]

Negative comparisons of Soviet and U.S. schools were given in Arthur Trace, Jr.'s descriptively titled 1961 book, *What Ivan Knows That Johnny Doesn't: A Comparison of Soviet and American School Programs*.[45] The book's cover warned, "By the time American schoolchildren get Jack and Jill up that hill, Soviet children of the same age will probably be discussing the hill's altitude, mineral deposits and geo-political role in world affairs."[46] Trace compared Soviet and U.S. textbooks, curricula, and study habits. Regarding science instruction, Trace made this ominous comparison, "whereas all Russian students who graduate from high school have studied physics for five years, chemistry for four years, biology for six years, and astronomy for one year, only some American high school graduates have studied biology or physics or chemistry for one year."[47] After comparing elementary school reading textbooks, Trace concluded that American students were "being seriously shortchanged.... One wonders how many students really succeed in overcoming the handicap which these basal readers [U.S. reading textbooks] place them under in learning other subjects."[48] Trace also found serious shortcomings in comparison to Soviet schools in the teaching of literature, foreign languages, history, and geography.

A dilemma was created for Americans who claimed that Soviet schools were superior to American schools. Did this mean that the communist system was superior to the U.S. system? If U.S. schools copied Soviet schools would students become communist? Trace's answers emphasized the ideological purposes of instruction. Literature and history could be taught with the same academic emphasis in the United States, Trace argued, but with a different goal for ideological control: "Thus, if Soviet education can use literature as highly effective means of persuading Soviet students of the superiority of the communist way of life, then American education can give our students a thorough enough understanding of ... the democratic way of life."[49] Trace asserted, "our schools will not be communistic if they adopt textbooks which can teach our children to read well by the end of the fourth grade."[50] And, regarding increased academic work, he contended, "Above all, it is not communistic for students to study hard in school and at home so that they can train their minds well enough to become the competent professional leaders and intelligent citizens that America and the free world desperately require."[51]

As reflected in Trace's comparisons, Sputnik I generated a feeling among some Americans that the United States should emulate Soviet schools, particularly those aspects resulting from Stalinization such as classroom discipline, difficult textbooks, demanding study requirements, and a focus on academic subjects. There were few questions raised about the value of the organization and curricula of Soviet schools. In fact, the organization, instructional methods, textbooks, and discipline of Soviet schools were often cited as superior to that of U.S. schools. For those lauding the quality of Soviet over U.S. schools, the only issue was ideological content with the content of Soviet instruction emphasizing communist ideology and U.S. schools implanting in students' minds a belief in the American way of life. The idea of using education to implant a particular ideology was never questioned. There seemed to be a general acceptance that the purpose of schooling was ideological control.

In the Soviet Union, Sputnik dramatically symbolized the accomplishments of Nikita Khrushchev. At launch time, according to Sergei Khrushchev, his son and frequent companion, the two of them were dining in Kiev with a group of Ukrainian officials. An aid informed his father that he had a telephone call. Sergei wrote, "I guessed what the call had to be about and became very tense."[52] On returning to the guests and announcing the success of the launch, he explained the importance of the event. Sergei wrote, "He emphasized that here we had succeeded in surpassing America. He dreamed of demonstrating the advantages of socialism in actual practice. And now there was such an opportunity."[53] According to Sergei, his father bragged, "The Americans have proclaimed to the whole world that they are getting ready to launch a satellite over the earth. Theirs is only the size of an orange. We, on the other hand, have kept quiet, but we now have a satellite circling the planet. And not a little one, but one weighing eighty kilos."[54] Under Nikita Khrushchev, changes in Soviet military and scientific policies led up to the launching of Sputnik.

Among other things, Sputnik ensured the triumph of science and mathematics as the most important subjects in the school curricula because they were considered necessary for national economic and military planning in the national security state. After Stalin's death in 1953, Khrushchev assumed a leadership role in De-Stalinization that included major changes in military policies. After World War II, Stalin hoped to build the world's most powerful armed forces including the largest navy and army. For a war-torn nation, this was an expensive burden. Khrushchev wanted to rebuild the Soviet economy and provide the population with better housing and consumer goods. This meant abandoning Stalin's aggressive military program and replacing it with a less expensive missile defense system.

The result of these changes in military policies and Khrushchev's rivalry with the United States were the Sputnik launchings that, in turn, motivated the U.S. Congress to pass the 1958 National Defense Education Act. It is important to note the title of this legislation: National Defense Education Act. As the title suggests, the U.S. federal government was assuming a leadership role in the making education a function of the needs of the national security state. For a country where education was primarily controlled by state governments, the National Defense Education Act was a major step in nationalizing the school system to meet the needs of the Cold War.

THE SOVIET EDUCATIONAL SECURITY STATE

In the 1950s, Nikita Khrushchev instituted reforms that more tightly integrated education into economic and military plans. What bothered Khrushchev was the strong emphasis given in Soviet schools to academic subjects, ironically, because the stress on academic subjects and the formal instructional methods in Soviet schools were the reasons some Americans believed Soviet education was superior to American. However, this was not the opinion of Nikita Krushchev, who, in 1953, criticized Soviet schools for being "divorced from life" and that its graduates were "insufficiently prepared for practical work."[55] Readers will recall that Stalinization of Soviet schools in the 1930s resulted in a formalistic and rigid system where student advancement was dependent on test performance. Abandoning progressive methods, Soviet schools in the 1930s primarily emphasized academic studies.

Khrushchev wanted to balance academic study with training workers for the national economy. This meant tying education more closely to specific economic goals. The Stalinization of schools resulted in preparing students for college and, one could argue, provided the nation with a strong corps of scientists. Khrushchev complained that Soviet education was elitist and neglected to prepare the majority of noncollege bound students for work. There were several reasons why Khrushchev wanted to abandon the academic emphasis of Soviet schools. One reason was the need for a skilled workforce to advance industrial development. The Soviet Union had a major shortage of skilled workers as a result of casualties during World War II.

The second reason was the cost of providing the academic model of schooling to all Soviet students. School graduates were primarily educated for entrance into universities. However, Soviet universities were not large enough to absorb all secondary school graduates. Consequently, universal academic schooling would have required a costly expansion of the higher education system. Rather than making the academic model universal, Khrushchev's 1958 reforms provided universal 8-year schools followed by a choice of part-time schools, vocational schools, specialized schools, and general polytechnic schools. Nigel Grant concluded, "the retreat from the overwhelmingly academic character of the old ten-year school, and the stress on practical work for all, was the keynote of the 1958 reforms."[56]

Khrushchev explained the creation of closer ties between education and national economic planning in a 1958 memorandum titled, "Strengthening the Ties of the School With Life, and Further Developing the System of Public Education." In the memo, Khrushchev explained the reasons for the reform: "We are striving to have our entire youth, millions of boys and girls through the ten-year secondary school. Naturally enough, they cannot all be absorbed by the colleges.... The greater part of them ... turn out to be quite unprepared for life and do not know in which direction to turn."[57] As a result, he observed, "these boys and girls have absolutely no knowledge of production, and society does not know how best to utilize these young and vigorous people ... this state of affairs can hardly be considered right."[58]

The third reason given for school reform was ideological. A third class was forming composed of government bureaucrats and professionals who were trying to ensure that their children inherited their status by receiving the "best" education. Similar to Mao, Khrushchev worried that education was separating theory from practice and creating class differences based on attitudes about work. Krushchev stated, "We still have sharp distinction drawn between mental and manual work.... This is fundamentally wrong and runs counter to our teachings.... If a boy or girl does not study well ... and fails to get into college, the parents ... frighten him by saying that ... he will have to work in a factory as a common laborer." This attitude, Krushchev stressed, was contrary to the values of a socialist society: "In socialist society work must be valued by its usefulness.... It must be constantly inculcated in the young people that ... work is a vital necessity for every Soviet person."[59]

Although some of these reforms were modified in 1964 because of the difficulty of actually having students working in factories, the major thrust of the reforms remained in place. The primary emphasis was now on preparing a skilled workforce that could meet the labor requirements of a planned economy. Of course, college attendance supplied part of the labor needs. Although these changes were made in the structure and curriculum of schools, formal methods of instruction remained in place. As noted in the previous discussion of Soviet influence on Chinese schools in the 1950s, Soviet rules and regulations governing student conduct supported classroom practices that primarily involved direct instruction from the teacher. There was no return to the progressive school practices of the 1920s.

THE AMERICAN EDUCATIONAL SECURITY STATE

Fears generated by the Cold War transformed American education from a local and state enterprise into a nationalized system tied to the national security state. As a nationalized system, schools became more focused on formal academic subjects with an emphasis on science and mathematics. As I discussed in chapter 1, some Americans by the 1940s and 1950s were linking progressive education with communism. With the launching of Sputnik, progressive education was now blamed for the United States falling behind in science. Even President Eisenhower joined the attack against progressive education by warning, "They [educators, parents, and students] must be induced to abandon the educational path that, rather blindly, they have been following as a result of John Dewey's teachings ... when he (or his followers) went freewheeling into the realm of basic education they, in my opinion, did a great disservice to the American public."[60]

Nationalization of the education system increased during World War II with federal funding of military research in universities. Prior to World War II, support of scientific research primarily came from private industry. During World War II and the Cold War, funding shifted from private sources to the federal government and large national philanthropic foundations. This pattern generated some resistance from professors and others who feared the loss of academic freedom. Despite this resistance, the federal government's research agenda, particularly in the area of weapons research, did have a controlling influence on university research. The result was, and is, a complex system of private and state universities with research agendas often determined by the central (federal) government's priorities.[61]

Trends towards nationalization of elementary and secondary schools emerged from the federal sponsorship of science research during World War II and the 1958 National Defense Education Act. Nationalization reached a high point in 2001 with the federal government's legislation "No Child Left Behind." Similar to higher education, elementary and secondary schools came to operate in a complex system of private schools, local and state controls, and national priorities. This complexity was a result of a historical reliance on local and state control of schools being transformed by federal involvement. The most important historical marker for the growing nationalization of elementary and secondary schools, and integration into an educational security state, was the 1958 National Defense Education Act.

Cold War educational policies were initiated by the activities of the World War II Office of Scientific Research and Development, its Director Vannevar Bush, and James Conant, the head of its S-I Section; the S-I Section was involved in the Manhattan Project's development of the atomic bomb. In response to a 1944 request from President Franklin Roosevelt,

Bush prepared a federal report, *Science—The Endless Frontier*, which stated that postwar national security was dependent on an increase of men and women educated in science and increased federal funding of research. The report called for the creation of a federally sponsored National Science Foundation to support research and to develop science curricula for elementary and secondary schools.[62] In Congressional testimony supporting National Science Foundation legislation, James Conant testified, "It is men that count. And today we do not have the scientific manpower requisite for the job that lies ahead."[63] Conant wanted more high school students to choose a scientific career. By 1956, National Science Foundation officials were supervising the development of science and mathematics curricula by the Physical Science Study Committee, and in 1958, by the School Mathematics Study Group. Not only did the National Science Foundation stress the importance of science instruction to national security, but it also contributed to the nationalization of science instruction.[64]

Like the Soviet Union and China, U.S. national leaders were also interested in the role of education in controlling the supply of human resources for economic planning. Whereas Khrushchev had used the rhetoric of communism to justify the use of schools to channel students according to their abilities into the Soviet workforce, President Eisenhower and other leaders used the rhetoric of democracy. For instance, the National Manpower Council, founded in 1951 at Columbia University when Eisenhower headed the institution prior to his election to the presidency, stated in a 1954 report, "A democratic society promises each individual the opportunity to develop his potentialities as fully as he can in accordance with his own desires."[65]

James Conant, an advocate of labor market planning as part of national defense preparation, emphasized throughout his career the importance of schools in providing vocational counseling to ensure that students entered careers that matched their abilities and national economic needs. In language very similar to that used by Khrushchev regarding the uniform academic nature of Soviet schools, Conant told the U.S. Congressional committee that was considering establishing the National Science Foundation, "We pay a price for the fundamental democracy of our undifferentiated system of public schools ... if we are wise the price need not be as high as it is at the present moment."[66]

Conant's writings provided the basic arguments for the establishment of the U.S. educational security state. Conant was a friend and supporter of President Eisenhower and had close ties to prominent educators. On March 1, 1957, he received financial support to study the U.S. high school from the Carnegie Corporation, a foundation that has had an important nationalizing influence on U.S. schools. The date, March 1, 1957, was important because it was seven months before the launching of Sputnik I. Conant's report was published in 1959 as *The American High School Today*.[67] Between 1957 and 1958, Conant lectured throughout the nation on the importance of high school reform for the Cold War. Consequently, his work had a direct impact on the 1958 National Defense Act. Conant wrote in his autobiography, "The timing was perfect. A wave of public criticism of the high schools which had started after Sputnik had reached its crest. School board members all over the country were anxious for specific answers."[68]

Conant's school recommendations were framed in the context of the Cold War. He was dismayed that "many people are quite unconscious of the relation between high school education and the welfare of the United States. They are still living in imagination in a world which knew neither nuclear weapons nor Soviet imperialism."[69] In recommending increased study of foreign languages, he asserted, "In the competition with the Communists in the uncommitted nations of the world, we need to send many engineers as well as other specialists to areas where English is spoken only by a thin layer of the elite and to other places where English is not spoken at all."[70]

His most important recommendation was the consolidation of small high schools into large institutions that could provide a wide range of students with "marketable skills." At the heart of these institutions were to be one counselor for every 250 to 300 students who would persuade students to enter careers that matched their interests and national needs. He wanted each academic course to be divided into three ability groups with some students being programmed for college and some for direct entrance into the labor market. Students not bound for college, he urged, should be educated to meet specific needs of the labor market. This would require a continual assessment of labor market needs. Conant insisted, "The school administration should constantly assess the employment situation in those trades included in the vocational programs. When opportunities for employment in a given trade no longer exist within the community, the training program in that field should be dropped."[71]

Similar to Mao's slogan of "red and expert" and the Soviet educational goal of the new socialist man/woman with useful work skills, Conant wanted marketable skills balanced by allegiance to U.S. institutions. To create a sense of democratic community, Conant recommended that students from all ability levels and vocational interests be mixed in homerooms, student governments, and in a 12th-grade course in U.S. problems and government. All of these combined activities he hoped would overcome the potentially undemocratic qualities of ability and vocational groupings.

Conant's ideological intentions were clear. Regarding the 12th-grade U.S. problems or government course, he claimed it would "develop not only an understanding of the American form of government and of the economic basis of our free society, but also mutual respect and understanding between types of students."[72] In referring to the "economic basis of our free society," it was quite clear that he did not envision high school debates about socialist versus capitalist economies where arguments for socialism might win. Reflecting a lack of knowledge of socialist youth groups in China and the Soviet Union that existed to create a sense of communist solidarity, he argued that totalitarian countries, meaning the Soviet Union and China, educated students in separate schools without the democratic mixing for students he proposed for homerooms, student governments, and senior problems and government courses. Conant claimed in his recommendation for a 12th-grade U.S. problem course, "This approach is one significant way in which our schools distinguish themselves from those in totalitarian nations. This course, as well as well-organized homerooms and certain student activities, can contribute a great deal to the development of future citizens of our democracy."[73]

Cold War concerns about progressive education, increasing the supply of scientific personnel, Sputnik, and educating students to meet specific needs of the labor market framed the discussions leading to the 1958 National Defense Education Act. One month after the launching of Sputnik I, President Eisenhower, in a speech in Oklahoma City, warned, "When such competence in things material is at the service of leaders who have so little regard for things human, and who command the power of an empire, there is danger ahead for freemen everywhere." The most important Cold War problem, he argued, was educating more scientists and engineers to match the output of Soviet schools. "My scientific advisors," he stated, "place this problem above all other immediate tasks of producing missiles, of developing new techniques in the armed forces." He urged a program "to stimulate good-quality teaching of mathematics and science."[74] On January 27, 1958, three and half months after the launch of Sputnik I, Eisenhower delivered a speech to Congress calling for a fivefold increase in funding for the education activities of the National Science Foundation; increased funding for science courses in elementary and high schools; and improved testing programs for identifying scientific talent and for matching student abilities with labor market needs. On September 2, 1958, President Eisenhower signed the National Defense Education Act.

From a global perspective, 1958 was an amazing year with the United States, the Soviet Union, and China following a similar educational reform path that more closely tied their school systems to national military and economic plans. The National Defense Education Act's Title V provided federal funds to high schools to improve and increase the testing, counseling, and vocational guidance of students. Funds were allocated to support the National Science Foundation's Physical Science Study Committee and its School Mathematics Study Group to improve science and math instruction and curricula.

America's influence on wars of liberation was also addressed in the legislation. Money was provided for improvement of foreign language instruction. President Eisenhower insisted, "Knowledge of foreign languages is particularly important today in the light of America's responsibilities of leadership in the free world. And yet the American people are deficient in foreign languages, *particularly those of the emerging nations in Asia, Africa, and the Near East* [my emphasis]." Also, he urged increased study of these world regions. Overall, Eisenhower felt the legislation was an "emergency" program stemming "from national need, and its fruits will bear directly on national security."[75]

CHINA AND THE GREAT LEAP FORWARD

In 1958, as U.S. and Soviet leaders launched post-Sputnik school reforms, Mao Zedong, emboldened by the idea that socialism could produce scientific and technological accomplishments like the Sputnik, made plans for a "Great Leap Forward" in agricultural and industrial production.[76] The Great Leap Forward's educational goals were given in a 1958 directive from the Central Committee of the Chinese Communist Party and the State Council: "The Great Leap Forward in industrial and agricultural production has brought about the beginning of an upsurge in the cultural revolution, characterized in the main by the rapid expansion of a literacy campaign and educational and cultural work. One of the great historical tasks … is to train tens of millions of red and expert intellectuals of the working class."[77]

Similar to Khrushchev, Mao was concerned about the creation of a third class that would pass on its educational advantages to its children while hindering the educational advancement of the children of peasants and workers. Mao's instructions for the Great Leap Forward in education were simple. On August 13, 1958 at the University of Tientsin he declared, "In [the] future, schools should have factories and factories schools. Teachers should do manual work. It will not do to move only their lips and not their hands. Colleges should grasp three things: party committee leadership, mass line, and the coordination of education and production."[78] The next month at the University of Wuhan, he commented, "It is a good thing that the students themselves spontaneously ask for part-time study and part-time work; this is a logical result of the campaign to build workshops at schools…. In school reform, notice must be paid to the development of the activism of the broad teaching staff and students and to the gathering together of the wisdom of the masses."[79] A more detailed explanation of education's role in the Great Leap Forward was given by Yang Husi-feng, Minster of Education, in a 1959 speech on the "Educational Work Achievements in 1958 and Arrangements for 1959" and in a 1960 speech with the commanding and descriptive title, "Actively Carry Out the Reform of the School System to Bring About Greater, Faster Better, and More Economical Results in the Development of Education."[80]

Reviewing the education program of the Great Leap Forward in his 1959 speech, Minister Yang emphasized the efforts to more closely align school policies with economic planning: "In 1958, educational undertakings of our country made two outstanding strides. One was successful implementation of the policy of *coordinating education with productive labor*, which brought about a big and comprehensive revolution in out educational undertakings [my emphasis]."[81] Part of the coordination of education with productive labor involved actual participation of teachers and students in industrial and agricultural work. Similar to Khrushchev's statements about teaching students to honor work, Yang stated, "Their [students and teachers] ignorance of productive labor and their view point concerning the class which exploited the laboring people in the past have been greatly changed, their viewpoints on labor and the broad masses have been strengthened.... They summed their achievements as 'Broken Palms, Transformed Stand, Sun-Blackened Face, and Trained Ideology'."[82] Regarding the Great Leap Forward in educational opportunities, Minister Yang reported that 30 million people were now enrolled in part-time schools, another 30 million children were in newly opened kindergartens, and primary and intermediate school enrollments increased 34% and 36% respectively between 1957 and 1958.

Also, similar to the Soviet Union, there was a mandate for students in full-time schools to experience some form of productive labor along with the creation schools in factories and on farms. This mandate, according to Minister Yang, could be carried out by full-time schools organizing model factories and farms or making arrangements with existing enterprises. Similar to Khrushchev's concerns, the goal was to prevent a disdain by the educated for ordinary labor. "Special attention," the Minister said, "should be given to prevent the unilateral emphasis on education which will give rise to the tendency of looking down on physical labor."[83]

The historical and philosophical reasons for combining formal education with the experience of productive labor was provided by Lu Ting-yi, Director of the Propaganda Department of the Central Committee of the Chinese Communist Party, in a 1958 directive titled, "Education Must Be Combined with Productive Labor." Lu argued that exploiting classes had for thousands of years championed divorcing manual labor from education. As an example, Lu quoted Mencius, a leading exponent of Confucian teachings (circa 371–288 B.C.E.), "Those who labor with their minds govern others; those who labor with their strength are governed by others. Those who are governed by others support them; those who govern others are supported by them. This is a principle universally recognized."[84] In opposition to this principle of the exploiting classes, Lu credited early 19th-century European socialists with first suggesting the combination of labor and learning. He quoted Karl Marx, "In a reasonable social order every child must become a productive worker starting at the age of nine."[85] And, according to Lu: "Lenin said, 'It is impossible to visualize the ideal of future society without combining the training and education of the younger generation with productive labor'."[86] Therefore, a real socialist education required a combination of educating workers and peasants, and having full-time students experience manual labor. Lu warned, "Education divorced from productive labor is bound to lead ... [to] divorcing education from the realities of our country and eventually causing right deviationist and doctrinaire mistakes."[87]

The Great Leap Forward in education also placed an emphasis on formal standards and methods of instruction. Foreshadowing the 1960s Cultural Revolution, formal instructional methods were to be balanced by the right of students to make proper criticisms of their teachers. In calling on teachers to adopt a strong supervisory role in teaching, Yang commanded that, "teachers are required to earnestly shoulder the tasks of 'preaching, giving lectures,' and 'clearing doubts.' ... At the same time, they should listen and accept the opinions of the students so as to improve both teaching and study."[88]

Similar to the increasing U.S. emphasis on science and math instruction, Minister Yang's 1960 speech devoted a long section to upgrading teaching in these areas. In "Actively Carry Out the Reform of the School System to Bring About Greater, Faster, Better, and More Economical results in the Development of Education," Yang opened with a list of statistics on the growth of educational opportunities including a claim that since 1958 more than 60 million illiterate people were now literate. He then complimented schools for establishing relations that allowed students to experience labor in factories, mines, and farms.

Minister Yang discussed the improvement of curricula and instruction in science, mathematics, and foreign languages. He called for a shortening the U.S. model of elementary and secondary education from 12 years to a 10- or 9-year model similar to the Soviet Union. He said there were too many courses with a poor selection of content, "all of which adversely affect the mastery of the most important courses by the students. Much of the mathematics, physics, and chemistry now taught in middle schools is old stuff from the nineteenth century."[89] He proposed, similar to changes in U.S. schools, that basic college courses in physics, chemistry, and mathematics be taught in senior middle schools and that simple algebra courses be transferred from junior middle to elementary schools.

SINO–SOVIET SPLIT
AND THE FAILURE OF THE GREAT LEAP FORWARD

The necessity of emphasizing "expert" over "red" was prompted by the disastrous failure of the Great Leap Forward and the withdrawal of Soviet experts as relationships deteriorated between the two countries. A famine between 1959 and 1960 resulted in 20 million Chinese starving to death. It was caused by a combination of the rush to organize peasants into rural communes and a drought that laid barren a third of China's agricultural lands. Plans for the Great Leap Forward required an increase in steel production that included a requirement of melting down household objects in small smelters. Industrial goals were not reached and many people were left without the use of ordinary utensils for cooking.[90] Mao's suspicions about the Soviet Union seemed confirmed when Khrushchev implemented a policy of peaceful coexistence with the United States and other capitalist countries. Mao accused Soviet leaders of failing to wield the "sword of Leninism" and he contended that as long as imperialism existed peaceful coexistence was impossible. At the February 1960 Warsaw Pact, Khrushchev denounced Mao as being "ultra-Leftist, an ultra-dogmatist and a left revisionist" who had become "oblivious of any interest but his own, spinning theories detached from realities of the modern world." China's representative, Peng Zhen responded by calling Khrushchev "patriarchal, arbitrary and tyrannical."[91] Three weeks later, Soviet experts in China boarded trains and returned to Russia.

The Sino-Soviet split and the disaster of the Great Leap Forward resulted in a need for more skilled workers and technical experts; red would have to take second place to expert. Economic problems meant a cut back in school expenditures and a return of many students to farms and factories. Between 1961 and 1962, university enrollments declined by 14%. Middle school enrollments dropped by 13% in 1961 and 8% in 1962, and elementary enrollments declined by 6% in 1960, 11% in 1961, and 4% in 1962.[92]

Exemplifying the shift in emphasis from red to expert were the 1962 forums on "Redness" and "Expertness" held by the Peking Young Communist League[93] and the Young Communist League of Tsinghau University. The forums' official summary provided the following description of "red and expert": "One who is expert but not 'red' is like a ship without a course and will eventually lose one's way. One who is 'red' but not expert will become at most a good-for-nothing 'empty politician'."[94] In context to the Forums' summary, being red was necessary for finding "one's way" or selecting a career in which to be an expert. This meaning is highlighted in the official summary's story of Wang Chih-yüan, a 5th-year student at the Peking Agricultural University. In middle school, Wang studied horticulture and then applied for entrance into the Peking Agricultural University. To his chagrin, University administrators decided the nation needed specialists in vegetable farming and placed him in a vegetable specialty. In his words, "At the time, I was not interested in this speciality. Later, *helped and educated by the Party,* I gradually came to realize the purpose of study.… I became keenly interested in the Vegetable Speciality [my emphasis]."[95] In this case, the ideological education of the Party taught Wang that careers should be selected according to the needs of the people and not for personal reasons. In this case, revolutionary training served the purpose of convincing students to become experts in careers needed by the state.

The increased stress on the academic model and expertness, as opposed to the revolutionary model and redness, would eventually lead to a backlash in 1966 with the onset of the Cultural Revolution which stressed Mao's revolutionary educational model. It would be misleading to suggest that after the failure of the Great Leap Forward and the resulting economic downturn that the revolutionary model was simply overwhelmed by the stress on expertness. Revolutionary educational concerns were never lost. Even in the United States education for expertness was to be balanced by ideological instruction in the American way of life. As the President of Peking University, Lu P'ing declared in 1963, "The basic tasks of our socialist universities is to implement the policy of making education serve proletarian politics and integrating education with productive labor and to bring up laborers with socialist consciousness and culture."[96] However, the increasing emphasis on expertness and the academic model did set the stage for the Cultural Revolution.

EDUCATION FOR EDUCATION'S SAKE

In the 1940s and 1950s, a revolution in thinking about the purposes of higher education was underway not only in China but also in the United States and many other countries. Leaders of educational security states were intolerant of the idea that people should pursue education for education's sake and seek a life of the mind for the personal joy it might provide. The pursuit of learning for private pleasure was considered a luxury and a waste of the financial and human resources needed for military and economic growth. In earlier years, scholars since the times of Plato and Confucius idealized the life of a mind freed from material concerns and devoted to the search for truth. For the educational security state, learning was a social and economic investment that should produce material gains for the individual and society; learning became an instrument of state power.

Just as Gorky dismissed "art for art's sake" as a bourgeois excuse for making luxury goods for the rich, the Chinese Communist Party criticized the idea of "education for education's sake" as a justification for creating a parasitic class of intellectuals. This was an important concern regarding the expansion of higher education. Speaking at the June 1, 1950 Conference on Higher Education, China's new Communist Minister of Education, Ma Hsu-lun warned, "The theoretical education must never fall into the old trap of 'academic for academic per se' again, nor neglect the need of our people and our country.... Therefore, we must be very careful in planning our curriculum reform. The basic principle for the curriculum reform is combining theory and practice; The classroom materials must meet the needs of national construction."[97] To eliminate the tendency of scholars to seek personal comfort in the image of "education for education's sake" and "academic for academic per se," Minister Ma suggested placing all institutions of higher learning under the centralized control of the Ministry of Education. Exercising centralized control, Ma argued, the Ministry could ensure that curriculum reform would "carry out the revolution in political education ... [and] meet the national needs in industry, agriculture, national-defense."[98] He reiterated the importance of leaving behind the model of learning for learning's sake: "The first and utmost point is that our higher education must meet the needs of national economics, politics, culture, and national defense."[99]

Two months after the June Conference, the Central Ministry of Education issued orders for the reorganization of higher education. Again, the orders pointed to the problem of education for education's sake: "we must get rid of the empty notion of 'academic for academic per se,' and to strike for the integration of national construction and practice, which is the direction of our higher education." However, the directives recognized the importance of theoretical work as long as it was instrumental in fulfilling national policies. The Ministry mandated that all institutions of higher education utilize a departmental structure "to train specialists; the curriculum must be closely in accordance with the present and long-term needs of economics, politics, national defense and cultural construction."[100]

An unspoken criticism of education for education's sake existed in the United States as schooling was integrated into economic planning. Students were no longer to simply pursue an education for the joy of learning. Education now had to fulfill economic and military needs. In the 19th century, secondary and college education was often justified as training the mind as opposed to meeting economic goals. The *Yale Report of 1828* established the 19th century goals for American collegiate education. The *Yale Report* stated that collegiate education should provide "the *discipline* and the *furniture* of the mind." The report rejected the idea that a college education should be practical: "The great object of a collegiate education, preparatory to the study of a profession, is to give that expansion and balance of the mental powers, those liberal comprehensive views, and those fine proportions of character, which are not to be found in him whose ideas are always confined to one particular channel."[101] The *Yale Report's* educational goals were in sharp contrast to developments in collegiate education after World War II when students were viewed as future man/woman power for economic and military development. Clark Kerr, Chancellor of the University of California at Berkeley, became a leading spokesperson in the 1950s and 1960s for the new conception of higher education. He argued that academics should no longer live in a ivory tower, but should think of their service to society. He likened the new university to a service station that provided help to business and government. There was little room in this new type of university for those wanting to pursue education for education's sake.[102]

A similar abandonment of education for education's sake took place in U.S. secondary education in the late 19th and early 20th century with the development of vocational education and vocational guidance. The *Cardinal Principles of Secondary Education* (1918) marked the transition from the contention that secondary education, similar to the arguments of the *Yale Report*, should train the mind through the study of classical languages and literature to a high school system that prepared students for entrance into the labor market or college.[103] Similar to later Chinese advocates of education for redness and expertness, U.S. secondary schools were to prepare students for democracy and careers. The *Cardinal Principles of Secondary Education* recommended that high schools provide a broad program so that students could be separated into different subject areas based on their future destination in the labor market: "Differentiation [separation of students into different curricula] should be, in the broad sense of the term, vocational ... such as agricultural, business, clerical, industrial, fine-arts, and household-arts ... the pupil through a wide variety of contacts and experiences [should be helped] to obtain a basis for intelligent choice of his educational and vocational career."[104] And, in language that paralleled the discussions of red and expert, the report stated: "The purpose of democracy is so to organize society that each member may develop his personality primarily through activities designed for the well-being of his fellow members and of society as a whole ... [and] education in a democracy ... should develop in each individual the knowledge, interests, ideals, habits, and powers whereby he will find his place and use that place to shape both himself and society toward ever nobler ends."[105]

CONCLUSION: THE EDUCATIONAL SECURITY STATE

By the 1960s, the three major world powers—China, the Soviet Union, and the United States—had made schooling an instrument for economic and military development. Gone were Confucian and Platonic models of the isolated scholar who pursued learning for personal joy and for an abstract knowledge of truth. The educational security state wanted human minds to be devoted to economic and military needs. This meant implanting an ideology in student minds that would cause them to frame and interpret personal experience and world events according to Marxism–Leninism, Marxism–Leninism–Mao Zedong thought, or the American way of life. It also meant educating students to believe that service to the state and society was more important than pursuit of personal pleasure. The fantasy lives of students were to be filled with Stakhanovite workers, Lei Feng's self-sacrificing fidelity, or the heroes of the American Revolution and fighters against communism. All aspects of the human mind were to be educated for service to the economy and military. What about progressive education and its goal of empowering students to participate in changing the state and economic system? As I discuss in the next chapter, this educational dream would find new life in wars of liberation, particularly in South America.

Chapter 5

Education for Cultural Revolution

In 1968, against the background of wars of liberation and China's Cultural Revolution, Paulo Freire completed *Pedagogy of the Oppressed,* a book that would significantly advance progressive education ideas and contribute to a global awareness of what would be known as "critical" methods of instruction.[1] As evidenced in his writings, Freire's theories were directly influenced by the global flow of educational ideas. He acknowledged the impact on his thinking of Latin American forms of Marxism that recognized the needs of peasant and indigenous cultures of the Americas; the Cuban Revolution; and Mao Zedong. In reference to his core idea that the pedagogy of the oppressed commits humans to permanent liberation or revolution, Freire wrote: "This appears to be the fundamental aspect of Mao's cultural revolution."[2] Regarding his important proposal for dialogical instruction that helps learners understand how their subjective beliefs shape their interpretation of the objective world, Freire noted,

> Mao Zedong declared, "You know I've proclaimed for a long time: we must teach the masses clearly what we have received from them confusedly." ... This affirmation contains an entire dialogical theory of how to construct the program content of education, which cannot be elaborated according to what the *educator* thinks best for his students.[3]

Although Freire acknowledged the influence of Mao Zedong, he lived in a world of evolving ideas about how to bring about social change in South and Central America and the upheavals of global wars of liberation. In South and Central America, people had to deal with two major waves of imperialism; first from Spain and then from the United States. After the end of Spanish imperialism, there remained in former colonies a ruling elite of Spanish descendants. In addition, many complained about the increasing control of U.S. government and businesses over local economies and political structures. There were complaints that the U.S. government was protecting its own interests by supporting the power of the former colonial elites. Consequently, many seeking political reform and social change felt they were carrying on a two-front war against local elites and U.S. political and economic control.

Therefore, Paulo Freire lived in a tumultuous world where Marxist ideology had to be adapted to societies with large indigenous and peasant populations. These adaptations of Marxism appeared in the 1952 Bolivian National Revolutionary Movement; the 1953 to 1959 Cuban Revolution; the revolutionary projects of Che Guevara; the 1960 overthrow of the Venezuelan government and 1963 creation of the Venezuelan Armed Forces of National Liberation (FALN); and the 1961 Nicaraguan insurgency led by the Sandinista National Liberation Front. These South and Central American movements for social change were part of a general global climate of social unrest caused by European, U.S., and Japanese imperialism in the Americas, Africa, Southeast Asia, China, and Korea.[4]

Vietnam's liberation war became an international symbol for struggles against imperialism. After the defeat of Japanese imperialism, Ho Chi Minh's international reputation was enhanced when he issued the 1945 Declaration of Independence of the Democratic Republic of Vietnam. The Declaration's opening words captured Ho's belief that he was following in an anti-colonial tradition that began with America's 18th century war of independence against British colonialism. Although always aware of American racism, Ho considered the United States an ally because of their fight against Japan during World War II.[5]

Declaration of Independence of the Democratic Republic of Vietnam

All men are created equal; they are endowed by their Creator with certain unalienable rights; among these are Life, Liberty, and the pursuit of Happiness.

This immortal statement was made in the Declaration of Independence of the United States of America in 1776. In a broader sense this means: All the peoples on the earth are equal from birth, all the peoples have a right to live, to be happy and free.

The Declaration of the French Revolution made in 1791 on the Rights of Man and the Citizen also states: "All men are born free and with equal rights, and must always remain free and have equal rights."

Those are undeniable rights.

Nevertheless, for more than eighty years, the French imperialists, abusing the standard of Liberty, Equality, and Fraternity, have violated our Fatherland and oppressed our fellow citizens. They have acted contrary to their ideal of humanity and justice.

In the field of politics, they have deprived our people of every democratic liberty.... They have built more prisons than schools. They mercilessly slain our
patriots; they have drowned our uprisings in rivers of blood....[6]

In this chapter, I will analyze the impact of wars of liberation on the global
flow of progressive educational ideas. In chapter 6, I discuss the continuation
of formal educational ideas in other countries experiencing wars of liberation, particularly in Africa and Islamic countries. Also, I decided to include a
discussion of China's Cultural Revolution because of its global impact in the
1960s and its importance for understanding the ideas of Paulo Freire.

I begin this chapter with an examination of the evolution of Marxist
ideas in South and Central America. Education of peasants and indigenous
peoples were central to the adaptation of Marxism to local circumstances. I
then discuss the Cuban Revolution and the Cuban Literacy Crusade as an
example of Latin American progressive educational ideas. The educational
ideas of China's cultural revolution influenced Latin American Marxists
and the work of Paulo Freire. Again, I would like to remind the reader that
not all wars of liberation resulted in the implementation of progressive
forms of education. In chapter 6, I examine wars of liberation that
maintained formal educational methods.

EDUCATION AND CULTURAL REVOLUTION IN SOUTH
AND CENTRAL AMERICA: JOSÉ CARLOS MARIÁTEGUI

Similar to Russia and China, South and Central America were primarily rural societies without a large industrial working class. In addition, South and
Central America included large indigenous populations whose interests
had to be considered in any efforts at meaningful social change. Many Latin
American Marxists believed that education of the rural masses and cultural
revolution should be part of an economic and political revolution. Unlike
Russia and China where communist revolutions were followed by efforts to
educate mainly rural and illiterate populations, Latin American revolutionaries believed that a revolutionary education should be concurrent with political and economic change.

José Mariátegui was an early influential Marxist scholar concerned about
the plight of indigenous peoples. Born on July 14, 1894, he grew up in the
small southern Peruvian coastal town of Moquegua in a family where his
mother abandoned the his father because of the father's anti-Catholic sentiments. Mariátegui was considered by many the originator of a Latin American form of Marxism that would influence Marxists throughout South and
Central America, including the thinking of Che Guevara, Fidel Castro, and
leaders of the Sandinistas. Marc Becker asserted, "He is widely regarded as
being the first truly creative and original Latin American Marxist thinker."[7]

In *Marxist Thought in Latin America*, Sheldon B. Liss concluded, "No Latin American Marxist receives more acknowledgments of intellectual indebtedness from fellow thinkers than José Mariátegui."[8]

Raised in poverty by his devout Catholic mestiza mother, Mariátegui, by providing a role for the Catholic Church in his Marxist theories, provided an intellectual justification for the later development of what would be known as liberation theology. Unlike the atheist component of European Marxism, many in South and Central America blended socialist ideas with their religious faith. Liberation theology was formally proclaimed at the 1968 Medellin Bishops Conference, which committed the Church to helping the poor and protecting human rights. Following the proclamation, a movement started called Christians for Socialism who believed, as stated by the Bishop of Cuernavaca, Mexico, Sergio Arceo that, "Only socialism can give Latin America the authentic development it needs.... I believe that a socialist system is more in conformity with the Christian principles of brotherhood, justice, and peace."[9]

Besides being an early advocated of liberation theology, Mariátegui called for mass political education of peasants and indigenous peoples as a necessary condition for the growth of Marxism in South America. He became a Marxist when, after receiving an eighth-grade education, he took a job at the Peruvian newspaper *La Prensa* and began writing political articles. The radicalism of his articles caused the Peruvian government to exile him in 1919 to Europe. In Europe he moved in communist circles in France and Italy. Although I don't know if he actually met Ho Chi Minh during his exile, he encountered many of the same Marxists that worked with Ho and the Comintern.[10] After returning to Peru in 1923, he declared that he was "a convinced and declared Marxist."[11]

Mass political education, Mariátegui believed, was necessary for adapting Marxism to South American conditions, particularly for the recruitment of peasants and indigenous peoples. Mariátegui argued, "The problem of Indian illiteracy goes beyond the pedagogical sphere. It becomes increasingly evident that *to teach a man to read and write is not to educate him* [my emphasis]."[12] He contended that Marxism should be adapted to South America's social and political conditions, which included a large peasant population and indigenous tribes.

Mariátegui believed that praxis, important for Freire's later work, was necessary for creating a free as opposed to an authoritarian Marxist society. He defined praxis as a "dialectic interrelation between objective and subjective conditions."[13] In other words, people were to understand how their subjective beliefs determined their interpretation of the objective world and how the objective world informed their subjective views. This form of education, Mariátegui stated in a manner similar to Freire's later use of consciousness as a liberating force, would "spark the revolutionary consciousness that would accelerate the socialist revolution, and thus help to compensate for the underdeveloped nature of the nation."[14]

Mariátegui, who had Inca ancestry, believed that Marxism could be adapted to indigenous cultures. He envisioned the creation of an "Indo-American" socialism. In his most widely read and translated book, *Seven Interpretive Essays on Peruvian Reality,* Mariátegui rejected industrialization as a necessary condition for a socialist revolution among the Inca people and called for recognition of a traditional Inca-communist society. He argued that traditional Inca society was socialist. "Faith in the renaissance of the Indian is not pinned to the material process of 'Westernizing' the Quechua [Inca] country," he asserted. "The soul of the Indian is not raised by the white man's civilization or alphabet but by the myth, the idea, of Socialist revolution."[15] After noting how Chinese and Hindu societies were able to incorporate socialist ideas, he questioned those who did not see indigenous cultures as incorporating Marxist ideas: "Why should the Inca people, who constructed the most highly-developed and harmonious communistic system, be the only ones unmoved by the worldwide emotion? The consanguinity of the Indian movement with world revolutionary currents is too evident to need documentation."[16] Quoting indigenous peoples' advocate González Prada, Mariátegui emphasized the importance of revolution for changing the conditions of Native Americans, "the condition of the Indian can improve in two ways: either the heart of the oppressor will be moved to take pity and recognize the rights of the oppressed, or the spirit of the oppressed will find the valor needed to turn on the oppressors."[17]

Although education was key to revolution by indigenous peoples, Mariátegui realized that education could also be used to oppress Native Americans by preparing them the work for the oppressor, such as educating indigenous peoples to administer government programs designed to Westernize and enslave native groups. Education for government service, he felt, was a typical method by which colonial governments used indigenous peoples to control other indigenous peoples. Mariátegui referred to the government administrative and social system that oppressed indigenous peoples as *gamonalismo.* "The literate Indian," he wrote, "who enters the service of gamonalismo turns into an exploiter of his own race."[18]

Therefore, it was important for Mariátegui, as it would be for Freire and other Latin American progressive educators, to distinguish between education for oppression and education for liberation. In "Public Education," one of the *Seven Interpretive Essays on Peruvian Reality,* Mariátegui discussed how education could support an oppressive and authoritarian society. In his discussion, he provided an important summary of the effect of the global flow of educational ideas on South and Central America.

Mariátegui identified three successive influences on the development of Peruvian public education: Spain, France, and the United States. The Spanish imposed a feudal system of education that was aristocratic and literary. After independence from Spain, the 1831 government declared that education was to be free, a measure that Mariátegui asserted was never carried out. According to Mariátegui, the colonial model of education continued into the new Republic with the goal of maintaining the ruling classes: "The liberals, the old landholding aristocracy, and the new urban middle class all studied together in the humanities. They liked to think of universities and colleges as factories producing writers and lawyers."[19] These educated lawyers and writers from the upper class, he asserted, filled high-ranking positions in government and business, thus ensuring the perpetuation of the power of the upper social class. Mariátegui summarized the social role of the education system inherited from the Spanish:

> The Spanish heritage was not only psychological and intellectual but above all economic and social. Education continued to be a privilege because the privileges of wealth and class continued. The aristocratic and literary concept of education was typical of a feudal system and economy. Not having abolished feudalism in Peru, independence would not abolish its ideas about education.[20]

Although continuing to experience the influence of the feudal educational model after independence, Peru modeled itself after the French republican government. Mariátegui claimed, "The French influence only added its defects to the original ones of the Spanish heritage."[21] He questioned the value of the French republican model because France in early 19th century was not an advanced capitalist nation like England, Germany, and the United States. Quoting and referencing French writers on education, Mariátegui argued that 19th-century France was never able to develop a uniform system of national primary education and that its educational system primarily enhanced the power of the new republican bourgeoisie. Consequently, like the Spanish, the French secondary school system was devoted to preparing bureaucrats and government officials that ensured continued access to political power of the bourgeoisie's children.

According to Mariátegui, this meant that the educational system, after independence from Spain, continued to perpetuate the power of former Spanish colonialists who remained in Peru. Mariátegui complained, "Our mistake derives from the viceroyal aristocracy [Spanish colonialists] which, disguised as the republican bourgeoisie, has maintained in the republic the privileges and principles of a colonial society. This class wanted its children to have, if not the severely dogmatic education of the mother country, as least the elegantly conservative education of the Jesuit colleges that existed in France during the Restoration."[22]

In the early 20th century, Peruvian education leaders called for the adoption of the U.S. model of education to aid in industrial development or, in other words, to more closely tie education to economic planning. The leading advocate of the U.S. model was Manuel Villarán, who argued, "education in Peru ... suffers from its failure to meet the needs of the developing national economy and from its indifference to the indigenous element."[23] He argued that the economic future of Peru depended on its educational system preparing workers rather than scribes to enter government bureaucracies and the legal profession. Villarán claimed, "the great nations of Europe today are remodeling their educational programs, largely along North American lines, because they understand that this century requires men of enterprise rather than men of letters ... we should also correct our mistakes and educate practical, industrious, and energetic men, the ones the country needs in order to become wealthy and by the same token powerful."[24]

The 1920 Organic Law of Education converted Peruvian schools to the U.S. model with primary and secondary schooling preparing students for jobs needed for economic development. However, Mariátegui argued that adoption of the U.S. model did not undercut the economic and political power of the descendants of colonial rule. He wrote, "the educational movement was sabotaged by the continued and widespread existence of a feudal regime. It is not possible to democratize the education of a country without democratizing its economy and its political superstructure."[25] The major failure of the Organic Law of Education, he believed, resulted from the American system of separating or tracking students according to their future place in the labor market. This created, he contended, a "dual school system according to whether or not the student will continue to secondary school, thereby restricting working-class children to a primary education in schools that do not prepare them to pursue a professional career."[26]

The school reforms based on the American model failed to undercut the power of the established upper class of Peru, Mariátegui argued, which therefore proved that countries must develop their own educational reforms based on national needs with foreigners acting as consultants. Similar to other progressive and Marxist educators, Mariátegui advocated the abandonment of idealist forms of education in which knowledge was never linked to its origins in economic and social conditions. He called for education to be linked to the real world of work. He quoted Mexican educational reformer Pedro Ureña, "To learn is not only to learn to know but also to learn to do."[27] Education separate from the real world of work relations, he argued, was antithetical to Inca culture, "in which idleness was a crime, and work, performed with devotion, the highest virtue."[28] Similar to Marx's idea of polytechnical education and in reference to continued domination of the former Spanish colonial aristocracy, he stated, "A modern concept of the school places manual and intellectual work at the same level, an equation that is not acceptable to the vanity of the aristocratic humanists. Contrary to the pretensions of these men of letters, the trade school is the authentic product of a civilization created by work and for work."[29]

THE BACKGROUND FOR PROGRESSIVE EDUCATION IN LATIN AMERICA

Most Latin American progressives would agree with Mariátegui that social change depended on eradicating illiteracy and raising the political consciousness of peasants and indigenous peoples. This required a politically oriented method of teaching literacy. Also, most Latin American Marxists rejected the Leninist idea of a dictatorship of the proletariat in favor of some form of social democracy. Cultural issues were also of paramount importance in Latin America because of its large population of indigenous peoples, descendants of enslaved Africans, and mestizos. Should the goal of education be to transform indigenous cultures into Western industrial culture? Mariátegui's proposal for the resurrection of an Inca communist culture suggested the protection or reformation of indigenous cultures rather than their transformation into a European industrial culture. In this context, progressive education had to respect cultural traditions when instituting literacy and mass education programs. Mariátegui believed that in a social democratic tradition, education could help reverse the dominance of European cultural imperialism and provide a means by which local cultures could serve as a basis for liberation from economic and political exploitation.

For many Latin American radicals, cultural issues, particularly cultural issues related to education, were central to political and social change. Latin American social progressives tended to talk about social conflict as opposed to class conflict. The reality was that in Central and South America social differences between European descendants, mestizos, descendants of enslaved Africans, and indigenous peoples added another dimension to the concept of class. These social groupings often paralleled economic and political differences with European descendants frequently holding dominant economic and political positions while indigenous peoples and descendants of enslaved Africans struggled with poverty and lacked political and economic rights. Racism by European descendants heightened the tensions caused by economic disparities between the rich and poor.

Also, culture and education became a central concern because of the influence of Italian Marxist Antonio Gramsci. Born in 1891, Gramsci helped found, in 1913, the socialist newspaper, *L'Ordine Nuovo*, and the Italian Communist Party in 1921. He worked with the Communist International in Moscow and Vienna between 1922 to 1924. This was the world of Ho Chi Minh and Mariátegui during their years of exile. Imprisoned in 1926, Gramsci made a major contribution to social theory in his book, *The Prison Notebooks*.[30] Reflecting Gramsci's influence, Liss concludes, "Almost all the *pensadores* [Latin American Marxists intellectuals] agree that the power of the of the oppressors exists only as long as the masses obey them."[31] One goal of a progressive education was to break the oppressor's control over the minds of the oppressed so that the oppressed would not unthinkingly obey authority or accept as true the ideologies that justify the power of the oppressors. Gramsci used the term *hegemony* to describe the ideological control of the ruling class. Through schooling, media, newspapers, and other means, the values of the ruling class were internalized by the population. The masses accepted their own subordination to the ruling class because they acted and reasoned from the same set of beliefs. According to Gramsci, and repeated by Latin American progressives, this explained why exploited workers, who were taught the value and righteousness of capitalism accepted their own exploitation and the dictates of the captains of industry.

The goal of a critical education was to make people conscious of this hegemony and how it resulted in their own subordination to an unjust economic and social order. According to Gramsci, before taking over the political instruments of the state, the Communist Party must first function as an educational institution to overcome the hegemony of the ruling classes. The leadership of this education should be, Gramsci argued, in the hands of *organic intellectuals* who, in the case of Latin America, would help peasants, workers, and indigenous peoples articulate their own needs and desires. This educational process would free the oppressed from the hegemony of the ruling classes. Organic intellectuals were to engage in a dialectical process with peasants, workers, and indigenous peoples to develop social theories that reflected each groups real-life circumstances and needs. Eventually, Paulo Freire would provide the instructional methodology for accomplishing this goal.

Therefore, progressive education in Latin American encompassed concerns about cultural differences, breaking the hegemonic control of the ruling classes, and helping cultural groups articulate their own needs and desires. In summarizing Marxist traditions, Liss wrote, "Latin American radicals believe that genuine education—the process of critical evaluation and questioning, not merely the dissemination of information—is a marvelous instrument of progress that will eventually help negate the 'truths' of the prevailing system."[32]

THE CUBAN REVOLUTION AND PROGRESSIVE EDUCATIONAL IDEOLOGY

On January 1, 1959, Fidel Castro's guerilla forces overthrew the dictatorship of Fulgencio Batista. My interest is not in the details of the armed struggle that had been waged from 1953 to 1959, but the success of the literacy crusade following the revolution. The methods and accomplishments of the literacy crusade influenced Paulo Freire and progressive educators around the world. Cuba's educational accomplishments continued to be recognized into the 21st century. Despite economic problems, created in part by U.S. economic sanctions, Cuban students attained the highest achievement scores of any Latin American country on international tests given by the United Nations Education, Scientific, and Cultural Organization (UNESCO) in 2001 in the areas of reading and language. The conservative U.S. weekly newspaper *Education Week* proclaimed that year, "Castro's Cuba outscores the rest of Latin America in literacy and math.... A political pariah in the eyes of the United States for more than four decades, Cuba has long drawn notice for its schools. Interest has heightened, though, since a 2001 study by an international task force reported that Cuban 3rd and 4th graders, based on UNESCO research, easily outscored all their Latin American peers in language and mathematics."[33]

The Inter-American Development Bank reported, based on a number of international tests,[34] that: "The only Latin American country which would score at a level similar to that of the United States would be Cuba."[35] Even children from upper-income Latin American families had lower achievement rates than Cuban students. The Inter-Development Bank concluded: "But even children in higher socioeconomic groups in the region do not perform very well. In the UNESCO/OREALC study children in private schools scored higher than children in public schools, but their scores were still 20 points below the average for all Cuban children."[36]

As noted in previous chapters, revolutionary movements in Russia and China inherited high illiteracy rates, particularly among rural populations. In general, high illiteracy rates continue among rural populations in Central and South America, Africa, India, and Asian nations. In 2002, the World Bank estimated more than a billion illiterate adults in the world.[37] And, of course, there was a direct link between illiteracy and the wealth of a particular country with the poorest countries having been victims of imperialism: "Data from the International Adult Literacy Survey indicate a high correlation between country levels of income inequality and inequality in the distribution of literacy."[38]

Fidel Castro initiated a literacy campaign among peasants while fighting in the island's mountains prior to the 1959 victory. In 1953, Castro expressed his belief that education would be key to the social development of Cuba after the Revolution.[39] His educational thought was influenced by the Argentine socialist Anibal Ponce who wrote *Education and the Class Struggle* (1936) which was later reprinted in Cuba.[40] Ponce maintained that since classical times the ruling class used education to control the masses. In *Fidel! Castro's Political and Social Thought*, Sheldon Liss provided the following summary of Ponce's thinking: "The state, in collusion with the church, taught irrationality, passivity, fatalism, and faith in the supernatural.... He [Ponce] showed how the ruling class controlled the social organization of the state through education, which conveyed information but did not teach people how to think for fear that they question the system that education was designed to support."[41] Reflecting Ponce's argument, Castro feared that if a revolutionary education stressing critical and dialectical thought was not initiated, then the Cuban people would never be free because of the hegemony of colonial masters. He stated education should "prevent cultural colonization from surviving economic colonization."[42] Similar to Mao and other Latin American Marxists, Castro emphasized the importance of relating theory to practice and schooling to work. He envisioned attaching schools to workplaces. Also, similar to Mao, he believed that all intellectuals, particularly scientists and engineers, needed a political education so that they could understand the impact of their theories on the lives of workers. Liss summarized Castro's educational ideas, "people do not learn by indoctrination, by having their heads filled with bits and pieces of theory. They learn by thinking, analyzing, and searching history for lessons and answers. In Castro's ideal revolutionary society, people go to school to learn, dissect, to understand."[43]

Other theoretical contributions, which had a worldwide impact, were expressed in the writings of French Marxist Régis Debray, and the writings and exploits of Che Guevara. The Cuban literacy campaign in 1961 provided Debray with his first contact with the Cuban revolution.[44] His summary of the ideas behind the Cuban revolution was published in 1967 with the title, *Revolution in the Revolution? Armed Struggle and Political Struggle in Latin America*. Editors for the Marxist Monthly Review Press, publishers of Debray's book, called the book "the first ... comprehensive and authoritative presentation of the revolutionary thought of Fidel Castro and Che Guevara."[45] Debray argued that the Communist Party was not able to establish itself in Latin American as it had in China and Vietnam. Consequently, without a vanguard political organization, the political and military had to be united as it had during guerilla warfare in Cuba. Debray wrote, "When the guerrilla army assumes the prerogatives of political leadership.... It alone can guarantee that the people's power will not be perverted after victory." Also, guerilla warfare provided the opportunity, according to

Debray, for establishing an alliance between the different social groups that existed in Latin America. In an important justification for creating a guerilla army, one that reflected Che Guevara's beliefs, Debray argued that it would serve as a unifying force:

> In the mountains, then workers, peasants, and intellectuals meet for the first time. This integration is not so easy at the beginning.... The peasants, especially if they are of Indian origin, stay to themselves and speak their own language (Quechua or Cakchiquel), among themselves. The others, those who know how to write and speak well, spontaneously create their own circle. Mistrust, timidity, custom, have to be gradually vanquished by means of untiring political work.... These men all have something to learn from each other, beginning with their differences.... Slowly the shared existence, the combats, the hardships endured together weld an alliance having the simple force of friendship.[46]

Similar to Debray's ideas on the unity generated by guerilla warfare, Castro wrote during the days of mountain fighting: "Here the word 'people', which is so often utilized in a vague and confused sense, becomes a living, wonderful and dazzling reality. *Now* I know who the people are: I see them in that invincible force that surrounds us everywhere."[47] Therefore, the guerilla armies composed of nonprofessional soldiers provided a new model for social change and political education. Debray concluded, the "absence of specialists in political affairs has the effect of sanctioning the absence of specialists in military affairs. The people's army is its own political authority. The *guerrilleros* play both roles, indivisibly. Its commanders are political instructors for the fighters, its political instructors are its commanders."[48]

Following the Revolution, Che Guevara declared that society must become a "gigantic" school. He gave this explanation of the role of the Cuban guerilla forces, "Then came the stage of guerrilla struggle. It developed in two distinct environments: the people, the still sleeping mass that had to be mobilized; and its vanguard, the guerrillas, the motor force of the mobilization, the generator of revolutionary consciousness and militant enthusiasm. This vanguard was the catalyzing agent that created the subjective conditions necessary for victory."[49] Referring to the literacy crusade, Che wrote in 1965 that the state should give direct political instruction to the people: "Education takes hold among the masses and the foreseen new attitude tends to become a habit. The masses continue to make it their own and to influence those who have not yet educated themselves. This is the indirect form of educating the masses, as powerful, as the other, structured one."[50]

Guevara rejected Stalinist forms of education for an educational concept based on revolutionary freedom. He warned, "We must not create either docile servants of official thought or 'scholarship students' who live at the expense of the state—practicing freedom in quotation marks."[51] He also rejected the tenets of socialist realism and argued for artistic freedom. For Guevara, there had to be a balance between freedom and antirevolutionary practices. "What is needed," he stated, "is the development of an ideological–cultural mechanism that permits both free inquiry and the uprooting of the weeds that multiply so easily in the fertilized soil of state subsidies."[52] Similar to traditional Marxist education arguments, he believed, work should be combined with education to produce a new socialist generation.

> Their [youth] education is every day more complete, and we do not neglect their incorporation into work from the outset. Our scholarship students do physical work during their vacations or along with their studies. Work is a reward in some cases, a means of education in others, but is never a punishment.... Our aspiration is for the party to become a mass party, but only when the masses have reached the level of the vanguard, that is, when they are educated for communism.[53]

Love of humanity was a very important aspect of Guevara's ideology and the educational work of Paulo Freire. For both thinkers, love was a motivating emotion that led people to want to liberate humanity. Frequently, Marxist leaders neglected the role of emotions in determining actions. Guevara wrote, "let me say that the true revolutionary is guided by great feelings of love.... Perhaps it is one of the great dramas of the leader that he or she must combine a passionate spirit with a cold intelligence and make painful decisions without flinching. Our vanguard revolutionaries must idealize this love of the people."[54] Part of the goal of education was to develop a love of the people. He declared, "The basic clay of our work is the youth; we place our hope in it and prepare it to take the banner from our hands."[55]

THE LITERACY CRUSADE

Only 2 months after the fall of the Batista regime, the literacy crusade was launched by the newly established National Literacy and Basic Education Commission. In keeping with his dialectical view of education, Castro declared to literacy workers, "You are going to teach, but as you teach you will also learn much more than you can possibly teach, and in the end you will feel as grateful to the campesinos as the campesinos will feel to you for teaching them to read and write."[56]

The work of the literacy crusade was documented in 1964 by observers from UNESCO. The UNESCO team reported that similar to other parts of Latin America illiteracy rates were highest in rural areas. According to statistics gathered in 1953, the Havana province had an illiteracy rate of 9.2%, with the rate in rural provinces ranging from 19.2% to 30.8%. Prior to the Revolution, 50% of school-age children, mostly in rural areas, did not attend school. In 1959 to 1960, shortly after Batista was deposed, 15,000 new classrooms were build in rural zones.[57]

The literacy crusade provided an opportunity for educating youth and older citizens to work for the good of the community. In 1960, Castro asked secondary school youth to volunteer to teach in rural areas. Although there were 9,000 unemployed teachers, most refused to work in the countryside. After a month of training in 1960, a group of 1,000 students were sent to the most isolated areas of the countryside followed by groups of other students. In accordance with Castro's slogan, "The people should teach the people," common citizens were recruited to use their free time to teach reading and writing.[58] Called *Alfabetizadores*, secondary school youth and citizen volunteers became the major literacy instructors. After recruitment and training of a large corps of Alfabetizadores, Castro declared 1961 to be the "Year of Education" and closed secondary schools in April so that students could join the crusade. Professional teachers acted as trainers and supervisors. At the end of 1961, the Cuban government reported that 707,212 illiterates (or 72.2%) had been taught reading and writing at the first-grade level by 120,632 Alfabetizadores under the supervision of 34,772 teachers. The 1961 literacy crusade and subsequent efforts were guided by Castro's formula: "to every illiterate, an Alfabetizador; to every Alfabetizador, an illiterate."[59]

The creation of literacy texts and thematic representations based on the vocabulary and lives of Cuban farmers and fishermen/women would influence other literacy campaigns and would later be adapted by Paulo Freire. The UNESCO mission reported,

> There was a need for a primer whose revolutionary and political content would not only have an adequate motivation from an historical and psychological point of view, but also would equally express this motivation in a comprehensible form and *as close as possible to the language of the Cuban farmer.*[60]

To capture the language of the farmer, 4 months were devoted to recording interviews with illiterates. The language captured on the recordings was used to write a primer called *Venceremos (We Shall Conquer)*. Reproductions of photographs of ordinary life were included in the *Primer*. The reproductions were thematic representations of the lessons and were to serve as items for discussions. Many of the lessons reflected the ordinary lives of Cubans. The reproductions were to stimulate dialogues between Alfabetizadores and illiterates about Cuban social life and revolutionary activities. This thematic method would later be advocated by Paulo Freire. The UNESCO mission summarized the purpose of the photographs:

The primer's illustrations were reproductions of photographs of Cuban life after the Revolution, which took into account the theme expounded. The photograph helped to capture the most essential aspect of the motivation, since it not only served as visual aid to the illiterate, but also helped the whole process of learning how to read and write, by solving in advance the doubts which may have arisen by providing conversational themes, and awakening the attention.[61]

Venceremos's lessons were graded according to difficulty. They contained themes of the Cuban revolution, politics, and Cuban social life. It should be noted in the following list that the 14th lesson was used to explain "The Year of Education."

Lessons in Venceremos

1. OEA (Organization of American States)
2. INRA (National Institute of Agrarian Reform)
3. The Cooperative Farm under the Agrarian Reform
4. The Land
5. Cuban Fishermen
6. The People's Store
7. Every Cuban, a Home Owner
8. A Healthy People in a Free Cuba
9. INIT (National Institute of Tourist Industry)
10. The Militia
11. The Revolution Wins all the Battles
12. The People at Work
13. Cuba Is Not Alone
14. The Year of Education
15. Poetry and the Alphabet[62]

Reflecting efforts to relate literacy to the real world of Cuban citizens, the Ministry of Education published pamphlets to stimulated reading about different occupations, such as woodcutters, fishermen/women, and charcoal makers. One booklet, *La Cultura y El Trabajo* (Culture and Work) encouraged fishermen/women to teach Alfabetizadores how to fish and Alfabetizadores to teach fishermen/women how to read.

A manual, *Alfabeticemos* (Let's Teach How to Read and Write), was prepared for literacy instructors. This manual taught instructional methodologies and inculcated revolutionary themes ranging from "The Revolution" and "Fidel is Our Leader" to "The Revolution Wins All the Battles." In other words, Alfabetizadores, who were students and ordinary citizens, were also receiving a political education. Study groups were formed that included Alfabetizadores, supervising professional teachers, technical assistants, and political instructors. Some of the time in the study groups was spent dialoging about instructional methods and the following revolutionary themes from the manual.

Revolutionary Orientation Themes in *Alfabeticemos*

 1. The Revolution
 2. Fidel is Our Leader
 3. The Land is Ours
 4. The Cooperative Farms
 5. The Right to Housing
 6. Cuba Had Riches and was Poor
 7. Nationalization
 8. Industrialization
 9. The Revolution Converts Army Barracks Into Schools
10. Racial Discrimination
11. Friends and Enemies
12. Imperialism
13. International Trade
14. War and Peace
15. International Unity
16. Democracy
17. Workers and Farmers
18. The People, United and Alert
19. Freedom of Religion
20. Health
21. Popular Recreation
22. The Abolition of Illiteracy
23. The Revolution Wins All the Battles
24. The Declaration of Havana[63]

In conclusion, the literacy crusade embodied many of the educational principles advocated by Latin American Marxists and leaders of the Cuban Revolution. First, the crusade used students and ordinary citizens as Alfabetizadores; this could be considered a response to Che Guevara's call for new socialist men and women serving the community by working for the greater good of society. Second, the literacy texts contained peasant's vocabulary, thematic photographs, and stories about peasant lives in order to preserve peasant and indigenous cultures. Third, concerns about relating theory to practice were accomplished by relating education directly to people's lives. And last, concerns about the hegemony of the ruling classes and imperialist powers were addressed in the dialogical methods employed in study groups and literacy instruction.

In closing this section, I want to express my own concerns about the literacy crusade's idolization of Castro, which, in the light of Krushchev's criticisms during this period about the cult of personality surrounding Stalin, detracted from the critical edge of the instructional methodologies that were employed. Study groups using the teaching manual *Alfabeticemos* were expected to discuss a section on "Fidel is Our Leader." As part of the final literacy test, students were required to write a letter to Fidel Castro. Writing the letter entitled students to receive a free textbook to continue their studies. According to the UNESCO mission, "the letter the pupil wrote to Fidel Castro at the end of the final test (a letter entitled him to receive a book for his future studies), were included in the personal files of the pupil and were kept in the Campaign's archives in each municipality of the island."[64] I imagine that students only wrote letters of praise rather than critical statements to Castro, and I might be wrong on this point because these letters remained in their permanent files.

MAO AND THE CULTURAL REVOLUTION

Around the globe, the 1966 Chinese Cultural Revolution sent students and educators into the streets waving Mao's Little Red Book and pasting posters of the Red Guard on walls and lamp posts. What was the attraction of the Cultural Revolution? Why did so many students and educators seize upon it as an alternative to the growing rigidity of educational security states' formal systems of education? What was the great appeal of a political movement designed to strengthen the power of Mao Zedong and which caused the brutalization of teachers, scholars, and other leaders?

The answer, I believe, was that the Cultural Revolution went to the heart of the problems inherent in educational security states' use of education to distribute human resources into the economic and military machinery of the state. One problem was that educational security states were alienating students by treating them as objects to be molded for economic and military needs. Secondly, social and economic inequalities were being reinforced by educational systems that were transforming family privilege into educational advantages and, as a result, into advantages in the labor market. Most of the educational reforms of the Cultural Revolution were designed to increase equality of educational opportunity, particularly for children of peasants and workers. And lastly, the Cultural Revolution provided the hope that more permanent social improvements might result from educational and cultural change rather than armed revolution.

The Cultural Revolution began with Mao Zedong's "May 7th Directive, 1966" and it was officially launched with the distribution of a May 16th circular from the Central Committee of the Chinese Communist Party.[65] Mao's "May 7th Directive" declared, "While their [students] main task is to study, they should in their studies, learn other things, that is industrial work, farming and military affairs. They should also criticize the bourgeoisie. *The school term should be shortened, education should be revolutionized, and the domination of our schools by bourgeois intellectuals should not be allowed to continue* [my emphasis]."[66]

There was nothing really new in the "May 7th Directive." Mao had always advocated, in the tradition of Marx's polytechnical education, the combining of learning and work, and theory and practice. Mao consistently criticized schools, beginning with his complaints about Confucian education, for being dominated by bourgeois intellectuals and an examination system that promoted elitism. Also, he always believed students were overburdened with the study of useless bits of information. What was different was his intention to truly carry out an educational revolution using the force of organized groups of educators and students. On May 24th, Mao's efforts received support when Nie Yanzi, Party Secretary of the Philosophy Department at Beijing University, put up a wall-poster outside the students' canteen. The poster criticized the university's president for ignoring Mao's calls for a cultural revolution and it urged students and faculty "resolutely, thoroughly, cleanly and completely to eliminate all demons and monsters, and all Khrushchev-type counter-revolutionary revisionists, and to carry the socialist revolution through to the end."[67] A week later, in a radio broadcast, Mao endorsed the poster. The endorsement rallied students to Nie's cause. During the same period, a nameless student organized a "Red Guard" at the Qinghua University Middle School. "Red Guard" organizations began to appear in schools around the country.[68]

In June, 1966, the Central Committee of the Communist Party, as part of the assault on the examination system that favored the admission into higher education of students from professional and government-employed families, took the bold step of postponing the enrollment of new students in colleges and universities by half a year. The Central Committee's directive stated, "the method of examination and enrollment for the higher educational institutions has failed in the main, to free itself from the set pattern of the bourgeois system of examination, and such a method is harmful to the implementation of the guiding policy on education formulated by the Central Committee of the Party and Chairman Mao."[69] The directive called for reforming the examination system for greater "absorption into the higher educational institutions of a still greater number of revolutionary young people from among the workers, peasants and soldiers."[70]

The call for reforming the examination system continued into the following year when an "Editorial on Importance of Transforming Chinese Educational System" was published in the Chinese journal *Current Background*. Like

Mao and many other Chinese, the editorialist compared the school and examination system to the social power of the old Confucian system: "A thoroughgoing revolution in the educational system will destroy the influence of the old, exploiting class educational ideas which have dominated for several thousand years, ever since Confucius, and will extirpate one of the important seats of power of the bourgeois 'authorities' and scholar-tyrants in the field of ideology."[71] The editorial applauded the postponement of admission of new students and warned that, "If the entrance examination of enrolling new students went ahead as usual just now, this would undoubtedly bring the great proletarian cultural revolution in the field of education to a stop half way, cripple the revolutionary enthusiasm of the Left students and encourage the counter-revolutionary arrogance of the bourgeois Right."[72] After providing examples of public anger about the college and senior middle school entrance examination system, the editorial lauded the introduction of a new system where students would be admitted based on "their outstanding moral, intellectual and physical qualities."[73]

In 1969, a new system of examinations was put into place that was supposed to end the class bias of the previous system and result in more children of workers and peasants entering senior middle schools and universities. The new plan invoked Mao's concern that, "The present method of examination is a method used to handle the enemy, which takes him by surprise with odd and out-of-the-way questions. It is a method of examination used in tests on stereotyped writings."[74] The new plan called for students to receive a systematic review of material that would appear on the examination. Also, examination results were to undergo review by a committee of students. Students, teachers, and parents were to engage in ideological discussions over the purposes of the examination system.

The new system of examinations was supposed to promote learning as opposed to being a method for selection and control of students. Later in the 20th and 21st centuries, as I discuss in other chapters, many people pondered the same issues as Mao Zedong as the use of standardized examinations increasingly determined advancement between school grades and admission to higher education. In 1969, the differences between the old and new Chinese examination systems were described as, "The examination in the past was solely for the purpose of obtaining marks which decided whether a student repeated or was to be dismissed and the teachers used the examination to suppress students and reject students who were children of workers and peasants."[75] Now the purpose of examinations, it was claimed, was to aid students to learn, including learning ideological material: "However the examination today is solely for the purpose ... [of] helping the students with their reviews and their consolidation of what they have learned, and cultivating the students' ability of analyzing and solving problems so as to improve the method of teaching and elevate the quality of teaching."[76] Secondly, the new examinations were not to be "surprise attack[s] using odd and out-of-the-way questions."[77] Before examinations, students were now to be told the nature of the material that would appear on the examination. And lastly, students who failed the examination were to be given assistance so that they could pass at a later date: "In this way those with high achievements are encouraged to do better and those with lower achievements are encouraged to catch up. Consciousness is heightened, enthusiasm is rallied, and knowledge is increased every time an examination is administered. Students welcome such examination[s]."[78]

Mao urged shifting educational control from an bourgeois elite of experts to "revolutionary" teachers, students, workers, and peasants. Schools were called upon to democratically elect committees of "revolutionary" teachers and students who would ensure the expulsion or reeducation of bourgeois teachers and administrators. Squads of the Red Guard conducted public condemnations of so called counterrevolutionary teachers. "Red Little Soldiers" were organized in elementary schools to "study quotations from Chairman Mao and learn to read characters and sing revolutionary songs with the revolutionary teachers and pupils in senior classes acting as their supervising personnel."[79] School administrators, were to be "strengthened or re-elected through mass discussion to take good care of the life of teachers and pupils."[80]

As part of the revolution in education, workers and peasants were to be given more control over the management of schools. A report from one rural commune stated, "The poor and lower-middle peasants are enthusiastic in running schools, considering them their own. Many old poor peasants have lectured to the pupils."[81] And, in keeping with the self-sacrificing image of the social realist figure Lei Feng, a peasant named Chien reportedly criticized a government request to build classrooms for a junior middle school: "Chien learned about it and made a special trip to the school to criticize it for the mistake of demanding money from the state. He suggested using self-reliance to build the classrooms, and when the commune members lent a hand six classrooms … were soon built."[82] Although the communal report stressed the benefits of peasant control of schools, it also stressed how the Cultural Revolution resulted in greater equality of educational opportunity for peasants, a focus on the political teachings of Mao Zedong, and the integration of teachers into the work life of peasants.

An important educational aspect of the Cultural Revolution was highlighted in the communal report's discussion of integrating teachers into the work life of peasants. As a result, the report claimed, teachers could now understand the relationship between what they taught and the real life of the people, and that they no longer looked down on the life of the peasant. Consequently, teachers were more sympathetic towards their students. Mao, as part of the campaign to have teachers and college professors experience the work life of industrial laborers and farmers, asserted, "The lowly are most intelligent; the elite most ignorant … [and] the intellectuals will accomplish nothing if they fail to integrate themselves with the workers and peasants."[83]

Exemplifying the general policy of having students, teachers, and professors laboring alongside workers and peasants, the communal report stated that, "they [teachers] teach in school while serving as pupils outside school. They are teachers when they give lectures but become pupils when poor and lower-middle peasants take the floor. In the past they feared contact with peasants and did not want to become soiled; now they work in mud alongside the peasants."[84] The result of working in the mud, according to the report, was that teachers expressed more sympathy for the living conditions of students: "If any pupil comes too late for class, the teacher promptly tutors him. Some teachers have used their own money to buy stationery for poor pupils or given their own cotton-padded coats to pupils who needed them."[85]

Forcing educators to labor alongside workers and peasants also ensured a linkage between theory and practice or, as it was called, praxis. Combining theory and practice in instruction was at the heart of progressive educational theories and Marxist ideology. One of Mao's clearest statements on praxis was in a 1963 essay titled, "Where Do Correct Ideas Come From?" Mao, similar to John Dewey and other progressive and Marxist thinkers, opened the essay by stating his belief that ideas resulted from material conditions and not from gods or God, or sources innate in the individual: "Where do correct ideas come form? Do they drop from the skies? No. Are they innate in the mind? No. They come from social practice, and from it alone."[86]

Mao identified three forms of social practice that generated and tested the value of ideas; industrial and agricultural production, class struggle, and scientific experiment. The formation of human consciousness, Mao argued, resulted from individuals' perceptions of the external world. Mao wrote, "It [perceptual knowledge] is the first stage in the whole process of cognition, the stage leading from objective matter to subjective, from existence to ideas." At the stage of perceptual knowledge forming ideas, Mao stated, it was not possible to determine whether these ideas correctly reflected the objective world. Correctness of ideas would be tested in "the second stage in the process of cognition, the stage leading from consciousness back to matter, from ideas back to existence, in which the knowledge gained in the first stage is applied in social practice to ascertain whether the theories, policies, plans or measures meet the anticipated success."[87]

It was the theory behind the second stage of cognition that Mao used to justify sending students, teachers, and professors into the fields and factories. Work provided an opportunity for students and educators to put subjective ideas and theories into social practice. "Generally speaking," Mao wrote, "those [ideas, theories, policies, and plans] that succeed are correct and those that fail are incorrect, and this is especially true of man's struggle with nature."[88] The testing of ideas and theories in social practice or praxis required repetition until correct thinking was approached or achieved.

The outcome of praxis, according to Mao and later Paulo Freire, was for workers and peasants to participate in social change. Mao declared, "the one and only purpose of the proletariat knowing the world is to *change it* [my emphasis]."[89] Mao summarized the theory of praxis that would make it possible for the proletariat to participate in revolutionary change: "Often, correct knowledge can be arrived at only after many repetitions of the process that is, leading from practice to knowledge and then back to practice. Such is the Marxist theory of knowledge, the dialectical materialist theory of knowledge."[90]

If theory was to be tested in social practice, the actual outcome of the Cultural Revolution was not pretty and proved some of its basic premises to be wrong. The Red Guard went to extreme lengths to carry out the admonition to criticize teachers and unseat bourgeois intellectuals. For example, Ken Ling, a Red Guard member, reported, "Teacher Chen, over 60 years old and suffering from high blood pressure, was ... dragged up to the second floor of a classroom building and ... beaten with fists and broomsticks.... He passed out several times.... He could hardly move his body, his feet were cut by glass and thorns."[91] Teacher Chen eventually died during this ordeal. Other teachers were executed by Red Guard members. "Some teachers were buried alive. On the roof of that building over there," a witness recalled, "four teachers were ordered to sit on a pack of explosives and [forced] to light them themselves."[92] The Red Guard burned and destroyed books, art work, and buildings that they felt embodied bourgeois thinking. Professors, teachers, students, and artists complained they learned little and their social consciousness was not raised by working side-by-side with peasants and workers.

However, despite the excesses of the Red Guard, the Cultural Revolution became a world symbol for student power; providing equal access to schools for lower income groups; turning examinations into learning experiences as opposed simply using them to give marks for promotion; praxis as an instructional method; and politicizing all school subjects. The goals of the Cultural Revolution spoke directly to the problems arising from educational security states making schools part of economic and military planning. As schools in educational security states became more important in determining students' future careers, they increasingly reinforced social class differences. Children of the rich received the best education and performed well on tests, whereas the opposite occurred for children of the poor. As I discussed in chapter 4, Krushchev's education proposals attempted to correct the educational advantages of the children of elite bureaucrats.

CRITICAL EDUCATION AND PROGRESSIVE THEORY: PAULO FREIRE

When Paulo Freire referred to the "fundamental aspect of Mao's Cultural Revolution," it was in support of Freire's assertion:

> The pedagogy of the oppressed, as a humanist and libertarian pedagogy, has two distinct stages. In the first, the oppressed unveil the world of oppression and through the praxis commit themselves to its transformation. In the second stage, in which the reality of oppression has already been transformed, this pedagogy ceases to belong to the oppressed and becomes a pedagogy of all men in the process of permanent liberation. In both stages, it is always through action in depth that the culture of domination is culturally confronted.[93]

Freire traces the beginning of his pedagogical ideas to 1947 when he rejected a career in law to work for Brazil's newly formed Division of Education and Culture of the Industrial Social Service. Born in 1921 in Recife, Brazil, he grew up in a middle-class family that experienced poverty and other hardships during the 1930s depression. When he abandoned his law career in 1947, he claimed that he realized that law served the oppressor whereas education could serve the oppressed.

An incident in reporting a research project completed for the Division of Education and Culture brought home to Freire the importance of a Marxist's dialectical materialist theory of knowledge and cultural differences. Similar to other Latin American Marxists and Mao Zedong, Freire realized the importance of dialogue in refining the truth of theoretical conclusions or, in other words, relating ideas to social practices. The incident involved a laborer's reaction to Freire's research findings. Later, Freire would write about his verbal exchange with the laborer, "This talk was given about thirty-two years ago. I have never forgotten it."[94] The research reported by Freire dealt with freedom, punishment, and reward in education and it was delivered to a large audience attending a 1-day seminar at the Division of Education and Culture's social center in Recife. Freire reported to the audience that he had found a marked difference in the punishment of children among poor city dwellers in contrast to poor fishing families along the coast. The urban poor, he found, frequently meted out violent and sometimes cruel punishments to their children. In contrast, fishing families allowed their children a maximum of freedom and seldom engaged in corporal punishment. Freire proposed that there were political consequences to these differences and that children of the urban poor were being prepared to accept the authority of the oppressor. Freire wrote, "One of my concerns, at the time, as valid then as it is now, was with the political consequences of that kind of relationship between parents and children.... It was as if family and school were so completely subjected to the greater context of global society that they could do nothing but reproduce the authoritarian ideology."[95]

Freire and the unnamed laborer clashed over Freire's interpretation of corporal punishment using the child development theories of Swiss psychologist Jean Piaget. This was an important issue because it highlighted the difference between dialectical materialism and idealism. Piaget had concluded that children's reasoning developed according to innate stages of development. During the 1920s and 1930s, Soviet psychologist Lev Vygotsky criticized Piaget's theories for failing to consider a child's development as depending on the interaction between the child and society.[96] Vygotsky accused Piaget of being an idealist who acted as if child development could occur outside the context of the real world. Vygotsky questioned Piaget's efforts to determine the innate development of reasoning by examining areas where the child supposedly had no knowledge and was not corrupted by outside learning. Piaget wanted to find the "pure" stages in the development of a child's reasoning. From Vygotsky's perspective, this was an example of "idealism" where human action was abstracted from social practice. Vygotsky asserted: "For Piaget, the index of the level of the child's thinking is to be found not in what the child knows or what he is able to learn but in his capacity for thinking in a domain where he has no knowledge. Here, instruction and thinking are placed in the sharpest possible contrast."[97]

Therefore, from the perspective of Marxists and followers of John Dewey, Paulo Freire was distorting his findings by explaining them with an idealist theory of human development that neglected the importance of social conditions and learning. This was the issue raised by Freire's unnamed laborer. Using Piaget's theories on moral codes, Freire suggested what was needed in urban families was a loving relationship between parents and children. After this meaningless spin on the research findings, the unnamed laborer raised his hand and asked Pablo Freire if he had ever visited any of their homes. "And," Freire recalled, "he began to describe their pitiful houses. He told me of the lack of facilities, of the extremely minimal space in which all their bodies were jammed. He spoke of the lack of resources ... of physical exhaustion, of the impossibility of dreams for a better tomorrow. He told me of the prohibition imposed on them from being happy—or even of having hope."[98] The laborer said he could describe Freire's home even though he had never seen it. He described Freire's home as having many bedrooms, a library, situated on its own lot, and filled with modern appliances. "But sir," he commented, "it's one thing to come home, even tired, and find the kids all bathed, dressed up, clean, well fed, not hungry—and another thing to come home and find your kids dirty, hungry, crying, and making noise. And people have to get up at four in the morning the next day and start all over again—hurting, sad, hopeless."[99] He concluded with the following explanation of violence towards children among poor urban families: "If people hit their kids, and even 'go beyond bounds,' as you say, it's not because people don't love their kids. No, its because life is so hard they don't have much choice."[100]

The laborer's comments, Freire claimed, made him aware of the importance of testing his subjective interpretation of objective facts by engaging in a dialogue with the people who are the objects of study. In the corporal punishment study, Freire had simply imposed his own subjective interpretation on his findings. However, this interpretation was corrected by the laborer's criticisms. This dialogical process of testing subjective judgements of objective data became an important part of Freire's teaching methods. In addition, during his research Freire used the language and syntax of the urban poor and fishing villages and gave his research presentations in the language and syntax of the audience. Similar to the Cuban Literacy Crusade, Freire would use the language and syntax of his students when implementing his instructional methodology.

In 1960, Freire left the Division of Education and Culture of the Industrial Social Service to help organize the Movement for Popular Culture under the leadership of Recife's mayor, Miguel Arraes. The Movement for Popular Culture implemented the conclusions of many Latin American progressives that social change should begin with the education of peasants, workers, and indigenous peoples. Government statutes declared the goals of the Movement for Popular Culture to be improving the education and cultural level of children and adults and the forming of "departments designed to interpret, systematize, and transmit the multiple aspects of popular culture."[101] All members of the movement, Freire recalled, were dedicated to bringing about the transformation of Brazilian society. This required a transformation of peasant, indigenous, and worker cultures into revolutionary cultures seeking to transform the world. This would become a central goal of Freire's instructional methods. Regarding the Movement for Popular Culture, Freire wrote, "Another part of the movement's nature was a critical understanding of the role of culture in the educational process, as well as in the political struggle for the change that Brazilian society needed then and still needs today; change in culture in general, in popular culture in particular, and to the progressive education of children and adults."[102]

The Movement for Popular Culture advocated a dialectical process for achieving cultural transformation; a method that would become central to Freire's pedagogy. "A dialectical view of the role of culture in the historical process aligned the movement," Freire explained. "In a dialectic ... the future evolves from the transformation of the present as it occurs. Thus, the future takes on a problematic and undetermined character. The future is not what it needs to be, but whatever we make of it in the present."[103] In other words, the Movement's cultural circles engaged in discussions with peasants, indigenous peoples, and workers about the historical reasons for the development of their cultures and their attitudes about the future. The future was presented as a problem so that participants would learn that the future was not already determined and that they could participate in making the future. In contrast to this dialectical view of culture and the future, the Movement for Popular Culture described: "In a mechanistic and authoritarian understanding in which the future, nonproblematized, is already known, already certain, education is reduced to the transfer of recipes, packages."[104] Freire would later call this mechanistic approach "banking education." Therefore, in the context of the Movement for Popular Culture, cultural circles were to engage in dialogues about their cultures and the future, and the dialog was to result in reflection and problematizing of their cultures and futures.

During these years, Paulo Freire made clear his commitment, like many other Latin American Marxists, to social democracy. He rejected the position of those who advocated democracy without advocating socialism. Real democracy, he argued, required socialism. He wrote, "While I am a radical and substantive democrat, I am a socialist. There is no way of countering the one with the other. To do so is one of the tragic errors of so-called realist socialism."[105]

In 1964, Freire went to Chile after being exiled following a coup d'etat by the Brazilian military elite, During his exile, Freire's socialist philosophy and instructional methods crystallized, and he wrote *Pedagogy of the Oppressed*. In 1964, Chile was in a political ferment which would eventually result in the first elected Latin American Marxist government in 1970 under the leadership of Salvador Allende. Freire was hired as a consultant to the Institute for the Development of Animal Husbandry by Jacques Chonchol, who would later serve as socialist Minister of Agriculture under Allende.[106] In the charged atmosphere of Chilean politics, Freire met socialists from many Latin American countries, including Cuba. It was here that he read Che Guevara's previously quoted statement, "the true revolutionary is guided by great feelings of love." In reference to the Cuban presence and

Guevara's statement on love, Freire wrote, "The Cubans showed that changes could be made.... Guevara's capacity for love was there."[107] In *Pedagogy of the Oppressed*, he used the quote on love from Guevara to justify the statement, "Dialogue cannot exist, however, in the absence of a profound love for the world and for men. The naming of the world, which is an act of creation and re-creation, is not possible if it is not infused in love."[108] He used Guevara's quote to footnote the following statement: "I am more and more convinced that true revolutionaries must perceive the revolution, because of its creative and liberating nature, as an act of love."[109]

According to Freire, his work with cultural circles in Brazil "were consolidated in Chilean practice, and in the theoretical reflection I made upon that practice."[110] Freire conducted cultural circles as part of the agricultural reform work of the Chilean Institute for the Development of Animal Husbandry. In one of these cultural circles a peasant apologized for talking because, he said, "You know things, sir. We don't."[111] Freire reflected that a progressive educator must seize the moment and to accept the comments of peasants as stepping stones in learning. "What I had to do," he wrote, "was to begin with the acceptance of something said in the discourse of the peasant and make a problem of it for them, and thereby bring them once more to dialogue."[112] Therefore, in response to the peasants comments, Freire drew a line down the middle of a chalk board. He told the circle of peasants that he would put a mark on one side for every question that he asked and they couldn't answer, and on the other side for every question they asked and he couldn't answer. Of course, marks were evenly distributed on both sides of the line and the peasants learned that they also had knowledge of the world. When the same circumstance occurred in another cultural circle, Freire asked, "I know. You don't. But *why* do I know and you don't?" The peasants responded that he had studied and been to school and they hadn't. "And why have I been to school?" Freire continued questioning. The peasants responded that Freire's parents could afford to send him to school whereas their parents couldn't because they were peasants. As peasants, they stated, they had nothing except working from sun-up to sundown. When Freire asked why these conditions existed, they responded that it was the will of God. After further questioning, they concluded, "No. God isn't the cause of all this. It's the boss!"[113]

During his exile in Chile, Freire made several trips to New York City where he experienced "thematic" lessons conducted by Catholic priests. In one these sessions, which he later reports in *Pedagogy of the Oppressed*, an educator presented to a group of Blacks and Puerto Ricans a photo of the street in front of the building in which they were meeting. The photo showed garbage on the sidewalk. Using an pedagogical method that would become central in Freire's work, the group leader asked the participants what they saw in the photo. The responses ranged from a street in Latin America to Africa. Participants refused to believe it was a street in the United States until one of them commented, "Might as well admit it's our street. Where we live."[114]

In trying to explain the initial unwillingness of the participants to admit the photo was of their street, Freire turned to the work of Erich Fromm whom he met while visiting Ivan Illich in Cuernavaca, Mexico. After explaining to Fromm the New York City session, Fromm declared, "This kind of educational practice is a kind of historico-cultural, political psychoanalysis."[115] Later, Freire would rely on Fromm's work to explain Guevara's admonishment that revolution should be a revolution of love. Freire related emotions to stages of consciousness about causal relationships that shape society with biophilic personality referring to a love and desire to free all people, and necrophilic personality to a desire to enslave everyone. The psychoanalytic sections of *Pedagogy of the Oppressed* verged on idealism similar to his use of Piaget to explain family violence. Forgetting his own Marxist commitment to apply a dialectical process, Freire used Fromm's writings to claim that educating a person to understand the world and to be an actor that changed history would change people's personalities. The new personalities resulting from the use of his educational method, he claimed, would be biophilic and they would be driven by an emotional desire to free others and lead a revolution of love.

Freire wrote the first three chapters of *Pedagogy of the Oppressed* during a 3-week vacation in July, 1967. These original three chapters explained his pedagogical methods and contained a critique of formal education, which he called "banking education." After reviewing the manuscript, he provided a broader theoretical framework by adding a fourth chapter. Freire justified chapter 4 by quoting Lenin, "Without a revolutionary theory, there can be no revolutionary movement."[116] Reflecting the global flow of ideas, the original manuscript was written in Portugese but was first published in 1968 in English in the United States followed by Spanish, Italian, French, and German translation. It wasn't until 1975 that a Portugese version was printed in Brazil.[117]

In *Pedagogy of the Oppressed*, Freire emphasized the lessons he learned in the Chilean cultural circles. He criticized educators who "approach the peasant or urban masses with projects which may correspond to their own view of the world, but not to that of the people."[118] Interestingly, he supported this conclusion with a lengthy footnote from the writings of Mao Zedong which ended, "There are two principles here: one is the actual needs of the masses rather than what we fancy they need, and the other is the wishes of the masses, who must make up their own minds instead of our making up their minds for them."[119] Freire believed that a dialogical interaction with peasants, indigenous peoples, and urban workers was the key to their involvement in social transformation. This approach, he believed, would overcome the constant concerns expressed by Latin American Marxists about the lack of participation of peasants in demands for social improvement and revolutionary activities. Regarding this concern, Freire quoted Che Guevara's frustration about the lack of peasant involvement in the revolutionary movement he was leading in Bolivia: "The peasant mobilization does not exist.... They are neither very rapid nor very efficient ... although they are losing their fear of us ... it is a slow and patient task."[120]

Pedagogy of the Oppressed answered the central problem facing Latin American Marxists, which was how to include peasants and indigenous peoples in a revolutionary movement. Freire attributed the apparent backwardness and lack of revolutionary ardor of these groups to their living in a culture of silence. Breaking the culture of silence required teaching people to engage in dialectical relationship with their material conditions. The genius of Freire's method was that it combined literacy instruction with revolutionary education without using propaganda and political slogans. Also, his method preserved cultures and languages while helping people to understand the causes of their misery. Educators presented themes about people's daily lives similar to the photograph used in the example just discussed in New York City. Literacy group members were to engage in a dialogue about thematic representations of the group's lives. The language used by the participants provided the words used in their literacy instruction. Through learning to read, participants were to name the world using their own words. As discussions evolved and literacy increased, participants were to engage in dialogical reflections about their different and changing views of their objective worlds. The more the participant learned to read about their world and the more they unveiled the causes of their existence, the better prepared they were to transform their world. As Mao Zedong stated,

> It is therefore necessary to educate our comrades in the dialectical materialist theory of knowledge, so that they can orient their thinking correctly, become good at investigation and study and at summing up experience, overcome difficulties, commit fewer mistakes, do their work better, and struggle hard so as to build China into a great and powerful socialist country and *help the broad masses of the oppressed and exploited through the world in fulfillment of our great international duty* [my emphasis].[121]

Reflecting the influence of Erich Fromm, Freire assumed that once people learned how to transform their worlds and participate in the making of history, they would become liberators and lovers of humanity.

Freire contrasted his methods with formal instruction that he called "banking" education. His discussion of banking education was a powerful critique of formal education. Banking education, Freire argued, mirrors oppressive societies where humans learn to serve their masters. The purpose of banking education was for students to accept existing forms of oppression as unchangeable. In other words, banking education ensured what Gramsci called the "hegemony of the oppressors." Achieving hegemonic control of the people required an education that filled students with facts and information without giving them the tools or knowledge to transform society. Students were never to be taught that they could be subjects of history who could participate in changing history. Banking education prepared students to think of themselves as objects of history whose lives were already determined. Freire provided the following list of reasons why formal or banking education maintained oppressive societies. This list contains some of the most important objections progressive educators have of formal methods of instruction. In Freire's banking education list, students are objects and not participants in their own education. This, supposedly, prepares them to submit as objects to the will of the oppressors.

Principles of Banking Education

1. The teacher teaches and the students are taught;
2. The teacher knows everything and the students know nothing;
3. The teacher thinks and the students are thought about;
4. The teacher talks and the students listen—meekly;
5. The teacher disciplines and the students are disciplined;

Besides being treated as objects, students learned to think of all knowledge as in the hands of the teacher and by extension the hands of rulers.

6. The teacher chooses and enforces his choice, and the students comply;
7. The teacher acts and the students have the illusion of acting through the action of the teacher;
8. The teacher chooses the program content, and the students (who were not consulted) adapt to it;
9. The teacher confuses the authority of knowledge with his own professional

authority, which he sets in opposition to the
freedom of the students;
10. The teacher is the subject of the learning
process, while the pupils are mere objects.[122]

When I first met Freire in 1970 at Ivan Illich's Center for Intercultural Documentation in Cuernavaca, Mexico, he stated that his method was like a cook-
book recipe involving the presentation of thematic representations of people's
objective lives, dialogue about the thematic representations, and codification
of people's language for use in literacy instruction. This recipe was meaningless, he claimed, without an understanding of his concept of what it meant to be
human. However, as I suggested earlier, his concept of humanness borders on
idealism in contrast to materialism. To be human, Freire argued, was to be able
to make conscious choices about the objective world. In making these choices,
the person becomes a subject of history consciously working to change history.
Based on Erich Fromm's work, Freire used the term *biophilic* to describe the
person who acted as a subject of history. In contrast, the *necrophilic* acted at the
will of an oppressor and did not make conscious choices to change history.
Necrophilics were mere objects of history and the will of the oppressor. In this
taxonomy, a biophilic person was free and wanted to liberate people and the
necrophilic was oppressed and wanted to enslave humanity. Consequently,
freedom and oppression were within the individual and, at the same time, in
political and social institutions. Formal schools using banking methods of education shaped a necrophilic personality that wanted to live in authoritarian societies and exert authority over others. The biophilic personality wanted to live
in a free society and wanted to free all people.

Although the objective existence of necrophilic and biophilic personalities that reflect particular social organizations can be questioned, Freire did
provide progressives with an educational methodology which promised to
educate peasants and indigenous peoples to be revolutionary without destroying their cultures. Freire believed that a Marxist revolution could be
conducted by rural people. In fact, one could imagine a cultural circle of In-
cas deciding that José Carlos Mariátegui was correct in proposing a resurrection of a traditional Inca-Communist society. Freire made it possible to
imagine a cultural revolution preceding a political and economic revolution. He also made it possible to think of progressive education as the
primary instrument for social improvement.

THE EDUCATION CRUSADE AND LIBERATION THEOLOGY: MEDELLIN CONFERENCE (1968)

Liberation theology played a major role in spreading Freire's educational
methods. As mentioned previously in this chapter, Jose Mariátegui advo-

cated relating Marxism to indigenous cultures and providing a role for the Catholic Church in revolutionary change. Of course, his reasoning ran counter to the atheistic dogmas of traditional Marxism and international communism. From his perspective and that of many other South and Central American Marxists, the Catholic Church was an integral part of people's lives and had adapted to indigenous cultures. Certainly, a lesson that could be learned from the Russian Revolution was that atheistic doctrines complicated revolutionary change by generating resistance from those with religious convictions. The easiest way out of this problem was to integrate religion into revolutionary practice.

Paulo Freire, although critical of the actions of the Church, never adopted an openly atheist position. In fact, *Pedagogy of the Oppressed* contains quotes from precursors to the liberation theology movement. In his book, he quotes without criticism Bishop Franic Split, one of the participants at the 1968 Conference of Latin American Bishops in Medellin, Columbia; a conference that coalesced the liberation theology movement:

> If the workers do not become in some way the owners of their labor, all structural reforms will be ineffective. [This is true] even if the workers receive a higher salary in an economic system but are not content with these raises. They want to be owners, not sellers, of their labor.... At present the workers are increasingly aware that labor represents a part of the human person. A person, however cannot be bought; neither can he sell himself. Any purchase or sale of labor is a type of slavery.[123]

The documents issued by the Medellin conference supported Freirean educational methods by emphasizing the importance of protecting cultures and by advocating "Concientización." The documents rejected violent revolution for peaceful methods. Similar to Freire, they advocated a cultural revolution through education. Using concepts of consciousness that parallels Freire's work, the Medellin Conference's declaration "Justice and Peace" stated, "The lack of political consciousness in our countries makes the educational activity of the Church absolutely essential, for the purpose of bringing Christians to consider their participation in the political life of the nation as a matter of conscience and as the practice of charity in its most noble and meaningful sense for the life of the community."[124] This idea was reiterated in a section on titled "Information and Concientización."

> We wish to affirm that it is indispensable to form a social conscience and a realistic perception of the problems of the community and of social structures. We must awaken the social conscience and communal customs in all strata of society and professional groups regarding such values as dialogue and community living within the same group and relations with wider social groups (workers, peasants, professionals, clergy, religious, administration, etc.).[125]

The Medellin Conference announced that the Church would actively work to raise the level of people's consciousness: "This task of 'concientización' and social education ought to be integrated into joint pastoral action at various levels."[126]

In addition to recognizing the educational role of the Church in raising political consciousness, "Justice and Peace" stressed the importance of recognizing cultural differences. "The lack of socio-cultural integration," the declaration argued, "in the majority of our countries, has given rise to the superimposition of cultures. In the economic sphere systems flourished which [sic] consider solely the potential of groups with great earning power. This lack of adaptation to the characteristics and to the potentials of all our people, in turn, gives rise to frequent political instability and the consolidation of purely formal institutions."[127]

Participants at the Medellin Conference believed that overcoming social and economic oppression was necessary for achieving Christian peace. The Conference refused to support armed revolution while recognizing that continued economic inequalities would disrupt peaceful relationships. "In the face of the tensions which conspire against peace, and even present the temptation of violence," the Conference declaration stated, "we believe that the Latin American Episcopate cannot avoid assuming very concrete responsibilities; because to create a just social order, without which peace is illusory, is an eminently Christian task."[128] The declaration went on to stress that pastoral work should include education, defending the rights of the poor and oppressed, denouncing economic inequalities, creating grass-roots organizations, ending the arms race, and denouncing the unjust actions of world powers. Regarding education, it was declared, "To us, the Pastors of the Church, belongs the duty to educate the Christian conscience, to inspire, stimulate and help orient all of the initiatives that contribute to the formation of man."[129]

Liberation theology included a criticism of the ongoing efforts at economic "development." At the 1969 Campine, Switzerland meeting of the World Council of Churches Peruvian theologian Gustavo Gutiérrez raised the question of "Why development? Why not liberation?" These ideas were later incorporated in Gutiérrez's 1971 book *A Theology of Liberation*; a book that supported Paulo Freire's educational methods.[130]

In *A Theology of Liberation*, Gutiérrez defined praxis in terms acceptable to the Catholic Church. Gutiérrez wrote, "The praxis on which liberation theology reflects is a praxis of solidarity in the interests of liberation and is inspired by the gospel.... This liberating praxis endeavors to transform history in the light of the reign of God."[131] By emphasizing the reign of God, liberation theology gave a meaning to liberation and consciousness that paralleled the ideas of Freire, but retained a Christian meaning. Gutiérrez distinguished three levels of liberation. The first was liberation from oppressive economic and marginalized living conditions. The second was gaining inner freedom which could be considered similar to Freire's concepts of critical consciousness and the freedom of the biophilic personality. "But it is not enough that we be liberated from," Gutiérrez wrote, "oppressive socio-economic structures; also needed is a personal transformation by which we live with profound inner freedom in the face of every kind of servitude, and this is the second dimension or level of liberation."[132] And finally, he argued there was liberation from sin.

Similar to many other radicals, Gutiérrez urged the development of a social theory adapted to the special needs of Central and South America. He asserted that "one of the most creative and fruitful efforts implemented in Latin America is the experimental work of Paulo Freire, who has sought to establish a 'pedagogy of the oppressed.'"[133] Gutiérrez cited the work of José Carlos Mariátegui who, as I previously discussed, urged the adaptation of Marxist theories to the needs of the indigenous peoples of South and Central America. "We must bring Indo-American socialism," Gutiérrez quoted Mariátegui, "to life with our own reality, in our own language."[134] Quoting Che Guevara, Gutiérrez emphasized the importance of a new theoretical approach: "One of the great dangers which threaten the building of socialism in Latin America—pressed as it is by immediate concerns—is the lack of its own solid theory, and this theory must be Latin American, not to satisfy a desire for originality, but for the sake of elementary historical realism."[135]

Did Freire offer this original theory? Gutiérrez asserted that "one of the most creative and fruitful efforts implemented in Latin America is the experimental work of Paulo Freire, who sought to establish a 'pedagogy of the oppressed.'"[136] Summarizing Freire's ideas, Gutiérrez emphasized the development of critical consciousness through dialogue and the eventual commitment to building a new society. In Gutiérrez words, "In this process, which Freire calls 'conscientization,' the oppressed reject the oppressive consciousness which dwells in them, become aware of their situation, and find their own language. They become, by themselves, less dependent and freer, as they commit themselves to the transformation and building up of society."[137]

Despite the difference between Freire's materialist approach and liberation theology's concern about the ultimate reign of God over the process of conscientization, advocates of liberation theology embraced Freirian methods. The educational efforts of advocates of liberation theology were primarily carried out by Base Ecclesial Communities (BECs). The formation of BECs were advocated by the bishops attending the 1968 Medellin meeting which called for "small communities," "grass-roots organizations," and "collaboration ... with non-Catholic Christian Churches and institutions dedicated to the task of restoring justice in human relations."[138] In his history of liberation theology, Christian Smith offered this summary of the BECs' work: "BECs offered not only a solution to the lack of clergy but also, for the liberation theology movement, a means of educating the masses at the grass roots. Pastoral workers, utilizing Paulo Freire's method of conscientization, taught community members how to do critical social analysis."[139]

Ivan Illich's Center for Intercultural Documentation (CIDOC) in Cuernavaca, Mexico helped to spread both liberation theology and Freirian educational ideas.[140] Liberation theologists, such as Gustavo Gutiérrez, and North and South American educators, including Paulo Freire, John Holt, and Clarence Karier, gathered at CIDOC to exchange ideas on radical change and education. Illich, a former priest and supporter of liberation theology, advocated abolishing formal schooling because it had become a method of oppression. Priests and educators provided a variety of descriptions of CIDOC's influence, ranging from "shock treatment" to "jolt[ing] ... foreigners into questioning what they were doing." I first met Paulo Freire at CIDOC in 1970 and for the first time learned about his educational theories. I was one of those who carried his ideas back to North America. At CIDOC, I coedited books with liberation theologist Father Jordan Bishop, *Formative Undercurrents in Compulsory Knowledge* and with Clarence Karier and Paul Violas, *Roots of Crisis*. These books contributed to discussions of radical school reform in the United States.[141]

NICARAGUA AND EL SALVADOR: LIBERATION THEOLOGY, FREIRE, AND NATIONAL LITERACY CRUSADES

By the end of the 1970s, wars of liberation in Nicaragua and El Salvador sparked literacy crusades that reflected the influence of liberation theology and Paulo Freire's pedagogical methods. Both countries were composed of ruling elites, impoverished peasants, and indigenous peoples. In 1961, the Sandinista National Liberation Front was formed in Nicaragua, which overthrew the dictatorship of the Somoza dynasty in 1979. In neighboring El Salvador, the Farabundo Marti National Liberation Front was formed in 1980 resulting in a decade of civil war with major areas of the country captured by the Liberation Front in 1989. In both countries, literacy crusades were considered fundamental parts of the revolutionary movement.[142]

Echoing educational arguments of other Latin American Marxists, Carlos Vilas, who worked at the Ministry of Planning in Nicaragua from 1980 to 1984, explained the transformation of education under the Sandinistas: "Education in the Sandinista revolution ... is no longer a mechanism of reproducing dependent capitalist society, but on the contrary a dimension of the process of *liberation of the great popular majorities from the material and ideological conditions in which they were reproduced as exploited and oppress classes.*"[143] According to Vilas' statistics, the Nicaraguan Literacy Crusade launched on March 23, 1980 eventually involved 80,000 literacy crusade workers, which included, similar to the Cuban literacy crusade, 55,000 high school and university students; 18,000 public workers, housewives, and workers; and 7,000 professional teachers. According to Vilas in the first 5 months of the crusade illiteracy was reduced from 50.4% to 12.9% with half a million adults learning to read.[144]

Similar to Cuba, the Nicaraguan Literacy Crusade embodied the philosophy of linking literacy and pedagogical methods to revolutionary social change. In addition, there was a belief that mass involvement in educational planning was necessary for creating a progressive educational agenda. In 1981, the Ministry of Education organized a variety of local and national groups in a 2-week discussion called the National Consultation with the goal of giving ideological direction to the education of the "so-called new man."[145] Vilas summarized the Ministry of Education report: "the National Consultation demanded new education that ties study to work and theory to practice.... The new education should be one that accompanies and promotes the revolutionary process, that eliminates individualism and opportunism, and that contributes to forming a new human being and a new society."[146]

The official director of the Literacy Crusade was liberation theologian Father Fernando Cardenal who proclaimed at the beginning of the crusade in language similar to that of Paulo Freire, "Literacy is fundamental to achieving progress and it is essential to the building of a democratic society.... You learn to read and write so you can identify the reality in which you live, so that you can become a protagonist of history rather than a spectator."[147]

The revolutionary intention of the Nicaraguan Literacy Crusade was captured in the song sung by the educational workers or Brigadistas.

Brigadistas' Hymn

Ever onwards, Brigadista,

Staunch guerrillas of the

Literacy Crusade.

Your Machete is the primer

To kill ignorance and error

With just one fell swoop.

Ever onwards, Brigadista,

Many centuries of ignorance

Will fall

We'll erect our barricades

Of notebooks and blackboards,

Let's go onwards

To the cultural revolt,

Fists on high! Books open!

Everybody's in the national

Crusade

We'll earn our destiny

As children of Sandino

Bringing clarity where there

Was only darkness before.[148]

In actual practice, literacy instruction deviated from Freire's dialogical model. Like the Cuban literacy crusade, instructional materials bordered on political indoctrination. Freirian methods required a dialogue about a thematic representation where the teacher assumed that the meaning of the theme would emerge from the participants. In the Nicaraguan crusade, the thematic approach was used to convey a particular political message. In other words, participants did not learn that their knowledge could be a direct source of understanding the world. For instance, the Brigadistas used a 10-step instructional formula which began: "1. The presentation of an evocative photo from the primer to stimulate dialogue within the class, *leading to the conclusion expressed by the short sentence that followed* [my emphasis]." The following eight steps dealt with separating words by syllables and reading and writing sentences using these syllables. The final step was: "The muestra, or demonstration—a phrase or motto to be copied in the student's best handwriting."[149]

Freire advocated using themes directly related to the lives of the participants. However, the primer created for the Nicaraguan literacy crusade had as its first thematic representation a photo of Augusto Sandino, after whom the Sandinistas were named, who led a guerrilla campaign against the U.S. presence in Nicaragua from 1927 to 1933. Besides being a photograph that was at least 47 years old, the photo hardly represented the working lives and culture of the people in the 1980s. Underscoring the political propaganda aspects of the literacy campaign, the first lesson was titled "Sandino—Guide of the Revolution."[150]

Sheryl Hirshon, who participated in the literacy crusade, reported the following dialogue about Augusto Sandino's thematic photo. There is little in this dialogue that represents the Freirian idea of the participants creating their own consciousness of their objective lives.

> Let's look, then, at this picture. Do any of you know who it
>
> is? That's right, it's Sandino. How do you know? Oh, you
>
> saw his picture in Muy Muy. Well, look at him here. What's
>
> he wearing.... What did he do that was so special? That's
>
> right, you got it. He fought against the Yankees when they
>
> invaded Nicaragua.... So we've come to a sort of
>
> conclusion here. You've said that it was Sandino that really
>
> began the revolution. Well here, to begin the lesson, is one
>
> way of putting the idea. I'll write it on the blackboard and
>
> then let's read the phrase.

Sandino-Guide of the Revolution[151]

The group leader continued the lesson by teaching the syllables in the words "the Revolution."

In El Salvador, the continuing guerrilla war interfered with the literacy crusade. Sociologist John Hammond concluded that liberation theology and the teaching methods of Paulo Freire played major roles prompting the armed struggle. In Hammond's words, "During the 1970s a political movement arose in the Salvadoran countryside that led to the decade-long revolt of the 1980s. Innovative church people inspired by liberation theology formed Christian base communities in rural parishes, and from these a new political consciousness emerged."[152] However, these Christian communities often gave a theological twist to Freirian methods of using thematic representation. In one typical situation, Hammond described the use of the Bible as the thematic representation used to explore local political and economic injustices.

Also, battlefield conditions did not allow for lengthy dialogues leading to conscientization. Rather than providing learners with thematic representations that were intended to provoke open-ended discussions, thematic representations were made specific to the war. For instance, consider the following answers from a battlefield literacy worker to questions posed by Hammond. In this case, the literacy worker indicated a specific direction for a discussion about the word "shovel" rather than letting the learners engage in an open-ended dialogue.

Literacy worker: We always taught class based on the situation we were living in.

Hammond: What aspects of the situation did you pay most attention to?

Literacy worker: Well, the course of the war, more than anything. For example, we could use the word *pala*, and we had a short dialogue about what a shovel was for: to dig trenches to fight the enemy.[153]

Because reading material was scarce on the front lines, the most available text was *The Fifteen Principles of the Guerrilla Combatant*, which contained illustrations representing principles such as "We will be aggressive and bold in combat," and "We will respect prisoners and work to convince enemy soldiers to abandon the army of the rich."[154]

Liberation theologist Father Rogelio Ponceele insisted that literacy instruction using the methods of conscientization was too slow. "I insisted," Father Ponceele stated, "that it had to be something quicker, the traditional method, because it was urgent to learn and the campas already had enough political instruction."[155] Some guerilla leaders believed political education was essential to the struggle. Therefore, there were open discussions of political principles among the guerillas. Hammond quotes guerrilla fighters: "We weren't guerrilla fighters just to fight, but to raise ourselves up and develop ourselves culturally. The purpose wasn't just to spew bullets, but to learn" and "We said we don't want to create an army that just thinks about taking up a rifle and killing, with a militarist attitude."[156]

Off the battlefield, El Salvador's literacy workers adhered more closely to Freirian methods. The frequently used text was *Literacy for Peace*, which contained photos to be used as thematic representations. Sociologist Hammond observed one group where the literacy worker presented the poster-size photograph of an illustration in the text depicting two men in straw hats with machetes walking down a road. The literacy leader asked the participants what they saw in the photo. After describing the details of the photo, the participants, in an ideal Freirian dialogue, led the dialogue to a consideration of the cost of seed and fertilizer, and the economics of farming in El Salvador. The dialogue provided the generative words for literacy instruction.[157]

In summary, wars of liberation in Nicaragua and El Salvador provided important arenas for the implementation of liberation theology and Freirian methods. Under the stress of revolution and guerilla warfare, Freirian methods were often dispensed with for direct political indoctrination. The reality was that the dialogical process required a great deal of time and instructional leaders who understood the basic principles of the method. Many leaders seemed more concerned about teaching a particular political ideology than letting a political ideology emerge from a dialogical process. In this manner, local cultures might not have been given the opportunity to develop political ideas tied to their own local conditions.

CONCLUSION

Conceived in the age of wars of liberation, Paulo Freire's *Pedagogy of the Oppressed* gave new life to progressive forms of education. Similar to other progressive forms of education since the time of John Dewey, Freire's method was to help people understand how material conditions produced knowledge and how they could participate in creating new knowledge and changing society. Besides the recognition of the importance of cultural and language differences, Freire added an important dimension to progressive theory by emphasizing the importance of how people's subjective views might distort their understanding of objective conditions. His dialogical method was designed to have people reflect on their subjective views of reality and change those views as they gained greater understanding of what caused the social conditions in which they lived.

Freire was not isolated from the global flow of educational ideas. He lived in the political turmoil of South American society where progressives were trying to adapt Marxists ideas to the particular conditions of the region. These influential Latin American Marxists were also influenced by global progressive ideas, particularly Gramsci's ideas about hegemony. Cuba's revolution and literacy crusade became a powerful symbol for social change and for how peasant language and culture could be protected and utilized in education. The Cultural Revolution and Mao's teachings influenced efforts to increase equality of educational opportunity and reduce the power of elites over school systems. As I suggested, there was a similarity between Freire and Mao's educational philosophies.

However, wars of liberation produced formal types of education along with progressive types. In the next chapter, I begin with a discussion of how wars of liberation in Korea, Africa, and India perpetuated formal methods of schooling. Freire's concept of "banking education" became a apt method for describing the formal school systems resulting from these other wars of liberation.

Wars of Liberation and Formal Schooling: India, Africa, the Middle East, Indonesia, and Korea

Formal educational systems introduced by imperialist powers remained in postcolonialist nations of the Middle East, the Indian subcontinent, Sub-Saharan Africa, and Korea. An important factor in the globalization of the Euroamerican school model was the transformation of Islamic education. Similar to Japan and China, Islamic nations were attracted to Western science and technology, but worried about Western ideas corrupting Islamic values. Traditional Islamic education was integrated into the formal structure of Euroamerican schools in the Middle East, the Indian Subcontinent, Malaysia, and Sub-Saharan Africa. In addition, new nations in Sub-Saharan Africa retained colonial education structures. In the Democratic People's Republic of Korea, Soviet educational traditions combined with the personal educational philosophy of the nation's leader Kim Il Sung to create an educational security state. In this context, the school system of the Democratic People's Republic of Korea could be considered a product of Soviet imperialism.

In reaction to imperialism, many of these countries used schools to promote new forms of nationalism. These new nationalistic movements supported authoritarian forms of pedagogy, particularly in Islamic nations. In addition, authoritarian pedagogy continued in former colonies in Sub-Saharan Africa. In India, English educational traditions remained along with attempts to protect tribal and local cultures. In the Democratic People's Republic of Korea, Kim Il Sung implement his own form of socialist education.

In this chapter, I first analyze the intersection of Western and Islamic educational traditions and the evolution of educational systems in Islamic countries after the collapse of Western imperialism. I then consider the evolution of schooling in Malaysia, Pakistan, India, and Sub-Saharan Africa after their liberation. And finally, the chapter concludes with an examination of socialist education in the Democratic People's Republic of Korea.

ARAB NATIONS:
ISLAMIC VALUES AND WESTERN TECHNOLOGY

Similar to Japan and China, Arab leaders in the 19th century were forcefully confronted with the dilemma of how to utilize Euroamerican military science and technology to resist imperialism without undermining Islamic moral values. Four factors influenced how Arab educational systems responded to this dilemma. First was the long standing religious conflict between Christianity and Islam. Second was the status of Islamic education in each Arab country. Third were regional and historical differences between Arab nations. And lastly, there were differences between colonial educational policies, particularly the French and British. In *Islam & Modernity*, Fazlur Rahman's list of factors is slightly different than mine. His list does not include the historical antagonism between Christianity and Islam. His four factors are:

> (1) whether a particular cultural region retained its sovereignty vis-à-vis the European political expansion ...; (2) the character of the organization of the ulema, or religious leadership ...; (3) the state of development of Islamic education ...; (4) the character of the overall colonial policy of the particular colonizing power—British, French, or Dutch.[1]

Differences in religious doctrines made Islamic scholars wary of wholesale adoption of Western science and technology. Of course, the major issue was the dispute over the divinity of Christ. Christianity was founded on the premise that Jesus Christ was the son of God, whereas Islam recognized Jesus Christ as a prophet. Jerusalem was important to both Christians and Moslems because the Prophet Mohammed was led by God to the city for a miraculous meeting with Moses and Jesus. The meeting of Mohammed, Jesus, and Moses represents the continuity of the divine message of Moslem faith. Both religions divided the world between believers and nonbelievers. Christian colonizers believed that it was their God-given duty to convert "pagans" to Christianity.[2] Islam saw the world as divided between Moslems and infidels. This view of a divided world is clearly stated in the *Qur'an*:

> God is the friend of those who believe, and leads them out of darkness into light; but the patrons of infidels are idols and devils who lead them from light into darkness. They are the residents of Hell, and will there forever abide. (2:257).[3]

This religious antagonism was heightened by years of war between Christianity and Islam. In 1095, the Christian Crusades began with the goal of capturing the city of Jerusalem. This effort continued until the 13th century. From the Christian perspective, the goal was to rescue the city where Christ was crucified from the pagan Moslems. From the Islamic perspective, the goal was to protect the holy city where Mohamed met with Jesus and Moses. For centuries, students in the West were taught that the Crusades were an heroic venture by knights in shining armor marching off to rescue the Holy Land. From the Moslem perspective, the Crusades were an unexpected invasion by a barbarous and heathen army dressed in white sheets marked with red crosses followed by a rag-tag crowd of religious fanatics and prostitutes. At the siege of Antioch in 1097, the Crusaders were described by Islamic historians as roasting Moslem spies on spits and eating them as crowds watched in horror from the city walls. Once inside the walls, the Crusaders purportedly raped and killed women and slaughtered all the men.[4]

The military expansion of the Ottoman empire in the late 13th century continued the ongoing military conflict between Islam and Christianity. Moslem Turks captured and renamed the holy city of Eastern Christian Orthodoxy, from Constantinople to Istanbul in 1453 and they were at the walls of Vienna by 1529. According to Amin Maalouf, the result of Ottoman penetration was that the best of Arab civilization in the form of mathematics, science, medicine, astronomy, and architecture was imitated, absorbed, and surpassed by Euroamericans after the Crusades. Exemplifying 19th- and 20th-century Arab nationalism, Maalouf claimed "The Franj (Euroamerican) learned much in the Arab school, in Syria as in Spain and Sicily. What they learned from the Arabs was indispensable in their subsequent expansion."[5]

In the 19th century, traditional Islamic education began to change as Arabs tried to equal Western military organization and technology and resist colonialism. Prior to roughly the 19th century, Islamic scholars teaching in madrasas focused on issues of theology and law. The *Qur'an* called for the creation of a society based on community, socioeconomic justice, and human egalitarianism. The goal of scholars was to achieve this type of society by formulating laws based on the *Qur'an* and the *Hadith*. The *Qur'an* was the very Word of God, whereas the *Hadith* was a collection of the sayings of Mohammed. Religious and legal scholars consulted both the *Qur'an* and the *Hadith* to determine how human relationships should be regulated. As human society changed, new laws were required to ensure a just society.

In their search for just laws and a just society, madrasa scholars wrote commentaries on the *Qur'an* and the *Hadith*, and commentaries on the commentaries. Fazlur Rahman argued that this involved a deductive form of scholarship using the following method: "First one must move from the concrete case treatments of the *Qur'an*—taking the necessary and relevant social conditions of that time into account—to the general principles upon which the entire teaching converges. Second, from this general level there must be a movement back to specific legislation, taking into account the necessary and relevant conditions now obtaining."[6] This scholarship formed the *Sharia* or Scared Law, which in the 20th century was included in the constitutions of many Arab nations.

Education of children was given in maktabs and kuttabs using oral instruction to help students memorize the *Qur'an* with some teaching of reading, writing, and arithmetic. Prior to the 19th and 20th centuries, primary education was self-contained and was not considered part of an educational ladder leading to study at a madrasa. In other words, there was no institutional structure similar to the Euroamerican educational ladder.[7]

The desire of their political rulers to study and utilize increasingly superior Western military technology and organization caused Islamic scholars to worry about how to protect Islamic values. Five so-called Islamic modernists (Syyid Ahamd Khan and Sayyid Amir' Ali of India, Jamal al-Din Al-Afhani and Namik Kemal of Turkey, and Shaykh Muhammad Abduh of Egypt) provided the rationalization for the teaching of Western science and technology. They argued that the West developed science by utilizing the early discoveries of Moslem scholars from the 9th to the 13th century. Islamic study of science was based on the *Qur'an*'s requirement that humans study the handiwork of God. In studying Western science, they argued, Muslims were recovering their past and fulfilling the demands of the *Qur'an*. Although Islamic scholarship declined during the middle ages, these scholars argued that it could be revived by combining the study of Islamic values with science.[8]

Of these Islamic modernists, Shaykh Muhammad Abduh is considered to have had the greatest influence over Arab education. In Egypt, he stressed that the true goal of education was the cultivation of human character according to the principles of Islam. He objected to the foreign schools in Egypt with declaration: "Let parents refrain from sending their children to foreign schools that tend to change their habits and religious faith."[9] Muhammad Abduh argued that national education systems should include religious education. Regarding Egyptian national education, Abduh wrote, "If one seeks to educate and improve the Egyptian nation without religion, it is as if a farmer would try to sow seed in unsuitable soil … his efforts will be in vain."[10]

After relocating to Beirut, Abduh wrote memorandums on school reform to religious authorities in Istanbul. A major complaint was that the curriculum of specialized schools, particularly military and science schools, lacked moral and religious instruction. He complained about the use of foreign textbooks that denigrated Islamic countries. In addition, he complained that Arab students in Euroamerican schools were being alienated from their Islamic cultures.

Of particular importance for Abduh was the use of Arabic as the medium of classroom instruction. Although foreign schools used Euroamerican languages as the medium of instruction, many Arab schools used Turkish because of the influence of the Ottoman empire. Abduh advocated the use of Arabic for religious and nationalist reasons. First, knowledge of Arabic was essential for reading the *Qur'an*. Second, because culture and language were intimately bound together, preservation of Arab culture against the inroad of Euroamerican culture required the preservation of the Arab language.[11] Thus, Abduh articulated a form of schooling that heightened Arab nationalism.

EUROPEAN IMPERIALISM AND ARAB EDUCATION

In the late 18th and 19th centuries, France, Great Britain, and Italy colonized Egypt, Algeria, Libya, and Tunisia. In 1798, Napoleon's armies marched into Egypt. During their 3-year occupation, the French impressed Egyptian leaders with their military organization. When Muhammad Ali came to power after the French withdrawal, he decided to study Euroamerican military organization. In *Putting Islam to Work: Politics and Religious Transformation in Egypt*, Gregory Starrett summarized Muhammad Ali's impact on Egyptian education, "It was his effort to consolidate control over Egypt and gain military parity with Europe that motivated the initial importation of the Euroamerican-style school to Egypt."[12]

Muhammad Ali sent young Egyptian men to France to study military science and technology and he opened a military school that taught Turkish, Italian, military tactics, the use of military equipment, and, of course, the *Qur'an*. In 1824, Muhammad Ali allowed a French military mission onto Egyptian soil as part of an effort to improve the military training of Egyptian troops. In addition, Muhammad Ali established medical, pharmaceutical, engineering, applied chemistry, and veterinary schools.[13]

Muhammad Ali's successor, Abbas I (1849–1854), expanded Euroamerican influence by sending Egyptian men on educational missions to Bavaria, Berlin, England, Italy, and Vienna. The largest missions were to Bavaria and Berlin. These missions played an important role in the development of Arab nationalism in the 20th century.[14] In addition, foreign Christian missionaries established schools. By 1878, it was reported that 52% of Egyptian students were in schools operated by foreign governments and missionaries.[15] In 1882, the British occupied Egypt bringing the country under increasing Euroamerican influence.[16]

In Egypt, kuttabs (local *Qur'anic* schools) were integrated into an educational ladder leading to secondary military and other specialized schools. The traditional kuttabs were quite different from Euroamerican primary schools and their transformation was an example of Euroamerican influence on Islamic education. In Egyptian kuttabs, the primary educational goal was memorization of *Qur'an* which provided little preparation for entrance in advanced specialized schools. In kuttabs, students recited the *Qur'an* while rocking back and forth. It was believed that the rocking motion jogged the memory. At the time of Muhammad Ali's ascendancy to power there were no printed texts and instruction relied on oral instruction with students writing on slates. The first printed book used in Egyptian schools appeared in 1834. It was a printed version of a 8th century legal commentary.[17]

The difference between instruction in kuttabs and Euroamerican primary schools was reflected in the reaction of Euroamericans to classroom instruction. Gregory Starrett provided many examples of how different Islamic education seemed to Euroamericans. For instance, an English writer, James Augustus St. John, visiting Egypt in 1832 and 1833, provided this Euroamerican perspective on Islamic instructional methods, "While studying, or rather learning to repeat, their lessons, each boy declaims his portion of the *Qur'an* aloud at the same time, rocking his body to and fro, according to their theory, to assist the memory; and as everyone seems desirous of drowning the voices of his companions, the din produced by so many shrill discordant notes reminds one of the 'laborers of Babel'."[18] In an 1892 publication, *England in Egypt*, Alfred Milner, the under secretary for finance during the British rule of Egypt, offered this disdainful description of Islamic educational methods: "... to sit on the ground swinging your body backwards and forwards, and continually repeating, in a monotonous chant, a quantity of matter which you are taught to regard with religious reverence, but never taught to understand, is, if anything, an anti-educational process."[19]

The British implemented policies that modeled England's primary schools. For the British, primary schools were considered a means of preparing future workers and providing a means of social control to avoid political and labor unrest. Through a system of grants, teacher certification and inspections, Egyptian officials attempted to convert kuttabs from simple centers for memorization of the *Qur'an* to schools that focused on the teaching of reading, writing, and arithmetic. These changes were intended to transfer the traditional responsibility for socialization for work from village life to the school.[20]

In addition, religious education was adapted to a Euroamerican model. In Euroamerican schools, religion served the purpose of teaching moral standards for the purpose of social control of masses of people. In the

United States, Horace Mann stressed the importance of avoiding controversial religious issues in favor of teaching basic moral standards of conduct. The same thing was true in British-government schools, particularly
as planned by Joseph Lancaster for charity schools. Religion would continue to be an important part of government schools in Islamic countries
with religion being studied in relationship to personal conduct and to Arab
nationalism. As Starrett concluded, "The traditional study of the *Qur'an*,
whose purpose had been to learn [memorize] how to use the scared word in
appropriate contexts, now became the study of Islam as a moral system, a
study removed from its living context and placed on the same level as other
secular categories of knowledge."[21]

In 1830, France occupied Algeria, which, at the time, was part of the Ottoman empire. After overcoming violent resistance by the local population,
the French implemented education policies to change the culture of the
country (Frenchification). By French law, Algeria was incorporated into
metropolitan France and large amounts of land were confiscated from the
local population. The French government sent mass numbers of French to
Algeria to settle on the confiscated lands. Schools, like those in France, were
established for French settlers. Franco-Musulman schools were established
for the indigenous population. These schools, along with those for French
settlers, used French as the medium of instruction and followed a French
curriculum. Arabic was taught in Franco-Musulman schools as a foreign
language.[22] However, similar to French policies in Indochina, educational
opportunities for the Arab population were severely limited. For instance in
1944 only 110,000 Moslem children were actually in school, out of a school
age population 1,250,000.[23]

The French followed similar policies of Frenchification in Tunisia, which
it claimed as a protectorate in 1881. French schools were established that
used the curriculum of metropolitan French schools with the medium of instruction in French. Separate Franco-Arab schools used the French curriculum with the addition of local instructors to teach Arabic and religion.[24] In
Syria, which France occupied as a League of Nation Trust after World War I,
France continued its colonial education policies by requiring the teaching
of French and adapting the local school curricula to French models.[25]

ARAB NATIONALISM AND EDUCATION

After World War I, Arab nationalism was ignited by the increasing European domination of the Arab world. World War I brought the end to the
far-reaching Ottoman empire and the establishment of a secular Moslem
republic in Turkey. After World War I, the British, Italian, and French
controlled Egypt, Libya, Algeria and Tunisia. Syria was divided into the

republics of Lebanon and Syria and became French-mandated territories. British gained control of Iraq and Palestine. Military conflict between Christian Euroamericans and Islamic Arabs continued after World I. In Libya, the Italians followed colonial policies similar to those of France. Shortly after occupation of Libya, the Italian minister for the colony declared that the primary purpose of elementary education in Libya should be "a progressive and efficient penetration of the native minds by the Italian language and spirit."[26]

Inevitably, Arabs revolted against European domination. Educational concerns were central to Arab concerns. A. L. Tibawi, Arab educator and Professor at University of London Institute of Education, provided the following summary of the status of Euroamerican and Arab relations after World War I: "The whole Arab world was up in arms against its European masters. The greatest scores to be settled were with Britain and France.... In a deeper sense, however, it [the Arab revolt] was cultural and educational: the Arabs were no where satisfied with the conduct of the education service by foreign masters."[27] According to Tibawi, the reaction of Arab leaders, many of whom had been educated in Europe, was "disillusionment with European liberalism and disappointment at the failure of two great powers to conduct their policy according to the best principles in their own tradition."[28]

Sati' al-Husri, a prominent advocate of Arab nationalism, was born into a Syrian family in Yemen in 1882. He studied in Paris, Switzerland, and Belgium. During World War I, he was appointed Ottoman Director of Education in Syria. After the War, he became responsible for Education and Archaeology at the University of Baghdad. After a number of other education posts, he moved to Egypt where he joined the Cultural Department of the Arab League in 1947 and founded the Institute for Advanced Arab Studies in 1953. Eventually, he became chair of Arab Nationalism at the Institute. His writings became compulsory readings in nationalist school systems throughout the Arab world. He died in December 1968 leaving behind a vast collection of writings on Arab nationalism. His ideas are included in many of the constitutions of the Arab world.

Al-Husri believed national education was the key to revitalizing the Arab world and awakening the oppressed people of the Islamic world. He argued that the teaching of history should emphasize the "glorious past in order to provide a basis for the national awakening."[29] He contended that national education was the key to Arab unity. He wrote, "The struggle for the national awakening requires much more effort and hardship to spread belief in the nation, and all available means must be used to strengthen this belief."[30]

Attracted to German romantic notions of nationalism, Al-Husri argued that history was the consciousness of a nation while language was its soul.

The foremost means of maintaining Arab culture and saving it from Euroamerican domination was the preservation of the Arab language. He wrote, "A common language and a common history is the basis of nation formation and nationalism. The union of these two spheres lead to a union of emotions, aims, sufferings, hopes, and culture."[31] In addition, Al-Husri was attracted to the militaristic aspects of German nationalism and considered military service a means for achieving a national education. He declared, "The barracks are as much institutes for national education as national schools."[32]

Arab nationalism received support from traditional Islamic ideas of the role of political authority. It was believed that political authority was needed to ensure that human desires for food and sex did not lead to human conflict and ultimately destruction of the human race. Of course, this political authority had to be guided by Sacred Law (the *Sharia*) in its restriction and punishment of human behavior. Early Islamic scholar al-Qasim ibu Ibrahim stated, "People need a guide to teach them these restrictions [religious], and this guide is the Imam [leader of the religious community and/or head of state]. Also the Imam punishes people if they disobey him, and reward them if they obey him. In this manner people are kept safe."[33]

In the context of this theory of the state, the head of the state has the obligation to follow the *Sharia* and to enforce its moral restrictions. In addition, the head of state is obligated to ensure that the population receives a religious education. In the context of Arab nationalism, this meant that the head of state was required to advance the study and use of Arabic, promote Arab history and patriotism in the schools, instill a sense of belonging to an Islamic community, ensure the religious instruction of children and youth, and follow the *Sharia*. The 1964 Covenant of Arab Cultural Unity states as its educational aim: "The creation of generations of Arabs, believing in God, loyal to the Arab homeland ... armed with science and morals, so as to share in the advancement of Arab society by maintaining the position of the glorious Arab nation."[34]

"Arab socialism" added another dimension to nationalistic impulses and to educational ideals. Today, socialism is frequently referred to in the constitutions of Arab nations. This form of socialism should not be confused with Marxism. The leading advocate of Arab socialism, Michel 'Aflaq explained,

> When I am asked to give a definition of socialism, I can say that it is not to be found in the works of Marx and Lenin. I say: socialism is the religion of life, and of its victory over death. By giving work to everyone and helping them to develop their talents it keeps the patrimony of life for life, and leaves for death only dried up flesh and scorched bones.[35]

Arab socialism embodied the teachings on charity expressed in the *Qur'an* along with the concept of *umma* (community). In Islamic thought, the *umma* stands above the individual. The individual in Islam is an organic part of the *umma*. This concept of community reinforces nationalistic ideals. Within Arab socialism and nationalism, the state is the organic community in which the person is an organic part. The goal of nationalistic education is to wed the individual to the *umma* as represented by the state.[36]

Islamic socialism was also portrayed as midway between the extremes of Euroamerican capitalism and Soviet-style communism. Islamic socialism recognized the right of private ownership of property, but in the context that God was the real owner. As trustees of God's property, human owners had a duty to provide for the poor. In 1949, the Prime Minister of Pakistan explained, "Islamic socialism ... means that every person in this land has equal rights to be provided with food, shelter, clothing, education, and medical facilities."[37]

ARAB WARS OF LIBERATION: EGYPT AND THE EDUCATIONAL SECURITY STATE

After World War II, Arab nations joined other colonies in throwing off the yoke of European imperialism. The resulting Arab educational systems retained the Euroamerican educational ladder with an emphasis on Arab nationalism. The goal of most new educational systems was to balance Islam and Euroamerican science and technology with requirements of the national security state. Writing about current Arab nationalism, A. L. Tibawi concluded, "The content of modern Arab education is now ... European.... In the scientific and technical field the subject matter is, to a great extent, European, and is mostly taught, particularly in universities, through the medium of one European language or another."[38] Arab nations adopted the Euroamerican education ladder of elementary or primary education leading to secondary education and from there to college or university. In keeping with Arab nationalism, most Arab countries used Arabic as the medium of instruction in elementary and secondary schools and they required some form of religious education. In addition, courses were taught on Arab history and Islamic civilization.

The Arab educational security state combined Islamic traditions, European influences, and Arab nationalism. The newly formed Arab states followed the model of Euroamerican constitutionalism. Arab constitutions established nation states in which education was integrated into economic and military development to support nationalism and militarism. Abiding by religious traditions, Arab constitutions recognized the governing power of the *Sharia* and the obligation for newly formed governments to provide schooling. Leaders in newly established Arab nations believed that religious instruction in national school systems would act as a form of social control by regulating the behavior of citizens. Also, Arab school systems promoted Arab nationalism through the teaching of national histories, Arab literature, and Islamic civilization. In various forms, Arab national school systems promoted patriotism through pictures of leaders and flags hung in classrooms, and nationalistic songs and ceremonies. Leaders of newly formed Arab states after World War II integrated education systems into economic planning. Therefore, the combination of using national school systems to control public behavior, promote nationalism, and aid in economic development made education central to these newly formed states.

Highly authoritarian and formal school systems emerged from Arab liberation movements. Progressive education never found its way into Arab Islamic traditions. Most teachers used instructional techniques that were a combination of formal Euroamerican and traditional Islamic methods. Reflecting Islamic traditions, emphasis was still placed on memorization of textual materials, oral recitation, and respect for the authority of the teacher. Textbooks replaced the oral teachings of kuttabs. Teachers were now transmitters and commentators on officially approved texts. There was frequent testing based on memorized sections of the text.[39]

In 1945, Egypt joined with Syria, Iraq, Lebanon, Saudi Arabia, Syria, Transjordan (later Jordan) to form the League of Arab States or, as it was more popularly known, the Arab League.[40] The Arab League promoted Arab nationalism. Article II of the 1945 Charter of the League of Arab States declared: "The league has as its purpose the strengthening of the relations between the member-states, the coordination of their policies in order to achieve co-operation between them and to safeguard their independence and sovereignty; and a general concern with the affairs and interests of the Arab countries."[41]

Arab League members wanted to protect the Arab language from the eroding forces of colonial European languages. An official Arab League document explained: "Arabs take pride in their language and give it great importance, as it is the one feature that identifies Arabs and giving them identity. Thus, a language center was established featuring some of the most prominent professors in linguistics and other fields to adapt the language with the new terminologies of the times and to maintain Arabic as a livening language as it has remained throughout the centuries."[42]

Arab League leaders linked Arab nationalism to the founding of the Islamic religion on Arab soil and to its spread as part of the "Arab/Islam Empire." It was the Arab/Islam empire, according to the Arab League's document on "Arab Civilization," that made possible the development of Western science.

The Prophet Muhammad appeared in the seventh century AD carrying the message of Islam. His followers soon spread the new faith in the West, across North Africa into Spain and France, and in the East, to the borders of China.

But these Muslim believers were not merely conquerors. They rapidly established a new and dynamic civilization that for centuries was the only bright light in an otherwise culturally and intellectually stagnant world. *While Europe was experiencing its "Dark Ages," the Arab/Islamic Empire was at its apogee. It was the same Islamic civilization, with its many contributions to science and the humanities that paved the way for the rise of the West to its present prominence* [my emphasis].[43]

Education was promoted as part of Arab nationalism. The Arab League stressed the importance of schooling by quoting the *Qur'an* that: "it is the duty of every Muslim man and woman to seek education." In the context of Arab nationalism, the Arab League provided this equalitarian description Islamic educational traditions to counter Euroamerican stereotypes.

Historians such as Ibn Khallikan reported that women also taught classes in which men took lessons. Few Westerners recognize the extent to which Arab women contributed to the social, economic and political life of the empire. Arab women excelled in medicine, mysticism, poetry, teaching, and oratory and even took active roles in military conflicts. Current misconceptions are based on false stereotypes of Arab life and culture popularized by some journalists and "Orientalists."

In the mosque schools, rich and poor alike attended classes freely. Classes were held at specific times and announced in advance by the teacher. Students could attend several classes a day, sometimes traveling from one mosque to another. Teachers were respected by their students and there were formal, if unwritten, rules of behavior. Laughing, talking, joking or disrespectful behavior of any kind were not permitted.[44]

Egypt exemplified the rise of Arab nationalism in education and the implementation of Euroamerican educational traditions. In 1952, Egyptian military officers overthrew a puppet monarchy created by the British and established a constitutional republic under the leadership of Gamal Abdel Nasser of the Revolutionary Command Council that had planned the revolution. In 1954 Nasser became prime minister and was elected president in 1956. Nationalistic spirit immediately infected the Egyptian school system with students being required to chant "Nasser! Nasser! Nasser!" and recited revolutionary slogans.[45]

The Egyptian constitution and educational system is a blend of historic Islamic doctrines, European influences, and Arab nationalism and socialism. In keeping with the tenets of Arab socialism, Article I of the Egyptian constitution declares: "The Arab Republic of Egypt is a Socialist Democratic State based on the alliance of the working forces of the people."[46] Article 2 links the Arab language with the *Sharia*: "Islam is the Religion of the State. Arabic is its official language, and the principal source of legislation is Islamic Jurisprudence (*Sharia*)."[47] Islamic political principles require the state to regulate moral values. In the Egyptian constitution, this obligation encompassed promotion of nationalism and socialism. Part Two, Article 12 of Chapter I of the Constitution, "Social and Moral Constituents," stated, "Society shall be committed to safeguarding and protecting morals, promoting the genuine Egyptian traditions and abiding by the high standards of religious education, moral and national values, the historical heritage of the people, scientific facts, socialist conduct and public manners within the limits of the law. The State is committed to abiding by these principles and promoting them."[48]

Religious education is identified as central by the Egyptian constitution. Article 19 of Chapter I specifically stated: "Religious education shall be a principal subject in the courses of general education."[49] Preceding this dictum, Article 18 declared: "Education is a right guaranteed by the State. It is obligatory in the primary stage. The State shall work to extend obligation to other stages. The State shall supervise all branches of education and guarantee the independence of universities and scientific research centers, with a view to linking all this with the requirements of society and production."[50]

First, it should be noted, Article 18 integrates schools into the new Egyptian nation state with the phrase "with a view to linking all this with the requirements of society and production." Second, Egyptian schools are to promote nationalism. Nationalism combined with religious education makes schooling a system of social control. Under Nasser, religious study in primary schools focuses on traditional religious values and students' obligations to society and duties to the government.[51] The use of textbooks in religious study transformed the traditional method of memorization of the *Qur'an*. Now, religious textbooks contained quotes from the *Qur'an* along with vocabulary lists and summaries. Stories were used to illustrate proper behavior according to Islamic traditions and, of course, to ensure an orderly society. And, in keeping the formal methods of Euroamerican traditions, textbooks contained lists of religious-behavioral rules to be memorized for examinations.[52]

Like other Arab countries, Egypt continues using the Euroamerican educational ladder with a compulsory requirement of 8 years of education broken down into 5 years of primary education (Grades 1–5) and three years of preparatory education (Grades 6–8). After preparatory school, students can choose to enter a variety of secondary schools, ranging from vocational, general, technical, and military. It is important to note that the organization of secondary education is geared to the economic needs of the nation.[53]

The equivalency between the Egyptian and United States educational ladder is shown in the guidelines used by the American Association of Collegiate Registrars and Admissions Officers for the placement of Egyptian students in U.S. schools. According to these guidelines, a student holding a certificate from a preparatory school (8 years of Egyptian education) should be placed in the 10th grade of a U.S. high school and those holding certificates from a general secondary school should be considered for admission as 1st-year students in U.S. universities.[54]

The merger of Islamic religious education, Western science and technology, Arab nationalism, and education for economic planning are exemplified by the curriculum for Egyptian primary schools (Grades 1–5). The greatest numbers of class periods in the curriculum are devoted to religious education, Arabic language, and mathematics.

Egyptian Primary Curriculum, 1990–1991

>Religious Education
>
>Arabic Language
>
>Mathematics
>
>Social Studies
>
>Science and Health
>
>Observation of Nature
>
>Technical Education (industrial subject, agriculture, or home economics)
>
>Physical Education
>
>Music and/or Art
>
>Practical/Technical Training[55]

ALGERIA: REVOLUTION AND THE STRUGGLE FOR A NATIONAL IDENTITY AND LANGUAGE

Following the Algerian revolution against France, schools were enlisted in an effort to create a national identity and language. In 1954, the National Liberation Front (FLN) led the revolt against French rule. With many casualties on both sides, the revolution lasted until 1962. After the war, the formation of a new national state was complicated by the large number of French European settlers who had colonized the country.[56] Post-revolutionary educational changes attempted to follow the FLN's credo that "Islam is our religion, Arabic is our language, Algeria is our fatherland."[57] In keeping with this credo, the overall goal for the new school system was to educate "a participant but obedient public, trained to assume the technical requirements of a scientifically developing society although maintaining, indeed reinforcing the Arab-Islamic identity."[58]

There were four important factors hindering the development of a common identity while pursuing a path of economic development. First, prior to French colonization it was not clear that Algeria had a "collective identity." This meant that revolutionary leaders had to invent a national identity; this task, in part, was eventually given to the school system. Second, Arabic was not the original language of all native peoples, such as the Berbers and Kabyles. Third, the Arabic spoken by the Algerian population was different from that identified as classical and modern literary Arabic. Fourth, revolutionary literature had been written in French and 95% of the its political leadership were educated in France along with almost all of its scientists and technical experts.[59]

Through teaching Arabic and national history, schools were enlisted in the process of creating a national identity; an essential process in nation building. The use of history to help people imagine a national identity was exemplified by the text of the Preamble to the 1976 Algerian constitution and Article 8: "The People set up institutions having as objectives: the safeguard [ing] and consolidation of the national identity and unity."[60] The Preamble presents this interpretation of the nation's history:

> Its history is a long series of struggles which always made Algeria a land of freedom and dignity. Being at the heart of great events witnessed by the Mediterranean area throughout history, Algeria has found in her sons, since the Numid [first Algerian kingdom established between 202–148 B.C.E. by a Berber chief allied with Rome] era and the Islamic epic and up to the wars of decolonization, the pioneers of freedom, unity and progress as well as builders of democratic and prosperous States during the periods of glory and peace. The 1st of November 1954 was a turning point for its destiny and a crowning for the strong resistance to aggressions carried out against its culture, its values and the fundamental components of its identity which are Islam, Arabity and Amazighity [common identity]. Its current struggles are well rooted in the glorious past of the nation.[61]

Recapturing a lost collective identity through schooling was difficult. Language was considered the key to developing a national identity and, as mentioned previously, the French neglected the education of the vast majority of the indigenous population and used French as the medium of instruction. This meant that the new government faced a shortage of local teachers who were trained to teach Arabic and Islamic values. In 1963, primary schools had 16,546 instructors who could teach through the medium of French and only

3,452 who could use Arabic. Consequently, Arabicization began in only the first grade of primary school. To increase the number of Arabic-speaking teachers, the government opened six Arabic training colleges and sent students to other Arab nations for training.[62]

However, speaking French remained the key to economic advancement in Algerian society. There developed a two-track educational system with one being an Arabic track and the other a bilingual track (Arabic and French). In the Arabic track, all subjects were taught in Arabic with French being taught as a foreign language. In the bilingual track, scientific subjects were taught in French and the other subjects in Arabic. The result was that few graduates of the Arabic track actually entered scientific and other professional careers and graduates found it difficult to get jobs in government and industrial areas.[63]

Consequently, the two-track system reinforced existing class differences. Rural and recently urbanized Algerians tended to enter the Arabic track whereas urban and middle class families sent their children to bilingual schools. John Ruedy concluded, "Thus, the way Arabicization was carried out only widened the social cleavages it was designed to bridge and exacerbated the tensions tearing at a still very fragmented society."[64]

Despite its goal of recapturing its collective identity, the new Algerian government retained the educational ladder introduced by the French, which included 6 years of primary school followed by 7 years of secondary education. In 1971, the government divided secondary education into a 4-year intermediate cycle followed by 3 years of secondary school. And similar to Egypt, the primary curriculum includes the study of Arabic and "Islamic education and morals" along with science, mathematics, and "practical training." Secondary education separates students into General and Technical, with both tracks studying Arabic and "Islamic science."[65] The Arab League defines Islamic science as the study of the *Qur'an*, *Hadith*, and *Sharia*.[66]

Also, the Algerian government, following the Euroamerican model, includes education its national economic planning. The America-Mideast Educational and Training Service reports, "The Algerians began considering vocational training as a necessary national investment in the 1970s, when development plans generated a significant demand for skilled workers. By 1990, nearly 120,000 trainees were enrolled in various vocation training centers, institutes, and in the distance education program."[67]

In the end, the legacy of colonialism compromised efforts to create a collective identity through Arabicization. French remained the preferred language of industrial development. However, through the teaching of history and the Islamic science, students could imagine a collective identity for Algeria.

SYRIA: EDUCATION AND ARAB SOCIALISM

In general, other Arab nations followed the pattern of adding the study of Arabic and Islam to a Euroamerican curricula and utilizing the Euroamerican educational ladder. For instance, Syria, which was given to the French as a mandated territory after World War I, experienced a fierce anti-French uprising in 1945. With independence, it became a charter member of both the Arab League and the United Nations. A cultural agreement was made with Egypt in 1957, with Syria adopting the Egyptian educational ladder.[68]

In 1963, the Socialist Arab Baath Party came to power in Syria with a platform supporting Arab socialist nationalism. The Preamble to the 1973 Syrian constitution articulates the nationalist goals of the Baath Party: "The Socialist Arab Baath Party is the first movement in the Arab homeland which gives Arab unity its sound revolutionary meaning, connects the nationalist with the socialist struggle, and represents the Arab nation's will and aspirations for a future that will bind the Arab nation with its glorious past and will enable it to carry out its role in achieving victory for the cause of freedom of all the peoples."[69] Also, the constitution declared that a "comprehensive Arab revolution is an existing and continuing necessity to achieve the Arab nation's aspirations for unity, freedom, and socialism. The revolution in the Syrian Arab region is part of the comprehensive Arab revolution. Its policy in all areas stems from the general strategy of the Arab revolution."[70]

The Syrian constitution decreed Arabic as the official national language and "Islamic jurisprudence" as the main source of education. The constitution specifically stated that the goal of education is to create a spirit of Arab national socialism:

Part 3 Educational and Cultural Principles

Article 21 [Goals]

The educational and cultural system aims at creating

a socialist nationalist Arab generation which is

scientifically minded and attached to its history and

land, proud of its heritage, and filled with the spirit

of struggle to achieve its nation's objectives of unity,

freedom, and socialism, and to serve humanity and

its progress.

Article 23 [Socialist Education, Arts, Sports]

(1) The nationalist socialist education is the basis for building the unified socialist Arab society. It seeks to strengthen moral values, to achieve the higher ideals of the Arab nation, to develop the society, and to serve the causes of humanity. The state undertakes to encourage and to protect this education.[71]

SAUDI ARABIA: RELIGIOUS FUNDAMENTALISM AND AUTHORITARIAN EDUCATION

Not part of the Arab League, Saudi Arabia was strongly influenced by Wahhabism, an Islamic fundamentalist movement originating in the 18th century. 'Abd al-Wahhab (1703–1791) objected to what he believed was the debauchery of Ottoman rulers and he called for a return to the pristine social conditions of the generation of Mohammad. He believed that only Arabs could carry on the true traditions of Islam. In 1744, he married into the House of Saud which then ruled part of the Arabian peninsula. 'Abd al-Wahhab preached an authoritarian political creed: "He who occupies the office of Caliph … must be obeyed, and insurrection against him is forbidden."[72] Today, among other things, Wahhabism rejects Euroamerican ideas about female equality along with the use of tobacco, Euroamerican-style dancing and music, and democracy. The result is a highly authoritarian government and educational system with strict regulation of public morality.

The teaching of modern science and the education of women are important issues for the followers of Wahhabism. As I discuss below, the Saudi Arabian government has ensured that the teaching of science is within the context of fundamentalist Islamic beliefs. Although the *Qur'an* calls for the education of women, they are strictly segregated in Saudi Arabian educational institutions.

Unlike other Arab nations, the nation of Saudi Arabia never experienced the direct effects of European colonialism. Under the leadership of Abd al-Aziz Bin Abd al-Rahman al-Faysal Al Sa'ud, the different regions of what is now Saudi Arabia were unified and a decree was issued in 1932 proclaiming the existence of the Kingdom of Saudi Arabia as an Islamic state with Arabic as its national language and the *Sharia* as its system of jurisprudence. In 1933, the Kingdom signed an oil exploration agreement with Standard Oil of California. In 1938, the discovery of a vast source of oil made the Saudi royal family one of the wealthiest in the world.[73]

As a wealthy monarchy, the Saudi royal family never embraced the principles of Arab socialism. However, it did support Arab nationalism. Its 1992 constitution describes its monarchical control:

Chapter 2 [Monarchy]

Article 5

(a) The system of government in the Kingdom of
Saudi Arabia is that of a monarchy.

(b) Rule passes to the sons of the founding King,
Abd al-Aziz Bin Abd al-Rahman al-Faysal Al Sa'ud,
and to their children's children. The most upright
among them is to receive allegiance in accordance
with the principles of the Holy Koran and the
Tradition of the Venerable Prophet.

The constitution states that legislation will be based on Islamic law and its official language is Arabic.[74]

The integration of fundamentalist Islamic ideas into a Euroamerican-style education system are exemplified in the 236 articles of the "Educational Policy in Saudi Arabia" issued in 1970 by the government's Higher Committee of Educational Policy and disseminated in the United States by the Relations Department of the Saudi Arabian Cultural Mission to the United States.[75] Besides stating that the principle goal of the nation's school system is the fostering of "a holistic, Islamic concept of the universe, man and life, such that the entire world is subject to the laws of God," official government policy provides guidelines for reconciling science with religious beliefs.[76] For instance, one article of the policy statement calls for the integration of an Islamic "orientation" into all aspects of the curriculum: "Integrate Islamic orientation in sciences and knowledge in all their forms, items, curricula, writing and teaching so that they would fall in harmony with sound Islamic thinking."[77] Another article states as an educational objective: "Demonstrating the full harmony between science and religion in the Islamic law, as Islam is a combination of religion and secularism, and Islamic thought meets all human needs in their highest forms and in all ages."[78] And, in another article of the government's official "Educational Policy in Saudi Arabia," modern science is to be brought into alignment with Islamic beliefs by:

> Encouraging and promoting the spirit of scientific thinking and research, strengthening the faculties of observation and meditation, and enlightening the student about God's miracles in the world and God's wisdom in His creatures; thus enabling the individual to fulfill an active role in building a social life and steering it toward the right direction.[79]

Whereas other Arab nations, such as Egypt, identify Islamic religion as a separate subject, Saudi Arabia's policies integrate religious studies into all aspects of the curriculum. Writing for the Relations Department of the Saudi Arabian Cultural Mission to the U.S.A., Hamad I. Al Salloom emphasized, "It is, however, important to note that in this respect, religious studies are not taught as separate entities but in their corresponding relation with the other fields of study such as education, economics, sociology, psychology, medicine, and law."[80]

In Saudi Arabia, there is strict segregation of the sexes at all levels of education except for nursery and kindergarten, and the first two grades in some private schools. There are separate school buildings, staffs, and in some cases separate institutions. Sexual segregation is so strictly applied that in higher education, female students can only listen to male teachers over closed-circuit television.[81]

Despite not experiencing colonialism, the Saudi Arabian educational system follows the Euroamerican style educational ladder of 6 years of elementary, 3 years of intermediate, and 3 years of secondary schooling. According to Saudi policies, elementary education should "Cultivate the correct Islamic creed in children's souls and provide them with a comprehensive moral and intellectual education shaped by Islamic values" along with developing basic skills in language, mathematics, and physical education. As stated previously, Islamic values are to be integrated into all of the following subjects in the elementary and intermediate school curriculum (the curriculum is the same for both levels of schooling).

Elementary and Intermediate School Curriculum

Islamic Studies

Arabic Studies

Social Studies

Science

Mathematics

Art Education

Physical Education (Boys Only)

Home Economics (Girls Only)[82]

Secondary education is integrated into national economic planning with specialized schools for technical training, agriculture, commerce, industrial, and pre-collegiate education. The official government's "Educational Policy in Saudi Arabia" states as a goal of the system: "Training the necessary manpower and diversifying education with special attention to vocational training."[83] Regarding the preparation of the necessary manpower for the nation's economy, the government's official education policy stresses that work is for good of the nation. This could be compared to the Soviet Union's goal of educating Stakhanovite workers. The Saudi Arabian government calls for: "Planting the zeal of work in the hearts of students, commending it in all its forms, urging individuals to excel in their work and emphasizing its role in the construction of the nation."[84]

Education for a national security state encompasses this Stakhanovite-like manpower goal for all levels of education as given in the following official goals:

Elementary School

Develop children's understanding of the rights and duties of citizenship and instill love of country and loyalty to the monarchy;

Cultivate a love for learning and the value of work, and train children to make constructive use of their leisure time;[85]

Intermediate School

Train students to serve their communities and country, and strengthen their loyalty to the monarchy;

Stimulate students to restore the glory of the Islamic nation and march on the path of dignity and glory;

Train students to devote their time to useful reading, invest their leisure time in constructive activities, and work toward strengthening and advancing their Islamic character;

Enable students to be aware of and confront misleading propaganda, subversive doctrines and principles foreign to Islamic values.[86]

Secondary Education

Instilling allegiance to the wide Islamic homeland and private homeland (the Kingdom of Saudi

Arabia);

Directing students' talents and skills into the most
fruitful paths to serve their personal goals and the
objectives of Islamic education;

Graduating technically and morally qualified
students *to fill the country's needs in elementary*
teaching, religious duties and occupations in
farming, trade, and industry [my emphasis].[87]

LANGUAGE AND WARS OF LIBERATION

Similar to Arab countries, the collapse of colonial empires in Asia resulted
in educational concerns about language, religion, and nationalism. Both
the British and French in Asia and Africa, along with other European colonial powers, made their languages the official languages of their colonial
governments. After independence, many former colonies instituted language policies and educational practices designed to replace imposed European languages with indigenous languages. This often proved to be a
problem because local elites, as in Algeria, continued to use the language of
the previous colonizer. In addition, former English colonies found it difficult to shed the use of English because English was quickly becoming the
language of globalization.[88]

For instance, consider the language issues in the former British colonies of Malaysia and India. In both countries, British authorities opened
English language schools for the local population to train low-level clerks
for the colonial government. Providing English language instruction to a
minority of the population heightened social class and ethnic tensions because knowledge of English provided the user with access to power and
wealth in the colonial empire.

In Malaysia, under British rule from the 18th century to the ratification
of the Malaysian constitution in 1957, language and education policies were
designed to keep the indigenous Malaysian population in traditional jobs
in agriculture and fishing while educating the ethnic Indian and Chinese
population for service in the colonial administration. The British in the
19th century had transported Chinese and Indians to Malaysia to work in
tin mines and on rubber plantations. To implement their educational policies, the British colonial government established English and vernacular
schools. The English schools were specifically designed to educate workers
for commercial enterprises and government administration. The English
schools contributed to making English the language of the upper class and

knowledge of English essential for advancement in Malaysian society. The large number of ethnic Chinese and Indians, in contrast to the small number of Malaysians, who attended English schools set the stage for future racial clashes between the ethnic Chinese and Indian populations and the indigenous Malaysian population. It was reported in 1924 that enrolled in English schools were 20,166 ethnic Chinese, 4,613 ethnic Indians, 3,858 Malaysians, and 3,504 Europeans/Eurasians.[89]

Reinforcing social class and ethnic divisions, the British government opened Malaysian vernacular schools. These schools provided a limited amount of education because, as explained in 1906 by the Governor-General Sir Frank Sweetenham, "the Government has never desired to give to the children a smattering, or even a larger quantity, of knowledge which will not help them to more useful and happy lives than they now lead. To the Malay the principal value of school attendance is to teach him habits of order, punctuality, and obedience."[90] The goal, he stated, "is to make the son of the fisherman or peasant a more intelligent fisherman or peasant than his father had been."[91] Sweetham worried that too much education would destroy the Malaysians as a rural people.

After independence, the 1957 constitution established a constitutional monarchy with Malay as the official language. The use of English was associated with British imperialism and the economic power of ethnic Chinese who had been educated in English schools. Therefore, making Malay the national language was both an expression of nationalism and an attempt to gain economic equality for the indigenous Malaysian population. However, because the government prior to 1957 had issued all laws in English and the courts operated in English, the constitution provided a 10-year transition period until all government functions were to be conducted in Malay.[92]

Ethnic tensions caused by economic inequalities flared up in 1969 in race riots between Malaysians and ethnic Chinese. The economic power associated with knowledge of English was an issue in the riots. To calm ethnic tensions and promote nationalism and economic equality, the government instituted a plan that made Malay the medium of instruction, with the gradual introduction of the requirement beginning in early primary grades. By 1983, first-year courses in universities were taught in Malay. Also, in recognition of ethnic tensions, primary and secondary schools offered language instruction in Tamil and Chinese.[93] Despite these new language policies, English remained the most important language in major businesses, particularly those associated with international trade. Instruction in English continued in secondary schools.

Similar issues arose with Indian independence. Colonial rule had made knowledge of English an important source of economic and political divisions. Most, if not all, the leaders of the independence movement received their advance education in England. When instituting England's educational policy in India, Thomas Macaulay, a member of the Supreme Council of India, established the policy of educating an administrative cadre of Indians in the English language and culture. This group of English-speaking Indians were suppose to owe their allegiance to England and were to help the English rule the vast Indian territory. Predicting the use of English as the global language, Macaulay argued, "In India, English is the language spoken by the ruling class. It is spoken by the higher class of natives at the seats of government. It is likely to become the language of commerce throughout the seas of the East."[94] In addition he believed that "a single shelf of a good European library was worth the whole native literature of India and Arabia."[95]

After independence, Jawaharlal Nehru, India's first Prime Minister (1947–1964), who had been educated in an Anglicized Indian household and attend school in England, argued: "Some people imagine that English is likely to become the *lingua franca* of India. That seems to me a fantastic conception, except in respect of a handful of upper-class intelligentsia. It has no relation to the problem of mass education and culture."[96] However, Nehru did not believe that independence from England should result in not teaching English in India. Recognizing the imperialism of the English language, Nehru argued, "English is ... undoubtedly the most widespread and important world language, and it is gaining fast on the other languages. It is likely to become more and more the medium of international intercourse and radio broadcasting."[97]

The issue of language was hotly debated during the writing of the India's 1949 Constitution. Hindi was decided on as the national language. However, there was still the question of other minority languages and the use of minority languages in education. Nehru worried, "The real problem will remain: as to what policy we shall adopt in a scheme of general mass education and the cultural development of people; how shall we promote the unity of India and yet preserve the rich diversity of our inheritance?"[98]

A problem in using Hindi as the national language was that at the time of the writing of the Constitution, it was not universally known in India. Consequently, a transitional period was needed to allow time for a general education program in Hindi. This paralleled the actions in Malaysia. English would be the official language for a 15-year period after the acceptance of the Constitution. The Constitution stated,

343. Official language of the union. (1)The official language of the Union shall be Hindi ... (2) For a period of fifteen years from the commencement of this Constitution, the English language shall continue to be used for all the official purposes of Union....[99]

Like Malaysia, English continues as India's major language for international business and politics. English continued as the medium of instruction in elite schools. In fact, the 1978 University Grants Commission's report complained that the educational system was not developing the character needed for a cooperative socialist society but still continued to emphasize the British values of "narrow individualism, unhealthy competition to the neglect of social good."[100] In 1998, the top arts and science college selected by the magazine *India Today* exemplified the continued interrelationship between the British model, the English language, and social class. The top college was St. Stephen's, Delhi which was described as "Perhaps the last repository of the Oxbridge culture in India, St. Stephen's has often been accused of being a finishing school, a networking society and even a dilettante's paradise.... To successive generations of Calcutta's elite, however, one of its attributes has remained constant: it is the place where you acquire that lifelong chip on the shoulder."[101] The reputation of the college was based in part on its "English literature faculties" and student societies, such as the Shakespeare and Wodehouse societies. Mixing class and caste in its description, *India Today* stated, "There are day scholars and boarders, but in the college hierarchy 'gentlemen (and since last year, ladies) in residence' are the brahmins."[102]

RELIGION AND INDEPENDENCE

Religious education was also central to national independence movements in Malaysia and India. In both countries, there was strong Islamic resentment of Christian proselytizing by missionaries. In Malaysia, language, social class, and religion were intertwined in the resentment of the Malaysian people with British occupation. Coexisting in Malaysia with English and vernacular schools were *Qur'anic* schools called *pondoks*; the name derived from an Arabic word referring to an inn or hotel. Most Malaysians were Moslem, and pondoks provided a free education. These schools followed a traditional Islamic curriculum, including the study of the *Qur'an*, the Sunna, and the Arabic language.[103]

In 1908, the first madrasa was established in Malaysia with a broader curriculum than the pondoks. Eventually madrasas offered curricula in Malay, English, and Arabic. Similar to what would happen in India, these madrasas supported resistance against English rule. After World War II, religion became a central issue as nationalist groups worked to finalize independence for the British. The 1957 constitution made Islam the official religion of Malaysia. Regarding educational institutions, the constitution declared, "Every religious group has the right to establish and maintain institutions for the education of children and provide therein instruction in its own religion."[104] One special clause allowed for government funding of Islamic schools: "Federal law or State law may provide for special financial aid for the establishment or maintenance of Muslim institutions or the instruction in the Muslim religion of persons professing that religion."[105] Following the adoption of the constitution, the government made Islamic religious instruction compulsory for all Moslem students.

Similar to Arab countries, Islamic morality is now part of the Malaysian primary and secondary school curriculum. Islamic morality is embodied in the 1987 New Education Philosophy report issued by the Malaysian government: "Education in Malaysia is an on-going effort towards further developing the potential of individuals ... based on a firm belief in and devotion to God."[106] Under the New Education Philosophy, the teaching of Islamic values served the secular purpose of social control by the state. The school system was to educate good citizen with the following values:

1. Have a firm belief in and obedience to God;
2. Be knowledgeable;
3. Possess living skills;
4. Possess high moral standards;
5. Be responsible to his self, society, and nation;
6. Contribute to the well-being of society and nation;
7. Have a balanced personality.[107]

In British India, there were two distinct Islamic educational movements, with one trying to accommodate British rule whereas the other educated for resistance to British imperialism. Eventually, these traditions would continue in modern-day Pakistan, which was carved out of India in 1947 as part of the British effort to resolve religious conflict between Islam and Hinduism. In 1875, Syed Ahmad founded Muhammadan Anglo-Oriental College (now Aligarh University) modeled on British institutions of higher learning. Syed believed that Moslems could improve their economic and political position through employment in the government and by showing loyalty to British rule. This required a Western-style education, which leading Hindus had already embraced.[108]

In conflict with this educational accommodation to British imperialism, there was a revival of madrasa education with the establishment of Darul Uloom Deoband (1867). These new madrasas were anti-imperialist in their teachings but followed a system of examinations based on the British model. In his study of contemporary madrasas in Pakistan, A. H. Nayyar states, regarding the madrasa revival in late-19th century British India, "The founders of *madrasahs* were strongly anti-imperialist, and communicated this spirit to their students.... They viewed the imperialism of the

West more as that of Christendom, and the modern technology brought in by the imperialists as a tool in the hands of adversarial religious force."[109]

Despite the madrasa movement, very few Moslems in India received an education. In 1949, two years after its creation, an education survey of Pakistan found that in the age group from 5–9 years (Grades 1–5) only 15.8% of males and 4.8% of females were in school. Of the secondary age group, (9–14 years, Grades 6–10) only 9.4% of males and 2.7% of females were in school.[110] These figures did not improve after the establishment of Pakistan. In *The State of the World's Children 2000* , UNICEF reported that in 1995, the adult literacy rate for males was 54% and females 24%, and the secondary school enrollment (for the secondary-age cohort group) between 1990 and 1996 was 33% for males and 17% for females.[111]

Today, an underfunded state system exists alongside a system of madrasas that continue their anti-imperialist and anti-Western traditions. In the 1990s, Pakistan had the lowest percentage of government expenditures (2%) on education of any Islamic nation.[112] Pakistan's current educational objectives promise that:

> The current literacy rate of about 39% will be raised to 55% during the first five years of the policy and 70% by the year 2010. Functional literacy and income generation skills will be provided to rural women of 15 to 25 age group and basic educational facilities will be provided to working children. Functional literacy will be imparted to adolescents (10–14) who missed out the chance of primary education. The existing disparities in basic education will be reduced to half by year 2010.[113]

Similar to other Islamic nations, Pakistan's government schools operate with a Euroamerican type educational ladder with elementary schools including Grades 1–8 and secondary schools being divided into pre-collegiate and various vocational training programs. An important educational goal is instilling Islamic values: "Education and training should enable the citizens of Pakistan to lead their lives according to the teachings of Islam as laid down in the *Qur'an* and Sunnah and to educate and train them as a true practicing Muslim."[114]

The lack of government schools aided the steady and rapid growth of madrasas since 1947.[115] Another important factor in the growth of madrasas is that they are able to provide free room and board, textbooks, and instruction through a combination of government subsidies and community. The free room and board is particularly attractive to low income families. Nayyar wrote,

> Madrasahs, unlike formal schools, are attractive because they are invariably boarding houses, providing free boarding and lodging, free books, and often even clothing.... This is an important, perhaps, overriding, factor for many

from the lower and lower-middle classes. Not only does it go to reduce the
burden on the tight family budget, it also keeps the children away from loiter-
ing and street crime.[116]

The Pakistani madrasas are famous throughout the Islamic world. They
attract foreign students associated with fundamentalist Islamic movements
including those who participate in the Taliban movement in Afghani-
stan.[117] In *Globalization and Educational Rights*, I reported a conversation in
2000 between a New York Times journalist Jeffery Goldberg and students
attending a Pakistani madrasa.[118] When Goldberg visited the Haqqania
madrasa in the year 2000, he found classes being conducted in the centu-
ries-old style of a white-bearded teacher reading from the text while students listened.[119] Interrupting the discussion of the *Hadith*, a student asked
Goldberg what he thought of Osama bin Laden. In response to the question
about Osama bin Laden, Goldberg quoted from the *Hadith* a passage which
forbids the killing of innocent people: "It is narrated by Ibn Umar that a
woman was found killed in one of these battles, so the Messenger of Allah,
may peace be upon him, forbade the killing of women and children."[120]
This passage suggests that God does not approve of terrorism directed at ci-
vilian targets such as airplane and car bombs. Students responded to
Goldberg by asking for proof that women and children were killed by
Osama bin Laden. One student said, "Osama wants to keep Islam pure
from the pollution of the infidels. He believes Islam is the way for all the
world. He wants to bring Islam to all the world."[121] A student replied to
Goldberg that there was no compulsion in religion but that the West was
forcing Moslems to live under the rule of infidels.

Therefore, because of historical circumstances, Pakistani education developed quite differently from that of Arab nations. Although the government school system shows the characteristic Euroamerican educational
ladder and an emphasis on teaching Islamic values, the anti-Western and
anti-imperialist madrasa tradition originating from 19th-century British
India now serves the Islamic world in educating students for continued resistance to Euroamerican values and domination. In contrast, Malaysia,
similar to the Arab world, has institutionalized Islamic instruction in public
schools where it serves as a mechanism of state social control.

NEO-COLONIALISM
AND SUB-SAHARAN AFRICAN EDUCATION

Sub-Saharan African education repeats in many ways the story of many
Arab and Asian countries, with European imperialism leaving in its wake
Euroamerican school structures, language and religious issues, and racial
turmoil. The major difference with Arab and Asian countries is the neo-co-

lonial impact of the World Bank in Sub-Saharan Africa. Also, European colonizers imposed different educational practices. For instance, the British
utilized missionaries to spread the word of Christianity and the value of the
English language and Anglo-Saxon culture while colonial authorities confiscated prime agricultural land and turned it over to settlers from England.
And the British transported laborers from India to Africa and the Carib-
bean creating populations with mixed ancestral backgrounds. Reverend
Metcalf Sunter is credited with spreading the model of English missionary
education beginning in Sierra Leone in 1873. Sunter considered local languages of little commercial value when compared to English. Sunter helped
spread missionary education throughout English controlled West Africa.
Similar to India and Malaysia, many Africans in Sierra Leone, Nigeria,
Kenya, Rhodesia, and Tanganyika attended missionary schools to get jobs
in the administration of the colonial government. The result was to make
English the language of government and commerce.[122]

As African scholar Nugugi stated, "the most coveted place ... in the [po-
litical] system was only available to holders of an English-language credit
card. English was the official vehicle and magic formula to colonial
elitedom."[123] By 1974, Nigeria followed India and the Philippines as having
the most students enrolled in English in the top 10 nations in which English
functions as a second language. The Republic of South Africa, Kenya, and
Ghana are fifth, eighth and ninth respectively.[124] Euroamerican school
structures remained in these previously English colonies.

Other imperialist languages continue to be prominent in former colonies. In 1906, Leopold of Belgium signed a Concordat with the Vatican
giving Catholic missionaries the leading role in establishing schools.[125]
French remains the official language and the language used in major businesses in the Democratic Republic of the Congo. The Cameroon experienced German, French, and British colonialism and after independence
French and English continues as official languages and mediums of instruction in schools.[126] In Angola, Portugese remains the official language
after Portugese colonialists used Catholic missionaries to convert the local
population.[127] After independence, Chad and most of French West Africa
(now the independent nations of Mali, Senegal, Burkina Faso, Benin,
Côte d'Ivoire, Guinea, Mauritania, and Niger) retained French as their official language.[128] Mauritania is the exception among the nations of the
former French West Africa, with Arabic being its official language. Of
course, many indigenous languages continue to exist side-by-side with
these official languages.

In many of the colonies and later nations, Islam and Christianity com-
peted for dominance over indigenous religions. Louis Brenner's *Controlling
Knowledge: Religion, Power and Schooling in a West African Muslim Society* de-

tails how Islamic education could serve colonial authority and also be a training ground for resistance to imperialism in a manner similar to India. Colonial authorities in French West Africa established their own forms of madrasas (the French called them *médersas*) in 1906 for the purpose of "teaching an elite of young Muslims how to speak and write in French and at the same time to give them proper views on the civilizing role of France in Africa."[129] These médersas were to serve the purpose of legitimizing French rule and as institutions to maintain social control over the colonized populations. The schools were also considered a method for countering anti-French sentiments among the Muslim population. The Governor General of French West Africa declared that these schools were "our most effective answer to Islamic propaganda."[130] In 1910, his successor William Ponty asserted, "Everyone knows that the study of French is the most effective cure one can employ against [religious] fanaticism, and experience teaches us that Muslims who know our language are less imbued with prejudice than those who know only Arabic."[131] This sentiment was reiterated in 1921 by the Inspector of Education for French West Africa: "The médersas are Muslim educational establishments designed, in principle, to divert to the profit of French policy the influence that the *marabouts* [Islamic cleric] exercise over the Muslim populations. The médersas are meant to dissipate the pretensions of the Muslim world against our civilization."[132]

French colonial authorities considered Islam to be a fanatical religion that threatened not only the work of their Catholic missionaries, but also the power of the colonial government. In establishing médersas they attempted to secularize Islamic teachings for the purpose of social control. For instance, Bouilliagui Fadiga, head of the Timbuktu madrasa, wrote in 1935, "The médersa is a mixed school [French and Arabic], a school for domestication, and also a school for pacification. Its existence reassures and gives confidence to the population. Besides being a symbol of tolerance with regard to the most fanatical of religions, it is a charitable institution."[133] In 1946, Islamic leaders in French West Africa began to open their own anti-imperialist schools using the Arabic word madrasa to distinguish them for the French médersas. Similar to Egypt and other countries, these madrasas had an educational ladder with a curriculum divided into a variety of subjects. Arabic was taught as a foreign language with the goal of eventually making Arabic the language of instruction. The overall purpose of these madrasas was to educate men who would lead the struggle for independence from French Rule.[134]

After independence, Sub-Saharan African nations tried to rapidly expand nationalistic forms of education. The overall goal was to increase equality of opportunity and create national identities. But by the 1970s, Sub-Saharan African nations experienced a rapid economic downturn requiring them to reduce their efforts to extend equality of educational opportunity. As the downturn took place, the World Bank and the International Monetary Fund began to play an increasing role in determining education policies.[135]

The acceptance of loans from the World Bank and the International Monetary Funds required that educational systems be tied to economic development. This was premised on a particular vision of economic organization involving privatization, free markets, and reduced government services. Educational systems were to develop human capital to meet the labor needs of corporate farming and industrialization using a Euroamerican education ladder. The World Bank's vision of development was that of continuous economic expansion and consumption driven by the quest for profit.[136]

One way of highlighting the World Bank's vision of economic development is to contrast it with a particular Islamic view of economics, namely that given in the constitution of Iran. The Preamble to the Iranian constitution includes the following economic statement:

The Economy Is a Means, Not an End

In strengthening the foundations of the economy, the fundamental consideration will be fulfillment of the material needs of man in the course of his overall growth and development. *This principle contrasts with other economic systems, where the aim is concentration and accumulation of wealth and maximization of profit. In materialist schools of thought, the economy represents an end in itself, so that it comes to be a subversive and corrupting factor in the course of man's development.* In Islam, the economy is a means, and all that is required of a means is that it should be an efficient factor contributing to the attainment of the ultimate goal [my emphasis].[137]

Louis Brenner found that the World Bank and government policies of the former French West African colony of Mali transformed madrasa education. After independence, madrasas had continued to function as private schools primarily teaching religion. In 1985, as a result of economic development plans, Mali's government leaders decreed that madrasas were now part of the state educational system and required them to adopt the government's educational curriculum. The schools were allowed to retain their religious orientation and instruction in Arabic. However, the general focus of the madrasas was no longer on religion, but on economic development. The teaching of Arabic was promoted as having value in trade with Arab nations and as an international language. A government report argued that it had a responsibility to ensure that students in madrasas were educated for national development: "These children [attending madrasas and *Qur'anic* schools] expect us to offer them the opportunity to become enlightened

Muslims, effective citizens, *effective producers and agents of national development* [my emphasis].[138]

In former nations of French West Africa and other Sub-Saharan nations, the World Bank helped to expand educational opportunities utilizing former colonial schools and linking schooling to economic planning. Still, educational opportunities remained limited for a majority of the population. The result, according to Patrick Boyle, was the education of elite economic and political groups who were privileged by their education in European languages. These languages proved profitable in large businesses, and international trade and politics.[139]

Another effect of World Bank policies was to increase the privatization of elite education. In the 1980s and 1990s, Sub-Saharan African governments faced staggering loan payments to the World Bank and they were forced to reduce public expenditures for education. This resulted, according to Patrick Boyle, in elite groups supporting the establishment of private schools as a means of passing on their educational privileges to their children. Boyle studied three urban centers: Kinhshasa, Congo; Yaoundé, Cameroon; and Nairobi, Kenya. Besides finding an expanding private sector education for elite families, he also found rapidly increasing illiteracy rates among non-elite children.

Boyle's findings contradicted the arguments of developmentalist theorists. These theorists had argued that investment in education would spur economic growth. However, the early stages of economic development did not provide enough economic growth to sustain educational investments. In Boyle's words,

> the contemporary situation of rapidly rising illiteracy in many of Sub-Saharan Africa's prominent capital cities, after years of efforts to establish universal primary education and eradicate illiteracy, gives one reason to revisit such recommendations [of developmental theorists]. Had Sub-Saharan Africa enjoyed a period of dynamic economic growth for several decades after independence these earlier policy recommendations [rapidly expanding educational opportunities] would perhaps today be seen in a more favorable light."[140]

In summary, former European colonies in Sub-Saharan Africa retained the educational structures and curriculum introduced by colonial governments and missionaries. Similar to Egypt, many of the traditional Islamic schools were secularized and absorbed into the economic and nationalistic goals of state education systems. Despite the desire to expand educational opportunities, governments relied on development strategies of the World Bank, which resulted in high government debts, a collapse of public schools systems, and the development of elite private schooling.

AUTHORITY AND SOCIALIST EDUCATION
IN THE DEMOCRATIC PEOPLE'S REPUBLIC OF KOREA

While progressive educators in South and Central American were attempting to adapt Marxism to local cultural conditions through a process of conscientization and ultimately personal liberation, Kim Il Sung, leader of the national liberation movement in Korea and head of the Democratic People's Republic of Korea articulated a socialist education model that fused human minds to the needs of the national security state. In 1961, at a National Conference of Active Educational Workers, Kim Il Sung explained, "To build this socialist society, the creation of material and technical foundations must go hand in hand with the *transformation of man's consciousness*. Even though the socialist transformation of the relations of production is completed ... *we cannot claim that the building of socialism has been completed as long as the people, the masters who control society, are not remolded* [my emphasis]." As an aside, Kim warned the audience of educators, "By the way remolding people is much more complicated and difficult than transforming the social system or developing technology."[141]

Similar to Vietnam, Korea underwent a major change when the grip of Japanese imperialism was broken after World War II. The 1905 treaty ending the Russian–Japanese War recognized Japan's interest in Korea and 5 years later the Japanese government ended the reign of the last Choson Emperor and completed its colonization of the country. Resistance against Japanese rule surfaced in 1919 when more than 2 million people took to the streets of Seoul. The Japanese military killed thousands while many fled to other countries. A government in exile was created in Shanghai, China under the leadership of Syngman Rhee. In 1925, the Korean Communist party was founded, which was eventually headed by Kim Il Sung. Exiled Koreans, including Kim Il Sung, joined Chinese forces in the 1930s to resist Japanese imperialism in Manchuria. The public memories of the struggle against Japanese forces would later be used by Kim Il Sung to promote a patriotic allegiance to the North Korean government. During World War II, allied governments agreed that when Soviet forces entered the war against Japan, they would be allowed to occupy Korea above a line drawn at the 38th Parallel. After the war, the Soviet Union rejected a United Nations proposal for elections to determine a national government. As a result, in 1948, the United States government installed Syngman Rhee as head of the Republic of Korea, which was geographically situated south of the 38th Parallel. North of the 38th Parallel, Kim Il Sung, supported by the Soviet Union, declared the existence of the Democratic People's Republic of Korea.[142]

The division of Korea into U.S.- and Soviet-backed governments set the stage for a major war in 1950. Both Korean governments claimed that the other was acting at the behest of a colonial power. Kim Il Sung asserted that Japanese imperialism was replaced by American imperialism whereas Syngman Rhee emphasized Soviet influence in the North. Dae-Sook Suh, Kim Il Sung's biographer maintained that although both sides accused the other of starting the war, "where the hostilities ended with neither victory nor defeat, it is difficult to arrive at a version to which both sides are willing to subscribe. While there is overwhelming evidence that North Korea launched what they themselves have alleged the 'fatherland liberation war,' it is impossible to pinpoint the extent of Soviet instigation or Chinese persuasion."[143] The war lasted until 1953 when the United Nations was able to achieve an uneasy peace between the two sides.

Influenced by the struggle against the Japanese and continuing worries about American imperialism, Kim Il Sung's socialist education model embraced a form of nationalism embodied in the concept "Juche." Shortly after coming to power, Kim expressed the following nationalistic sentiments, "If you are to become revolutionaries, you must have a passionate love for your country and people as the anti-Japanese guerrillas did ... you must always keep a sharp lookout for the aggressive schemes of the American imperialists."[144] The Juche idea encompassed a nationalist form of communism and the doctrines of historical materialism. This nationalist form of communism included patriotic fervor. Similar to what was happening to Marxist thought in other countries, Kim argued that communist ideas had to be adapted to the history, culture, and environment of each country. Like other Marxists, Kim believed that people should be taught that they were masters of their own fate; that knowledge was created by material conditions and not by supernatural powers or that they were innate in people; and that people had the power to shape their future.

In Kim's "Theses On Socialist Education" written for a 1977 meeting of the Workers' Party of Korea, he declared, "Juche must be established in education. Socialism and communism is built with each national state as a unit and master of the revolution and construction in each country.... Socialist education is a creative work to develop the people who live and act in specific conditions."[145] To prepare people to carry out socialist work under specific conditions required an education, Kim stated, focused on local history geography, and natural conditions. "Only when our people know about their own country and revolution," Kim wrote, "can they solve the difficult problems that arise ... fight [ing] selflessly for our revolutionary cause with pride that they are working for the Korean revolution under our Party's leadership and with love for the country and the people."[146]

Kim's form of nationalism combined emotional attachments to Korea's communist government and its revolution with an obligation to work for the people. Patriotic ardor was to be kept alive through the usual methods of nationalistic music, marches, pledges, and symbols. These patriotic exercises were to build loyalty to the Korean Communist Party. Kim clearly stated, "The establishment of the Party's monolithic ideological system in education is aimed at training people to be revolutionaries *who are totally loyal to the Party* [my emphasis]."[147] Kim considered all media—newspapers, movies, radio, and televisions—as part of the monolithic structure of socialist education. "All media of socialist education," he declared, "must be made to serve in training people as revolutionary fighters *faithful to the Party, and education in loyalty to the Party should be the keynote in the whole process of education* [my emphasis]."[148] In describing political education, Kim emphasized loyalty to the Party and used the image of "molding" students: "All children and students will thus be molded into revolutionary fighters boundlessly loyal to the Party, who will resolutely defend the Party and rally closely around it to carry out is policies *without reservations*."[149]

Kim wanted patriotic feelings to include protection of the state's property. At a 1961 National Conference of Active Educational Workers, Kim included protection of the state's property in the idea of patriotism:

> Patriotism is not an empty concept. Education in patriotism cannot be conducted simply by erecting the slogan, "Let us arm ourselves with the spirit of socialist patriotism!" Educating people in the spirit of patriotism must begin with fostering the idea of caring for every tree planted on the road side, for the chairs and desks in the school.... There is no doubt that a person who has formed the habit of *cherishing common property from childhood will grow up to be a valuable patriot* [my emphasis].[150]

Also, Kim gave another twist to the meaning of theory and practice by relating it to the needs of the national security state. Progressive educators emphasized the importance of testing theory in practice while, at the same time, using tested theory to guide practice. In contrast, Kim used these terms to describe working for the Party and national construction. In "Theses on Socialist Education," he wrote, "In socialist education universal principles and theories should be taught to the students in close combination with practice, and education be conducted in such a way that *all theories and knowledge can actively help in dealing with the problems that arise in the revolution and construction*."[151] Unlike Mao's teachers and students who were sent to factories and farms so that they could adjust and reflect on their learning in the light of real working conditions, Korean students were to have this experience as part of job training. Kim emphasized that, "School lessons and lectures should be properly combined with experiments and practical training, so that students *digest* what they have learned in class and develop the ability to apply it [my emphasis]."[152] There is a difference between *digesting* knowledge and *reflecting* on it. *Digesting* knowledge suggests Freire's image of banking education with the teacher spoon feeding bits and pieces of information to students.

Juche was supposed to influence theory and practice, which meant that knowledge was to be shaped by nationalist needs as defined by the Korean Communist Party. For instance, fears of imperialism fed the nationalistic fervor of Kim's government and resulted in the application of Juche to foreign science and technology. Reflecting the realistic pressures from U.S. support of South Korea combined with memories of Japanese imperialism, Kim's writings contained a consistent fear of foreign influence. Kim warned that, "The purpose of learning and introducing foreign things should always be to get to know our own things better and to carry out our revolution and construction more efficiently."[153] Regarding foreign science and technology, Kim argued, "they should be taught from a Juche standpoint to suit our own conditions, or actual situation. If we fail to accept even advanced science and technology critically to suit our actual situation, so far from benefitting us they affect our revolution and construction adversely."[154]

Similar to the concept of theory and practice, Kim gave a dogmatic twist to the progressive idea of learning through discovery. In a section on "Heuristic Teaching"—heuristic meant enabling persons to discover or learn something themselves—Kim asserted that all subjects should be taught by heuristic methods because they were compatible with a socialist education and improved student understanding. However, the purpose of heuristic methods was not to prepare students to apply them outside of school. Learning through discovery was presented as an ideal method for inculcating Party doctrines in students. In the section on "Heuristic Education," Kim wrote, "Only when the students themselves understand and respond to communist ideology can it become a firm faith. Therefore, ideological education *should be neither coercive nor yet crammed but always done by explanation and persuasion,* so that students understand and sympathize with the advanced ideas of themselves."[155]

The Stalinist-like school organization advocated by Kim Il Sung indicated that heuristic teaching methods were not intended to spark independence and freedom in classrooms. Heuristic methods were just a means for instilling a fixed body of knowledge. This interpretation of Kim's intentions are supported by his 1962 speech to the Cabinet of the Democratic People's Republic of Korea on "Improving and Strengthening the Work of Education."[156] In this speech, Kim outlined a very controlled and, from a progressive standpoint, oppressive classroom organization. In the speech, Kim urged an intensification of educational discipline as necessary preparation of students to enter the workforce: "Only when it [discipline] is established thoroughly in the schools of general education will the pupils study well and, after leaving school and going out into society, live, and *do all their work, including fulfillment of state plans,* as they should [my emphasis]."[157] By educational discipline, Kim meant being punctual, completing school work on time, and obeying school authorities. "Those who are *not* accustomed to a life of discipline," Kim maintained, "are unpunctual in reporting for work and leaving the workplace every day, absent themselves from duty at will, and fail to perform their duties without compunction."[158]

Kim's concept of school discipline was linked to the needs of the national security state. School discipline required teachers to closely follow a standardized curriculum that Kim likened to the state's economic plans: "To fulfill the national economic plan is the legal responsibility of factories and enterprises, and to carry out the education program is the legal responsibility allotted by the Party, the state and the people to the schools."[159] Teachers were not to deviate from the prescribed state curriculum. "At schools," Kim urged, "all subjects should be taught strictly according to the curricula and the teaching schedules and, thus, the education program should be carried out 100 percent."[160] In turn, students were to fulfill their obligations to the state by studying hard. Kim's concept of discipline also included an emphasis on order, dress, and cleanliness as preparation for the workplace. Kim warned that, "The pupils of the school which fails to give them proper education put their school bags and caps all over the house, keep their exercise books in poor condition, and neglect their home leaving it in disorder. It is hard to believe that the pupils, who are to living this way … will keep their workplaces clean and lead a cultured life when they … go to work at factories or public institutions."[161]

Students were suppose to transfer their love of meeting the requirements of the state curriculum to the workplace where they were to display zeal in fulfilling the state's economic plans. To accomplish this goal, Kim suggested combining communist education with instruction in science and technology. The communist education Kim advocated focused on teaching people to love to work for the state. "The most important thing in communist education," Kim declared, "is to cultivate a communist attitude towards labor … it is very important in socialist education to teach all people to have a correct attitude towards labor."[162] This correct attitude entailed a joy of working for the good of the people. Kim suggested that the joy of working for the common good could be developed by students cleaning their classrooms, taking care of school gardens, and helping parents at home.

Communist education, according to Kim, included teaching a love for state property and an acceptance of a collective society. Students were urged to sacrifice their own personal property when it might result in protecting state property. As previously mentioned, Kim considered protection of state property as part of patriotism. Regarding education, Kim asserted, "We must implant in the people the habit of caring more for the property of the state and society even if they have to sacrifice their own private possessions."[163]

In summary, the socialist education in the People's Republic of Korea epitomized a formal education model for a national security state. Nationalism was promoted through a study of Korean history, culture, and geography wedded to a communist education that taught dedication to the state, including a willingness to sacrifice personal property to protect state property. Strict school discipline was considered necessary preparation to fulfill the state's economic and military plans, and to maintain order in factories and public institutions. Teachers were required to strictly follow the state's prescribed curriculum in order to prepare students to accomplish the state's economic plans.

CONCLUSION:
THE GLOBALIZATION OF EUROAMERICAN SCHOOLING

In summary, formal Euroamerican school structures remained in place after independence from colonial rule in the Middle East, the Indian subcontinent. Sub-Saharan Africa, and Korea. The impact of imperialism transformed *Qur'anic* schools and madrasas and enfolded religious instruction into formal Euroamerican school structures, curricula, and pedagogy. Imperialism had ensured the global adoption of the Euroamerican style educational ladder. European languages, particularly English, remained important in the educational programs of these newly liberated countries. Nevertheless, the liberation movements in South and Central America had spawned a progressive education agenda that would eventually reverberate around the world. One of the lasting aspects of this progressive education movement was the focus on indigenous knowledge. Indigenous knowledge would become an important factor in the environmental education revolution. and in developmental plans.

The Educational Security State: China, Japan, the United States, and the European Union

Schools were in turmoil in both countries as President Richard Nixon's plane landed in 1972 at Peking's airport for his historic meeting with Chairman Mao Zedong. Protesting the Viet Nam War and the decline of democracy, U.S. students in high schools and universities were demanding an end to the expanding educational security state. The crown jewels of the American educational system, its great research universities, were under attack for conducting military research for the government and private industries. In the early 1960s, President Clark Kerr of the University of California called upon research universities to service the needs of American industry and government. Waving Mao's *Little Red Book*, protesting students demanded curricula and instructional methods that served their needs and interests as opposed to those of an industrial-military complex. In part, student protests were in reaction to the chain of events leading to and from the 1958 National Defense Education Act; primarily the push from business and the military to make math and science central to the curricula of secondary and higher education. In addition, the Civil Rights movement raised concerns about racial and social class inequalities in the U.S. school system. Many protestors worried about the lack of education for social change, justice, and increased democracy, and the commitment of schools to equal educational opportunity.

Ironically, China's Cultural Revolution was encountering stiff resistance as it tried to dismantle the early beginnings of its national security state. Originally, the Cultural Revolution hoped to end social class bias, reactionary political instruction, separation of theory from practice, and formal teaching methods; the very issues that concerned protesting American students. But more conservative Chinese leaders were worried that economic development was being undermined by sending professors, researchers, and teachers to factories and rural areas to labor alongside the ordinary worker and peasant. The requirement of worker approval for admission to higher education obstructed the educational security state's goal of recruiting the best and brightest to be educated for service to the economy and military. Dismantling an examination system designed to select future experts for economic development touched the very heart of the labor recruiting power of the educational security state.

This period was the crucial test for the educational security state. Could it withstand the international student protests against its service to business and the military? Could it withstand the criticisms that social class and racial inequalities were being reinforced by the examination and sorting of students for education for service to business and the military? What about political education? The educational security state requires that political education results in students supporting the goals of economic growth and consumption, and service to the state. Could it withstand a movement for political education dedicated to participation in social change, promotion of human rights and social justice, and support real participatory democracy? In China and the United States, the answer to all of the above questions was "Yes!" In 2005, the European Union developed a master plan for the educational security state.

DENG XIAOPING: FROM CONFUCIANISM TO THE SOCIALIST ROAD

After Mao's Zedong's death in 1976, Deng Xiaoping rose to power as he reconstructed the Chinese economy and educational system. Paralleling the lives of Mao Zedong and Ho Chi Minh, Deng Xiaoping was born on August 22, 1904 into a merchant family in Sichuan where a preschool tutor taught him Confucian ethics embedded in nursery rhymes in *Three Character Classics* and *Article of One Thousand Words*. Some of his ancestors had passed the Confucian-based imperial examinations. At the age of 6, he attended a modern Confucian primary school. What was "modern" about the school was the study of mathematics and the Chinese language along with traditional Confucian texts. In 1915, at the age of 11, Deng experienced the educational reforms that were sweeping China when he was sent to a junior secondary school. At the school, the traditional study of Confucianism and classical Chinese was replaced with a Westernized curriculum of mathematics, geography, history, natural sciences, music, painting, and vernacular Chinese. After graduating from junior secondary school, Deng enrolled in a modern high school that he attended for only a short time between September 1918 and January 1919.[1]

In June, 1919, Deng Xiaoping joined a work study program that sent him to France where he eventually moved in communist circles and might have crossed paths with Ho Chi Minh and José Mariátegui. In preparation for the trip to France, Deng attended a preparatory school where he studied French and industrial technology. Similar to Indochinese workers like Ho Chi Minh, the French government recruited Chinese to fill the void left in the French labor market by the shortages caused by World War I. Between 1915 and 1918 more than 10,000 Chinese workers had been brought to France. Work-study programs were another method of recruiting Chinese to work in French factories. Between 1919 and 1920, Deng, at the age of 15, along with more than 1,500 students traveled to France under a work-study program.

Working and educational conditions were deplorable. The experience radicalized many of the Chinese students and, like Ho Chi Minh, some joined the newly formed French Communist Party. He Changgong, a work-study student and future Communist China's minister of the coal industry, recalled his experience in France in 1920: "Just like toilers, we would pick up any kind of job—light job, temporary job—whatever job was available. We got up in the middle of the night to help with the market, pulling vegetable carts, pushing milk bottles.... There used to be many horse carts, and we were hired to collect and remove horse and mule dung."[2] Financially, Deng struggled trying to balance working in factories with study. The difficult working conditions caused many Chinese students to demonstrate, which eventually led to a mass riot in Lyons in 1921. Deng joined the French Communist Youth League sometime between 1923 and 1924, and the Communist Party in early 1926 when he arrived in Moscow.[3]

In Moscow, Deng attended the University of the Toilers of China, which in 1928 was renamed the Sun Yat-Sen University. There he studied Marxist theory, the history of international labor movements and social developments, and the history of Chinese and East Asian revolutionary movements. In the spirit of Russification and the attempt to create Soviet hegemony in communist movements, he also studied Russian, the history of the Russian Communist Party, and the structure and operation of the Soviet government. In late 1926, Feng Yuxiang, who headed an army composed of nationalists and communists, requested help from the Soviet Union. The Soviet Union sent arms and the leadership of the Chinese Communist Party in Moscow sent 20 communists, including Deng, to work in Feng's army. Deng arrived in 1927 in Wuhan where he met Mao Zedong and participated in an armed uprising against the nationalists and became a staff worker at the underground Chinese Communist Party headquarters in Shanghai.[4] Deng remained an important player in the Communist Party during the revolutionary years and until the Cultural Revolution.

Thus, Deng's educational career followed the path of many other Asian revolutionaries with an early Confucian education followed by exposure to Western and communist education. Although Deng's career after the completion of the Chinese Communist Revolution is important, my interest is primarily in the central role he played in shaping China's policies after Mao's death in 1976. In the 1960s, Deng's power within the Chinese Communist Party faced an important setback during the Cultural Revolution. Restored to favor in the 1970s, he would eventually ensure China's economic development and the organization of China's educational security state.

During the 1950s, he did articulate some of the ideas that would later play a role in building contemporary China. First was the importance of creating an industrial base for the growth of socialism. After Mao's death, he would criticize Mao for neglecting economic development during the Cultural Revolution. Second, Deng proclaimed, along with Mao, the importance of giving a "Chinese essence" to communism.[5] Similar to statements in the early 20th century that use of Western science and technology should be in the context of Chinese values, many Chinese communists were to emphasize the importance of adapting communist doctrines to Chinese circumstances and culture. Also, an emphasis on Chinese essence was used to distance the country from the Soviet Union.

In 1956, Deng elaborated on the two ideas of economic development and adapting communism to China's needs in a speech to an international youth group titled, "Integrate Marxism–Leninism with the Concrete Conditions of China." As Deng explained to the youth group, China was now on the socialist road to communism: "Following Marxist–Leninist principles, China first had to accomplish a bourgeois democratic revolution. Following this step, China now is building socialism, and then, in the future, advance from socialism to communism."[6] The main problem facing China, he stated, was that it was primarily a peasant society and not an industrial one. The important step on the socialist road was the economic development of China. But this economic development must not, Deng warned, be a simple copy of the experience of other countries. Deng asserted, "The universal truth of Marxism–Leninism must be integrated with the concrete practice of a country—a formulation which is itself a universal truth. It embraces two aspects—universal truth and the integration of that truth with a country's concrete conditions."[7] Deng went on to elaborate the importance of following the socialist road or as he would later call it, the road to socialist modernization:

It is the view of our Chinese Communist Party that the universal truth includes abolishing feudalism and capitalism and realizing socialism, to be followed by communism. Can we do without taking the socialist road? No, we cannot. If we deviate from this universal truth and give up our efforts to establish socialism, the People's Republic of China and the Chinese Communist Party would have no need to exist. How then can China abolish feudalism and capitalism and realize socialism and communism at an earlier date? We have to study the characteristics of our own country. Otherwise, if we mechanically copy the experience of other countries this universal truth will not be realized.[8]

By the 1980s, Deng would argue that the socialist road was superior to the capitalist road in developing industrial economies. In this speech, he warned, "The universal truth calls for abolishing capitalism and exploitation, and realizing socialism. If we depart from it, socialist transformation of capitalist industry and commerce would be out of the question, and we shall find ourselves on the capitalist, not the socialist, road."[9]

Foreshadowing China's educational security state, Deng in the 1950s stressed the importance of using education for industrial development. He gave more stress to the expert side of the "red and expert" education slogan. In a 1954 speech to the Government Administration Council, Deng complimented the Council for "paying close attention to production and capital construction."[10] However, he said they were not paying enough attention to the role of education in industrial development: "They [the Council] are not paying enough attention to the training of cadres, as can be seen from the little attention they have paid to the schools they run. They barely seem to realize that running schools well and training cadres *are the fundamental of our construction program* [my emphasis]."[11] He warned that the failure of secondary vocational schools would hinder future economic development. In 1958, Deng emphasized, "Socialist construction requires well-educated workers and all workers need to be educated."[12]

Like some American leaders in the 1950s, Deng held up the Soviet school system as a model of academic discipline. In his 1954 speech, Deng explained, "Discipline in schools in the Soviet Union is very rigorous. If our students there do not study hard, they are sent back. We should learn from the Soviet schools and set such strict demands on our students. Bad students should be expelled from school, a weapon that schools must wield and that they simply cannot do without."[13] In his 1958 speech on education, Deng called for quality instruction using a centralized curriculum with local control of schools. He complained that "It is inconceivable that our country has not a set of unified teaching materials for secondary schools.... The Ministry of Education should work out ideas and plans with regard to the teaching materials and educational system."[14] A centralized curriculum with local control of schools would later be a hallmark of Deng's educational security state.

And, in line with his later pronouncements that material rewards on the socialist road should be according to ability and contribution to economic growth, Deng called for raising the salaries of professors, engineers, doctors, and other professionals; the very intellectual class attacked during the Cultural Revolution. In Deng's words, which he would reiterate during his economic reforms of the late 1970s and 1980s, "In future wage differentials should be widened, so that genuinely capable people who have contribute greatly to the country receive much higher pay than others."[15] He recommended composing a list of the best academics to receive increased material rewards.

Like many other revolutionaries that were educated in Europe and the Soviet Union, Deng returned home to try and adapted Marxist ideas to local conditions. He had made the educational transition from a Confucian village school, to a Westernized elementary and junior secondary school, to the progressive curriculum of Sun Yat-Sen University. Like others of his generation, including Islamic, Hindu, Japanese, Chinese, Korean, and Indochinese leaders, Western education emphasizing science and mathematics was seen as the key to Euroamerican-style economic development. Of course this meant accepting the Western industrial and consumer model for organizing China's economic system. Deng would eventually throw open China's doors to foreign technology and investments. As he strove to build the socialist road to economic growth, Deng incorporated schools into the educational security state.

MARKET ECONOMY:
"PRACTICE IS THE SOLE CRITERION FOR TESTING TRUTH"
AND "TO EACH ACCORDING TO HIS WORK"

"While the early Bolsheviks stressed education as a means to political democratization," Kalpana Misra explains regarding China's post-Maoist era, "and the Maoists aimed at eliminating class and status distinctions through an increasingly accessible education of uniform quality, Dengist educational reforms focused primarily on the achievement of economic modernization."[16] The focus on education for economic modernization resulted in some major reinterpretation of Marxist ideas regarding the role of socialism in economic development; the role of a market economy under socialism; the criteria of truth; the meaning of social class, and the dictatorship of the Communist Party.

For Deng, education was linked to the socialist road to economic development. One of the things he stressed was that socialism was superior to capitalism in helping "underdeveloped" countries. The conceptualization of China as an underdeveloped country was an important element in

Deng's justification for the major changes he introduced into China's economy and educational system. He articulated this idea in his "Three Worlds" speech before the United Nations in 1974 shortly after Mao restored him to power. In part, the speech was designed to ensure that the rest of the world did not see China as a lackey of the Soviet Union. Deng declared the "First World" to be the two superpowers, the United States and the Soviet Union. He attacked the Soviet Union with the comment, "the superpower that flaunts the banner of socialism is particularly vicious and dangerous."[17] The "Second World" were the developed nations of Europe and Japan, which sometimes accepted the hegemonic control of the two superpowers whereas at other times resented it. Deng included China in the "Third World" of developing nations. He portrayed the "Third World" as the revolutionary force struggling against the imperialism of the "First World" superpowers.

In 1976, Chinese Communist Party announced the Four Modernizations, which included increased development of foreign trade; more technological innovation; stronger central planning; and pay incentives based "from each according to his ability, to each according to his work." The Four Modernizations would profoundly effect education as schools shifted from the emphasis on "Red" during the Cultural Revolution to an emphasis on "Expert." The Four Modernizations became the basis for Deng's plan to put China on the socialist road to modernization. Later, Deng linked, as I explain later in this section, a reconceptualization of social class conflict in China to what he called the Four Cardinal Principles.[18]

For Deng, socialism was superior to capitalism in expanding the economies of third world nations. In 1979, while Deng was explaining why a market economy could function under socialism, he asserted, "We believe that socialism is superior to capitalism. This superiority should be demonstrated in that socialism provides more favorable conditions for expanding the productive forces than capitalism does."[19] Deng then attacked the Cultural Revolution as retarding China's economic accomplishments: "This superiority [of socialism] should have become evident, but owing to our differing understanding of it, the development of the productive forces has been delayed, especially during the past ten-year period to 1976 [the year of Mao's death]."[20]

The benchmarks for development, Deng felt, were to be found in the United States and the Soviet Union. For instance, 3 years after his United Nations speech, Deng told a forum on science and education: "We must admit that the number of China's scientific research personnel is still small and cannot compare with that in the major developed countries. The United States has 1,200,000 scientific research people. The Soviet Union had 900,000 the year before last.... We have only about 200,000."[21] This statement was made after Deng declared in the same speech that, "China must catch up with the most advanced countries in the world."[22]

The introduction of a market economy was a major step in Deng's plans for education and economic development. Under a market economy, there would be both public and private schools regulated by the state. Deng explained the justification for a market economy under socialism in an interview conducted in 1985 by the Editor-in-Chief of *Time Magazine*, Henry Grunwald. Deng told Grunwald: "There is no fundamental contradiction between socialism and a market economy.... If we combine a planned economy with a market economy, we shall be in a better position to liberate the productive forces and speed up economic growth."[23] The important thing in this explanation was that a market economy would still be part of a planned economy. Would this lead to capitalism? "No," Deng stated, "because in the course of reform we shall make sure of two things: one is that the public sector of the economy is always predominant; the other is that in developing the economy we seek common prosperity, always trying to avoid polarization."[24] Will a market economy result in economic inequality? "Of course," Deng explained, "some regions and some people may prosper before others do, and then they can help other regions and people to gradually do the same."[25]

Therefore, market economies operated as one part of planned economy which was designed to place China on the socialist road by increasing economic development. For example, as part of China's economic planning, Special Economic Zones were created that allowed foreign businesses to operate under market conditions. These foreign businesses were given tax holidays and lower tax rates. However, it is clear that these Special Economic Zones were still under the control of the state and were part of a planned economy.[26] For Deng, market economies, foreign investment, Special Economic Zones were experiments in speeding up economic development. Regarding the Special Economic Zones, Deng commented, "By quickening the pace of development, the situation in the four special economic zones, in the Yangtze Delta, and in China as a whole, will be quite different from what it is at present. From now on, we must speed up reform and development."[27]

Deng's advocacy of experimenting with different forms of economic organization, including allowing privately operated schools, was based on a particular Marxist definition of "truth." For Deng, truth was found through practice. If a particular economic method worked to speed China down the socialist road then that economic method was proven true in practice. Deng explained his position on seeking truth in an important keynote address in 1978 to the Central Working Conference planning the Third Plenary Session of the Eleventh Central Committee of the Chinese Communist Party.

In part, Deng was attempting to correct what he considered to be the over-emphasis on political theory in judging truth during the Cultural Revolution. Deng's theoretical campaign was known by the slogan, "Practice is the sole criterion for testing truth."[28] Deng told the Conference, "Only if we emancipate our minds, seek truth from facts, proceed from reality in everything and integrate theory with practice, can we carry out our socialist modernization program."[29] Later in the speech, he declared, "Seeking truth from facts is the basis of the proletarian world outlook as well as the ideological basis of Marxism."[30]

It is not my intention in this book to analyze the implications for Marxist thought of Deng's slogan, "Practice is the sole criterion for testing truth." Kaplan Misra does a good job of this in his book on Post-Maoism.[31] My interest is that the slogan allowed for economic and social experimentation where the major criteria for judging success was economic development as part of socialist modernization. Misra summarized the debate over truth:

> Deng's advocacy of "seek truth from facts" legitimized a reductionist attitude toward practice to the exclusion of any theoretical validation, whatsoever. Such a trend marked a radical departure not only from Mao, but from the Leninist position that "facts do not interpret themselves," and spontaneous theorization resulting from a particular practice is not necessarily true of that practice, hence, the need for a vanguard armed with a scientific theory. Indeed, the whole notion of false consciousness and the science/ideology distinction were ignored in post-Mao discussions on practice, and the epistemological position adopted in relation to the relativity of truth, by most theorists, was decidedly pragmatic.[32]

By unshackling the mind from what he viewed as the heavy hand of theory, Deng argued that the proposition "practice is the sole criterion for testing truth" would generate new ideas about how to keep China on the socialist road to modernization. "To make a revolution," Deng said to the 1978 Central Working Conference, "and build socialism we need large numbers of path breakers who dare to think, explore new ways and generate new ideas. Otherwise, we won't be able to rid our country of poverty and backwardness or catch up with—still less surpass—the advanced countries."[33]

Allowing for "path breakers" raised the issue of the role of the intellectual on the socialist road. Maoist reaction to Confucianism and the attacks on intellectuals during the cultural revolution had seriously undermined the social position of intellectuals. However, Deng's concerns with economic development resuscitated the intellectuals' role. Now the value of intellectuals was to measured by their contribution to economic development. And accordingly, intellectuals should be rewarded. In his speech to the 1978 Central Working Conference, Deng demanded, "All enterprises, schools, research institutes and government offices should set up systems for evaluating work and conferring academic, technical and honorary titles. Rewards and penalties, promotions and demotions should be based on work performance. And they should be linked to increases or reductions in material benefits."[34] After suggesting that material benefits should be linked to work, Deng stressed that "In economic policy, I think we should allow some regions and enterprises to earn more and enjoy more benefits sooner than others, in accordance with their hard work and greater contributions to society."[35]

Resolving problems of social class, and differences in ability and material rewards were key to Deng's restructuring of the educational system and the introduction of a market system. During the cultural revolution, professors and teachers were branded as capitalist roaders and sent to factories and farms for re-education. University students were chosen on the basis of worker support rather than proven ability in secondary school classes and on examinations. Cooperation was to replace competition in the educational system. Mao's fear was that the educational system would support social class differences by giving preferred treatment to children of professionals, state officials, and intellectuals.

Deng resolved these problems by stating that social differences no longer existed in China and that differences in material rewards would not create social class divisions. In 1979, at a forum on the Communist Party's theoretical work, Deng announced that differences between Marxist-defined social classes no longer existed in China: "We do not believe that there is a bourgeoisie within the Party, nor do we believe that under the socialist system a bourgeoisie or any other exploiting class will re-emerge after exploiting classes and the conditions of exploitation have really been eliminated."[36] Deng made it clear that any future problems would not be a result of class struggle but of violation of the laws:

> But we must recognize that in our socialist society there are still counter-revolutionaries, enemy agents, criminals and other bad elements of all kinds who undermine socialist public order, as well as new exploiters who engage in corruption, embezzlement, speculation and profiteering. And we must also recognize that such phenomena cannot be all eliminated for a long time to come. The struggle against these individuals is different from the struggle of one class against another, which occurred in the past (these individuals cannot form a cohesive and overt class).[37]

Because class conflict was eliminated, it meant that all people were now members of the proletariat. Consequently, this reformulation of class in China allowed Deng to continue supporting the idea of the Chinese Communist Party being the dictatorship of the proletariat. Under Deng's interpretation of social class in China, the dictatorship of the proletariat now meant the dictatorship of all people except those criminals trying to undermine socialist public order. In the same 1979 speech when he announced that class conflict no longer existed in China, Deng stressed the importance of what he called the Four Cardinal Principles:

> The Central Committee maintains that, to carry out China's four modernizations, we must uphold the Four Cardinal Principles ideologically and politically. This is the basic prerequisite for achieving modernization. The four principles are:
>
> 1. We must keep to the socialist road.
> 2. We must uphold the dictatorship of the proletariat.
> 3. We must uphold the leadership of the Communist Party.
> 4. We must uphold Marxism–Leninism and Mao Zedong Thought.[38]

Interpreted in the framework of Deng's announcement that social class conflict no longer existed, "the dictatorship of the proletariat" and the "leadership of the Communist Party" meant the dictatorship of the people and the leadership of a political party that represented all people. Political theorist Kalpana Misra argued that Deng's reasoning harkened back to the 1920s when there was a call for "collaboration of the four classes" and "a people's democratic dictatorship":

> Mao's emphasis on violent and disruptive class struggle through the 1960s and 1970s marked a deviant trend that was reversed soon after his passing. The re-adoption of the phrase 'people's democratic dictatorship' and the replacement of class struggle by social struggle signified a return to the dominant tradition.[39]

With the freeing of Communist China from the burden of the class struggle, Deng could now justify inequality in material rewards and educational achievement. In a 1978 talk to the Office of Research on Political Affairs with the descriptive title, "Adhere to the Principle 'To Each According to His Work'," Deng declared. "We must adhere to this socialist principle which calls for distribution according to the quantity and quality of an individual's work.… Political attitude should also be taken into account, but it must be made clear that a good political attitude should find expression mainly in a good performance in socialist labor and a greater contribution society."[40] Unlike Mao, Deng made a link between correct political attitudes and increased material rewards, with good political attitudes meaning hard work for the socialist cause of modernization.

Although Deng supported the principle of "to each according his work," as necessary on the socialist road, he claimed that when communism was finally achieved "the principle of each according to his ability and to each according to his needs will be applied."[41] In a 1984 speech, "Building A Socialism With a Specifically Chinese Character," he summarized his views on the socialist road leading to communism.

> The superiority of the socialist system is demonstrated, in the final analysis, by faster and greater development of those forces than under the capitalist system. As they develop, the people's material and cultural life will constantly improve. One of our shortcomings after the founding of the People's Republic was that we didn't pay enough attention to developing the productive forces. Socialism means eliminating poverty. Pauperism is not socialism, still less communism.[42]

In summary, development under the Four Modernizations and the Four Cardinal Principles would enfold education into economic planning. Schools would be affected by the market economy; acceptance of foreign investment; "To Each According to his Work"; and the end of social class struggle. As Deng stressed throughout his transformation of the Chinese economy, the worth of everything would be measured by its contribution to helping China down the socialist road.

EDUCATION AND THE SOCIALIST ROAD

In May of 1977, Deng announced the end to Mao's fears of creating a powerful intellectual class. He told two members of the Central Committee of the Chinese Communist Party: "To improve education we must walk on two legs, that is we must raise the standards of education at the same time as we make it available to more and more people. It is necessary to establish key primary schools, key secondary schools and key colleges and universities."[43] These "key" schools were to be elite schools. These elite schools would educate the best students. As Deng explained, "It is necessary to bring together, through stiff examinations, the outstanding people in the key secondary schools and the key colleges and universities."[44] In addition to elite schools serving the most qualified students, he proposed identifying the best scientists and technologists and providing them with better living conditions and increased wages. And, in reference to Mao's concerns about correct political attitudes among the intelligentsia, Deng stated, "The political requirements set for these people must be appropriate: they should love the motherland, love socialism and accept the leadership of the Party. If they do their research work well and achieve results, that will be helpful politically and will benefit China."[45] And, in keeping with the idea that all people were members of the proletariat, Deng called for a renewed respect for learning: "The erroneous attitude of not respecting intellectuals must be opposed. All work, be it mental or manual, is labor."[46] In August of 1977, in a speech to a forum on work in science and education, Deng reiterated that scientists and other intellectuals were members of the proletariat: "Both scientific researchers and educational workers are working people. Scientific research and educational work are mental labor—and doesn't mental labor count as labor."[47] Again, he stressed the importance of higher material rewards for scientists and the identifying of key secondary and universities for elite educational training. Students and intellectuals were now essential for the march on the socialist road.

In what might be called the re-Stalinization of student life, Deng called for a return to the student discipline that existed before the Cultural Revolution. Referring to the pre-Cultural Revolution years in his August, 1978 speech, Deng stated, "For quite some time after the founding of the People's Republic, the general atmosphere in our society was good, as were public order and discipline. Students and pupils willingly observed discipline. Young Pioneers wearing red scarves could frequently be seen holding megaphones and helping to direct traffic."[48] The leaders of the cultural revolution, he charged, had led youth astray. To achieve modernization required, according to Deng, the re-institution of formal discipline of students. "If we are to bring about a complete change in the general atmosphere in society as a whole, a good atmosphere must be fostered in the schools. Good attitudes and habits should be cultivated: love of labor, readiness to observe discipline, the desire to make progress, and so on. Teachers are duty-bound to foster such attitudes."[49]

Deng outlined other educational proposals in a September, 1977 speech with the commanding title, "Setting Things Right in Education." The speech strongly criticized officials in the Ministry of Education for not completely abandoning the legacy of the Cultural Revolution. "How can we dismiss," Deng reasoned, "nearly 10 million of China's intellectuals at one stroke? Weren't most of the professionals now at work trained in the first 17 years after 1949?"[50] Turning to the problems in the Ministry of Education, Deng complained, "You people in charge of educational work have yet to emancipate your minds … you don't speak out in defense of the masses of intellectuals…. Educational workers in general are complaining about your Ministry of Education."[51]

How were things to be set right? Deng told the Ministry of Education to abandon the placement of students in workplaces after graduation from secondary school. Students should be directly recruited from secondary school for admission to colleges and universities. Deng admitted that, in the past, he supported policies requiring secondary students to do 2 years of physical labor after graduation. "Facts have shown," he claimed, "that after a couple of years of labor, the students have forgotten half of what they learned at school. This is a waste of time."[52] And, in a critical move against the Cultural Revolution's attempts to create equality between teachers and students, and between teachers themselves, Deng called for a restoration of academic titles: "In colleges and universities, the titles of professor, lecturer and assistant should be restored. The question of re-instituting the system of professional titles has been on many comrades' minds for years. Recently, this question was settled by the Central Committee."[53]

By 1977, Deng was clearly in the process of building an educational system that would compliment the socialist road to modernization. Gone were attempts to govern the system according to political principles that demanded the elimination of bourgeois teachers; an emphasis on equality of educational opportunity; elimination of competitive exams; and the political training of students and teachers through required factory and farm work. Elite secondary schools and universities were to be created under the direct control of the Ministry of Education. The control of other schools would be decentralized to the provincial and city level. The political component of entrance requirements to secondary institutions were dramatically changed. Correct political attitudes, according to Deng, simply involved support of China's process of socialist modernization. In contrast to the requirement of political approval by workers during the Cultural Revolution, Deng stated, "we must stress the applicant's own political conduct. A clear political record, love of socialism and labor, readiness to observe discipline and a determination to support the revolutionary cause—that is all we should require. In short, we should have two main criteria for admitting college students: first, good conduct; and second, a good academic record."[54]

Strengthening the examination system was given priority in a major 1978 address by Deng to the National Conference on Education. Doing well on examinations would become a key element in receiving increased material rewards in China. Similar to other educational security states, government controlled examinations were to exercise power over how well teachers were teaching the official curriculum and in the selection of students for secondary schools and higher education. Typical of many people who think that the primary purpose of schooling is service to the economic system, Deng compared students to factory products: "Examinations are a necessary way of checking on the performance of students and teachers, just as the testing of factory products is a necessary means of quality control."[55]

Deng's 1978 speech to the National Conference on Education gave an official mandate to institute the educational security state. "First," he said, "we must improve the quality of education and raise the level of teaching in the sciences, social sciences and humanities so as to serve socialist construction better.... We must ... build a vast army of working-class intellectuals who are both 'red and expert.' Only then will we be able to master and advance modern science and culture.... Only then will we be able to attain a productivity of labor higher than that under capitalism, transform China into a modern and powerful socialist country and ultimately defeat bourgeois influences in the superstructure."[56]

CHINA'S EDUCATIONAL SECURITY STATE
AND NEON SOCIALISM

China's educational security state determines career and educational futures, causes suicides, promotes cheating, requires high-tech surveillance of exam centers, and exerts moral and economic control. Consider the following article on the happy student embracing the state's right to exam and select people for future material and social benefits. "Deng gives me a chance to develop myself: says former city educated girl," was the headline to a August 20, 2004 article in the *People's Daily* referring to school graduate Zhang Manling and Deng's reinstatement of the examination system. Zhang had appeared in the U.S. weekly, *Time Magazine* as an example of Deng's economic and educational reforms. After completing secondary school in 1969, she was sent back to her native city where she contracted arthritis and began doing low-level jobs in a local hospital. "Though back home," she related, "and with a job, I felt very depressed and disheartened all day long. My fate remained a mystery to me although I spent a great deal of time pondering over it. I wondered what the survival of the fittest is."[58] The article's writer explained, "During the ten-year turmoil, all the institutions of higher learning did away with entrance exams based on merits. Recruitment of college students was decided in compliance with recommendation of farmers and workers."[59]

Then Zhang's prospects improved, according to the article, when Deng called for the reinstatement of entrance examinations. "I felt a fresh wind blowing into my life and a new hope emerging before me," Zhang related. "I postponed my wedding day and braced myself for the entrance examination."[60] She passed and was admitted into one of Deng's "key" universities, the Beijing University. As a model of the Deng's changes in the educational system, she is now, appropriately, deputy director of the Film and TV Center of the Publicity Department of the Yunnan Committee of the Communist Party of China.

In contrast to Zhang's embracing of the examination system, an unidentified mother reportedly sued the Shanghai police for failing to give prompt care to her daughter on June 3, 2004. Depressed at twice failing the college entrance examination, her daughter committed suicide by jumping from their apartment.[61] Besides reports of suicides, there were rumblings about increased cheating on the exams through the use of cell phones and tiny cameras. In response, Beijing government introduced high-tech devices in exam centers that could detect cell phone use within a 30-meter distance.[62] In 2005, a delegate to the National People's Congress, Guo Zeshan, president of the Zhanjiang Teacher's College, introduced an "examination law" to fight exam fraud. Guo explained, "Such a law will involve judicial authorities in exam fraud investigation, prevent examiners and examinees from cheating and maintain the dignity, authority and impartiality of the examination system that has been an effective means of selecting and qualifying professionals since ancient times."[63] He suggested the law should cover domestic and international examinations.

At the heart of China's educational security state is the Education Law of the People's Republic of China. Article 2 of the law makes it clear that all aspects of education, including private educational institutions operating within a market economy are controlled by the state: "This Law shall be applicable to education of all types and at all levels offered within the territory of the People's Republic of China."[64] In keeping with educational security state's enfolding education into economic planning, Articles 3, 4, 5, and 11 place education in the context of socialist modernization and a market economy. Article 3 states: "In developing the cause of socialist education, the State adheres to taking Marxism, Leninism, Mao Zedong Thought and the theory of *building socialism with Chinese characteristics as its guidelines* [sic] ... [my emphasis]."[65] Article 4 asserts: "Education is the basis of the socialist modernization drive ..."[66]

In supporting socialist modernization, Article 5 states a goal is reminiscent Marx's concept of polytechnical education and Mao's concerns about combining education and labor. Under Deng, requirements for students to work in factories and agriculture were suspended. Article 5 declares: "Education must serve the socialist modernization drive and must be combined with production and physical labor in order to train for the socialist cause builders and successors who are developed in an all-around way—morally, intellectually and physically."[67]

And, in reference to a market economy, Article 11 states: "To meet the needs of developing a socialist market economy and promoting social progress, the State carries forward educational reform, fosters a coordinated development of education at various levels and of various types, and establishes and improves a system of life-long education."[68]

A key role of schools in an educational security state is the promotion of nationalism and loyalty to the state. Article 6 requires: "The State conducts education among educatees in patriotism, collectivism, socialism as well as in the importance of ideals, ethics, discipline, the legal system, national defense and national unity."[69]

China has adopted an administrative control system similar to the United States and that advocated by the World Bank. In Western nations, this system is often referred to as *neo-liberal* or *neo-conservative*. It combines centralized control of what is taught in schools through a system of state-mandated tests and curriculum with decentralization and a combination of private and public schools. In general, the neo-liberal or neo-conservative vision is of states turning over their traditional services, such as schooling, to a market economy but retaining control through regulation.

Under China's Education Law the "State encourages enterprises, institutions, public organizations and other social organizations, as well as individual citizens to establish and run schools or other institutions of education in accordance with the law."[70] The basic conditions for establishing a school include organizational structure, qualified teachers, an approved building, and a source of funding. These privately established schools are given the power to organize their own administrative system. Article 29 ensures that these privately operated schools conform to state policies and educational goals.

> Article 29—Schools and other institutions of
> education shall fulfil the following obligations:

1. to observe laws and regulations;
2. to implement the State's educational policies, apply the standards set by the State for education and teaching and guarantee the quality of education and teaching;
3. to safeguard the lawful rights and interests of the educatees, teachers and other staff and workers;
4. to provide convenience in appropriate ways for educatees and their guardians to have access to the educatees' academic performance and other relevant information;
5. to collect fees according to the regulations of the State and publicize the individual items of such fees;
6. to be subjected to supervision according to law.[71]

Of course, the national examination system, which determines entrance into secondary and higher education, indirectly controls the content of education. In reality, the content of instruction in public and private schools is governed by the requirement of passing national exams. Thus, exams determine instruction and the knowledge that students will be taught. Article 20 of the Education Law gives the power of control over national examinations to the education department of the State Council. Article 20 states: "The State applies a national education examination system. The administrative department of education under the State Council shall determine the types of national education examination which shall be undertaken by the institutions that conduct such education examination as approved by the State."[72]

In conclusion, Deng's reforms set aside Mao's political objectives and efforts to provide greater equality of educational opportunity and to ensure that education did not reinforce social classes. The introduction of a market economy and the goal of socialism with a Chinese essence are incorporated into the State's educational plans. Schools are now key to selecting the talent that will help China march down the socialist road of modernization. By declaring an end to class struggle, Deng was able to claim that increased material rewards resulting from educational advantages did not reinforce social class differences because they contributed to the economic prosperity of all the people. Privatization and decentralization of the management of state schools is for the purpose of making schools more efficient in carrying out the State's agenda. Examinations and curricular regulation ensure direct control over what is taught to students. Therefore, after Mao's experiments with different forms of progressive education, the People's Republic of China's educational policies are closely tied to the economic needs of socialist modernization.

JAPAN AND THE UNITED STATES: EDUCATIONAL SECURITY STATES

In the last half of the 20th century, Japanese and United States' educational policies were intertwined in the construction of educational security states. But in the 21st century, Japan's school system was backing away from exam-driven instruction as the United States was embracing an exam-driven system to educate workers for the global labor market. This story is filled with ironic twists and turns in policies. The story's plot line contains the U.S. conquest of Japan during World War II and the imposition of a U.S. educational structure; the conflict between progressives and educational conservatives in the United States and Japan during the 1950s, including similar charges of communism; the ensuing development of Japan's school system as a model of test-driven instruction tied to economic development; American fear in the 1980s that they were losing ground in the global economy because of an inferior school system; American admiration of Japan's schools and exam system and the adoption of a similar model to improve America's competitive edge in global markets; and Japan's concerns that its test-driven schools were stifling creativity, cultivating uniformity, and, consequently, slowing its economic development.

It will be recalled from previous chapters that in the 19th-century Japan was the first nation in the region to adopt a Western model of education in order to develop the science and military technology necessary to stop the spread of Western imperialism. Its early Westernized schools attracted scholars from throughout the area. In keeping with the idea that Westernizing the Japanese educational system was protection against Western colonialism, Japan's official surrender to the United States at the end of World War II on August 15, 1945 was accompanied by an announcement by Emperor Hirohito, that "we declared war on America and Britain out of our sincere desire to ensure Japan's self-preservation and the stabilization of East Asia."[73]

U.S. occupiers quickly engaged in purging the Japanese school system of nationalism and reorganizing for more democratic control.[74] The Civil Information and Education Section of the Supreme Command Allied Powers ordered the removal from textbooks any mention of Japanese colonialism, Japanese superiority, and "Concepts and attitudes which are contrary to the principles set forth in the Charter of the United Nations."[75] Schools were given a list of designated pages to be removed from textbooks.[76] The 1946 Japanese Constitution, written under the influence of U.S. occupation, states in Article 26: "All people shall have the right to receive an equal education correspondent to their ability, as provided by law. All people shall be obligated to have all boys and girls under their protection receive ordinary education as provided for by law. Such compulsory education shall be free."[77] And, similar to American schools, schooling was to be separated from established religions: "The State and its organs shall refrain from religious education or any other religious activity."[78] The separation of religion from education became important in the 21st century as Japanese officials tried to introduce more moral instruction in the public schools. Under the guidance of U.S. educators, the Japanese educational system was organized around the U.S. model of schooling. Compulsory education was mandated for 6 years of primary schooling for ages ranging from 5 to 12, and for 3 years of middle school for ages ranging from 12 to 15. Graduates of middle schools could enter technical schools or high schools for ages 15 to 18. Those graduating from high school could enter a university or junior college.[79]

Decentralization of educational control occurred with the 1948 Board of Education Law. Modeled on the U.S. school system, the law created local school boards with elected members and an appointed superintendent of education. Of particular importance were powers granted to local school boards regarding: "Matters concerning the curriculum contents to be taught and their treatment"; "Matters concerning selection of textbooks"; and "Matters concerning social education."[80]

Similar to some public officials in the United States in the 1950s, United States occupiers were concerned with communist influences in Japanese schools. Consequently, despite claims that they were trying to make Japanese schools more democratic, U.S. occupiers tried to purge the schools of supposed communist influences. In the end, this meant that the democratic reform of schools was not accompanied by progressive educational practices. Like U.S. conservatives, Japanese conservatives balked at the idea of progressive reform. Exemplifying these conservative concerns was a 1953 magazine article written by a college professor, Kitaoka Juisha, resurrecting Confucian arguments for the necessity of state control of morality. "The Japanese people ... are apt to misuse the freedom that they have been granted ... when the control of morals is relaxed, the harlots shamelessly parade the streets, when censorship is abolished, the book-shops bury their counters with erotic magazines. It is doubtful whether such a people should in fact be granted too much freedom."[81]

Western-styled Japanese progressive-liberals, socialists, and communists struggled with conservatives over the democratic control of schools. Progressive-liberals objected to state domination of education and the use of education to control national morality. Progressive-liberals worried about the possible resurrection of the Imperial Rescript on Education and the growing recentralization of control over the educational system.

Central control of education returned when the United States withdrew its opposition to nationalistic education and centralization. As Teruhisa Horio argued, "Of course this gave rise to the contradiction, still visible in Japanese life today, of a form of patriotism that is subordinated to American global interests."[82] Released from the bonds of pro-democratic education rhetoric, Minister of Education Amano Teiyu released the 1951 "An Outline for National Moral Practice," which reiterated traditional Japanese concepts of the individual to the state. "The State is the womb of our existence, the ethical and cultural core of our collective existence ... the nation depends on those activities which the individual willingly performs so as to contribute to the well-being of the State."[83]

In 1955, the Law Concerning the Management and Operation of Local School Administration undermined liberal-progressive hopes of a democratically controlled and empowering education. The legislation caused an uproar in the Japanese legislative body, the Diet, and police were called in to maintain order. In its final form, the legislation replaced elected school boards with appointed ones. In 1958, the Education Ministry's course of study was made legally binding on local schools and rigorous textbook inspection was instituted. Drawing on traditional beliefs regarding the subordination of individuals to the state, Minister of Education Kiyose Ichero justified these changes: "It is simply not good enough to speak about the rights that accrue to individuals as the members of a democratic society; we must also make as concerted an effort as possible to advocate and nurture ... loyalty and devotion to the State."[84]

There was a close parallel between the United States and Japan during the late 1950s and early 1960s regarding education and national human power planning. Japanese political and education leaders began resurrecting and refining the 19th century goal of schooling for economic development. During the same period, U.S. leaders advocated human capital development as part of military competition with Soviet Union; proposed human power policies found their way into the U.S.'s National Defense Education Act. The Japanese adopted language similar to that used in the United States by calling for "human resource" development and "manpower planning." Educational and political leaders in both countries instituted plans to "sort" students to meet human power needs.[85] In the 1960s, Japan implemented a system of national examinations. In addition to human resource development, national examinations ensured that teachers would follow the state curriculum. Inevitably, teachers were forced to teach to the test. "Now," in the words of Teruhisa Horio, "through this new mechanism [national testing] for controlling teachers, the Ministry attempted to bring the remaining loose ends of educational freedom within the purview of its administrative control."[86]

National testing was basic to using education for economic development. In 1960, the Japanese government's Economic Advisory Committee captured the spirit of these policies in the title of its report, "The Advance of Manpower Capability and the Promotion of Scientific Technology." The language of the report captured the educational spirit of school systems serving the global economy. Students were "human resources" rather than future citizens or human beings. The goal of education was serving the economic system. "It is essential to promote manpower development as part of economic policy," asserted the Economic Advisory Committee, "Human resource development and deployment will become increasingly significant in the future."[87] The same themes appeared in the 1984 report of the Education Council of the Japan Committee for Economic Development. Worried about continued economic expansion, the report expressed concern about human resource strategies for the next century. The report claimed, "In such an environment, 'acquisition and fostering of human resources' are considered to be more significant than any other aspects of society."[88]

Testing was the key to state control of the curriculum and the implementation of human resource development. Testing was used to identify the talented while weeding out workers who would fill low-paying jobs. In 1960, the Japanese Minister of Education announced, "A broadly based policy to develop human talent to support the long-term economic planning.... To this end it is critically important to discover outstanding talent at an early age and cultivate it through an appropriate form of education."[89]

Japanese authorities identified the end of junior high school as the important time for administering a national examination. Like later policies in China, an entrance examination was required for secondary schooling. In the words of the Education Ministry, "it is necessary at the end of the period of compulsory education [junior high school] to measure the child's competencies and aptitudes, and on the basis thereof to provide guidance regarding *the path that will lead in the future to both individual success and usefulness to the nation as a whole* [my emphasis]."[90] Examinations for university admissions completed the sorting process for human resources. Testing resulted in students engaging in juken senso or "examination preparation war." In preparation for the examinations, parents began to send their children to private cram schools.[91]

JAPAN AS THE OTHER IN U.S. EDUCATIONAL POLICY

It was this examination-driven Japanese school system that some American leaders began to admire by the 1980s. The 1960s and 1970s were a difficult time for American conservative educators as student protests, paralleling China's Cultural Revolution, demanded an end to the domination of human capital planning in education and a return to progressive educational goals. Student walkouts, demonstrations against corporate involvement in universities, and the rise of the Students for Democratic Society created a climate antithetical to formalistic education. Progressive reforms, such as alternative schools, open classrooms, unification of the curriculum, and learning through real-life experiences dominated educational policy discussions.

The revolt against U.S. formalistic educational practices and links between schools and national human power planning would provide a backdrop to conservative criticisms of U.S. schooling into the 21st century. Particularly after the 1980s, conservatives would demand a return to academic "rigor" and a school system controlled by examinations. In addition, the struggle for equal educational opportunities during the 1960s, again paralleling similar efforts by Mao in China, complicated the issue of academic rigor for conservatives. Critics of formal education claimed that intelligence and achievement tests discriminated against the poor and cultural and racial minorities groups in the United States. In addition, some cultural minorities began to demand culturally relevant curricula.

American conservatives would consider multiculturalism a threat to academic standards.

Therefore by the 1980s, American supporters of formal education were seeking some excuse for moving U.S. schools away from a progressive agenda and support of minority cultural rights. Global economics provided that excuse with the issuance of the 1983 report of the U.S. government-sponsored National Commission on Excellence in Education: *A Nation at Risk*. In fact, Diane Ravitch and Chester Finn, two of the drum beaters for a return of U.S. Schools to traditional formal academic instruction, recalled that their founding in 1981 of the Education Excellence Network received little attention until the issuance of the *Nation at Risk* report. Both Ravitch and Finn served in the U.S. Department of Education and dedicated their professional lives to the creation of government-mandated standardized curriculum and high-stakes examinations. "To put it mildly," they remembered, "this bombshell [*A Nation at Risk*] awakened parents, educators, governors, legislators, and the press…. Its warning of 'a rising tide of mediocrity' helped launch what came to be called the excellence movement, which included a mass of other commissions, studies, and reports."[92]

The *Nation at Risk* report made education central to economic globalization. U.S. Secretary of Education Terence Bell requested the National Commission on Excellence in Education to compare "American schools and colleges with those of other advanced nations."[93] The Commission was created as a legal U.S. government advisory committee to the Secretary of Education who appointed its chair and membership. It conducted 17 Commission meetings, public forums, and panel discussions in 11 different sites across the United States.[94]

After making this comparison, the Commission dramatically opened its report: "Our nation is at risk. Our once unchallenged preeminence in commerce, industry, science, and technological innovation is being overtaken by competitors throughout the world."[95] And, using military images appropriate for an educational security state, the report asserted: "If an unfriendly foreign power had attempted to impose on America the mediocre educational performance that exists today, we might well have viewed it as an act of war."[96] The Commission blamed the public schools for the declining place of the United States in world markets.

The problem, which supported the contentions of educational conservatives, was identified as the decline of the educational security state that had been created in the 1950s in response to Soviet technological gains. "We have squandered," the report claimed, "the gains in student achievement made in the wake of the Sputnik challenge."[97] And again using military imagery, the report asserted, "We have, in effect, been committing an act of unthinking, unilateral educational *disarmament* [my emphasis]."[98]

Although the goals of U.S. schooling had been frequently attuned to world issues such as the Cold War, the *Nation at Risk* placed the educational objectives squarely in the arena of global economics. Under the report's section titled "The Risk," there appeared the following statement on globalization:

> The World is indeed one global village. We live among determined, well-educated, and strongly motivated competitors. We compete with them for international standing and markets, not only with products but also with the ideas of our laboratories and neighborhood workshops. America's position in the world may once have been reasonably secure with only a few exceptionally well-trained men and women. It is no longer.[99]

Who were the "others" threatening U.S. dominance in the global economy. The report specifically identified Japan, South Korea, and Germany.

> The risk is not only that the Japanese make automobiles more efficiently than Americans and have government subsidies for development and export. It is not just that the South Koreans recently built the world's most efficient steel mill, or that American machine tools, once the pride of the world, are being displaced by German products. It is also that these developments signify a redistribution of trained capability throughout the globe.[100]

What evidence was presented that American schools, and particularly the progressive reforms touted in the 1960s and 1970s, had brought down the American economy? None! There was evidence presented of declining test scores on college entrance examinations and standardized achievement tests. However, there was no evidence presented of a relationship between test scores and U.S. economic decline. If fact, there are so many factors determining economic growth and expansion that it is difficult to blame one factor let alone placing the burden on education. Could it have been the federal debt left from the Vietnam War, the surge in oil prices, or a failure of American corporate management? Besides, graduates do not leave school and immediately bring down an economy. In fact, the graduates of the supposedly educationally superior 1950s were more than 40-years old by 1983. They were the ones holding the leadership positions in business and the military. David Berliner and Bruce Biddle would eventually title their book about this heavy handed criticism of public school, *The Manufactured Crisis: Myths, Fraud, and the Attack on America's Public Schools*.[101]

The real concern was enfolding schools into the economic and military needs of the educational security state. In its list of "Indicators of the Risk," the report stated:

Business and military leaders complain that they are required to spend millions of dollars on costly remedial education and training programs in such
basic skills as reading, writing, spelling, and computation. The Department of
the Navy, for example, reported to the Commission that one-quarter of its recent recruits cannot read at the ninth grade level.... Without remedial work
they cannot even begin, much less complete, *the sophisticated training essential in
much of the modern military* [my emphasis].[102]

Similar to China's Deng Xiaoping during the same time period, the
Commission on Excellence in Education recommended tight governance
of the educational system through "standardized tests of achievement."[103]
The first recommendation of the Commission was increasing academic requirements for high school graduation "for all students."[104] I am emphasizing phrase "for all students" because after the Commission's report, there
would be a push for uniform graduation requirements that would undercut
any attempt to individualize the curriculum based on student interests. The
second recommendation initiated the drive to create centralized control of
the curriculum and exam system similar to Japan. "We recommend," the
Commission said in words that were harbingers to future strict government
control of the knowledge disseminated by schools, "that schools, colleges
and universities adopt more rigorous and measurable standards...." Certainly worrisome to defenders of academic freedom in higher education
was the inclusion of colleges and universities in the call for "measurable
standards." In this recommendation, the Commission stated, "Standardized tests of achievement (not to be confused with aptitude tests) should be
administered at major transition points from one level of schooling to another and particularly from high school to college or work."[105]

The testing recommendation raised the issue of political power, similar
to what happened in Japan in the 1950s, over the control of the content of
instruction. In the United States, state governments had the constitutional
power to control local schools. Could there be nationwide examinations
that would control the content of instruction similar to those in Japan? Political control of knowledge or the context of instruction was an important
issue. Obviously, teachers would be required directly or indirectly to teach
students the material that would be on the standardized tests of achievement. This would be particularly true if the tests were used to determine
promotion between grades and graduation from high school.

The Commission avoided a discussion of which branch of government
would attempt to control knowledge in schools by leaving the issue unre-
solved. In a confusing statement, the Commission called for *nationwide* tests
administered through local and state governments. The implication was
that all U.S. students would be subjected to the same tests. The Commission

recommended: "The tests should be administered as part of a nationwide (but not federal) system of state and local standardized tests."[106]

It was President George H. W. Bush who, after being elected in 1988, recommended a federal system of achievement tests as part of an educational plan called "Goals 2000." In 2001, federal legislation called "No Child Left Behind" would require states to administer standardized achievement tests at different transition points in the students' progress through schools. Under "No Child Left Behind," the control of knowledge in the schools would be given to state governments under federal supervision.[107]

Also, the Commission advocated absorbing an increasing amount of the lives of children and adolescence in efforts to achieve global economic and military dominance. One could argue that the ultimate goal of an educational security state would be engaging the entire lives of children and youth in preparation to meet economic and military needs. Penetration into family life and after-school life would give schools greater space and time to enfold student lives into the needs of the educational security state. The Commission recommended more homework and a longer school day and year. "We recommend," the Commission's report stated, "that significantly more time be devoted to learning the New Basics. This will require more effective use of the existing school day, a longer school day, or a lengthened school year. Students in high schools should be assigned far more homework than is now the case."[108]

The "New Basics" referred to a uniform curriculum recommended for all high school students. These basics were attuned to what Commission members believed were required to ensure the United States' ability to compete in world markets. Therefore it is not surprising to find the arts missing from the New Basics. The recommended New Basics were 4 years of English, 3 years of mathematics, 3 years of science, 3 years of social studies, and a ½ year of computer science.[109]

For some Americans, the recommendation for nationwide testing brought into sharper focus the organization of Japanese schools and Japan's economic achievements. Typical of U.S. corporate fans of Japanese education was Louis Gerstner, Chair and CEO of IBM. Applauding the accomplishments of the Japanese school system, Gerstner and his colleagues in U.S. school reform in the 1990s wrote, "The Japanese, who boast one of the most successful school systems in the world, tell interviewers that they have the best bottom half in the world. They do. They have perfected mass education, and educate nearly everyone."[110] William Bennett, former Secretary of Education and conservative critic of U.S. schools, revered the Japanese schools. He claimed, "Our educational ideals are better realized on a large scale in Japan."[111]

Admirers of Japanese workers such as Benjamin Duke, in his book *The Japanese School: Lessons for Industrial America*, praised the amount of time of a child's life absorbed by the Japanese exam system, particularly the sending of children to private cram schools for exam preparation. This was readying the student for work in the global economy. In keeping with the military imagery of the educational security state, Duke praised "ronin" or masterless warriors who, after failing university entrance examinations, attended full day courses at Yobiko schools. In the Japanese system of exam preparation, Yobiko schools enroll as many 35,000 in branches across the country. Jukus are privately operated neighborhood schools focusing on examination preparation. They operate outside the hours of regular schools. So, parents might send their children to a juku in the evenings or on Saturdays or Sundays. In addition, there are commercially published home tests and drill books for practice at home. Similar to the recommendations of the Commission on Excellence in Education, a large proportion of the life of the Japanese child is committed to preparation for work in the global economy.[112]

JAPAN AND THE UNITED STATES: THE EDUCATIONAL SECURITY STATE IN THE 21ST CENTURY

Japanese education was reaching a crisis point as U.S. politicians were pushing their schools to adopt standardized curricula and high-stakes examinations, and filling the life of the children and adolescence with preparation for a global workforce. The American goal would reach some completion with the passage of the 2001 federal legislation "No Child Left Behind."[113] Ironically, "No Child Left Behind" was passed 1 year after the Japanese exam-driven system was declared "on the verge of crisis" by the Japanese Prime Minister's National Commission on Educational Reform. The Commission's report was submitted to Prime Minister Yoshiro Mori and contained the fearful warning: "At the threshold of the 21st century ... the reality is the Japanese education is deteriorating, and this cannot be overlooked. Continued occurrences of bullying, students who refuse to go to school, school violence, classroom disruption, violent juvenile and other problems concerning education have become serious."[114] Using language similar to *A Nation at Risk*, the report tried to sound an emergency call to change Japanese education: "We are on the verge of a crisis; our society will be unable to carry on if the current situation continues."[115]

The Japanese Ministry of Education asserted that the Commission's report showed that "through the standardization of education resulting from excessive egalitarianism, and the cramming of immoderate levels of knowledge, education oriented toward the individuality and competence of the children has been given to neglect."[116] One Commission member, Ikuyo Kaneko, principal of Keio Yochisha Elementary School, applauded the actions of the Ministry of Education after the issuance of the report for reducing required learning standards for each subject by 30%. Principal Ikuyo commented, "The 30% cut is the deregulation the education ministry has made over the nation's education system. It means schools will have more flexibility over *what and how* they teach students [my emphasis]."[117]

Consequently, Japanese educational reformers were blaming standards and the examination system for increased problems with children at the same time that this agenda was being nationalized in the United States with the 2001 passage of "No Child Left Behind." The Commission's report was very explicit as to what it thought needed to be corrected in its test driven educational system. The report's "Introduction" contained the following bulleted objectives:

- Remedy standardized education and introduce an educational system that develops individuality.
- Remedy the excessive emphasis on rote learning and diversify university entrance examinations.[118]

The report warned, "The trend of stressing similarity to others has created the tendency to hamper the creation of new values and the emergence of leaders who can lead society."[119]

It is important to note that raising these concerns did not mean changing the overall goal of schooling to produce workers for competition in the global economy. The report was simply stating that an educational system controlled by government curriculum standards and examinations might not be the best way to ensure a growing economy. In fact, the report suggested that standardization and exams were contributing to major social and psychological problems among Japan's young people. The report specifically called for promoting "education that cultivates a view of a career and work."[120] In fact, the report suggested that globalization required major changes in the test-driven educational system.

> People in the world are linked directly, information is instantly shared, and the globalization of the economy is progressing. The structure and aspects of society have been changing on a global scale, and complexities have emerged which are difficult to cope with given existing organizations and systems.... The traditional educational system is lagging behind the current of the times.[121]

The Commission's major reform proposals blamed national examinations for creating conditions that promoted rote learning and stifled creativity. "It is noted," the report stated, "that children in Japan become dull as they advance to junior and senior high schools and universities, although elementary school children are lively. The reason behind this is that students are so conscious of university entrance examinations that ... their study is mainly concentrated on rote learning."[122] Consequently, the Commission proposed that universities use a variety of measures for determining college admission, including essays, interviews, and recommendations, and that entrance exams be changed to measure a diversity of academic talents and critical thinking skills. It was also proposed that the secondary school entrance examination be eliminated by merging lower and upper secondary schools. In keeping with neo-liberal global trends and the desire to promote more intellectual diversity, the report called for decentralization of control, greater parental involvement in schools, and community schools. This greater local control over the curriculum was aided by the Ministry of Education's 30% reduction in curriculum requirements.

For some Japanese educators, these proposals did not go far enough. For instance, Daisaburo Hashizume, a sociology professor at the Tokyo Institute of Technology (TIT) called for abolishing entrance examinations: "University entrance exams are not meeting the goals they're supposed to achieve. To make a rational system that creates less strain for a student, we should abolish entrance exams. Unless we do that, 'reforms' are never really going to reform." He objected to the "exam hell" that had become part of Japanese student culture.

Similar to Japan's educational reformers, U.S. critics of the implementation of an exam-driven educational system expressed their outrage at educational trends in books with descriptive titles, such as *One Size Fits Few: The Folly of Educational Standards* by Susan Ohanian and Kathy Emery; *The Case Against Standardized Testing: Raising the Scores, Ruining the Schools* by Alfie Kohn; *Standardized Minds: The High Price of America's Testing Culture and What We Can Do to Change It* by Peter Sacks; and *Why is Corporate America Bashing Our Schools?* by Susan Ohanian.[123]

GLOBALIZATION AND NATIONALISM: THE EDUCATIONAL SECURITY STATE IN JAPAN AND THE UNITED STATES

In the 21st century, public officials in Japan and the United States expressed concern about maintaining a strong nation in the face of globalization and disruptive student behavior. The report of Japan's National Committee on Educational Reform and the U.S. legislation "No Child Left Behind" dealt with the issue of character education and national identity. I remind the reader that what I mean by "nation" is the emotional and imaginary feeling of personal belonging and attachment to the people and territorial boundaries encompassed by the political authority of the state.

In Japan, the issue of character education centered on protection of traditional values. The report of Japan's National Commission on Educational Reform blamed the loss of traditional values on its youth crisis. The report claimed:

> Self-discipline, consideration for others, love of nature, a feeling of deep respect for that beyond an individual's capability, respect for traditional culture and social norms, *fostering a mentality and attitude which show affection toward one's own home country or nation, learning basic knowledge or culture required for life in society must be the basis for all education.* Today's educational crisis in Japan is rooted in the neglect of these basics of a natural and fundamental education. Not only schools and homes but also society as a whole are required to share this understanding and address the situation in order to realize these basics of education [my emphasis].[124]

The report made it clear that the fostering of traditional values did not mean a narrow nationalism but the maintenance of a Japanese identity in the context of globalization or, in the words of the report, "fostering people who, while having identity as a Japanese, are able to contribute to mankind in the progress of globalization."[125] The report advocated the teaching of morals in elementary, junior, and senior high schools. It should be noted that the teaching of morality had been part of the Japanese curriculum since the restoration of state control in the 1950s. In the 2000 report, moral instruction is specifically tied to the problem of Japanese identity in a globalized environment. The report calls for instruction in Japanese "classics, philosophy, [and] history" as part of moral instruction.[126]

In discussing globalization, the report emphasized the importance of maintaining a Japanese identity through teaching traditional culture while recognizing the importance of modern science and technology. This discussion was similar to that captured in the 19th-century phrase "Western Science, Eastern Morals" which marked the introduction of Western educational forms. In referring to the new globalized age of science and technology, particularly information technology and life science, the report emphasized: "Under such conditions, it is also necessary to develop and give a great deal of respect for our traditions, culture, and other elements to be handed down to the Japanese in future generations from the viewpoint of contributing generally to mankind while possessing an awareness and identity as a Japanese person."[127]

Similar to Japan's National Commission on Educational Reform, the United States's legislation "No Child Left Behind" advocates moral instruction in the form of "Partnerships in Character Education" and "School Prayer." "Character education," according to a press release from the U.S. Department of Education, "is a key feature of No Child Left Behind, the landmark education reform law designed to change the culture

of American schools."[128] For self-identified "compassionate conservatives" such as President George W. Bush, who claimed responsibility for
the passage of "No Child Left Behind," there is an assumption that in
most cases poverty, crime, and other social problems result from a failure
in personal character and values. President Bush frequently combined his
religious views with a high degree of patriotism.[129] Consequently, direct
charity or government welfare doesn't solve the problem, in fact, it might
reinforce negative character traits. The solution is providing the conditions by which people can help themselves. Self-help, compassionate conservatives believe, will result in a transformation of character and the
acquisition of positive values. This character transformation is aided by
exposure to religious values. Consequently, the imposed discipline of educational standards and testing is to help students, according to compassionate conservatives, to develop the character traits of self-discipline and
hard work. Aiding in this process are character education, student-initi-
ated school prayer, and exposure to religious values as provided for in the
School Prayer section of "No Child Left Behind."[130]

Therefore, in both countries, leaders linked traditional values with
moral character; of course traditional values were different in both countries with the Confucian emphasis on social harmony in Japan and individual responsibility in the United States. In addition, both countries
promoted the teaching of a nationalistic history in schools as a means of
maintaining national identity. In the development of national standards
and tests in the United States in the 1990s, the subject of history proved to
be the most politically contentious subject. What interpretation of history
should appear in U.S. textbooks? American neo-conservatives wanted a
highly nationalistic history reflecting what they considered to be traditional
American values. "No Child Left Behind" specifically addressed this issue
by providing grants for the teaching of traditional U.S. history. In this context, traditional U.S. history refers to the content of history prior to an emphasis on social and cultural history that occurred in the 1960s. American
neo-conservatives believe that social and cultural history eroded the nationalistic spirit of public school history.[131] The dispute highlights significant
differences regarding the teaching and interpretation of U.S. history. For
neo-conservatives, the major purpose of teaching history is to create national unity by teaching a common set of political and social values. These
common values, according to the neo-conservative approach, should be
based on the beliefs underlying U.S. institutions. In the words of historian
Arthur Schlesinger Jr., "For better or worse, the White Anglo-Saxon
Protestant tradition was for two centuries—and in crucial respects still
is—the dominant influence on American culture and society.... The language of the new nation, its laws, its institutions, its political ideas, its litera-

ture, its customs, its precepts, its prayers, primarily derived from Britain."[132] "No Child Left Behind" states that grants are to be given

> (1) to carry out activities to promote the teaching of traditional American history in elementary schools and secondary schools as a separate academic subject (*not as a component of social studies*); and

> (2) for the development, implementation, and strengthening of programs to teach traditional American history as a separate academic subject (*not as a component of social studies*) within elementary school and secondary school curricula.[133]

The militaristic parts of "No Child Left Behind" heightened the nationalistic spirit embodied in those parts of the legislation that address traditional history, English acquisition, character education, and school prayer. This is in keeping with the military and economic goals of an educational security state. The legislation specifically gives U.S. military recruiters access to public schools to recruit students for duty in the armed forces: "each local educational agency receiving assistance under this Act shall provide, on a request made by military recruiters or an institution of higher education, access to secondary school students names, addresses, and telephone listings."[134] This was required even if a state had a law barring the military from public schools: "A local educational agency prohibited by Connecticut State law (either explicitly by statute or through statutory interpretation by the State Supreme Court or State Attorney General) from providing military recruiters with information or access as required by this section shall have until May 31, 2002, to comply with that requirement."[135] In addition, the legislation suggests hiring former military personnel as school teachers and counting military service as training for vocational education.[136] In a section of supporting innovative preretirement teacher education certification programs it is required that these programs "shall (1) provide recognition of military experience and training as related to certification or licensing requirements"[137] The equating of military training and duty with teacher training reflects an educational security state where public schools are required to serve the economy and military.

JAPAN, CHINA, AND KOREA: THE HISTORY TEXTBOOK CONTROVERSY

On April 5, 2005, the Japanese Ministry of Education approved eight history textbooks for use in junior high schools. The action sparked protests in China and Korea, with Chinese demonstrators demanding a boycott of Japanese goods. The ministry's approval of a highly nationalistic history textbook paralleled a similar situation in the United States. In Japan, the textbook that sparked the international controversy was written by a nationalistic group of academics called the Japanese Society for History Textbook Reform. This group accused other Japanese history textbooks of being "biased against" Japan and filled with "self-denigration."[138] Before the 2005 decision by the Minister of Education, protests in Japan had already occurred when the Ehime Prefecture announced that it would be using the nationalistic textbook. In response to the protests, a spokesman for the Japanese Society for History Reform declared, "We respect the Ehime Prefectural Board of Education's decision. Japan's education has been based on view of the Allied forces [after World War II] that try to describe *the nation as a sole evil*. The textbook is a model *to alter such a prejudiced thought*."[139] One day after the 2005 Minister of Education's decision an editorial in the Chinese *People's Daily* reported that the Japanese Society for History Reform wrote the book to counter "a historical conception of maltreatment" and "anti-Japanese education." The goal of the Society's text was to make Japanese "feel proud."[140]

In Japan and the United States, conservative nationalist groups want textbooks to present a positive view of their nation's past without giving attention to unsavory incidents and time periods. This is exemplified by the Japanese Society for History Textbook Reform references to "biased against Japan," "self-denigration," and "the nation as a sole evil." Similar language was used by neo-conservatives when national history standards were released in the United States in 1994. Lynne Cheney (her husband was famed neo-conservative and, later Vice President, Dick Cheney), who at the time was head of the National Endowment for the Humanities, attacked the standards for making "it sound as if everything in America is wrong and grim."[141] When history standards more in line with what neo-conservatives wanted were issued in 1995, *Education Week's* reporter Karen Diegmueller recounted that the criticisms of the history standards were primarily from neo-conservatives who contended, in Diegmueller's words, that "the standards undercut the great figures that traditionally have dominated the landscape of history and portray the United States and the West as oppressive regimes that have victimized women, minorities, and third-world countries."[142] What the critics wanted, Diegmueller wrote, was a history that emphasized U.S. accomplishments and provided students with uplifting ideals.

The reality is that both countries' histories contain what must be considered as violent acts against humanity. U.S. history contains stories of genocide against Native Americans, slavery, discrimination against minority groups and women, terrorism against religious and racial minorities, and the brutal conquest of Native American nations, Hawaii, the northern part of Mexico, and Puerto Rico. Should U.S. textbooks detail these crimes against humanity? In Japan, the issues are the country's list of atrocities before and during World War II, including forcing Korean women into sexual slavery for Japanese soldiers; the impressment of Koreans to work in war plants; the brutal treatment of civilians during colonization and occupation of Korea and Taiwan; and the mass killing of civilians during the capture of Nanjing, China in 1937 (known as "the rape of Nanjing").

A week after the 2005 approval of Japanese textbooks that failed to mention or glossed over these atrocities in Japanese history, the Prime Minister of China Wen Jiabao demanded during a visit to India that Japan "face up to" its wartime atrocities. As the Prime Minister was speaking, massive protests against Japan were occurring in China. The Prime Minister continued, "The massive war waged by Japan inflicted huge and tremendous suffering and hardships in China, Asia and the world at large. The core issue in China–Japanese relationship is that Japan needs to face up to history squarely."[143] An editorial in the *People's Daily* emphasized the international importance of Japanese history textbooks: "But these textbooks are not ordinary books, they involve accounts on the neighboring Asian countries, and involve the concealment and adulteration of the historical facts about Japanese militarist expansionism. Obviously, this has gone beyond the scope of Japan's internal affairs, it concerns Japan's relations with neighboring countries."[144]

Although international attention was directed at the textbook written by the Japanese Society for History Textbook Reform, there was also the issue of changes in other history texts that seemed to downplay the history of the nation's atrocities. The newspaper *Japan Today* reported that textbook publishers blamed the mounting pressure from the Japanese Society for History Textbook Reform on the glossing over of negative aspects of Japanese history. "'Education boards tend not to choose textbooks that contain a lot of the self-denigrating content,' one publisher said."[145] In regarding the removal of negative material from textbooks, the *Japan Today* noted that textbooks approved in 2001 listed the number of civilians killed in the rape of Nanjing as about 200,000, while those approved in 2005 used the term "many." In 2001, three of the eight approved history textbooks used the term "comfort women" or "comfort facilities" to refer to the sexual enslavement of Korean women. In 2005, only one textbook used the term "comfort facilities."[146]

Nationalism also reared its head in other forms in Japanese and U.S. schools. In 1999, the Japanese government identified Hinomaru flag and Kimigayo as the national flag and song, respectively. On March 6, 2005, one month before the eruption of the textbook controversy, the Minister of Education Nanaki Nakayama called on "teachers to teach students to respect the national flag and anthem regardless of what their beliefs maybe. If children are not taught to pledge allegiance to the national flag and anthem, they will feel ashamed and ridiculed when they go abroad."[147] The Minister's words added fuel to the controversy caused by the Tokyo school system requiring teachers to have students face the flag while singing the national anthem. Fifty-two Tokyo teachers' salaries were cut for disobeying the order to sing the national anthem and another 36 for refusing to sing it during graduation ceremonies.[148] Acting under a ruling by the Ministry of Education that schools require the singing of the national anthem, the Fukuka Prefecture school board announced that it had measured the volume of singing and reprimanded six of its schools for having "small" volume.[149] The school board of the Tottori Prefecture issued a warning to a teacher who refused to sing the national anthem during graduation ceremonies.[150] Tokyo District Court ruled in favor the Tokyo school board for reprimanding a teacher who refused to play the national anthem on a piano during a school ceremony.[151]

Although the above stories indicate a resistance to growing nationalism in Japanese schools, they also indicate the extent of its official sanction. Similar events have occurred in the United States. After the September 11, 2001 attacks on the World Trade Center politicians urged saying the Pledge of Allegiance and singing the national anthem in public schools. The U.S. newspaper, *Education Week* reported,

> State lawmakers around the country have been crafting legislation that would have schools begin the day with the Pledge of Allegiance, post the national motto "In God We Trust" in classrooms, or require students to take classes that teach patriotism. The flurry of bills, many of which are still pending, has emerged against a broader backdrop of renewed national pride following the terrorist attacks of Sept. 11.[152]

Although U.S. court rulings allow students and teachers not to participate in these nationalistic rituals, the ceremonies can be performed in the presence of all. This led to atheists objecting to the words "under God" in the American Pledge of Allegiance. A parent objected in California because his daughter was required to "watch and listen as her state-employed teacher in her state-run school leads her classmates in a ritual proclaiming that there is a God, and that ours is 'one nation under God.'"[153]

In summary, Japanese and U.S. educational policies have been intertwined since World War II, with the United States imposing its educational structure on Japan; Japan centralizing its control of curriculum and examinations; the United States admiring the Japanese testing and adopting a similar method of control; conservatives in both countries objecting to any textbook material that detracted from a positive image of their nations; and the growth of militarism and nationalism in public schools.

THE NEW RUSSIA:
MILITARISM, STATE EXAMS, AND HUMAN POWER PLANNING

"Anti-patriotic sentiments widespread among Russia's youth pose a threat to national security," declared Oleg Smolin, the head of the State Duma committee for education and science. "This is a direct threat to Russia's national security comparable to terrorism," Smolin told a 2005 video conference on "Youth—Future of Russia."[154] Patriotic plans were already stirring in Russia's Ministry of Education with the 2004 announcement of a campaign called, "Ready for Work and Defense of the Motherland." The new patriotic campaign was the work of the Russian Ministries of Education, Culture, and Defense. The picture accompanying the announcement in *MosNews* showed three young girls dressed in World War II Soviet uniforms exemplifying the attempt to recapture the patriotic fervor for the Motherland that had once existed in the Soviet Union. In fact, "Ready for Work and Defense of the Motherland," was considered a revival of a Soviet-era program. The revised program was planned to instill patriotism for work and the nation through sporting events, rallies, clubs, military training games, and patriotic video games.[155]

The attempt to revive Soviet-style patriotism was accompanied by the institution of nationwide college entrance examinations as a means for the Ministry of Education to gain control over a school system that had become increasingly diversified after the 1991 demise of the Soviet Union; an event that Russian Prime Minister Vladimir V. Putin later called the "greatest geopolitical catastrophe of the century."[156] With only minor changes to the educational structure, the uniformity of Stalinist education had continued until the collapse of the Soviet Union.[157] Afterwards, there developed a diversified system of private, for-profit, and public institutions with each university being able to define its own admission standards.[158] However, the actual power still remained in the Ministry of Education. The 1993 Russian Constitution stated: "The Russian Federation *shall institute federal state educational standards* and support various forms of education and self-education."[159]

Similar to the United States and Japan, Russia is becoming highly nationalistic, particularly towards Europe and the United States. Similar to the program "Ready for Work and Defense of the Motherland," this nationalism is based in part on the past glory of the Soviet Union. In a 2001 speech to the State Council it was reported by the *St. Petersburg Times* that Prime Minister Vladimir Putin directly praised the previously existing Soviet school system. In the words of reporter Oksana Yablokova, "Putin praised the *Soviet* education system and warned against blindly emulating Western standards, 'even the most progressive ones [my emphasis]'."[160] When the

U.S. administration criticized Russia in 2005 for lack of democratic reform, Prime Minister Putin shot back, "We will move forward considering our own internal circumstances. As a sovereign country, Russia can and will independently determine for itself the time frame and the conditions of its movement along that path."[161]

Militarism is an issue with regard to the right to free higher education. Similar to the United States in the 1950s, Russia has a military draft where exemptions are granted for attending college. Both the United States in the 1950s and currently the Russian government equate military duty with college attendance. In a 2001 interview by the *St. Petersburg Times*, a member of Moscow City Duma and prize-wining math teacher Yevgeny Bunimovich estimated that up to 40% of male students "go to college with 'zero interest' in studying and only to avoid the draft."[162] It would be difficult to determine the accuracy of Bunimovich's figures, but there appears to be tremendous pressure on colleges to admit students. This pressure has led to widespread rumors of corruption in college admission offices with school officials receiving bribes from prospective students. For instance, when nationwide standardized examinations were introduced in 2004, a group of 420 educators signed a petition against it because they feared "that corruption in low-salary admission boards—where bribes are notorious and expensive tutors often serve only as a pretext for further bribes—will only increase with a nationwide standardized test."[163]

Protests against the possibility of nationwide standardized exams began in 2001 after the Minister of Education Valentina Matviyenko and Minister of Economic and Trade Development Berman Gref suggested a national examination for college admissions with high scorers paying lower college tuition and being able to attend the more prestigious schools. Demonstrating the international importance of the U.S.-based Educational Testing Services, the two ministers compared the proposed test to the American Scholastic Aptitude Test. The last 2 years of high school were to be devoted to preparation for this standardized exam. The two government ministers said a national exam would also reduce the cost and problems for students from remote areas having to travel to individual colleges to seek admission. Now they could just send their application papers and along with the exam score. The Ministry of Education press secretary also told reporters, in contrast to the previously mentioned 420 educators, that the exam would end bribery among students and examiners: "when parents hire tutors to prepare their kids for entrance exams and then those tutors sit at admission boards as examiners."[164]

The U.S.-based Educational Testing Services was hired as a consultant in the development of the nationwide exam implemented in 2004. Besides demonstrating the global influence of Educational Testing Services, the use of the company raised issues about Russia copying the United States.

Yevgeny Senchenko, head of the education control department in the Education Ministry, warned reporters, "Don't compare this exam with SAT [Scholastic Aptitude Test]. Then people will think we copied the United States. China has been using a standardized exam for 20 years, but that doesn't mean we copied them."[165]

Although the institution of a national examination was to create some uniformity and end some bribery in the post-Stalinist school system, Prime Minister Putin called for more controls over private and for-profit education, and an alignment of the educational system with the needs of the labor market. Before the State Council, Putin declared that, "People must clearly understand where they can count on the state and where they must rely on their own resources. The private-education system must be fully transparent and people must know exactly what ... they get for their money."[166] In addition, Putin demanded that the educational system be readjusted to the needs of the labor market.

These recent events do not indicate that Russia is rapidly returning to a Stalinist educational security state. However some the elements are appearing, such as nationalism, militarism, national examinations, and discussions of attuning schools to labor market needs. There has even been some suggestion that history is now being written to glorify the Soviet past much as conservative historians in Japan and the United States want to gloss over anything negative about their countries. Yuri Afanasiev, historian and honorary president of the Russian State University, argues that Stalinism is currently being revived in Russia. "Attempts to pass an official or semi-official history of Russia have been made. It is the same as history in Stalin's times—falsified, biased, ideologized," he said at a conference marking the 20th anniversary of *perestroika*. "We are going back to the epoch of Stalin's dictatorship. Many historical facts are presented in the way he used to interpret them."[167] Referring directly to school textbooks, Afanasiev charged the textbook authors for failing to mention that the Soviet Union began the war fighting on the side of the Nazis. Similar to conservative textbook authors in Japan who felt it was necessary to forget their country's World War II atrocities in order to maintain the nationalism required by the educational security state, Afanasiev said that current school textbooks avoided mentioning that when veterans returned after the World War II: "Tens of thousands of invalids were sent to the northwestern island of Valaam so they did not spoil the 'aesthetic view' of Soviet cities. They all were buried at the same cemetery, which was later destroyed."[168]

MOBILIZING THE BRAINPOWER OF EUROPE

In the 21st century, nation states were committed to integrating educational into economic planning and establishing assessment-driven school systems. Retaining a national identity proved problematic with the growth of global languages, particularly English, and the cultural homogenization of global media and social contacts. Despite the difficulties encountered in the 2005 adoption of the European Union (EU) constitution, the EU represents both the highpoint of the educational security state and the problems of identity and language. National identity and language policies are an important issue for the EU not only in the face of global cultural trends but in the problem of uniting differing national groups. More than any other political system, the EU has directly tied schooling to global economic competition, reduced students to objects for psychological manipulation to serve economic interests, implemented assessment-driven educational policies, and created plans for a system of lifelong learning from preschool to retirement that would occupy a majority of a person's years in occupational training. With lifelong learning, there is no escape from the devouring power of the educational security state.

Banished from nation states, progressive education in the 21st century could be found in the rapidly growing civil society of global nongovernment organizations. In all of its various forms, the general goal of progressive education has been teaching people to understand how they can change society to achieve some form of human justice. As national school systems became increasingly dedicated to serving economic interests, their civic education policies were increasingly tied to nationalism and social control. Outside of the nation state, progressive education found a home in nongovernment organizations dedicated to human rights, social justice, and environmental protection. The three major objectives of Civicus, the World Alliance of Citizen Participation, exemplifies traditional progressive educational goals:

Three Objectives of the Civicus Mission Statement

1. Civic Existence—to promote the rights of citizens to organize and act collectively towards defined goals for the public good.
2. Civic Expression—to increase the effectiveness and improve the governance of civil society organizations, as well as their capacity to set and achieve their individual and collective goals.
3. Civic Engagement—to foster interaction between civil society and other institutions in order to increase the voice of citizens in public life.[169]

THE EUROPEAN UNION: THE EDUCATIONAL TECHNOCRACY

A number of factors are making the EU the most advanced educational security state. First, consider the very language used in the title to the European Commission's[170] report on linking university work to the EU's competitive position in the global economy: "Mobilizing the Brainpower of Europe: Enabling Universities to Make their Full Contribution to the Lisbon Strategy;"[171] The Lisbon Strategy was formulated at the March 2000 meeting in Lisbon of the European Council (the Heads of State or Government of the EU countries). At the meeting, the European Council adopted the following global economic goal to be reached by 2010: *To become the most competitive and dynamic knowledge-based economy in the world, capable of sustainable economic growth with more and better jobs and greater social cohesion.*[172] The Commission's title "Mobilizing the Brainpower" conceptualizes students and faculty as objects to fulfill a global economic objective.

Second, the EU was primarily organized to serve economic goals, particularly making its members major competitors in the global economy; this results in EU educational policy primarily being shaped to meet global economic competition. Third, the breakdown of traditional borders between member nations requires some common methods for assessing employment skills as people move between member nations; this requires an elaborate testing system linking schools to the job market. Fourth, the emphasis on global economic competition increases the importance of science and mathematics in EU schools and lessens the importance of the humanities and arts. Fifth, the creation of the EU requires the construction of a new national identity where students learn to see themselves primarily as European and secondarily as residents of member nations; this requires schools to teach a European identity and a recognition of the EU flag and national anthem. And sixth, to ensure that the language of a particular EU member does not become dominant and that local cultures are preserved, the EU schools require students to study their mother-tongue and two other languages; this educational practice falls under the slogan "Unity through diversity."

Another factor that makes the EU an exemplar of an educational security state is the subordination and psychological manipulation of children and youth to serve economic interests. As I discuss in the following section, the educational objectives resulting from the 2000 Lisbon Strategy call for using psychological methods to shape child and adolescent development so that their interests will meet the needs of EU's labor market. Of course, child and adolescent interests will have to be continually manipulated as the labor market changes.

Since its founding and expansion, the EU has enfolded its educational planning into its economic objectives. Historically, the EU evolved from a series of treaties for economic cooperation beginning with the 1957 Treaty of Rome establishing the European Economic Community (EEC) and the 1961 Organization for European Economic Cooperation (OECD) leading to the adoption on February 7, 1992 of the Treaty on European Union. On June 20, 1996, Romano Prodi, President of the Council of Ministers of the EU, defined the EU's economic purposes:

> The competitive challenge coming from the rest of the world today, particularly from Asia, should be tackled openly by placing in common the capacities, the inventiveness and the production quality of the Union's Member States. Regionalization, in its positive meaning as an area open to global competitiveness, is the only real instrument available to cope.[173]

To achieve the Lisbon Strategy, the European Council asked the Education Council (the education ministers of EU countries) to *"undertake a general reflection on the concrete objective of education systems, focusing on common concerns while respecting national diversity."*[174]

The phrase "concrete objective" meant objectives that could be measured either quantitatively or qualitatively. The image was that of a highly controlled educational system with social scientists applying measures that would keep the system on track. The student was the human resource to be developed for the global economy. Consequently, the objectives were divided into neat lists under three strategic objectives. For instance, the first strategic objective and its sub-objectives were:

Strategic Objective 1: Improving the quality and

effectiveness of education training systems in the

EU, in the light of the new requirements of the

knowledge society and the changing patterns of

teaching and learning.

Objective 1.1: Improving education and training for

teachers and trainers

Objective 1.2: Developing skills for the knowledge

society

Objective 1.3: Ensuring access to ICT [information

and communication technology] for everyone

Objective 1.4: Increasing recruitment in scientific

and technical studies

Objective 1.5: Making the best use of resources[175]

All of the above objectives are related to making the EU "the most competitive and dynamic knowledge-based economy in the world." For instance, the report identified two key issues in educating teachers (Objective 1.1) that are related to preparation of students for a knowledge-based economy. The other two deal with the recruitment of teachers to meet the EU's teacher shortage. The two key issues related to the knowledge economy are:

- identifying skills that teachers and trainers should have, given their changing roles in a knowledge society;
- providing the conditions which adequately support teachers and trainers as they respond to the challenges of the knowledge society, including through initial and in-service training in the perspective of *lifelong learning* [my emphasis].[176]

It is important to note the reference to lifelong learning. This is an important component of what is considered a knowledge society. Lifelong learning does not mean educating people so that they will spend leisure time reading novels and nonfiction books. It means constantly upgrading work skills as technology changes. Teachers are to prepare students for a knowledge economy that requires this constant upgrading of skills. For teachers, it means constantly upgrading their knowledge and skills as the economy changes. In 1996, Commissioner Edith Cresson launched the European Year of Lifelong Learning stressing the view that students were human resources to be developed for the good of the economy: "Developing human potential by investing in education and training is a masterkey to Europe's future economic and social well-being."[177] Within the context of this human resource model, Cresson asserted, "We face a dual challenge in this respect. Across Europe, the task is both to broaden access to education and training and to raise people's motivation for learning experiences on a lifelong basis."[178]

Cresson made the testing of skills an important component of lifelong learning to ensure that workers had actually improved their skills and to ensure recognition of these skills throughout the EU. "A central issue related to building lifelong learning systems," Cresson argued, " is the recognition and transferability of qualifications and competencies between Member states, and between workplaces and education and training institutions."[179] At the time, Cresson proposed a skills card containing work-related scores from assessment tests that the graduating student or an established worker could present to prospective employers. This proposal envisions an assessment-driven school system linked to an assessment-driven labor market.

This vision of an assessment-driven educational and economic system appears in "Objective 1.2: Developing skills for the knowledge society." This objective calls on schools to teach the "basic skills" of a knowledge-based economy. Basic skills include "not only numeracy and literacy (foundation skills) but also basic competencies in science, foreign languages, the use of

ICT and technology, learning to learn [lifelong learning], social skills, entrepreneurship, and what might be called general culture."[180] Certainly, the identification of "entrepreneurship" as a basic skill is a unique contribution to school instruction. The phrase "what might be called general culture" appears as an afterthought; it is never defined and there is no inclusion in assessment tools of any mention of "general culture."

Objective 1.2 also implies that the EU's major economic competitors are Japan and the United States. Included in the objective is a table comparing the EU's numeracy/mathematics and literacy scores with those of Japan and the United States.[181] There is no explanation given of the meaning of the scores for the Lisbon objectives. Consequently, the reader is given the impression that as test scores increase in relationship to Japan and the United States, the EU's position in the world economy will be enhanced.

The following quantitative measurements are specified as measuring improvement in these so-called basic skills. These measurements indicate how the EU's educational system will be assessment driven. In another report, these indicators are identified as "European benchmarks" for: "Making education and training systems in Europe a worldwide quality reference."[182]

Objective 1.2

- Quantitative tools: indicators
  people completing secondary education;
  continuous training of teachers in areas of emerging skills needs;
  literacy attainment levels (a PISA indicator; PISA is the program
  for international student assessment coordinated by OECD [Organization for Economic Cooperation and Development]);
  numeracy/mathematics attainment levels (also a PISA indicator);
  learning to learn attainment levels [lifelong learning];
  percentage of adults with less than upper secondary education who
  have participated in any form of adult education or training, by age
  group.[183]

The relationship of these quantitative indicators to global economic competition is highlighted in the table preceding the above list of indicators. Titled "Skills for the Knowledge Society," the table compares numeracy/mathematics and literacy PISA test scores between the EU, the United States, and Japan. Implied again is that the competition for high test scores between these three reflects global economic competition. Besides secondary school completion rates and adult participation in education and training, the indicators focus on training teachers to impart new skills, literacy and numeracy testing, and lifelong learning skills. Absent are any suggestions of measuring knowledge of "general culture," which is listed as a basic skill. This absence supports the idea that "general culture" was simply added on to the basic skills list without any explanation about how it would contribute to the EU being "the most competitive and dynamic knowledge-based economy in the world."

The most important influence of the Lisbon Strategy on the curriculum of higher education is the de-emphasis of the humanities and an increasing focus on science, mathematics, and technology. This is evident in the educational Objective 1.4 which is titled "Increasing Recruitment to Scientific and Technical Studies." Objective 1.4 opens: "Scientific and technological development and innovation are a sine qua non requirement in a competitive knowledge-based society and economy."[184] The lack of concern about the humanities and the objective of "general culture" are clearly evident in the Objective 1.4's report on the joint 2001 meeting of EU Ministers of Education and Ministers of Research. It was reported that the meeting:

> stressed the need to increase the recruitment to scientific and technological disciplines throughout the whole education and training system, including through a general renewal of pedagogy and closer links to working life and industry. To those already engaged in scientific and research professions, Europe needs to offer career prospects and rewards sufficiently satisfactory to keep them there.[185]

The desire to manipulate personal interests for achieving human resource needs is evident in the statement just presented and in what are listed as key issues in meeting Objective 1.4. Listed as the first key issue is: "increasing the interest in mathematics, science and technology from an early age."[186] In other words, EU educational systems are called on to consciously manipulate the interests of the child to meet the economic goals of the Lisbon Strategy. Manipulating children's development is part of the plan for enhancing the EU's global economic competition. This approach takes human resource planning beyond the stage of vocational training to the manipulation of the child. The child becomes a simple educational pawn serving economic interests.

Adolescent development is also made subordinated to global economics in what is identified as the second key issue:

> motivating young people to choose studies and careers in the fields of mathematics, science, and technology in particular research careers and scientific disciplines where there are shortages of qualified personnel, in a short and medium perspective, in particular through *the design of strategies for educational and vocational guidance and counseling* [my emphasis].[187]

In order words, psychological strategies are to be developed for guiding and counseling adolescents to choose scientific and technical studies in areas needed for global competition. Like children, adolescent interests are to be controlled and directed through psychological techniques to serve the interests of the economic system.

Following a similar pattern, the EU is shaping higher education to serve global economic goals. This effort is made explicit in the European Commission's 2005 report "European Higher Education in a Worldwide Perspective," which was published as an extension of the previously mentioned "Mobilizing the Brainpower of Europe." The written section of the report opens with a restatement of the Lisbon Strategy and a quote from the European Councils 2005 review of that strategy: "In advanced economies such as the EU, knowledge, meaning R&D, innovation and education, is a key driver of productivity growth. Knowledge is a critical factor with which Europe can ensure competitiveness in a global world where others compete with cheap labor or primary resources."[188]

Embedded in the quote just noted is a particular view of the economic division of the world. A vision that fits the term neo-colonialism. Implied is a world where some countries will compete with knowledge, such as the EU, Japan, and the United States, whereas other countries will supply cheap labor and resources. This could be considered a continuation of the colonial view of the world, where some nations, particularly previous colonial powers, will provide the knowledge base and research for technological development, whereas other previously colonized countries will be the manufacturing areas using cheap labor and importing natural resources from other previously colonized countries. If this vision of the world is indeed what is implied in the quote, then colonial powers retain their power and wealth while previously colonist countries remain poor and exploited.

This neo-colonial world view is reflected in the EU's efforts to cause a brain drain from other countries to the EU. In the following quote, low-income countries are identified as manufacturing sites: "To counterbalance the effects of the outsourcing of labor-intensive industries to low-income countries, countries compete in attracting the best talents to get a competitive advantage in the knowledge-based industry."[189] This means global competition for brains: "Globalization and the challenges of the modern knowledge-based economy have induced an increasing competition for the best brains."[190] Consequently, according to the report, "EU Ministers of Education have already set the objective of transforming the EU into 'the most favored destination of students, scholars and researchers from other world regions.'"[191]

Equating global economic competition with competition for "brains," the EU Education Ministers worry that the EU's brainpower is not pursuing research careers. The report concludes: "The EU produces significantly more graduates in mathematics, science and technology than the USA and Japan.... However, with a growth of over 30% China overtook the EU in 2003."[192] Russia is included in the table accompanying these statistics. The EU's Ministers of Education define the major competitors for global economic domination and control of brainpower as being between the EU, the United States, Japan, China, and Russia. However, Russia is dropped from its comparative table on PhD graduates. In this educational comparison the EU is ranked first followed in order by the United States, Japan, and China.[193]

Using education as an instrument of economic policy as opposed to education being determined by the interests and desires of students and parents is explicitly stated in the Commission's 2005 report on the progress made in achieving the educational objectives of the Lisbon Strategy: "Education has always been a powerful formative influence on society, yet its *instrumentality* has taken on new dimensions as a result of globalization and the knowledge revolution [my emphasis]."[194] Certainly, education has "a powerful formative influence on society." But this "influence" does not necessarily have to be as an instrument of the state or economic power. It could be the result of personal choices about education or an education resulting from contacts within a community as opposed to learning in a formal school setting. The report's writers seem to think of "education" as the schooling of a population in the interests of the state or some other power. Working from this conception of education, it is logical for the writers to make education an instrument for competition in a global economy. The student is simply considered as an instrumental resource for global economics. The sentence following the quote just discussed, which completes a two sentences paragraph, is: "Every serious long-term strategy to increase economic competitiveness, prosperity and social cohesion in the European Union is built on a foundation of education and training."[195]

How well have EU countries used education as an 'instrument' to fulfill the Lisbon Strategy? The Commission's 2005 report expresses disappointment at the high number of school dropouts which is estimated as 16% of the cohort between ages 18 to 24. In contrast, the report sounds confident about the increasing supply of scientists. Regarding the promotion of lifelong learning, the report urges Member States to increase their efforts "to develop an integrated, coherent and inclusive lifelong learning strategy."[196] The report finds fault in literacy test scores and the recruitment of teachers. Also the report states: "The EU suffers from under-investment in *human resources*, especially in higher education."[197]

THE EUROPEAN UNION AND LANGUAGE DIVERSITY

Although Japan is trying to maintain Japanese identity while stressing the teaching of English as the global language and U.S. schools operate under the assumption that English has already triumphed as the global language, the European Union is faced with language issues that are more about EU unity than globalization. Member states are reluctant to give up their national language for a common European language. Consequently, there is an emphasis on equality between languages and on educating students to be multilingual.

The EU's language policy is reflected in the Treaty on the European Union and in the Union's education policies. The acceptance of a multiple language policy is part of the Final Provisions (Title VII) of the Treaty on the European Union. Article S of the Final Provisions emphasizes equality between languages.

> This Treaty, drawn up in a single original in the Danish, Dutch, English, French, German, Greek, Irish, Italian, Portuguese and Spanish languages, the texts in each of these languages *being equally authentic* [my emphasis], shall be deposited in the archives of the government of the Italian Republic, which will transmit a certified copy to each of the governments of the other signatory States.[198]

In order to maintain "unity through diversity" within the EU there is a stress on multiple language instruction in schools. Objective 3.3 of the educational goals for the Lisbon Strategy states: "Europe's diversity is nowhere clearer than in its languages. Yet citizens can only benefit from this diversity if they are able to communicate with others across the linguistic lines and thus to learn about differences, tolerance, and mutual respect."[199] The objective is for every EU citizen to speak two foreign languages with training beginning in early childhood. However, EU schools were criticized in the 2005 report on the progress in reaching the educational objectives of the Lisbon Strategy: "Most EU pupils do not reach the objective of proficiency in at least two languages."[200]

The European Commission urges teaching the child's mother-tongue along with instruction in two foreign languages beginning in the early grades along with the lifelong learning of other languages. In contrast to U.S. language policies, the Commission report, "Promoting Language Learning and Linguistic Diversity," claims that early learning of a foreign language improves the learning of the mother tongue.[201] Of course, the problem is which foreign languages to teach? The Commission report that the major "foreign" languages taught in EU schools are English, French, German, and Spanish. This means that many EU students are not studying the languages of smaller member states, such as Danish, Italian, and so forth. In addition, there is the problem of maintaining regional and minority languages.

The possibility of English as the common EU language haunts the Commission's report. After stating the general support by Commission members of a multilingual policy, the report comments, "*The propositions that English alone is not enough*, and that lessons should be made available in a wide variety of languages were widely supported [my emphasis]."[202] And more ominously, the report warns, "In non-Anglophone countries recent trends to provide teaching in English may have unforeseen consequences on the vitality of the national language."[203]

Despite Commission efforts and the protests of non-Anglophone member states, English might become the common language of the EU. This trend would be more supportive of the Lisbon Strategy than a multilingual policy to foster EU unity. If this occurs, it might ensure that English becomes or remains, depending on one's perspective, the global language.

In summary, the Lisbon Strategy has clearly turned EU educational systems into instruments for global competition, with the EU hoping to become the richest and dominant force in the global knowledge industry while so-called developing countries with low-cost workers becoming the main manufacturing centers. To achieve this objective, psychological techniques are to be used on human resources, namely children and adolescents, to choose careers in science and technology. In addition, the EU will try to drain "brain power" from other countries to enhance its global competitiveness. Lifelong learning policies will ensure that more and more of a person's life from childhood to retirement will be devoted to education for fulfilling the Lisbon Strategy. As brainpower is mobilized for the Lisbon Strategy, universities will be less concerned with education in the humanities and more concerned with education of scientists, mathematicians, and technologists.

However, the difficulty experienced in 2005 in ratifying the new EU constitution raised doubts about the public acceptance of the EU's global economic plans and its accompanying educational agenda. Would the European public continue to commit itself to an educational plan geared primarily to global economic competition? The future of the EU educational security state would depend on a resolution of this question.

CONCLUSION

At the beginning of this chapter, I raised a series of questions about the viability and strength of an educational security state faced with criticisms about its service to business and the military, the possibilities of state examinations reinforcing class and racial differences, and concerns about political education. In the 21st century, the answers to these questions seemed to by a resounding "Yes!" The governments of China, Japan, the United States, and the European Union moved swiftly to ensure that their educational systems remained a function of their economic and military needs. In

Japan and the United States, nationalistic school teachings were implemented to ensure loyalty to the nation state and its economic and military programs. Russia appeared to be heading towards a resurrection of some form of its pre-Stalinist educational system with its trappings of economic planning and nationalistic militarism.

However, conservative leaders were not able to quiet the voices of dissent. A contradiction in the educational security state appeared between Japanese government's desire to control the future labor supply and concerns that the creativity and ingenuity needed for economic growth were being lost to an exam system that bred uniformity and rote learning. Would this contradiction produce a new synthesis that would balance state control of what is taught and how students are politicized with the need for creativity? Was negative public reaction in France and England to the new EU constitution a sign of disenchantment with educational policies designed to meet the needs of competition in a global economy?

Conclusion: The Triumph of the Industrial-Consumer Paradigm and English as the Global Language

Walking along Singapore's Orchard Road, advertising bombards the pedestrian with quickly changing electronic tabloids along the sidewalk; huge video billboards hanging on a multitude of shopping malls; illuminated shop windows; booming sounds from tents offering Citibank™ and American Express™ memberships and views of the latest electronics; seductive smells and offerings of globally franchised feeding venues like Starbucks™, McDonalds™, and Burger King™; and painted crosswalks announcing that Mastercard is the official credit card of the Great Singapore Sale.[1]

Singapore, the friendly authoritarian state, along with Communist China, the United States, Japan, India, and much of the rest of the world, is rushing to provide everyone with the opportunity to "shop 'til you drop." In Singapore, even authoritarianism is a consumer item as souvenir shops sell tee-shirts labeled at the top "The 'Fine' City" with appropriate illustrations below accompanying written text such as: "No Urination in Public Area, Fine $500;" "No Importing of Chewing Gum, Fine $1,000;" and "Forget to Flush Public Toilet, $500." In China, the Great Wall is now accompanied by the Great Malls with four existing malls in 2005 bigger than the Mall of America and the Golden Resources Mall in Beijing listed as the world's largest at 6 million square feet.[2]

Regardless of the political nature of the state, the industrial-consumer paradigm is used as the indicator of economic well-being. As I discussed at beginning of chapter 1, the industrial-consumer paradigm is based on the following:

- a fear that industrialism will create more leisure time that will corrupt workers and make them more difficult to control;
- the goal of industrialism should be the constant production and consumption of new products promoted by the psychological techniques of the advertising profession;
- advertising and production of new products should create new "needs" for consumers and seduce them into working harder so that they can be purchased;
- the consumption of products is suppose to provide personal fulfillment;
- planned obsolescence, particularly by changing designs of products and adding new features, is to heighten the desire to continually consume;
- brand names are used to create consumer desires for higher status and new personal images.

Singapore, which Allan Luke called the post-postcolonial state,[3] is a model of the consumer society. In order to achieve this status, the government has tightly coordinated its educational and economic planning. It is a model of the educational security state. At Singapore's 2005 Conference on Redesigning Pedagogy: Research, Policy, Practice, the Minister of Education Tharman Shanmugaratnam emphasized: "Schools have to respond and adapt to a number of imperatives. New knowledge and technologies are rapidly shaping the economic marketplace, and broadening the choices that individuals and communities have to make." As part of the requirements of the economic marketplace, the Minister asserted, "Cultural flexibility is an increasingly important life skill, in a globalizing world. Singapore's education landscape is itself moving progressively towards a greater diversity and flexibility."[4] In a similar tone, the Director of the National Institute of Education, Professor Leo Tan, stressed, "The National Institute of Education is proud to host this inaugural conference which will explore the ways in which pedagogy must change to meet the challenges posed by changes in the social, cultural, economic and learning environments. Both developed and developing country systems face these challenges."[5]

Singapore's educational policies have paralleled those of other countries bent on integrating educational and economic policies. Like the EU, Singapore wants to be a leading knowledge-based economy. In other books, I have discussed Singapore as an example of a strong neo-Confucian state that pioneered the coordination of education policy with economic planning.[6] Singapore's government carefully crafted its education and economic policies resulting in the transition from a developing to a developed nation. As Singapore emerged as a developed nation or post-postcolonial nation in the 1990s, it began to shift its emphasis from an assessment-driven school system to one that would meet the needs of a knowledge-based economy. Professor S. Gopinathan of Singapore's National Institute of Education explains,

> The Singaporean government's reading of the emergent new economy was that it required of school leavers entirely new sets of skills. The growth of the service sector and a speeding up of market liberalization for banking and telecommunication and the possibilities emergent in a technology-driven economic environment put a high premium on innovation, flexibility, entrepreneurship, creativity and a commitment to lifelong learning.[7]

Social cohesion and national identity are important issues as Singapore's government initiates plans to adapt their school system to the needs of a knowledge-based economy. Its three major ethnic groups—Chinese, Indian, and Malaysian—achieve linguistic unity through a common knowledge of English while each ethnic language is supported through school instruction and continued use in the home. In addition, the schools try to inculcate a strong sense of national identity and loyalty to the Singapore government while citizens are expected to participate in the global economy. The concern with maintaining national identity in a global economy is captured in the phrase: "Think Global, But be Rooted to Singapore."[8]

Singapore's example raises important questions about language and identity and the role of the educational security state in supporting an industrial-consumer economy. Is consumerism becoming the global culture with English as the international language? Besides the issue of whether an industrial-consumer model for the entire world can be supported by the earth's resources, there is the question of its desirability. Are there educational alternatives that will promote other ways of thinking about the economic organization of society?

ENGLISH AS THE GLOBAL LANGUAGE
AND THE INDUSTRIAL-CONSUMER PARADIGM

In the 21st century, the English language plays a different function in the global economy than it did during the 19th century when it was used as an instrument of cultural imperialism. Today, English serves as a vehicle for participation in the global economy. It is now chosen as a language to learn rather than it being imposed by outside forces. Also, it is often adapted to local linguistic traditions creating a world of "Englishes." In some cases it is the local language that is dubbed into movies and television programs that serves to spread Western cultural attitudes. In this complex multilingual world, global English might be spreading the ideal of an industrial-consumer economy.

A good example of the global role of English is Viniti Vaish's study of a primary school serving students from a slum area in Delhi, India. Most of the parents at this school want their children to learn English as means of economic upward mobility. Viniti provides the example of parents, who are earning about $80 USD a month in low-level jobs, wanting their children to learn English so that they can enter jobs with beginning salaries of about $200 USD a month "which is what a young English-knowing person would earn in a call center or as a data entry clerk in a multinational."[9] Many parents are spending money to send their children to nongovernment schools that provide instruction in English when local government schools do not provide similar instruction. This parental choice is putting pressure on government schools to provide more English instruction.

In the government school studied by Viniti, the English instruction textbooks are focused on Indian traditions rather than conveying to students a Western culture. Of the seventeen stories in one English instruction textbook, only two stories are related to Western culture, "Rumpelstiltskin" and "William Tell," whereas the other 15 stories are based on Indian mythology. India's National Council for Educational research and Training recommends that textbooks, "In order to make education a meaningful experience, it has to be related to the Indian context."[10] In contrast to the local cultural content of English instruction, Western mass media is in Hindi. The children interviewed by Vindi reported that they watched Western television and movies dubbed in Hindi, and read comic books, such as Mickey Mouse, in Hindi. Ironically, if one wanted to claim this media exposure to be a form of cultural imperialism it would be occurring in Hindi.

In summary, in countries such as India and Singapore, English is a means of upward mobility in a global economy. English taught through texts based on local cultural traditions is not a form of cultural imperialism but can be considered a means of achieving a post-postcolonial status. However, the very act of learning English can be considered preparation for participation in a global economic structure which, in the end, will affect local cultures. Alastair Pennycook argues that those who claim that "English is no longer tied to any culture since it is now the 'property of the world' overlook some of the values implied in teaching English."[11] These values involve the relationships of global economic development. After all, many learn English, as point by Viniti Vaish regarding India, for the purpose of joining the global economy. The very nature of this economy can change traditional cultures. In Pennycook's words, "to advocate … a more secular curriculum with greater access through English to certain jobs, economies, and cultural forms, is to advocate a set of changes that may have profound affects on families, religious affiliations, social movements, and so on."[12]

Religious identity for Moslems becomes a factor when English is considered necessary for participation in an industrial-consumer society. This issue is highlighted in an important printed exchange, "Islam, English, and 9/11," between Sohail Karmani of the University of Sharjah, United Arab Emirates and the previously mentioned Alastair Pennycook of the University of Technology, Sydney, Australia in the *Journal of Language, Identity, and Education*.[13] Whereas, historically, many Islamic leaders worried about the effect of learning English and Western science on Islamic values, Karmani asserted that these "days the general feeling in Arab-Moslem classrooms vis-à-vis the recent wars in the Moslem world (led more visibly these days by an alliance of powerful English-speaking nations) is one of increasing revulsion that complicates and overrides any serious efforts to challenge educational systems through the teaching of English."[14] He noted that a frequent justification given by Islamic leaders for teaching English is: "Learn the language of your enemy!"[15]

Karmani provided two powerful examples that suggest that knowledge of English does not result in domination by Western values. The first is the fact that the hijackers who flew the planes into the World Trade Center buildings on 9/11 were "well-integrated into U.S. mainstream society and in all probability spoke fluent English."[16] Indeed, Karmani argues, international terrorists need an international language like English to carry out their operations. The other example is the increasing use of English by Al-Jazeera and other Arab satellite-TV networks, while the United States government pours money into Arab-language newscasts to improve its country's image in Islamic nations.[17] In these two media examples, the important element is the content of the newscasts and not the language of the broadcast. A similar argument could be made about English instruction in schools; cultural imperialism might occur if students in English language courses read nothing but British or American literature as opposed to reading local stories translated into English.

Although knowledge of English enables people to participate in the global economy and/or international warfare, it also divides economic classes. Non-English speakers often resent English speakers. In Viniti Vaish's study, there were marked differences in income between those who spoke English and non-English speakers. Tariq Rahman found a similar situation in Pakistan along with a strong negative attitude towards English speakers by non-English speakers. A professor at the Quaid-i-Azam University in Islamabad, Pakistan, Rahman surveyed the attitudes of students in schools that used English as the medium of instruction and those that used Urdu. In terms of social class, children from low-income families often attend schools using Urdu as the language of instruction whereas Pakistan's elite send their children to English medium schools. Many of the schools attended by the poor are madrasas that inculcate anti-Western attitudes. In response to the question "Should English medium schools be abolished?," Rahman reported almost 100% of those students attending elite schools responded "no" whereas a significant majority in other schools responded "yes." To the question: "Do you think higher jobs in Pakistan should be available in English?," a majority of students in elite schools responded "yes," whereas a majority in other schools responded "no."[18]

The differences between the elite schools and the madrasas highlight how economic inequalities based on language might contribute to strong anti-Christian and anti-Western feelings. In addition, these anti-Western attitudes include a rejection of the industrial-consumer paradigm for a religious way of life. Rahman provided the following summary: "The state ... created market conditions which made English an expensive product to which the elite of wealth or power had privileged access. As such, English became a constructor of the modern, Westernized, secular identity in South Asia. It became a class marker and the basis of a new kind of social division and polarization of society."[19]

The issue of English and Islam is more complicated in Islamic nations with multiple religious and ethnic populations. Recently, ethnic Chinese and Indian populations in Malaysia have been critical of their government's policy of requiring government school instruction in Malaysian and the inculcation of Islamic values. Malaysian government leaders argue that the policy is necessary for maintaining a single Malaysian national identity. However, some ethnic Chinese and Indian leaders want Malaysia to adopt a policy similar to that of the EU by seeking unity through diversity, with the unifying language being English. For instance, Steven Gan, an ethnic Chinese, believed that he benefitted from attending schools when the classrooms were multiethnic and the shared language was English. As reported in the June 7, 2005 issue of the *International Herald Tribune:* "'We got a good education then at state schools and it was genuinely multiracial,' Gan said. The language of instruction was English until race riots struck the nation in 1969, after that, instruction was in Malay."[20]

Besides the language issue, religious issues divide Malaysians. I found outspoken tension in both Singapore and Malaysia between ethnic Chinese and Moslems. An ethnic Chinese taxi driver in Singapore assured me that I didn't have to worry about Moslems in Singapore because "The Chinese have them under control." In the predominately Chinese-ethnic Malaysian city of Malacca, a local resident in a casual street conversation with me praised the U.S. President George W. Bush for "bombing those Moslems."

Razak Baginda, who like Gan wistfully dreams of a return to multiethnic schools with English as the unifying language of instruction, complained that when he sent his daughter to a state school, there was pressure for her to conform to Islamic traditions including the wearing of a head scarf. Razak reported, "My daughter told me the religious teachers are the culprits. They indicate very negative views of the other religions. They always have them-and-us attitude that is very destructive, I think."[21]

Therefore, Malaysia presents the interesting situation of ethnic minorities who seek cultural unity through the use of English as the medium of instruction in schools, whereas Malaysians seek unity through the use of the Malay language. However, the Malaysian Islamic population does not simply dismiss the importance of teaching of teaching English. Among the Malaysians and ethnic minority populations, English is seen as the language needed for participation in the global economy.

Ratnawati Mohd-Asraf of the International Islamic University of Malaysia reported that attitudes about learning English have changed significantly from the period immediately following the end of English colonialism when English was treated as the language of imperialism. Now studies show that Malaysian and ethnic minorities view the learning of English as simply utilitarian. In sharp contrast to earlier reaction against the teaching of English, Ratnawati reported a study of three rural Malaysian schools on attitudes about the learning of English. In classes of Moslem and ethnic Chinese students, all of the students disagreed with the statement: "Learning English is a waste of time." All but one disagreed with the statement: "It is not important to learn English."[22] A survey of university students found many believing that English could be learned for utilitarian purposes without undermining religious and local cultural values. The following statements were made by different students: "Western culture does not necessarily mean negative culture. We can learn English but not copy the 'Western' way of life." "Learning the language doesn't mean adopting the culture." "We won't develop if we reject a language because of its culture. A language is just a tool.… That's why we learn English."[23]

The reaction against French and the demand for English language instruction in Cambodia supports the contention that English is primarily chosen as a tool to participate in the global economy. A former French colony, the Khmer Rouge (1975–1979) banned the use of French and all other foreign languages. During the Vietnamese occupation (1979–1989), language policies favored the use of Vietnamese and Russian. After the withdrawal of the Vietnamese, foreign aid particularly from the French flowed back into Cambodia. Because much of the educational aid came from France, French was reestablished as the medium for instruction in institutions of higher education.[24]

Beginning in 1993, university students began to resist the use of French as a medium of instruction. Effigies labeled "French" were burned in protest. Students demanded that English become the medium of instruction. Students worried about "never being able to find jobs … in this region of the world where English is the language of communication."[25] Students began to use part of their university stipends to purchase private instruction in English. University officials agreed to offer instruction in English as a foreign language. A university administrator explained, "The aim of the [the

Institute of Technology] is to train students to work in industry and business. In industry and business, French is [becoming] less and less important, and English is [becoming] more and more important."[26]

International forces are also pushing Cambodia away from French usage to English. Cambodia was admitted in 1999 to the Association of Southeast Asian Nations (ASEAN). English is the official language of communication of ASEAN. The Cambodian government could not fully participate in the committee work of the organization because it did not have enough English speakers. In addition, international aid agencies, such as the World Bank, the Asian Development Bank, the International Development Fund, and the United Nations along with international NGOs communicate in English.[27]

Similar to other countries, English usage creates a social class divide in Cambodia. Eighty-two percent of Cambodians are subsistence farmers living outside a cash economy that would allow them to purchase private English instruction. Only 32% of children entering primary school go on to secondary school where English instruction is provided. The result, according to Thomas Clayton, is that "English language skills stand as a barrier, prohibiting them from contributing their knowledge and experience to conversations about the country's political, economic, and development future."[28]

Like Viniti Vaish's evaluation of language choices in India, Thomas Clayton concluded that the adoption of English is now a matter of choice based on the realities of international economics and political alliances rather than a direct imposition by an imperialistic power. In fact, in the case of Cambodia, the direct imperialistic power is France that wants French retained as the medium of instruction. English is chosen for its utility in the global economy. If the international language was Urdu than Cambodian students would be demanding instruction in Urdu. Clayton concluded,

> While Cambodians have chosen English because of the functions that language serves in facilitating the country's political, economic, and development transitions, those functions were nevertheless created outside the country. Indeed, were it not for the language choices made in enterprises with wide ranging national and multinational attachments—including ASEAN, most commercial ventures, and most assistance agencies—Cambodians would have little reason to choose English. Thus, even if we reject the necessary association between English language spread and English-speaking countries, we must acknowledge a weaker version of the international-critical thesis: that language decisions in the developing world are significantly influenced—indeed, constrained—by the language policies, preferences, and programs of international political, economic, and development enterprises. To put it another way, international organizations have set the parameters of language choice for Cambodians and, in doing so, are exerting considerable control over the language decisions made in the country.[29]

In conclusion, for a variety of historical reasons, the primary one being the history of English imperialism, English has apparently become the language of the global economy. Despite fears of Western cultural being transmitted through English, many of the world's peoples are rushing to learn English so that they can participate in the global economy. In making the choice to learn English for purposes of participating in the global economy, people are accepting the economic paradigm of the global economy, whether it is outsourcing work in India or joining the staff of international corporations. In other words, English learned for participation in the global economy is not culturally neutral. In the 19th century, the British tried to spread their culture, as embodied in English literature, arts, religion, and manners, by making English the language for administration of the empire. Today, that 19th-century cultural content of English has been replaced by an economic paradigm that people willingly choose to participate in by learning English.

As noted in the examples of India, Pakistan, and Cambodia, knowledge of English has created a economic divide. Could this occur on a global scale? Could speakers of English from India and Cambodia who work for multinational corporations have more in common than they might have with poor, nonspeakers of English in their own countries? Will the global use of English create a global social and economic class? As exemplified by Cambodia, will a knowledge of English be necessary for participation in international political organizations? Or, in other words, will knowledge of English be necessary for participation in a global power elite?

ENGLISH AND NATIONAL IDENTITY IN JAPAN, THE UNITED STATES, AND CHINA

Japan and China exemplify nations wanting to maintain a strong national identity while promoting the learning of English. The United States represents a nation wanting to maintain English as a national language to ensure cultural unity while promoting the learning of other languages for military and economic reasons. I will first explore the language issues in Japan and the United States.

Maintaining Japanese identity as English becomes the language of the global economy was discussed in the 2002 Japanese Minister of Education's report, "Developing a strategic plan to cultivate 'Japanese with English Abilities'."[30] The report recognized the importance of English in the global economy: "With the progress of globalization in the economy and in society, it is essential that our children acquire communication skills in English, which has become a common international language, in order for living in the 21st century."[31] The report recommends strengthening the teaching of English at all levels of schooling, promoting overseas study, and giving students opportunities to practice conversational English. However, in the same report, the teaching of Japanese is emphasized: "it is not possible to state that Japanese people have sufficient ability to express their opinions based on a firm grasp of their own language."[32] Consequently, the strengthening of English instruction for the global economy was to be accompanied by improvements in instruction in the Japanese language, which, of course, is key to maintaining Japanese culture.

Historically, Japanese leaders struggled with the potential threat of learning foreign languages to national identity. In the 19th century, learning foreign languages was associated with the process of modernization. But after Japanese victories in the Sino-Japanese (1894) and Russo-Japanese (1904–1905) wars, a period of nationalism set in with the use of Japanese being promoted over the use of English. The Minister of Education declared: "Education in Japan in Japanese."[33] After this nationalistic period and prior to World War II, English was made a requirement for university entrance examinations. The emphasis was on memorizing grammar and vocabulary to translate English into Japanese. There was no requirement for spoken English. During World War II, English was discouraged as the "enemy's language."[34] During the American occupation, English was again made an important academic language and in 1956 was included in entrance examinations to Japanese secondary schools. Currently, 97% of all junior-high school graduates are going to secondary schools and have to be prepared to be tested for their abilities in English. In addition, English is taught in all secondary schools. However, like the early 20th century, the emphasis is on grammar and vocabulary and not aural/oral skills.[35]

Consequently, the Japanese Minister of Education's 2002 report reflects a concern about the actual ability of Japanese to speak English. According Yuko Goto Butler and Masakazu Iino, the new emphasis on conversational English is sparked by a downturn in the Japanese economy and a belief that Japan must change in the face of globalization. As a result, according to Yuko and Masakazu, "It is widely believed that Japanese people must be equipped with better communicative skills in English and that raising the ability to communicate with foreigners is a key remedial measure to boost Japan's position in the international economic and political arena."[36] In the minds of Japanese educational planners, English is the language of globalization as exemplified by the fact, as Yuko and Masakazu state, that there is "very little opportunity for Japanese students to learn other foreign languages besides English in the public school system of Japan."[37]

Similar to Japan, U.S. policymakers assume that English is the global language as implied in the U.S. legislation "No Child Left Behind" that supports an English-only policy in schools and the use of English as the only medium of instruction. The legislation gave the government's Office of Bilingual Education a new title, Office of English Language Acquisition, and the legislation placed emphasis on the learning of English. This change should be understood against the background of a long campaign by cultural conservatives in the 20th century for an "English-only" policy and making English the official language of the United States. "English-only" proposals were made in the context of nationalism and the promotion of Anglo-Saxon ideals as fundamental to the U.S. nation-state. The emphasis on English acquisition was also in reaction to a campaign by Native Americans, Puerto Ricans, and Mexican Americans to have the public schools maintain their languages. In fact, a campaign by representatives of these three groups had resulted in the original establishment of the Office of Bilingual Education.[38]

Therefore, "No Child Left Behind" promotes a national language while neglecting instruction in other languages. Why? Most likely U.S. politicians appear to feel that it is not necessary to learn other languages when English is the global language. Even if U.S. politicians worried about the possibility of Mandarin sharing the global stage with English, they would be more inclined to only emphasize instruction in English in hopes that it would continue to be the global language.

In contrast to the English-only bias of "No Child Left Behind," the U.S. military is worried about the nation's international language capabilities. The U.S. Defense Department is advocating the teaching of foreign languages "and greater understanding of other cultures in order to address the country's economic and security needs."[39] In a policy statement, "A Call to Action for National Language Capabilities," the following warning is made, "Gaps in our national language capabilities have undermined cross-cultural communication and understanding at home and abroad."[40] The U.S. publication *Education Week* reported, "since the Sept. 11, 2001, terrorist attacks, national-security experts have warned that the United States' foreign-language capabilities are insufficient to meet the demands for translators, analysts, and other critical positions in government and business."[41] It should be noted that the first language center being established under U.S. Defense Department policies is devoted to the language of America's major economic competitor, China.

In other words, like Japan and many other countries in the 19th century, the U.S. Defense Department is advocating: "Know the language of your enemies." Do the combined U.S. policies of English-only and learning foreign languages mean: "Learn other languages but protect American essence?"

Like Japan, China is emphasizing instruction in English as part of its effort to participate in the global economy. During the Cultural Revolution,

English was viewed as the language of the enemy and almost all English teaching programs were eliminated. After the rise of Deng Xiaoping to power, the teaching of English became an important part of his modernization program. In 1978, the Chinese Ministry of Education issued a syllabus for English instruction. There was established a universal requirement for English instruction in secondary schools. According to Guangwei Hu, "English was recognized as an important tool for engaging in economic, commercial, technological and cultural exchange with the rest of the world and hence for facilitating the modernization process; however, it was first and foremost a vehicle for 'international class struggle' and 'revolutionary diplomacy.'"[42] Thus, English was justified within communist rhetoric of class struggle while being a tool for modernization.

In 2001, the Ministry of Education issued a directive requiring primary schools in cities and county seats to offer English instruction. Guangwei argued that this policy was prompted by the Chinese government's desire to join the World Trade Organization and its desire to host the 2008 Olympic games.[43] Clearly, Chinese government leaders consider English as the vehicle for participating in the global economy and community of nations. It is important to note that, with more than 20% of the world's population, which was estimated in 2005 as 1,306,313,800, and 90% of the people speaking Mandarin, China could justly claim that Mandarin should be the global language. However, the reality of the historical spread of English by imperialism, popular media, missionaries, and economics has forced the Chinese government to recognize that knowledge of English is necessary for full participation in the global economy and community.

Therefore, the two nations, Japan and China, who have been most resistant to foreign influences have succumbed to the requirement of English for participation in global economic and international policy organizations. In contrast, U.S. education officials have acted under the assumption that English will be the global language while its military forces support the learning of foreign languages, particularly Mandarin, for security purposes.

GLOBAL AND LOCAL LANGUAGES: ENGLISH, COMMERCIAL SIGNAGE, AND BRAND LOGO

The overwhelming majority of non-English speakers and non-English speaking nations choose to learn English because it provides access to global economic and political organizations. Despite claims that English is now merely a utilitarian tool freed from older forms of cultural imperialism, the very fact that English is chosen as a tool for participation in the global economy means an acceptance of the values inherent in that economy. My contention, as I stated previously, is that the basic value of the global economy is that a good society is a result of economic growth spurred by the increased consumption of goods. Globally, this basic value of the industrial-consumption paradigm cuts across religious and political lines. Hindus, Moslems, Christians, Confucianists, pagans, dictatorships, communists, welfare socialists, representative democracies, monarchies, and authoritarian states all embrace the consumer model. Differing economic systems, like free market and planned economies, claim that they have a superior system for stimulating economic growth for the production of consumer goods.

On the other hand, consumer products are marketed in local languages. Advertising, mall signs, brand labels, and media commercials are most often in local languages. Sometimes there is a mixture of English and the local language in signage. Foreign movies and television programs are dubbed with the local vernacular. Store window displays and advertising occasionally show a mixture of foreign images. Along Singapore's Orchard Road and in Kuala Lumpur's Golden Triangle, European-looking models stare at you from ads for Boss, Calvin Klein, and Prada, and in store windows, some mannequins look European whereas others look like the local population.

Brand symbols are now more of a global language than English. Non-English and English speakers easily recognizes universal brand icons. Elissa Moses' advertising study, *The $100 Billion Allowance: Accessing the Global Teen Market* asked global teens to identify 75 brand icons, she found the most recognized to be Coca-Cola, Sony, Adidas, Nike, and Kodak.[44] Of course, McDonalds' Golden Arches are close to the top in recognition.

Therefore, although knowledge of English provides access to the highest paying jobs and economic power in the global economy, the actual consumer market tends to preserve local languages while incorporating global brand icons. This can create a hybridity of language and culture. When two immigrant students speaking different languages meet in a U.S. high school, they share a common language of global brands. Their shared culture is global consumerism.[45]

IS THERE ANYTHING WRONG WITH THE INDUSTRIAL-CONSUMER PARADIGM?

People have always shopped in bazaars, at street stands, in shops, public markets, and they have eaten fast food in night kitchens and stalls. Fine clothes, ornate furnishings, decorated carriages, and jewelry were desired for centuries. Conspicuous consumption has traditionally created ostentatious displays of social status and personal image. Most people have never run from consumption. Although some might argue that advertising creates an avaricious need to consume, shoppers are not directed at gun point to buy. By their own choice, people "shop 'til they drop."

Maybe, the industrial-consumer paradigm does fulfill human needs and desires. I certainly don't have the data or wisdom to simply dismiss this possibility. People do vote with their feet when they go to the malls and shops in China, Singapore, Saudi Arabia, France, Nigeria, Argentina, and the United States.

Although the industrial-consumer paradigm cannot be simply dismissed as a source of human satisfaction, there are certain problems inherent in the model. Though I don't have the answers for these problems, I would suggest the abandonment or modification of the educational security state if we are to educate enough people to develop solutions to these problems. Here are the major problems with the industrial-consumer paradigm:

1. There is no concern with happiness and satisfaction in employment. The emphasis is on happiness and satisfaction through consumption. This is a problem because most people spend more time at work then they do at consuming.
2. The emphasis is on working hard, often meaning longer hours, to increase consumption activities. Of course, many subsistence farmers and poor people work long hours just to survive. However, the industrial-consumer model doesn't promise fewer working hours, only more products.
3. The model is premised on a fear that industrialism might provide more personal freedom by reducing work time. Some people fear that more leisure time would make the masses uncontrollable.
4. The issue of what makes humans happy has been clouded by the advertising emphasis on personal satisfaction through consumption.
5. Can the world's natural resources sustain an industrial-consumer society for all the world's peoples?
6. If the world's natural resources cannot provide an industrial-consumer society to all the world's peoples, then will the world continue to be divided between the rich and poor and the hungry and overfed?
7. Will the industrial-consumer model with its voracious appetite for resources and disregard for the environment destroy Mother Earth?

WHAT HAPPENED TO PROGRESSIVE EDUCATION?

In *How Educational Ideologies are Shaping Global Society*, I detailed how progressive education in its many forms is now primarily utilized by nongovernment organizations (NGOs) operating in the global civil society as a countervailing force to the nation-state and the consumer-industrial society. The largest of these organizations are devoted to human rights and environmental issues.[46] The educational programs of human rights and environmental NGOs are designed to empower learners to actively protect human rights and the environment using progressive methods that were developed from the time of John Dewey to Paulo Freire.[47]

The educational efforts of environmental organizations pose the greatest challenge to the continuation of a consumer-industrial society. Many environmentalist advocate replacing the industrial-consumer paradigm with a biospheric paradigm. In this paradigm, humans become just one species existing among other animal and plant species. In addition, environmental education teaches that the meaning and pleasure of life is dependent on the quality of human interaction with nature. The biosphere paradigm is to act like a mental filter that interprets human experience in the context of a web of relations with the land, air, water, and other plant and animal species. It also results in seeing human knowledge as dependent on the same web of relationships. Consequently, environmental education is considered as something that must be wholistic and interdisciplinary where the student learns through experience, self-interest, and participation in social change.[48]

CONCLUSION:
THE NECESSITY OF ALTERNATIVE EDUCATIONAL
MODELS TO THE EDUCATIONAL SECURITY STATE

The globalized educational security state is primarily concerned with managing human resources to fulfill the needs of the industrial-consumer paradigm. Similar to English as the global language, historical factors have made the educational security state the global model. In this book, I have traced the evolution and eventual dominance of this educational model. Along the way other educational models have either been discarded or disregarded.

In this book, I have discussed the historical interplay between classical and progressive education and the educational security state. I also discussed efforts, particularly in South America, to accommodate the traditional learning of indigenous peoples with modern progressive education. Therefore, I would argue, there is available for consideration three alternative educational models to the current dominant global model. These are:

1. The classical search for the source of human happiness and the just society through the explication of texts as exemplified by Confucianist, Islamic, Christian, Buddhist, and Hindu traditions. Personally, I am very impressed by the work of neo-Confucianists.
2. The progressive educational goal of achieving human happiness and the just society by empowering people as actors in the reconstruction of society. I would identify the major thinkers in this tradition as John Dewey, Mao Zedong, and Paulo Freire.

3. The use of traditional knowledge particularly of indigenous peoples. This knowledge is based on centuries of experience with how humans interact with each other and the environment. It provides an understanding of the human species' place in the biosphere of Mother Earth.

These three educational models provide an alternative to the educational security state and might educate people capable of solving some of the inherent problems of the industrial-consumer model. Based on my list of the problems associated with the industrial-consumer model, I would hope that we could educate a generation who could provide answers to the following questions.

1. How can we organize technology and industry so that work is a source of happiness and satisfaction for all people? Rather than thinking about technology as a source of profit and new products, we should think about it as a way of freeing people from meaningless, harmful, and dissatisfying occupations.
2. How can we organize the economy so that all people have the nutrition, medical care, and shelter necessary to survive and have long and satisfactory lives?
3. How can we organize the economy so that people have more leisure time?
4. What are the social, political, and economic conditions that promote human happiness?
5. How can we organize the economy to maximize human happiness without depleting the world's resources while protecting the biosphere?

These are the questions that are not addressed by the model of the educational security state that now dominates global educational systems.

Notes

1. I define and illustrate these differing pedagogies later in this chapter and in subsequent chapters. Some readers might not be familiar with the concept "industrial-consumer" that I explain in this chapter.

2. My use of "global flow" and the "other" are derived respectively from Arjun Appadurai's *Modernity at Large: Cultural Dimensions of Globalization* (Minneapolis, MN: University of Minnesota Press, 1996) and Edward Said's *Culture and Imperialism* (New York: Knopf, 1993). I recognize the influence of their work on my own analysis of global schooling. However, I do not strictly adhere to their usage and definitions of these terms.

3. Simon Patten was the late 19th-century economist to first articulate the industrial consumer model. See Simon N. Patten, *The New Basis of Civilization* (Cambridge, MA: Harvard University Press, 1968). The following is a sample of the many books that trace the history of the industrial consumer model: Susan Strasser, *Satisfaction Guaranteed: The Making of the American Mass Market* (Washington, DC: Smithsonian Institution Press, 1989); Gary Cross, *An All-Consuming Century: Why Commercialism Won in Modern America* (New York: Columbia University Press, 2000); Jennifer Scanlon, Ed., *The Gender and Consumer Culture Reader* (New York: New York University Press, 2000); John Philip Jones, *What's in a Name? Advertising and the Concept of Brands* (Lexington, MA: D.C. Heath, 1986); William Leach, *Land of Desire: Merchants, Power, and the Rise of a New American Culture* (New York: Vintage Books, 1993); Richard Ohmann, *Selling Culture: Magazines, Markets, and Class at the Turn of the Century* (New York: Verso, 1996); Jackson Lears, *Fables of Abundance: A Cultural His-*

tory of Advertising in America (New York: Basic Books, 1994); Roland Marchand, *Advertising the American Dream: Making Way for Modernity 1920–1940* (Berkeley, CA: University of California Press, 1985); Stephen Fox, *The Mirror Makers: A History of American Advertising and Its Creators* (Urbana, IL: University of Illinois Press, 1997); Ruth Schwartz Cowan, *More Work for Mother: The Ironies of Household Technology from the Open Hearth to the Microwave* (New York: Basic Books, 1983); Ellen Gruber Garvey, *The Adman in the Parlor: Magazines and the Gendering of Consumer Culture, 1880s to 1910s* (New York: Oxford University Press, 1996); and Kathy Peiss, *Hope In A Jar: The Making of America's Beauty Culture* (New York: Henry Holt & Company, 1998).

4. I discuss the development of the industrial-consumer model and its integration into school practices in Joel Spring, *Educating the Consumer-Citizen: A History of the Marriage of Schools, Advertising, and Media* (Mahwah, NJ: Lawrence Erlbaum Associates, 2003).

5. Alex Williams, "What Women Want: More Horses," *The New York Times* (12 June 2005), Section 9, p. 1.

6. Ibid.

7. See Joel Spring, *Education and the Rise of the Global Economy* (Mahwah, NJ: Lawrence Erlbaum Associates, 1998); *Globalization and Educational Rights: An Intercivilizational Analysis* (Mahwah, NJ: Lawrence Erlbaum Associates, 2001); and *How Educational Ideologies are Shaping Global Society: Intergovernmental Organizations, NGOs, and the Decline of the Nation-State* (Mahwah, NJ: Lawrence Erlbaum Associates, 2004).

8. W. John Morgan, *Communists On Education and Culture 1848–1948* (New York: Palgrave Macmillan, 2003), p. 135.

9. See Ivan Illich, *De-Schooling Society* (New York: Harper & Row, 1971) and *Celebration of Awareness: A Call for Institutional Revolution* (New York: Doubleday, 1971).

10. For example, see the reprint of the New York State Criminal Anarchy Act of 1902 in "The Criminal Anarchy Law," in *Anarchy: An Anthology of Emma Goldman's Mother Earth* edited by Peter Glassgold (Washington, DC: Counterpoint, 2001), pp. 6–9.

11. Quoted in Ibid., p. 6.

12. I discuss this public school campaign against "radical" political ideologies in Joel Spring, *Images of American Life: A History of Ideological Management in Schools, Movies, Radio, and Television* (Albany: State University of New York Press, 1992), pp. 31–49, 159–185.

13. As quoted in Howard Beales, *Are American Teachers Free?* (New York: Scribner's, 1936), pp. 108–109.

14. Ronald Price, *Marx and Education in Russia and China* (Totowa, NJ: Rowan and Littlefield, 1977), p. 225.

15. Quoted by Morgan, p. 123.
16. See Barry Keenan, *The Dewey Experiment in China: Educational Reform and Political Power in the Early Republic* (Cambridge, MA: Harvard University Press, 1977) and David L. Hall and Roger T. Ames, *The Democracy of the Dead: Dewey, Confucius, and the Hope for Democracy in China* (Chicago: Open Court, 1999).
17. Nigel Grant, *Soviet Education* (Harmondsworth, Middlesex, England: Penguin Books, Inc. 1970), p. 19.
18. E. Thomas Ewing, *The Teachers of Stalinism: Policy, Practice, and Power in Soviet Schools of the 1930s* (New York: Peter Lang, 2002), p. 60.
19. Sergei N. Khrushchev, *Nikita Khrushchev and the Creation of a Superpower* (University Park, PA: The Pennsylvania State University Press, 2000), p. 6.
20. See Harry Warfel, *Noah Webster: Schoolmaster to America* (New York: Macmillan, 1936).
21. Morgan, p. 133.
22. Ibid.
23. Nigel Grant, p. 17.
24. An example of radical atheism in the United States is Emma Goldman's 1916 article "The Philosophy of Atheism" in *Anarchy! An Anthology of Emma Goldman's Mother Earth* edited by Peter Glassgold (Washington, DC: Counterpoint, 2001), pp. 88–96.
25. Sergei Khrushchev, pp. 11–12.
26. Karl Marx, *Capital: A Critique of Political Economy* (New York: Modern Library, 1936), p. 534.
27. Ibid.
28. Maurice Shore, *Soviet Education: Its Psychology and Philosophy* (New York: Philosophical Library, 1947), p. 129.
29. For a general description of the unified labor school see Jann Pennar, Ivan Hakalo, and George Bereday, *Modernization and Diversity in Soviet Education* (New York: Praeger, 1971), pp. 34–39.
30. Shore, p. 173.
31. Larry Holmes, *Stalin's School: Moscow's Model School No. 25, 1931–1937* (Pittsburgh: University of Pittsburgh Press, 1999), pp. 8–9.
32. Holmes, p. 10.
33. William Heard Kilpatrick, *The Project Method* (New York: Teachers College Press, 1918).
34. Ibid., p. 6.
35. Ibid., p. 14.
36. Ibid., p. 14.
37. Holmes, p. 11.
38. Shore, p. 193.
39. Anton Makarenko, *A Book for Parents* (Amsterdam: Fredonia Books, 2002), p. 7.

40. Anton Makarenko, *The Road to Life* (Moscow: Foreign Languages, 1955), p. 265.
41. Ibid., p. 267.
42. Ibid., p. 265.
43. Makarenko, *A Book for Parents ...*, p. 20.
44. Ibid., p. 21.
45. Holmes, pp. 21–30.
46. Ibid., p. 48.
47. Ibid., p. 53.
48. Ibid., p. 48.
49. Ibid., p. 48.
50. Ibid., p. 76.
51. Ibid., pp. 68–69.
52. John Dunstan, "Atheistic Education in the USSR," in *The Making of the Soviet Citizen* (London: Croom Helm, 1987) edited by George Avis, p. 53.
53. Ibid., p. 63.
54. Ewing, p. 51.
55. Ibid., p. 26.
56. Ibid., pp. 27–31.
57. William Gellerman, *The American Legion as Educator* (New York: Teachers College Press, 1938), pp. 90–91.
58. Ibid., pp. 90–91.
59. Ibid., p. 122 and Harold Hyman, *To Try Men's Souls: Loyalty Tests in American History* (Berkeley, CA: University of California Press, 1959), pp. 323–326.
60. C. A. Bowers, *The Progressive Educator and the Depression: The Radical Years* (New York: Random House, 1969), p. 15.
61. Quoted in ibid., p. 19.
62. As quoted in Mary Anne Raywid, *The Ax-Grinders: Critics of Our Public Schools* (New York: Macmillan, 1963), p. 51.
63. Augustin G. Rudd, *Bending the Twig: The Revolution in Education and Its Effect on Our Children* (New York: New York Chapter of the Sons of the American Revolution, 1957), pp. 26–27.
64. Paul Bailey, *Reform The People: Changing Attitudes Towards Popular Education in Early 20th Century China* (Vancouver: University of British Columbia Press, 1990), p. 163.
65. "Constitution of the People's Republic of China (Adopted on December 4, 1982)" in *Education and Socialist Modernization: A Documentary History of Education in the People's Republic of China, 1977–1986* edited by Shi Ming Hu and Eli Seifman (New York: AMS Press, 1987), p. 156.

66. Deng Xiaoping, "Building A Socialism With A Specifically Chinese Character, June 30, 1984," *Selected Works of Deng Xiaoping*, www.peopledaily.com.cn/english/, p. 1.

67. William J. Duiker, *Ho Chi Minh: A Life* (New York: Hyperion, 2000), pp. 15–16.

68. Ibid., p. 18.

69. Ibid., pp. 21–22.

70. I discuss these educational developments in Japan and China in Spring, *Education and the Rise of the Global Economy* ..., pp. 37–69 and *Globalization and Educational Rights* ..., pp. 20–56.

71. "Sakuma Shozan: Reflections on My Errors, 1855," in Herbert Passin, *Society and Education in Japan* (New York: Teachers College Press, 1965), p. 202.

72. Ibid., p. 202.

73. Byron Marshall, *Learning To Be Modern: Japanese Discourse on Education* (Boulder, CO: Westview Press, 1994), pp. 25–26.

74. "Preamble to the Fundamental Code of Education, 1872" in Passim, p. 210.

75. Marshall, pp. 63–65.

76. Bailey, p. 140.

77. Ibid., pp. 139–142.

78. Ibid., p. 156.

79. Ibid., p. 137.

80. Spring, *Globalization and Educational Rights* ..., pp. 20–23.

81. Barry Keenan, *The Dewey Experiment in China: Educational Reform and Political Power in the Early Republic* (Cambridge, MA: Harvard University Press, 1977), pp. 9–36.

82. David L. Hall and Roger T. Ames, *The Democracy of the Dead: Dewey Confucius, and the Hope for Democracy in China* (Chicago: Open Court, 1999), pp. 141–144.

83. Keenan, pp. 14–15.

84. Ibid., pp. 30–33.

85. Ibid., p. 68.

86. Ibid., pp. 69–71.

87. As quoted in Ibid., p. 78.

88. Julia Kwong, *Chinese Education in Transition: Prelude to the Cultural Revolution*, (Montreal: McGill-Queen's University Press, 1979), p. 67.

89. Ibid., p. 76.

90. Quoted in Julia Wong, *Chinese Education in Transition: Prelude to the Cultural Revolution* (Montreal: McGill-Queen's University Press, 1979), p. 71.

91. Hall and Ames, pp. 143–145.

CHAPTER 2

1. Philip Short, *Mao: A Life* (New York: Henry Holt and Company, 1999), p. 24.
2. Ibid., p. 26.
3. Ibid., p. 27.
4. Ibid., p. 31.
5. Philip Short, *Mao: A Life* (New York: Henry Holt and Company, 1999), p. 33.
6. William Duiker, *Ho Chi Minh: A Life* (New York: Hyperion, 2000), p. 32.
7. Ibid., p. 31.
8. Ibid., pp. 26–27.
9. Ibid., p. 40.
10. Ibid., p. 45.
11. As quoted by Short, p. 44.
12. Ibid., p. 52.
13. Ibid., p. 61.
14. Ibid., p. 71.
15. Ibid., p. 79.
16. Ibid., p. 87.
17. Ibid., p. 110.
18. Ibid., p. 113.
19. Ibid., p. 113.
20. Ibid., p. 67.
21. Ho Chi Minh, "Speech at Tours." in *Ho Chi Minh on Revolution* ..., p. 21.
22. Ho Chi Minh, "Report on the National and Colonial Questions at the Fifth Congress of the Communist International," in *Ho Chi Minh on Revolution* ..., p. 81.
23. Ho Chi Minh, "The Path Which Led Me To Leninism," in *Ho Chi Minh on Revolution: Selected Writings, 1920–1966*, edited by Bernard B. Fall (New York: Signet Books, 1968), pp. 24–25.
24. Duiker, p. 63.
25. Ho Chi Minh, "Report on the National and Colonial Questions at the Fifth Congress of the Communist International," in *Ho Chi Minh on Revolution* ..., pp. 63–64.
26. Duiker, p. 50.
27. Mary L. Dudziak, *Cold War Civil Rights: Race and the Image of American Democracy* (Princeton, NJ: Princeton University Press, 2000), p. 6.
28. See Max Elbaum, *Revolution in the Air: Sixties Radicals Turn to Lenin, Mao, and Che*(New York: Verso, 2002).
29. Ho Chi Minh, "Lynching," in *Ho Chi Minh on Revolution* ..., p. 51.
30. Ibid., p. 55.

31. Ho Chi Minh, "The Klu Klux Klan," in *Ho Chi Minh on Revolution* ..., pp. 55–58.

32. Ho Chi Minh, "French Colonization on Trial," in *Ho Chi Minh on Revolution* ..., p. 77.

33. Ibid, p. 64.

34. Ibid., p. 64.

35. Dhananjay Keer, *Dr. Ambedkar: Life and Mission* (Bombay: A. V. Keer, 1954), p. 17.

36. Ibid., p. 29.

37. Ibid., p. 29.

38. Ibid., p. 26.

39. Ibid., p. 38.

40. Ibid., p. 39.

41. Ibid., p. 80.

42. Ibid., pp. 121–122.

43. For a discussion of the role of the U.S. Constitution in shaping the Indian Constitution, see Granville Austin, *The Indian Constitution: Cornerstone of a Nation* (New Delhi: Oxford University Press, 1966), pp. 50–113.

44. Quoted by Short, p. 97.

45. Mao Zedong, "Women," in *Quotations from Chairman Mao Tse-Tung* (Peking: Foreign Languages Press, 1967), p. 294.

46. Ibid., p. 295.

47. Short, p. 310.

48. Ibid., p. 310.

49. Mao Zedong, "Women Have Gone to the Labor Front," *Quotations* ..., p. 297.

50. Quoted by Short, p. 119.

51. Ibid., p. 62.

52. Ibid., p. 123.

53. Ibid., pp. 126–127, 154.

54. J. V. Stalin, "The Political Tasks of the University of the Peoples of the East: Speech Delivered at a Meeting of Students of the Communist University of the Toilers of the East, May 18, 1925," in J. V. Stalin, *Works* (Moscow: Foreign Languages Publishing House, 1954), Vol. 7, p. 147.

55. See Isolda Tsiperovich, "Rare Chinese Editions published in the 1920s in Moscow: The Collection in the Library of the St. Petersburg Branch of the Institute of Oriental Studies," http://www.library.cornell.edu/wason/iaol/Vol.43/tspirovitch.htm and "Deng Xiaoping," http://www.humanrights-china.org/meetingchina/Meeti20031017104619.htm.

56. Ho Chi Minh, "The U.S.S.R. and the Colonial Peoples," *Ho Chi Minh on Revolution* ..., p. 44.

57. Ibid., p. 44.
58. Stalin, p. 141.
59. Ibid., p. 142.
60. Ibid., p. 140.
61. Short, p. 33.
62. Kim Il Sung, "Worthwhile Work Places for Building A New Country Await the Graduates of Democratic Educational Institutions: Speech Delivered at a Meeting to Welcome the Graduates of Various Schools in Pyongyang July 21, 1947," in Kim Il Sung, *On Socialist Pedagogy* (Honolulu: University Press of the Pacific, 2001), p. 1.
63. Mao Zedong, "Speech at the Meeting Celebrating the Completion of the Buildings of the Anti-Japanese Military and Political University 1937," in *Mao Papers: Anthology and Bibliography* edited by Jerome Ch'en (London: Oxford University Press, 1970), p. 12.
64. Mao Zedong, "Stalin's Sixtieth Birthday," in *Mao Papers* ..., p. 16.
65. Mao Zedong, "On Practice: On The Relation Between Knowledge and Practice—Between Knowing and Doing" *Chinese Education Under Communism* edited by Chang-Tu Hu (New York: Teachers College Press, 1962), pp. 51–61.
66. "Constitution of the People's Republic of China (Adopted on December 4, 1982)" in *Education and Socialist Modernization: A Documentary History of Education in the People's Republic of China, 1977–1986* edited by Shi Ming Hu and Eli Seifman (New York: AMS Press, 1987), p. 155.
67. See Paulo Freire, *Pedagogy of the Oppressed Thirtieth Anniversary Edition* (New York: Continuum International Publishing Group, 2000).
68. Mao Zedong, "On Practice," in *Chinese Education Under Communism* ..., p. 51.
69. See Freire, *Pedagogy*....
70. Mao, *"On Practice"* ..., p. 52.
71. Ibid., pp. 54–57.
72. Ibid., p. 61.
73. Ibid., p. 58.
74. Ho Chi Minh, "Report (1939)," in *Ho Chi Minh on Revolution* ..., p. 131.
75. Ho Chi Minh, "Letter from Abroad (1941)," in *Ho Chi Minh on Revolution* ..., p. 133.
76. Ibid., pp. 133–134.
77. Dae-Sook Suh, *Kim Il Sung: The North Korean Leader* (New York: Columbia University Press, 1988), pp. 1–107.
78. Kim Il Sung, "Worthwhile Work Places ...," p. 7.
79. Kim Il Sung, "You Must Learn and Learn To Be Excellent Cadres Of The New Korea," *On Socialist Pedagogy* ..., p. 13.

CHAPTER 3

1. Matthew Cullerne Bown, *Art Under Stalin* (New York: Holmes & Meier, 1991), p. 91.
2. Ibid., p. 91.
3. Maxim Gorky, "My Universities," in *The Autobiography of Maxim Gorky* (New York: Collier Books, 1962) translated by Helen Altschuler, p. 572.
4. Ibid., p. 573.
5. Maxim Gorky, "Soviet Literature: Address Delivered to the First All-Union Congress of Soviet Writers, August 17, 1934," in *On Literature: Selected Pieces by Maxim Gorky* translated by V. Dober (Honolulu: University of the Pacific, 2001), p. 233.
6. Ibid., pp. 233–234.
7. Ibid., p. 252.
8. Ibid., pp. 252–253.
9. Ibid., p. 232.
10. Ibid., p. 241.
11. Ibid., p. 263.
12. Ibid., p. 264.
13. Ibid., p. 264.
14. Quoted by W. John Morgan, *Communists on Education and Culture 1848–1948* (New York: Palgrave Macmillan, 2003), pp. 181–182.
15. Gorky, "Soviet Literature ...," p. 261.
16. "Year of the Stakhanovite," http://www.soviethistory.org/index.php?action=L2&SubjectID=1936stakhanov&Year=1936.
17. Ibid.
18. A. S. Makarenko, *A Book for Parents* (Amsterdam: Fredonia Books, 2002), pp. 314–315.
19. Ibid., p. 331.
20. Ibid., p. 332.
21. Ibid., p. 353.
22. Ibid., p. 353.
23. Olga Yanovskaya, *Stakhanovites in a Box at the Bolshoi Theater, 1937,* reproduced in Brown, p. 71.
24. Ilya Lukomski, *The Factory Party Committee, 1937,* reproduced in Brown, p. 69.
25. Vasili Efanov, *An Unforgettable Meeting* reproduced in Brown, p. 61.
26. Brown, pp. 61–62.
27. Ibid., p. 183.
28. Philip Short, *Mao: A Life* (New York: Henry Holt, 1999), p. 516
29. Ibid., p. 517.
30. For a review of these early works on controlling public opinion, including Lippmann's *Public Opinion,* see Stuart Ewen, *PR! A Social History of Spin* (New York: Basic Books, 1996), pp. 131–174.

31. For a general history of role of attempts to mold public opinion in the United States, see Joel Spring, *Educating the Consumer Citizen: A History of the Marriage of Schools, Advertising, and Media* (Mahwah, NJ: Lawrence Erlbaum Associates, 2003).

32. Ibid., p. 84.

33. Reprints of World War I posters can be found in Stephen Vaughn, *Holding Fast the Inner Lines: Democracy, Nationalism and the Committee on Public Information* (Chapel Hill, NC: The University of North Carolina Press, 1980), pp. 131–188.

34. Adolf Hitler, *Mein Kampf* (New York: Houghton Mifflin Company, 1971), p. 181.

35. Ibid., p. 180.

36. Ibid., p. 180.

37. Ibid., pp. 180–181

38. Ibid., p. 184.

39. Ibid., p. 185.

40. Walter Lippman, *Public Opinion* (New York: Free Press, 1965), p. 31.

41. Ibid., p. 158.

42. Ibid., p. 132.

43. Quote by Ewen, p. 149.

44. Ibid., p. 167.

45. Ibid., p. 163.

46. Ibid., pp. 297–298.

47. Ibid., p. 303.

48. Quoted by Ewen, p. 304.

49. Ibid., pp. 322–323.

50. Photos of billboards shown in Ewen, p. 323.

51. Ibid., p. 306.

52. See Felicity O'Dell, "Forming Socialist Attitudes Towards Work Among Soviet School Children," in *The Making of the Soviet Citizen: Character Formation and Civic Training in Soviet Education* edited by George Avis (London: Croom Helm, 1987), p. 81.

53. Ibid., p. 82.

54. Ibid., p. 86.

55. Ibid., p. 86.

56. Ibid., pp. 84–85.

57. Ibid., p. 314.

58. Ibid., p. 315.

59. Kelly Schrum, "Teena Means Business: Teenage Girls' Culture and 'Seventeen Magazine,' 1944–1950," in *Delinquents & Debutantes: Twentieth-Century American Girls' Cultures* (New York: New York University Press, 1998), p. 149.

60. Ibid., p. 149.

61. Ibid., p. 156.

62. Spring, pp. 125–154.

63. Lendol Calder used this magazine cover for the cover of his book, *Financing the American Dream: A Cultural History of Consumer Credit* (Princeton, NJ: Princeton University Press, 1999). Calder discussed the artist's original intentions on p. 305.

64. Michael Kammen, *Mystic Chords of Memory: The Transformation of Tradition in American Culture* (New York: Vintage Books, 1991), p. 573.

65. Ibid., pp. 572–581.

66. Ibid., p. 181.

67. John Bodnar, *Remaking America: Public Memory, Commemoration, and Patriotism in the Twentieth Century* (Princeton, NJ: Princeton University Press, 1992), p. 15.

68. Ibid., p. 15.

69. See "Twentieth Century History: Stalin's Death," http://history 1900s.about.com/library/weekly/aa040600a.htm.

70. Ibid.

71. Ibid.

72. Quoted by Kammen, p. 31.

73. Spring, pp. 193–197.

74. Kammen, p. 367.

75. "Frequently Asked Questions," http://www.history.org/Foundation/newsroom/faqs.cfm.

76. John D. Rockefeller Jr., "Our Mission: That the Future May Learn from the Past," http://www.history.org/foundation/mission.cfm.

77. Archibald MacLeish, "The Strategy of Truth," *A Time to Act: Selected Addresses* (Boston: Houghton Mifflin, 1943), pp. 29–30.

78. As quoted by John Blum, *V Was For Victory: Politics and American Culture During World War II* (New York: Harcourt Brace Jovanovich, 1976), p. 31.

79. See Allan Winkler, *The Politics of Propaganda: The Office of War Information, 1942–1945* (New Haven: Yale University Press, 1978), pp. 82–83.

80. William J. Duiker, *Ho Chi Minh: A Life* (New York: Hyperion, 2000), p. 283.

81. Ibid., p. 283.

82. Boris Tchechko, "The Conception of the Rights of Man in the U.S.S.R. based on Official Documents," in *Human Rights: Comments and Interpretations: A Symposium Edited by UNESCO* (Westport, CT: Greenwood Press, 1973), p. 169.

83. Ibid., pp. 169–170.

84. Ibid., pp. 160–161.

85. For a discussion of the early development of the U.S. national security state and the National Security Act of 1947 see Michael J. Hogan, *A Cross of Iron: Harry S. Truman and the Origins of the National Security State 1945–1954* (Cambridge, England: Cambridge University Press, 1998), pp. 1–69.

86. "Background of the Present Crisis," *NSC–68: United States Objectives and Programs for National Security (April 14, 1950), A Report to the President Pursuant to the President's Directive of January 31, 1950,* http:www.fas.org/irp/offdocs/nsc-hst/NSC–68.htm, Section I, p. 1.

87. These phrases in Truman and other's speeches are discussed by Hogan, pp. 15–18.

88. Ibid., p. 17.

89. "The Underlying Conflict in the Realm of Ideas and Values Between the U.S. Purpose and the Kremlin Design," *NSC–68 …,* Section IV, p. 1.

90. "Conclusions and Recommendations," *NSC–68 …,* p. 6.

91. "Kuklick's Commentary," in *American Cold War Strategy: Interpreting NSC–68* (Boston: Bedford/St. Martin's, 1993) edited by Ernest R. May, p. 158.

92. Ibid., p. 158.

93. Ibid., p. 159.

94. Ibid., p. 159.

95. As quoted by Hogan, p. 319.

96. "Possible Courses of Action," *NSC–68 …,* Section IX, p. 19.

97. Ibid.

98. Ibid.

99. See Ron Robin *The Making of the Cold War Enemy: Culture and Politics in the Military–Intellectual Complex* (Princeton, NJ: Princeton University Press, 2001), pp. 101–102.

100. Quoted by Frances Stonor Saunders in *The Cultural Cold War: The CIA and the World of Arts and Letters* (New York: The New Press, 1999), p. 148.

101. Robin, p. 10.

102. Ibid., pp. 94–95.

103. Ibid., pp. 101–102.

104. Ibid., p. 103.

105. Ibid., p. 102.

106. Ibid., p. 106.

107. Ibid., p. 118.

108. Heather Timmons, "Publicist Hired to Tell Iraqis of Democracy," *The New York Times on the Web* (March 31, 2004), p. 1.

109. Ibid.

110.   Robin, p. 110.
111.   Ibid., p., 109.
112.   Reproduced in Mary L. Dudziak, *Cold War Civil Rights: Race and Image in American Democracy* (Princeton, NJ: Princeton University Press, 2000), pp. 49, 54.
113.   Ibid., p. 49.
114.   Quoted by Dudziak, p. 28.
115.   Thomas Borstelmann, *The Cold War and the Color Line: American Race Relations in the Global Arena* (Cambridge, MA: Harvard University Press, 2001), p. 2.
116.   Dudziak, p. 58.
117.   Borstelmann, p. 4.
118.   Ibid., pp. 81–82.
119.   Quoted by Borstelmann, p. 75.
120.   Reproduced in Dudziak, p. 196.
121.   Quoted by Dudziak, pp. 99–102.
122.   Dwight Eisenhower, *Waging Peace, 1956–1961* (New York: Doubleday, 1965), p. 150.
123.   Ibid., p. 152.
124.   Ibid., pp. 162, 169.
125.   "Eisenhower's Address on the Situation in Little Rock, September 24, 1957," *New York Times* (September 25, 1957, p. 14); reprinted in *Civil Rights Movement 1942–1968* edited by Albert Blaustein and Robert Zangrando (New York: Trident Press, 1968), pp. 456–458.
126.   Joel Spring, *The Sorting Machine: National Educational Policy Since 1945* (New York: Longman, 1989) and *Images of American Life: A History of Ideological Management in Schools, Movies, Radio and Television* (Albany, NY: State University of New York Press, 1992). Also, the crusade was well documented at the time in four books: Mary Anne Raywid, *The Ax Grinders* (New York: Macmillan, 1963); Jack Nelson and Gene Roberts, Jr., *The Censors and the Schools* (Boston: Little, Brown, 1963); C. Winfield Scott and Clyde M. Hill's, *Public Education Under Criticism* (New York: Prentice-Hall, 1954); and David Hulburd, *This Happened in Pasadena* (New York: Macmillan, 1951). In addition, a number of books have been written about the effect of the anti-communist crusade on mass media, including, Richard Randall's *Censorship of the Movies: The Social and Political Control of a Mass Medium* (Madison, WI: University of Wisconsin Press, 1970); Terry Christensen, *Reel Politics: American Political Movies from Birth of a Nation to Platoon* (New York: Basil Blackwell, 1987); Murray Schumach, *The Face on the Cutting Room Floor: The Story of Movie and Television Censorship* (New York:

Morrow, 1964); and Lary May, *Recasting America: Culture and Politics in the Age of the Cold War* (Chicago: University of Chicago Press, 1988).

127.   Raywid, p. 50; Hulburd, pp. 90–108.
128.   Hulburd, pp. 107–108.
129.   Nelson and Roberts Jr., pp. 40–53.
130.   Quoted by Ronald W. Evans, *The Social Studies Wars* (New York: Teachers College Press, 2004), p. 114.
131.   See Larry Ceplair and Steven Englund, *The Inquisition in Hollywood: Politics in the Film Community, 1930–1960* (Berkeley, CA: University of California Press, 1983).
132.   Christensen, pp. 89–92.
133.   As quoted in Erik Barnouw, *The Golden Web: A History of Broadcasting in the United States, 1933–1953* (New York: Oxford University Press, 1968), p. 257.
134.   Ibid., pp. 253–257, 265.
135.   Robin, 170.
136.   "Possible Courses of Action," *NSC–68 ...*, Section IX, p. 19.
137.   See Saunders, *The Cultural Cold War ...*
138.   Ibid., pp. 22, 30–31.
139.   Quoted in Ibid., pp. 82–83.
140.   Quoted in Ibid., p. 98.
141.   Quoted in Ibid., p. 100.
142.   There was an important commercial side to the support of abstract art as discussed by Serge Guilbaut in *How New York Stole the Idea of Modern Art* (Chicago, University of Chicago Press, 1985).
143.   Saunders, p. 276.
144.   Quoted in Ibid., p. 254.
145.   Ibid., pp. 253–267.

CHAPTER 4

1.   "Constitution of the People's Republic of China (Adopted on December 4, 1982)" in *Education and Socialist Modernization: A Documentary History of Education in the People's Republic of China, 1977–1986* edited by Shi Ming Hu and Eli Seifman (New York: AMS Press, 1987), p. 155.
2.   Philip Short, *Mao: A Life* (New York: Henry Holt and Company, 1999), p. 357.
3.   Mao Zedong, "On the New Democracy (1940)" in *Chinese Education Under Communism* edited by Chang-Tu Hu (New York: Teachers College Press, 1962), p. 77.
4.   Ibid., p. 419.
5.   The differences in school ages reported for China (5–19) and the United States (5–17) is simply a matter of how population figures

have been reported and not in official policies regarding school ages. I realize that these differences in age groups distorts the percentage figures on students enrolled in school. However, there is still a big gap, and room for error, between the roughly 15% of school-age children in school in China and the 83% in the United States.

6. The International Institute for Applied Systems Analysis, "China's population by age groups, 1950–2050, United Nations Population Projection, 1998 Revision, United Nations Population Division: World Population Prospects." The 1998 Edition. New York (Data on CD-ROM), http://www.iiasa.ac.at/Research/LUC/ ChinaFood/data/pop/pop_7.htm; "Table 36.—Historical summary of public elementary and secondary school statistics: 1869–1870 to 1999–2000," *U.S. Department of Education, National Center for Education Statistics, Statistics of State School Systems; Statistics of Public Elementary and Secondary School Systems; Revenues and Expenditures for Public Elementary and Secondary Education, FY 1980; Common Core of Data Surveys; and Council of Economic Advisers, Economic Report of the President* (Washington, DC: National Center for Education Statistics, 2002), p. 49; and historical world population estimates can be found at www.census.gov/ipc/www/worldhis. html.

7. Chinese People's Political Consultative Conference, "Common Program of the Chinese People's Political consultative Conference (September 29, 1949)" in *Toward a New World Outlook: A Documentary History of Education in the People's Republic of China, 1949–1976* edited by Shi Ming Hu and Eli Seifman (New York: AMS Press, 1976), pp.10–11.

8. Ibid., p. 11.

9. Ibid., p. 11.

10. Ibid., p. 11.

11. Ibid., p. 11.

12. Mao Zedong, "Red and Expert (1958)" in *Mao Papers: Anthology and Bibliography* edited by Jerome Ch'en (New York: Oxford University Press, 1970), p. 82.

13. Ibid., pp. 82–83.

14. Theodore Hsi-en Chen, *Chinese Education Since 1949: Academic and Revolutionary Models* (New York: Pergamon Press, 1981), p. 121.

15. Ibid., pp. 122–123.

16. Ibid., pp. 123–124.

17. Government Administration Council of the Central People's Government, "Implementation of New Educational System Promulgated (October 1, 1951)" in *Toward a New World Outlook: A Documentary History ...*, pp. 30–33.

18. Kuo Mo-jo, "Cultural and Educational Work During the Past Year (September 30, 1950)" in *Toward a New World Outlook: A Documentary History* ..., p. 20.
19. Ibid., p. 20.
20. Ibid., p. 19.
21. "Rules of Conduct for Primary School Students (1955)" in *Toward a New World Outlook: A Documentary History* ..., p. 72.
22. "Rules of Conduct for Middle School Students (1955)" in *Toward a New World Outlook: A Documentary History* ..., p. 73.
23. Ma Hsu-lun, "The Policy and Tasks of Higher Education (1953)" in *Toward a New World Outlook: A Documentary History* ..., p. 49.
24. Ibid., pp. 49–50.
25. See Short, pp. 459–461.
26. Mao Zedong, "On the Correct Handling of Contradictions Among the People" in *Chinese Education Under Communism* ..., pp. 80–81.
27. Quoted in Short, p. 460.
28. Ibid., p. 460.
29. Lu Ting-yi, "Let All Flowers Bloom Together, Let Diverse Schools of Thought Contend" in *Toward a New World Outlook: A Documentary History* ..., pp. 77–79.
30. Ibid., p. 77.
31. Ibid., p. 78.
32. Ibid., p. 78.
33. Ibid., p. 78.
34. Ibid., p. 79.
35. Ibid., p. 79.
36. Ibid., p. 79.
37. Ibid., p. 79.
38. Short, pp. 457–470.
39. Short, p. 478.
40. Barbara Barksdale Clowse, *Brainpower for the Cold War: The Sputnik Crisis and National Defense Education Act of 1958* (Westport, CT: Greenwood Press, 1981), p. 8.
41. Ibid., p. 11.
42. Ibid., p. 15.
43. Ibid., p. 16.
44. Ibid., p. 113.
45. Arthur S, Trace, Jr., *What Ivan Knows That Johnny Doesn't: A Comparison of Soviet and American School Programs* (New York: Random House, 1961).
46. Ibid., statement printed on book cover.
47. Ibid., p. 3.
48. Ibid., p. 29.

49. Ibid., p. 186.
50. Ibid., p. 186.
51. Ibid., p. 187.
52. Sergei Khrushchev, *Nikita Khrushchev and the Creation of a Superpower* (University Park, PA: Pennsylvania State University Press, 2000), p. 259.
53. Ibid., p. 260.
54. Ibid., p. 260.
55. As quoted in Nigel Grant, *Soviet Education* (Harmondsworth, England: Penguin Books Ltd., 1964), p. 98.
56. Ibid., p. 98.
57. Quoted by Grant, p. 99.
58. Ibid., p. 99.
59. Ibid., p. 101.
60. Quoted in Clowse, pp. 106–107.
61. See Rebecca S. Lowen, *Creating the Cold War University: The Transformation of Stanford* (Berkeley, CA: University of California Press, 1997), and Hugh Davis Graham and Nancy Diamond, *The Rise of American Research Universities: Elites and Challengers in the Postwar Era* (Baltimore, MD: Johns Hopkins University Press, 1997).
62. Vannevar Bush, *Science—The Endless Frontier: A Report to the President* (Washington, DC: Government Printing Office, 1945).
63. *Hearings Before the Committee on Interstate and Foreign Commerce, Eightieth Congress, First Session on Bills Relating to the National Science Foundation, March 6 and 7, 1947* (Washington, DC: Government Printing Office, 1947), p. 147.
64. See Joel Spring, *The Sorting Machine Revisited: National Educational Policy Since 1945* (New York: Longman, 1989), pp. 63–65.
65. National Manpower Council, *A Policy for Scientific and Professional Manpower* (New York: Columbia University Press, 1953), p. 255.
66. *Hearings Before the Committee on Interstate and Foreign Commerce ...*, pp. 155–157.
67. James B. Conant, *The American High School Today* (New York: McGraw-Hill, 1959).
68. James B. Conant, *My Several Lives: Memoirs of a Social Inventor* (New York: Harper & Row, 1970), p. 621.
69. James B. Conant, *The Child, the Parent and the States* (Cambridge, MA.: Harvard University Press, 1959), p. 39.
70. Ibid., pp. 42–43.
71. Conant, *American High School ...*, p. 52.
72. Ibid., pp. 75–76.
73. Ibid., pp. 75–76.
74. Dwight D. Eisenhower, "Our Future Security," reprinted in *Science and Education for National Defense: Hearings Before the Committee on*

Labor and Public Welfare, United States Senate, Eighty-fifth Congress, Second Session (Washington, DC: Government Printing Office, 1958), pp. 1357–1360.

75. For a complete text of the speech see Dwight D. Eisenhower, "Message from the President of the United States Transmitting Recommendations Relative to Our Educational System," reprinted in Ibid., pp. 195–197.

76. Linking the success of Sputnik to the Great Leap Forward is made by Short, p. 482.

77. Quoted in Julia Kwong, *Chinese Education in Transition: Prelude to the Cultural Revolution*, (Montreal: McGill University, 1979), pp. 89–90.

78. Mao Zedong, "At the University of Tientsin (August 13, 1958)" in *Mao Papers ...*, p. 84.

79. Mao Zedong, "At the University of Wuhan (September 12, 1958)," Ibid., pp. 84–85.

80. Yang Husi-feng, "Educational Work Achievements in 1958 and Arrangements for 1959 (1959)" in *Toward a New World Outlook ...*, pp. 105–110 and "Actively Carry Out the Reform of the School System to Bring About Greater, Faster, Better, and More Economical Results in the Development of Education" in *Chinese Education Under Communism ...*, pp. 98–114.

81. Yang Husi-feng, "Educational Work Achievements in 1958 ...," p. 105.

82. Ibid., p. 105.

83. Ibid., p.108.

84. Lu Ting-yi, "Education Must Be Combined With Productive Labor" in *Chinese Education Under Communism ...*, p. 127.

85. Ibid., p. 127.

86. Ibid., p. 123.

87. Ibid., p. 121.

88. Yang Husi-feng, "Educational Work Achievements in 1958 ...," p. 109.

89. Yang Husi-feng, "Actively Carry Out the Reform of the School System to bring About Greater, ...," p. 103.

90. See Short, pp. 504–505.

91. Quoted by Short, pp. 503–504.

92. Kwang, p. 11.

93. Peking is now Beijing.

94. "Peking Young Communist League Committee and Young Communist League Committee of Tsinghua University Call Separate Forums on 'Redness' and Expertness" in *Toward a New World Outlook ...*, p. 148.

95. Ibid., pp. 148–149.

96. Lu P'ing, "Energetically Train a Force of Red and Expert Teachers," in *Toward a New World Outlook* ..., p. 154.
97. Ma Hsu-lun, "Speech Made by the Minister of Education, Mr. Ma Hsu-lun at the Conference of Higher Education on June 1, 1950" in *Toward a New World Outlook: A Documentary History* ..., p. 13.
98. Ibid., p. 13.
99. Ibid., p. 13.
100. Central Ministry of Education, "The Central Ministry of Education Announcement on Carrying out Curriculum Reform of Higher Education in Order to Achieve the Combination of Theory and Practice Step by Step (August 3, 1950)" in *Toward a New World Outlook: A Documentary History* ..., p. 16.
101. "*Yale Report* (1828)," in *The Colleges and the Public, 1787–1862* edited by Theodore Crane (New York: Teachers College Press, 1963), p. 90.
102. See Clark Kerr, *The Uses of the University* (Cambridge, MA: Harvard University Press, 1963).
103. From the very beginning of its existence, there was a tension in U.S. high school education over a practical versus an academic–classical education. The *Cardinal Principles of Secondary Education* ensured the triumph of the practical. For the early history of the U.S. high school see William Reese, *The Origins of the American High School* (New Haven, CT: Yale University Press, 1995).
104. Commission on the Reorganization of Secondary Education, National Education Association, *Cardinal Principles of Secondary Education, Bureau of Education Bulletin* (Washington, DC: U.S. Government Printing Office, 1918). Discussion of *Cardinal Principles*, the comprehensive high school, and extracurricular activities is taken from Joel Spring, *Education and the Rise of the Corporate State* (Boston: Beacon Press, 1972), pp. 108–125 with this quote from p. 109.
105. Spring, *Education and the Rise of the Corporate State*, pp. 109–110.

CHAPTER 5

1. The Portuguese manuscript was completed in 1968 and it was published in the United States as *Pedagogy of the Oppressed* (New York: Herder and Herder, 1970).
2. Ibid., p. 40.
3. Ibid., p. 82.
4. The best general summary of global wars of liberation is Daniel Moran's *Wars of National Liberation* (London: Cassell, 2001)
5. See William J. Duiker, *Ho Chi Minh: A Life* (New York: Hyperion, 2000), pp. 283–294.

6. Ho Chi Minh, "Declaration of Independence of the Democratic Republic of Vietnam" in *Ho Chi Minh on Revolution: Selected Writings, 1920–1966* (New York: Signet Books, 1967) edited by Bernard B. Fall, pp. 141–143.

7. For a study of his lasting influence see Marc Becker, *Mariátegui and Latin American Marxist Theory* (Athens, OH: Ohio University Center for International Studies, 1993).

8. Sheldon B. Liss, *Marxist Thought in Latin America* (Berkeley, CA: University of California Press, 1984), p. 129.

9. Ibid., p. 284.

10. Ibid., pp. 1–30.

11. Ibid., p. 31.

12. José Carlos Mariátegui, *Seven Interpretive Essays on Peruvian Reality* (Austin, TX: University of Texas Press, 1971), p. 122.

13. Becker, p. 38.

14. Ibid., p. 37.

15. Mariátegui, *Seven Interpretive Essays ...*, p. 28.

16. Ibid., p. 29.

17. Ibid., p. 25.

18. Ibid., p. 30.

19. Ibid., p. 79.

20. Ibid., p. 79.

21. Ibid., p. 83.

22. Ibid., p. 85.

23. Quoted in Ibid., p. 86.

24. Quoted in Ibid., p. 87.

25. Ibid., p. 88.

26. Ibid., p. 90.

27. Ibid., p. 119.

28. Ibid., p. 118.

29. Ibid., p. 121.

30. For an understanding of Gramsci's place in the theoretical development of Marxism see David McLellan, *Marxism After Marx* (New York: Houghton Mifflin Company, 1981), pp. 175–195.

31. Ibid., p. 272.

32. Ibid., pp. 272–273.

33. Robert C. Johnston, "A Revolutionary Education," *Education Week on the Web* (March 5, 2003), pp. 1–2.

34. These tests included the 1992 IEA study of literacy; Educational Testing Service's study of eighth grade reading and mathematics achievement in 1992 (IAEP); the Third International Math and Science Survey (TIMSS) of 1997 and 1999; UNESCO/OREALC's studies of third and fourth grade achievement in math and language in 1992 and 1997; and the OECD's PISA (Progress in Stu-

dent Achievement) study undertaken in the year 2000. Laurence Wolff, Ernesto Schiefelbein, and Paulina Schiefelbein, *Primary Education in Latin America: The Unfinished Agenda* (Washington, DC: Inter-American Development Bank, 2002), p. 11.

35. Ibid., p. 11.
36. Ibid., p. 11.
37. World Bank, *Education and Development* (Washington, DC: The World Bank, 2002), p. 4.
38. Human Development Network Africa Region and Education Department, World Bank, *Achieving Education for All by 2015: Simulation Results for 47 Low-Income Countries* (Washington, DC: The World Bank, 2002), p. 6.
39. Sheldon Liss, *Fidel! Castro's Political and Social Thought* (Boulder, CO: Westview Press, 1994), pp. 136–140.
40. Liss, *Marxist Thought in Latin America* ..., pp. 49–51.
41. Liss, *Fidel! Castro's Political and Social Thought* ..., p. 137.
42. Ibid., p. 137.
43. Ibid., p. 139.
44. Régis Debray, *Revolution in the Revolution? Armed Struggle and Political Struggle in Latin America* (New York: Monthly Review Press, 1967), p. 11.
45. Ibid., pp. 7–8.
46. Ibid., p. 110.
47. Ibid., p. 113.
48. Ibid., p. 114.
49. Che Guevara, "Socialism and Man in Cuba," *Global Justice: Liberation and Socialism* (Melbourne, Australia: Ocean Press, 2002), p. 30. This book was published in cooperation with Che Guevara Studies Center in Havana, Cuba.
50. Ibid., p. 35.
51. Ibid., p. 42.
52. Ibid., p. 41.
53. Ibid., p. 43.
54. Ibid., p. 44.
55. Ibid., p. 46.
56. Liss, *Fidel! Castro's Political and Social Thought* ..., p. 139.
57. Anna Lorenzetto and Karel Neys, *Report on the Method and Means Utilized in Cuba to Eliminate Illiteracy* (Ciudad Libertad, Cuba: Ministry of Education, 1965), pp. 15–16.
58. Ibid, p. 40.
59. Ibid., p. 43.
60. Ibid., p. 18.
61. Ibid., p. 23.
62. Ibid., p. 23.

63. Ibid., p. 24.
64. Anna Lorenzetto and Karel Neys, p. 37.
65. Philip Short, *Mao: A Life* (New York: Henry Holt, 1999), p. 532
66. Mao Zedong, "May 7th Directive," in *Toward A New World Outlook: A Documentary History of Education in the People's Republic of China, 1949–1976* edited by Shi Ming Hu and Eli Seifman (New York: AMS Press, Inc., 1976), p. 201.
67. Short, p. 536.
68. Short, pp. 235–236.
69. "Decision of C.P.C. Central Committee and State Council on Reform of Entrance Examination and Enrollment in Higher Education," in *Toward A New World Outlook: A Documentary History ...*, p. 202.
70. Ibid.
71. "Editorial on Importance of Transforming Chinese Educational System," in *Toward A New World Outlook: A Documentary History ...*, p. 212.
72. Ibid., p. 210.
73. Ibid., p. 211.
74. "Establish a New Proletarian System of Examination and Assessment," in *Toward A New World Outlook: A Documentary History ...*, p. 239.
75. Ibid., p. 240.
76. Ibid., p. 240.
77. Ibid., p. 240.
78. Ibid., p. 240.
79. Central Committee of the Chinese Communist Party, "Chinese Communist Party Central Committee's Notification (Draft) Concerning the Great Proletarian Cultural Revolution in Primary Schools (February 4, 1967)" in *Toward A New World Outlook: A Documentary History ...*, p. 203.
80. Ibid., p. 203.
81. The Investigation Group of the Chekiang Provincial Revolutionary Committee, "The Question of Prime Importance in the Revolution of Education in the Countryside is That the Poor and Lower-Middle Peasants Control the Power in Education," in *Toward A New World Outlook: A Documentary History ...*, p. 227.
82. Ibid., pp. 227–228.
83. As quoted in Ibid., p. 227.
84. Ibid., p. 227.
85. Ibid., p. 227.
86. Mao Zedong, "Where do Correct Ideas Come From? (May 1963)," in *Selected Readings From the Works of Mao Tsetung* (Peking: Foreign Language Press, 1971), p. 502.

87. Ibid., p. 503.
88. Ibid., p. 503.
89. Ibid., p. 503.
90. Ibid., pp. 503–504.
91. As quoted by Short, p. 545.
92. As quoted by Short, p. 545.
93. Freire, p. 40.
94. Paulo Freire, *Pedagogy of Hope: Reliving Pedagogy of the Oppressed* (New York: Continuum, 2004), p. 26.
95. Ibid., p. 20.
96. For a discussion of Vygotsky and Piaget see Lois Holzman, *Schools for Growth: Radical Alternatives to Current Educational Models* (Mahwah, NJ: Lawrence Erlbaum Associates, 1997), pp. 55–59.
97. Ibid., p. 56.
98. Freire, *Pedagogy of Hope* ..., p. 25.
99. Ibid., p. 25.
100. Ibid., pp. 25–26.
101. Statutes governing the Movement for Popular Culture are reprinted in Paulo Freire, *Letters to Cristina: Reflections on My Life and Work* (New York: Routledge, 1996), p. 228.
102. Ibid., p. 111.
103. Ibid., p. 111.
104. Ibid., p. 112.
105. Ibid., p. 114.
106. Freire, *Pedagogy of Hope* ..., p. 34.
107. Ibid., p. 43.
108. Freire, *Pedagogy of the Oppressed* ..., p. 77.
109. This quote is taken from footnote #4 of *Pedagogy of the Oppressed*, p. 77.
110. Freire, *Pedagogy of Hope* ..., p. 43.
111. Ibid., p. 45.
112. Ibid., p. 45.
113. Ibid., pp. 44–45.
114. Ibid., p. 55.
115. Ibid., p. 55.
116. Freire, *Pedagogy of the Oppressed* ..., pp. 119–120.
117. Freire, *Pedagogy of Hope* ..., pp. 61–63.
118. Freire, *Pedagogy of the Oppressed* ..., p. 83.
119. This is footnote #10 on p. 83 of Freire's *Pedagogy of the Oppressed* which is cited as "From the *Selected Works of Mao-Tse-Tung*, Vol. III. 'The United Front in Cultural Work' (October 30, 1944) (Peking, 1967)," pp. 186–187.
120. Freire, *Pedagogy of the Oppressed* ..., p. 166.
121. Mao Zedong, "Where Do Correct Ideas Come From? (May 1963)" ..., pp. 503–504.

122. Freire, *Pedagogy of the Oppressed ...*, p. 59.

123. Freire, *Pedagogy of the Oppressed*, pp. 139–140.

124. Medellín Conference (1968), *Medellín Conference Documents: Justice and Peace*, Latin American Studies Program of Providence College (November 20, 2004), http://www.providence.edu/las/documents.htm#Medellín%, p. 3.

125. Ibid., pp. 3–4.

126. Ibid.

127. Ibid., p. 1.

128. Ibid., p. 10.

129. Ibid., p. 10.

130. Christian Smith, *The Emergence of Liberation Theology: Radical Religion and Social Movement Theory* (Chicago: The University of Chicago Press, 1991), pp. 15–21.

131. Gustavo Gutiérrez, *A Theology of Liberation; 15th Anniversary Edition* (Maryknoll, NY: Orbis Books, 1988), p. xxx.

132. Ibid., p. xxxviii.

133. Ibid., p. 57.

134. Ibid., p. 56.

135. Ibid., p. 56.

136. Ibid., p. 57.

137. Ibid., p. 57.

138. Ibid., p. 19.

139. Ibid., p. 107.

140. In 1970 and 1971, I worked with Ivan Illich at the Center for Intercultural Documentation. It was there that I first met Paulo Freire.

141. The influences of CIDOC, Ivan Illich, and Paulo Freire are represented in my book, Joel Spring, *A Primer of Libertarian Education* (New York: Free Life Editions, 1975). The books coedited at CIDOC are Joel Spring and Jordan Bishop, *Formative Undercurrents in Compulsory Knowledge* (Cuernavaca, Mexico: CIDOC, 1970) and Clarence Karier, Paul Violas, and Joel Spring, *Roots of Crisis* (Chicago: Rand McNally, 1973).

142. See Sheryl Hirshon with Judy Butler, *And Also Teach Them to Read: The National Literacy Crusade of Nicaragua* (Westport, CT: Lawrence Hill & Company, 1983) and John L. Hammond, *Fighting to Learn: Popular Education and Guerilla War in El Salvador* (New Brunswick, NJ: Rutgers University Press, 1998).

143. Carlos M. Vilas, *The Sandinista Revolution: National Liberation and Social Transformation in Central America* (New York: Monthly Review Press, 1986), p. 216.

144. Ibid., pp. 215–216, 218.

145. Ibid., p. 219.

146. Ibid., p. 221.
147. Quoted in Hirshon, p. 5.
148. Quoted in Ibid., p. 2.
149. Ibid., p. 50.
150. Ibid., pp. 52–53.
151. Ibid., p. 53.
152. Hammond, p. 25.
153. Ibid., p. 57.
154. Ibid., p. 58.
155. Quoted in Ibid., p. 62.
156. Quoted in Ibid., p. 63.
157. Ibid., pp. 1–3.

CHAPTER 6

1. Fazlur Rahman, *Islam & Modernity: Transformation of an Intellectual Tradition* (Chicago: University of Chicago Press, 1982), p. 43.
2. Anthony Pagden, *Lords of All the World: Ideologies of Empire in Spain, Britain and France c.1500–c.1800* (New Haven, CT: Yale University Press, 1995). Pagden argued that an important ideological justification for Euroamerican colonialism was the Christian belief that world was divided between Christians and pagans.
3. *Al-Qur'an* translated by Ahmed Ali (Princeton, NJ: Princeton University Press, 1988), p. 45.
4. Amin Maalouf, *The Crusades Through Arab Eyes* (New York: Shocken Books, 1984), pp. 19–36.
5. Ibid., p. 264.
6. Rahman, p. 20.
7. Rahman found that certain colleges in the Ottoman empire were graded. Ibid, p. 35.
8. Rahman, pp. 50–51.
9. A. L. Tibawi, *Islamic Education: Its Traditions and Modernization into Arab National Systems* (London: Luzac & Comapany Limited, 1972), p. 71.
10. Bassam Tibi, *Arab Nationalism: Between Islam and the Nation-State* (New York: St. Martin's Press, 1997), p. 93.
11. Tibawi, p. 74.
12. Gregory Starrett, *Putting Islam to Work: Politics and Religious Transformation in Egypt* (Berkeley, CA: University of California Press, 1998), p. 26.
13. J. Heyworth-Dunne, *An Introduction to the History of Education in Modern Egypt* (London: Luzac & Company Limited, 1938), pp. 96–208.
14. Heyworth-Dunne, pp. 303–304.

15. Ibid., p. 436.
16. Ibid., pp. 425–443.
17. Starrett, p. 27.
18. As quoted by Starrett, p. 35.
19. Ibid., p. 36.
20. Ibid., pp. 50–54.
21. Starrett, p. 71.
22. Tibawi, p. 62–63, 165–167.
23. Ibid., p. 168.
24. Ibid., pp. 156–164.
25. Ibid., p. 141.
26. Ibid., p. 149.
27. Tibawi, p. 87.
28. Ibid., p. 87.
29. Ibid., p. 148.
30. Tibi, p. 148.
31. Ibid., p. 148.
32. Ibid., p. 148.
33. Ibid., p. 40.
34. Tibawi, pp. 206–207.
35. Ibid., p. 208.
36. Ibid., pp. 203–208.
37. As quoted by Antony Black, *The History of Islamic Political Thought: From the Prophet to the Present* (New York: Routledge, 2001), pp. 342–343.
38. Tibawi, pp. 201–202.
39. Ibid., pp. 211–214.
40. Other countries that would later join the Arab League were Algeria (1962), Bahrain (1971), Comoros (1993), Djibouti (1977), Kuwait (1961), Libya (1953), Mauritania (1973), Morocco (1958), Oman (1971), Qatar (1971), Somalia (1974), Southern Yemen (1967), Sudan (1956), Tunisia (1958), and the United Arab Emirates (1971).
41. "Charter of the League of Arab States," Retrieved from http://www.arableagueonline.org on January 19, 2005.
42. "Arabic Language," Retrieved from http://www.arableagueonline.org on January 19, 2005.
43. "Arab Civilization," Retrieved from http://www.arableagueonline.org on January 19, 2005.
44. "Education," Retrieved from http://www.arableagueonline.org on January 19, 2005.
45. Starrett, p. 79.
46. "Egyptian Constitution Ratified September 11, 1971," http://www.parliament.gov.eg retrieved on 1/13/05.

47. Ibid.
48. Ibid.
49. Ibid.
50. Ibid.
51. Starrett, p. 78.
52. Ibid., pp. 131–132.
53. See Leslie S. Nucho, Editor, *Education in the Arab World Volume I: Algeria, Bahrain, Egypt, Jordan, Kuwait, Lebanon, Morocco* (Washington, DC: AMIDEAST Publications,), pp. 145–300 and Lee Wilcox, *Arab Republic of Egypt: A Study of the Educational System of the Arab Republic of Egypt and a Guide to the Academic Placement of Students in Education Institutions of the United States* (Washington, DC: International Education Activities Group of the American Association of Collegiate Registrars and Admissions Officers, 1988).
54. Wilcox, p. 57.
55. Nucho, p. 150.
56. Moran, pp. 109–127.
57. John Ruedy, *Modern Algeria: The Origins and Development of a Nation* (Bloomington, Indiana: University of Indiana Press, 1992), p. 224.
58. Ibid., p. 228.
59. Ibid., pp. 224–225.
60. "Algerian Constitution Ratified November 9, 1976," http://www.oefre.unibe.ch/law/icl/index.html retrieved on 1/13/05.
61. Ibid.
62. Tibawi, pp. 168–169.
63. Ruedy, pp. 227–228.
64. Ibid., p. 228.
65. Nucho, pp. 13–83.
66. "Education," Retrieved from http://www.arableagueonline.org on January 19, 2005.
67. Nucho, p. 27.
68. Tibawi, p. 146.
69. "Syrian Constitution Ratified March 13, 1973," http://www.parliament.gov.eg retrieved on 1/13/05.
70. Ibid.
71. Ibid.
72. Tibi, p. 89.
73. Hamad I. Al Salloom with the support and aid of the Relations Department of the Saudi Arabian Cultural Mission to the U. S. A., *Education in Saudi Arabia, Second Edition* (Beltsville, MD: Amana Publications, 1991), pp. 3–6.

74. "Saudi Arabian Constitution ratified March 1992," *http://www.par-liament.gov.eg* retrieved on 1/13/05.
75. Hamad I. Al Salloom, p. 15.
76. Ibid., p. 15.
77. Ibid., p. 16.
78. Ibid., p. 17.
79. Ibid., p. 18
80. Ibid., p. 19.
81. Ibid., p. 20.
82. Ibid., p. 33.
83. Ibid., p. 18.
84. Ibid., p. 18.
85. Ibid., p. 32.
86. Ibid., p. 36.
87. Ibid., p. 40.
88. On the global spread of the English language see Robert Phillipson, *Linguistic Imperialism* (Oxford, England: Oxford University Press, 1992) and Braj B. Kachru, *The Alchemy of English: The Spread, Functions, and Models of Non-Native Englishes* (Urbana, IL: University of Illinois Press, 1990).
89. Rosnani Hashim, *Educational Dualism in Malaysia: Implications for Theory and Practice* (Kuala Lumpur: Oxford University Press, 1996), p. 51.
90. Ibid., p. 45.
91. Ibid., p. 45.
92. "Constitution of Malaysia ratified on August 31, 1957," Retrieved from http://confinder.richmond.edu/local_malaysia.html on January 25, 2005.
93. Hashim, p. 63.
94. Joel Spring, *Education and the Rise of the Global Economy* (Mahwah, NJ: Lawrence Erlbaum Associates, 1998), p. 16.
95. Ibid., p. 16.
96. Jawaharlal Nehru, "English" in *Jawaharlal Nehru: An Anthology* edited by Sarvepalli Gopal, (Delhi: Oxford University Press, 1980), p. 507.
97. Ibid., p. 507.
98. Jawaharlal Nehru, "The Question of Language" in *Jawaharlal Nehru: Anthology* ..., p. 508.
99. "Constitutional Basis of Education (1950), Constitution of India" in J. C. Aggarwal, *Land marks in the History of Modern Indian Education* (New Delhi: Vikas Publishing House, 1984), pp. 95–96.
100. Ibid., p. 359.
101. "Top 10 Colleges of India," Retrieved from *India Today*, http://www.India-today.com October 29, 2000.

102. Ibid.
103. Hashim, pp. 21–24.
104. Constitution of Malaysia ...
105. Ibid.
106. Hashim, p. 130.
107. Ibid., p. 131.
108. A. H. Nayyar, "Madrasah Education Frozen in Time," in *Education and the State: Fifty Years of Pakistan* edited by Pervez Hoodbhoy (Karachi: Oxford University Press, 1998), pp. 225–226.
109. Ibid., p. 226.
110. Nasir Jalil, "Pakistan's Education: The First Decade," *Education and the State ...*, p. 35.
111. UNICEF, *The State of the World's Children 2000* (New York: UNICEF, 2000), pp. 96–99.
112. Ibid., pp. 100–107.
113. "Aims and Objectives of Education and Islamic Education," Retrieved from Pakistan's official government Web site http://www.moe.gov.pk on January 23, 2005.
114. Ibid.
115. Nayyar provided a series of tables demonstrating the growth in numbers of madrasas and in the number students and graduates, pp. 228, 229, and 232.
116. Ibid., p. 233.
117. Ibid., p. 230.
118. Joel Spring, *Globalization and Educational Rights: An Intercivilizational Analysis* (Mahwah, NJ: Lawrence Erlbaum Associates, 2001), pp. 57–61.
119. Jeffrey Goldberg, "The Education of a Holy Warrior," *The New York Times Magazine* (25 June 2000), pp. 32–37, 53,63–64,70.
120. Ibid., p. 35.
121. Ibid., p. 35.
122. Phillipson, pp. 115–116.
123. Quoted in Phillipson, p. 130.
124. Kachru, p. 133.
125. Patrick Boyle's *Class Formation and Civil Society: The Politics of Education in Africa* (Hampshire, England: Ashgate, 1999) focuses on the evolution of education policies in the Congo, the Cameroons, and Kenya.
126. Solomon Shu, "Education in Cameroon," in *Education in Africa: A Comparative Survey* edited by A. Babs Fafunwa and J.U. Aisiku (London: George Allen & Unwin, 1982), pp. 28–48
127. See Michael Anthony Samuels, *Education in Angola, 1878–1914: A History of Culture Transfer and Administration* (New York: Teachers College Press, 1970).

128. See Ahmadou Toure, "Education in Mali" in *Education in Africa ...*, pp. 188–204.

129. Louis Brenner, *Controlling Knowledge: Religion, Power and Schooling in a West African Muslim Society* (Bloomington, IN: Indiana University Press, 2001), p. 41.

130. Ibid., p. 41.

131. Ibid., p. 41.

132. Ibid., pp. 44–43.

133. Ibid., p. 45.

134. Ibid., pp. 54–84.

135. Boyle, pp. 18–25.

136. For an expanded discussion of the World Bank's educational plans see Joel Spring, *How Educational Ideologies Are Shaping Global Society* (Mahwah, NJ: Lawrence Erlbaum Associates, 2004), pp. 28–65.

137. "Iran Constitution," *International Constitutional Law*, retrieved from http://www.oefre.unibe.ch/law/icl/index.html on February 10, 2005.

138. Brenner, p. 264.

139. Boyle, pp. 61–86.

140. Ibid, p. 82.

141. Kim Il Sung, "On the Duty of Educational Workers in the Raising of Children and Young People," *Kim Il Sung on Socialist Pedagogy* (Honolulu: University Press of the Pacific, 2001), pp. 22–23.

142. See Dae-Sook Suh, *Kim Il Sung: The North Korean Leader* (New York: Columbia University Press, 1988), pp. 55–107.

143. Ibid., p. 111.

144. Kim Il Sung, "Following the Will of Revolutionary Forerunners," *Kim Il Sung on Socialist Pedagogy ...*, p. 18.

145. Kim Il Sung, "Thesis on Socialist Education," *Kim Il Sung on Socialist Pedagogy ...*, p. 324.

146. Ibid, pp. 324–325.

147. Ibid, p. 322.

148. Ibid, p. 322.

149. Ibid, p. 329.

150. Kim Il Sung, "On the Duty of Educational Workers ...," p. 29.

151. Kim Il Sung, "Thesis on Socialist Education ...," p. 339.

152. Ibid, p. 339.

153. Ibid, p. 325.

154. Ibid, p. 325.

155. Ibid, p. 337.

156. Kim Il Sung, "Improving and Strengthening the Work of Education," *Kim Il Sung on Socialist Pedagogy ...*, pp. 66–92.

157. Ibid, p. 69.

158. Ibid, p. 69.
159. Ibid, p. 70.
160. Ibid, p. 70.
161. Ibid, p. 74.
162. Ibid, p. 71.
163. Ibid, p. 72.

CHAPTER 7

1. Benjamin Yang, *Deng: A Political Biography* (Armonk, NY: M.E. Sharpe, 1998), pp. 14–24.
2. Ibid., p. 35.
3. Ibid., pp. 34–46.
4. Ibid., pp. 47–55.
5. See Wei-Wei Zhang, *Ideology and Economic Reform Under Deng Xiaoping 1978–1993* (New York: Kegan Paul International, 1996), pp. 19–81.
6. Deng Xiaoping, "Integrate Marxism–Leninism with the Concrete Conditions of China, November 17, 1956," *Selected Works of Deng Xiaoping* available on the *People's Daily Online* http://english.peopledaily.com.cn/. This article was retrieved on March 29, 2005.
7. Ibid.
8. Ibid.
9. Ibid.
10. Deng Xiaoping, "Run Our Schools Well and Train Cadres, (July 9, 1954)," *Selected Works of Deng Xiaoping* available on the *People's Daily Online* http://english.peopledaily.com.cn/. This article was retrieved on March 29, 2005.
11. Ibid.
12. Deng Xiaoping, "Education Should Be Made Universal and Educational Standards Raised," April 7, 1958, *Selected Works of Deng Xiaoping* available on the *People's Daily Online* http://english.peopledaily.com.cn/. This article was retrieved on March 29, 2005.
13. Deng Xiaoping, "Run Our Schools Well ..."
14. Deng Xiaoping, "Education Should Be Made Universal ..."
15. Deng Xiaoping, "Run Our Schools Well ..."
16. Kalpana Misra, *From Post-Maoism to Post-Marxism: The Erosion of Official Ideology in Deng's China* (New York: Routledge, 1998), p. 164.
17. As quoted by Yang, p. 179.
18. Deng Xiaoping, "Uphold the Four Cardinal Principles, March 30, 1979," *Selected Works of Deng Xiaoping* available on the *People's Daily On-*

line http://english.peopledaily.com.cn/. This article was retrieved on April 2, 2005. Also for an analysis of Deng's rise to power see Maurice Meisner, *The Deng Xiaoping Era: An Inquiry into the Fate of Chinese Socialism 1978–1994* (New York: Hill and Wang, 1996), pp. 61–187.

19. Deng Xiaoping, "We Can Develop a Market Economy Under Socialism, November 26, 1979," *Selected Works of Deng Xiaoping* available on the *People's Daily Online* http://english.peopledaily.com.cn/. This article was retrieved on February 26, 2005.

20. Ibid.

21. Deng Xiaoping, "Some Comments on Work in Science and Education, August 8, 1977," *Selected Works of Deng Xiaoping* available on the *People's Daily Online* http://english.peopledaily.com.cn/. This article was retrieved on February 26, 2005.

22. Ibid.

23. Deng Xiaoping, "There Is No Fundamental Contradiction Between Socialism and a Market Economy, October 23, 1985," *Selected Works of Deng Xiaoping* available on the *People's Daily Online* http://english.peopledaily.com.cn/. This article was retrieved on February 26, 2005.

24. Ibid.

25. Ibid.

26. See Michael E. Marti, *China and the Legacy of Deng Xiaoping: From Communist Revolution to Capitalist Evolution* (Washington, DC: Brassey's Inc., 2002), pp. 1–30.

27. Ibid., p. 104.

28. See Misra, p. 19.

29. Deng Xiaoping, "Emancipate the Mind, Seek Truth From Facts and Unite as One in Looking to the Future, December 13, 1978," *Selected Works of Deng Xiaoping* available on the *People's Daily Online* http://english.peopledaily.com.cn/. This article was retrieved on February 26, 2005.

30. Ibid.

31. Misra, pp. 19–53.

32. Misra, p. 52.

33. Deng Xiaoping, "Emancipate the Mind ..."

34. Ibid.

35. Ibid.

36. Deng Xiaoping, "Uphold the Four Cardinal Principles ..."

37. Ibid.

38. Ibid.

39. Misra, p. 150.

40. Deng Xiaoping, "Adhere to the Principle 'To Each According to his Work', March 28, 1978," *Selected Works of Deng Xiaoping* available on

the *People's Daily Online* http://english.peopledaily.com.cn/. This article was retrieved on February 26, 2005.

41. Deng Xiaoping, "Building a Socialism With a Specifically Chinese Character, June 30, 1984," *Selected Works of Deng Xiaoping* available on the *People's Daily Online* http://english.peopledaily.com.cn/. This article was retrieved on February 26, 2005.

42. Ibid.

43. Deng Xiaoping, "Respect Knowledge, Respect Trained Personnel, May 24, 1977," *Selected Works of Deng Xiaoping* available on the *People's Daily Online* http://english.peopledaily.com.cn/. This article was retrieved on February 26, 2005.

44. Ibid.

45. Ibid.

46. Ibid.

47. Deng Xiaoping, "Some Comments on Work in Science and Education, August 8, 1977," *Selected Works of Deng Xiaoping* available on the *People's Daily Online* http://english.peopledaily.com.cn/. This article was retrieved on February 26, 2005.

48. Ibid.

49. Ibid.

50. Deng Xiaoping, "Setting Things Right in Education, September, 1977," *Selected Works of Deng Xiaoping* available on the *People's Daily Online* http://english.peopledaily.com.cn/. This article was retrieved on February 26, 2005.

51. Ibid.

52. Ibid.

53. Ibid.

54. Ibid.

55. Deng Xiaoping, "Speech at the National Conference on Education, April 22, 1978," *Selected Works of Deng Xiaoping* available on the *People's Daily Online* http://english.peopledaily.com.cn/. This article was retrieved on February 26, 2005.

56. Ibid.

57. *Neon Socialism,* is a term proposed to describe the Post-Mao China by Jennifer Adams, in my class on the Pedagogies of Globalization at the Graduate Center of the City University of New York.

58. "Deng gives me chance to develop myself: says for City educated girl," *People's Daily Online* (20 August 2004) http://english.peopledaily.com.cn/. This article was retrieved on February 26, 2005.

59. Ibid.

60. Ibid.

61. "Shanghai Cops Sued in Jumper's Death," *People's Daily Online* (February 25, 2005) http://english.peopledaily.com.cn/. This article was retrieved on March 2, 2005.

62. "Anti-Cheating Device to be Used in Exams," *People's Daily Online* (October 13, 2004) http://english.peopledaily.com.cn/. This article was retrieved on February 26, 2005.

63. "Lawmaker Proposes Legislation Against Exam Fraud," *People's Daily Online* (March 12, 2005) http://english.peopledaily.com.cn/. This article was retrieved on April 2, 2005.

64. "Education Law of the People's Republic of China—Chinese Laws and Regulations—People's Daily Online News Letter," *People's Daily Online*, http://english.peopledaily.com.cn/. This law was retrieved on March 5, 2005.

65. Ibid.

66. Ibid.

67. Ibid.

68. Ibid.

69. Ibid.

70. "Article 26," Ibid.

71. Ibid.

72. Ibid.

73. Quoted in Sheldon Garon, *Molding Japanese Minds: The State in Everyday Life* (Princeton, NJ: Princeton University Press, 1997), p. 149.

74. This brief discussion of post-World War II Japanese education is based on my previous published book: Joel Spring, *Education and the Rise of the Global Economy* (Mahwah, NJ: Lawrence Erlbaum Associates, 1998), pp. 37–70. In *Education and the Rise of the Global Economy*, I discuss the development of Japanese education from the time of 19th century Westernization until roughly the 1990s. What is different about the discussion in this book is the analysis of the impact of Japanese education on U.S. educational policies and the analysis of the changes in both countries in the 21st century.

75. Quoted in Byron Marshall, *Learning to Be Modern: Japanese Discourse on Education* (Boulder, CO: Westview Press, 1994), p. 157.

76. Ibid., pp. 157–159.

77. The Japanese Constitution can be found on the official Web site of the Prime Minister of Japan, http://www.kantei.go.jp/foreign/government_e.html. This document was retrieved on April 18, 2005.

78. Ibid.

79. Marshall, p. 163.

80. "The Board of Education Law," in *Japanese Education Since 1945: A Documentary Study* (Armonk, NY: M.E. Sharpe, 1994) edited by Edward R. Beauchamp and James Vardaman, Jr., p. 118.

81. Quoted in Marshall, pp. 177–178.
82. Teruhisa Horio, *Educational Thought and Ideology in Modern Japan* (Tokyo: University of Tokyo Press, 1988), p. 147.
83. Quoted by Horio, p., 146.
84. Quoted by Horio, p., 149.
85. See Joel Spring, *The Sorting Machine Revisited: National Educational Policy Since 1945* (White Plains, NY: Longman Inc., 1988).
86. Horio, p. 215.
87. "The Advance of Manpower Capability and the Promotion of Scientific Technology: Economic Advisory Committee" in *Japanese Education Since 1945* ..., pp. 148–149.
88. "A Proposition from Businessmen for Educational Reform: In Pursuit of Creativity, Diversity, and Internationality, Education Council, Japan Committee for Economic Development, July 1984" in Ibid., p. 285.
89. Quoted in Horio, p. 215.
90, Quoted in Horio, p. 216.
91. See Benjamin Duke, *The Japanese School: Lessons for Industrial America* (New York: Praeger, 1986), pp. 93–97, 216–217.
92. Chester Finn, Jr., & Diane Ravitch, "Educational Reform 1995–96 Introduction." Available: www.edexcellence.net, p. 2. Retrieved on September 24, 2004.
93. The National Commission On Excellence in Education, *A Nation at Risk: The Full Account* (Portland, OR: USA Research, 1984), p. 1.
94. See "Appendix," Ibid., pp. 87–114.
95. Ibid., p. 5.
96. Ibid., p. 5.
97. Ibid., p. 5.
98. Ibid., p. 5.
99. Ibid., p. 6.
100. Ibid., pp. 6–7.
101. David Berliner and Bruce Biddle, *The Manufactured Crisis: Myths, Fraud, and the Attack on America's Public Schools* (New York: Perseus Books, 1995).
102. The National Commission on Excellence in Education ..., pp. 9–10.
103. Ibid., p. 70.
104. Ibid., p. 70.
105. Ibid., pp. 73–74.
106. Ibid., p. 74.
107. I detail this history in Joel Spring, *Political Agendas for Education: From the Religious Right to the Green Party Third Edition* (Mahwah, NJ: Lawrence Erlbaum Associates, 2005). Also see *No Child Left Behind Act of 2001, Public Law 107–110* (January 8, 2002) http://www.ed.gov/policy/elsec/leg/esea02/107-110.pdf.

108. The National Commission on Excellence in Education ..., p. 75.
109. Ibid., p. 70.
110. Louis V. Gerstner, Jr., et al., *Reinventing Education: Entrepreneurship in America's Public Schools* (New York: Dutton, 1994), p. 59.
111. William Bennett, "Epilogue, *Japanese Education Today* (Washington, DC: Department of Education, 1987)," p. 69.
112. See Benjamin Duke, *The Japanese School: Lessons for Industrial America* (New York: Praeger, 1986), pp. 93–97, 216–217.
113. On the politics leading up to "No Child Left Behind" see Spring, *Political Agendas ...*
114. The National Commission on Educational Reform, *Report by the National Commission on Educational Reform, December 22, 2000*, Official Government Web site for the Prime Minister of Japan and His Cabinet, http://www.kantei.go.jp/foreign/index-e.html., p. 2. Retrieved on April 6, 2005.
115. Ibid., p. 2.
116. Ministry of Education, "Educational Reform: Education Reform Plan for the 21st Century," Official Government Web site for the Japanese Ministry of Education http://www.mext.go.jp/english/org/. Retrieved on April 25, 2005.
117. Eriko Arita, "Education Expert Calls for Radical Reforms," *Japan Times on the Web*, http://www.japantimes.co.jp/cgi-bin/makeprfy.pl5?nn20010724b5.htm. Retrieved on April 25, 2005.
118. The National Commission on Educational Reform, p. 1.
119. Ibid., p. 4.
120. Ibid., p. 1.
121. Ibid., p. 3.
122. Ibid., p. 10.
123. Kathy Emery and Susan Ohanian, *Why is Corporate America Bashing Our Schools?* (Portsmouth, NH: Heinemann, 2004); Susan Ohanian, *One Size Fits Few: The Folly of Educational Standards* (Portsmouth, NH: Heinemann, 1999); Alfie Kohn, *The Case Against Standardized Testing: Raising the Scores, Ruining the Schools* (Portsmouth, NH: Heinemann, 2000); and Peter Sacks, *Standardized Minds: The High Price of America's Testing Culture and What We Can Do to Change It* (New York: Perseus Publishing, 2001).
124. The National Commission on Educational Reform, p. 3.
125. Ibid., p. 5.
126. Ibid., p. 7.
127. Ibid., p. 18.
128. Press Release, "Character Education Grants Awarded," (Washington, DC: U.S. Department of Education, September 29, 2003), http://www.ed.gov/news/pressreleases/2003/09/09292003.html.

129. See George W. Bush, *On God and Country* edited by Thomas Freiling (Washington, DC: Allegiance Press, Inc, 2004).

130. The major statement of the ideology of compassionate conservatism can be found in Marvin Olasky, *Renewing American Compassion* (Washington, DC: Regenery, 1997). An example of the relationship between religious values and "No Child Left Behind" can be found in the document from the U.S. Department of Education, "No Child Left Behind and Faith-Based Leaders: Working Together So All Children Succeed" (Washington, DC: US Government Printing Office, 2004), http://www.ed.gov/nclb/freedom/faith/leaders.pdf.

131. On the controversy about historical interpretations to be included in American textbooks and curricula see Catherine Cornbleth & Dexter Waugh, *The Great Speckled Bird: Multicultural Politics and Education Policymaking* (Mahwah, NJ: Lawrence Erlbaum Associates, 1995). For an American neo-conservative guide to textbooks see Diane Ravitch, *A Consumer's Guide to High School History Textbooks* (Washington, DC: Fordham Institute, 2004).

132. Arthur M. Schlesinger, Jr., *The Disuniting of America* (Knoxville, TN: Whittle Direct Books, 1991), p. 8.

133. *No Child Left Behind Act of 2001 ...*, p. 243.

134. Ibid., p. 559.

135. Ibid., p. 560.

136. Ibid., pp. 201, 226.

137. Ibid., p. 230.

138. "Gov't oks nationalist text; sex slavery glossed over (6 April 2005)," *Japan Today* http://www.japantoday.com/. Retrieved on April 26, 2005.

139. "Ehime give go-ahead on use of controversial text (15 August 2002)," *Mainichi Shimbun* http://mdn.mainichi.co.jp/. Retrieved on April 26, 2005.

140. "Japan's right-wing textbook is teaching material by negative example: Comment (6 April 2005)," *People's Daily Online* http://english.people.com.cn/. Retrieved on April 11, 2005.

141. "Plan to Teach U.S. History Is Said to Slight White Males," *New York Times*, 26 October 1994, p. B12.

142. Karen Diegmueller, "Revise History Standards, Two Panels Advise," *Education Week*, 18 October 1995, p. 11.

143. "Japan must 'face up to history,' China Wen says, (12 April 2005)," *The Globe and Mail* http://www.theglobeandmail.com/. Retrieved on April 12, 2005.

144. "Japan's Right-wing textbook ..."

145. "Gov't Oks Nationalist Text ..."

146. Ibid.

147. "Teachers urged to tell students to respect flag, anthem (6 March 2005)," *Japan Today* http://www.japantoday.com/. Retrieved on April 28, 2005.

148. "36 Tokyo teachers seek reversal of reprimands over anthem (6 April 2005)," *Japan Today* http://www.japantoday.com/. Retrieved on April 28, 2005.

149. "Board checked to see how loud students sang anthem (31 May 2004)," *Japan Today* http://www.japantoday.com/. Retrieved on April 28, 2005.

150. "Teacher warned for refusing to sing nat'l anthem (24 March 2005)," *Japan Today* http://www.japantoday.com/. Retrieved on April 28, 2005.

151. "Court rules against teacher refusing to play anthem on piano (December 4, 2003)," *Japan Today* http://www.japantoday.com/. Retrieved on April 28, 2005.

152. John Gehring, "States Weigh Bills to Stoke Students' Patriotism (27 March 2002)," *Education Week Online* http://www.edweek.org/. Retrieved April 18, 2005.

153. Rhea R. Borja, "Pledge of Allegiance in the Legal Spotlight (10 July 2002)," *Education Week Online* http://www.edweek.org/. Retrieved April 18, 2005.

154. "Unpatriotic Russian Youth as Dangerous as Terrorism-Duma Official (3 March 2005)," *Mosnews* http://ww.mosnews.com/. Retrieved on April 20, 2005.

155. "Russia to Instill Youth with Patriotism Through War, Video Games (2 November 2004)," *Mosnews* http://ww.mosnews.com/. Retrieved on April 20, 2005.

156. C.J. Chivers, "Russia will Pursue Democracy, but in Its Own Way, Putin Says (26 Spring 2005)," *The New York Times on the Web* http://www.nytimes.com/. Retrieved on April 26, 2005.

157. See Anthony Jones, "The Educational Legacy of the Soviet Period," in *Education and Society in the New Russia* edited by Anthony Jones (Armonk, NY: M.E. Sharpe, 1994), pp.3–23.

158. See Stephen T. Kerr, "Diversification in Russian Education," Ibid., pp. 47–75.

159. Russian Constitution http://www.departments.bucknell.edu/russian/const/ch2.html. Retrieved on April 18, 2005.

160. Oksana Yablokova, "Education System to Get a Financial Boost, (31 August 2001)," *St. Petersburg Times* http://www.sptimesrussia.com/. Retrieved on April 26, 2005.

161. Chivers, "Russia will Pursue Democracy...."

162. Yablokova, "Education System...."

163. "Hundreds Protest Standardized Exam (31 May 2004)," *Mosnews* http://ww.mosnews.com/. Retrieved on April 20, 2005.

164. Irina Titova, "Education Plans Meet National Protests (2 March 2001)," *St. Petersburg Times* http://www.sptimesrussia.com/. Retrieved on April 26, 2005.

165. "Hundreds Protest Standardized Exam...."

166. Yablokova, "Education System...."

167. "Russia Returning to Ways of Stalin (4 April 2005)," *Mosnews* http://ww.mosnews.com/. Retrieved on April 20, 2005.

168. Ibid.

169. "This is Civicus, About Civicus, Our Mission," http://www.civicus.org/. Retrieved on May 16, 2005.

170. The Commission is the politically independent institution that represents and upholds the interests of the EU as a whole. It is the driving force within the EU's institutional system: it proposes legislation, policies and programs of action and it is responsible for implementing the decisions of Parliament and the Council.

171. Commission of the European Communities, "Communication from the Commission, Mobilizing the Brainpower of Europe: Enabling Universities to Make Their Full Contribution to the Lisbon Strategy," (Brussels: The European Commission, April 4, 2005).

172. Directorate-General for Education and Culture, *Education and Training in Europe: Diverse Systems, Shared Goals for 2010* (Luxembourg: Office for Official Publications of the European Communities, 2002), p. 7.

173. Quoted in Joel Spring, *Education and the Rise of the Global Economy* (Mahwah, NJ: Lawrence Erlbaum Associates, 1998), p. 97. Chapter 4 of this book provides a pre-21st century analysis of education and the EU.

174. Directorate-General for Education and Culture, *Education and Training in Europe ...*, p. 7.

175. Ibid, p. 12.

176. Ibid, p. 14.

177. Quoted in Joel Spring, *Education and the Rise of the Global Economy ...*, p. 110.

178. Ibid., p. 110.

179. Ibid., p. 108.

180. Directorate-General for Education and Culture, *Education and Training in Europe ...*, p. 16.

181. Ibid., p. 17.

182. Commission of the European Communities, "Annex to the: Communication from the Commission, Mobilizing the Brainpower of Europe: Enabling Universities to Make Their Full Contribution to

the Lisbon Strategy, European Higher Education in a Worldwide Perspective," (Brussels: The European Commission, April 4, 2005), p. 23.

183. Directorate-General for Education and Culture, *Education and Training in Europe* ..., p. 17.
184. Ibid., p. 19.
185. Ibid., p. 19.
186. Ibid., p. 19.
187. Ibid., p. 19.
188. Commission of the European Communities, "Annex to the: Communication from the Commission, Mobilizing the Brainpower of Europe ...," p. 4.
189. Ibid., p. 17.
190. Ibid., p. 17.
191. Ibid., p. 17.
192. Ibid., pp. 14–15.
193. Ibid., p. 17.
194. Commission Staff Working Paper, "Progress Towards the Lisbon Objectives in Education and Training, 2005 Report, (Brussels: Commission of the European Communities, March 22, 2005)," p. 12.
195. Ibid., p. 12.
196. Ibid., p. 5.
197. Ibid., p. 6.
198. Quoted in Spring, *Education and the Rise* ..., p. 101.
199. Directorate-General for Education and Culture, *Education and Training in Europe* ..., p. 29.
200. Commission Staff Working Paper, "Progress Towards the Lisbon Objectives ...," p. 6.
201. Communication from the Commission to the Council, the European Parliament, the Economic and Social Committee and the Committee of the Regions, "Promoting Language Learning and Linguistic Diversity: An Action Plan 2004–2006," (Brussels: Commission of the European Communities, August 24, 2003), p. 7.
202. Ibid., p. 4.
203. Ibid., p. 8.

CHAPTER 8

1. I walked Singapore's Orchard Road several times while participating in the conference "Redesigning Pedagogy: Research, Policy and Practice" held at the Centre for Research in Pedagogy & Prac-

tice National Institute of Education, Nanyang Technological University, Singapore from May 30 to June 1, 2005.

2. David Barboza, "China, New Land of Shoppers, Builds Malls on Gigantic Scale," *New York Times on the Web* (25 May 2005) retrieved on May 26, 2005.

3. Allan Luke is Dean of the National Institute of Education, Nanyang Technological University, Singapore.

4. Tharman Shanmugaratnam, Minister of Education, "Message," *International Conference on Education, Redesigning Pedagogy: Research, Policy, Practice* (Singapore: National Institute of Education, Nanyang Technological University, 2005), p. 5.

5. Leo Tan, "Message," *International Conference on Education …*, p. 7.

6. See Joel Spring, chapter 3, "Singapore: Schooling for Economic Growth," *Education and the Rise of the Global Economy* (Mahwah, NJ: Lawrence Erlbaum Associates, 1998), pp. 70–92 and chapter 1, "Nationalist Education in the Age of Globalization: Global Workers Carrying Their Nations in Their Hearts," *How Educational Ideologies are Shaping Global Society: Intergovernmental Organizations, NGOs, and the Decline of the Nation-State* (Mahwah, NJ: Lawrence Erlbaum Associates, 2004), pp. 1–28.

7. S. Gopinathan, "Globalization, the Singapore Developmental State and Education Policy: A Thesis Revisited," (Singapore: Centre for Research in Pedagogy and Practice, National Institute of Education, Nanyang Technological University, 2005), p. 10. Also see S. Gopinathan, "Preparing for the Next Rung: Economic Restructuring and Educational Reform in Singapore," *Journal of Education Work*, Vol. 12, No. 3, 1999.

8. See Spring, *How Educational Ideologies are Shaping Global Society …*, pp. 13–27.

9. Viniti Vaish, "A Periherist View of English as a Language of Decolonization in Post-Colonial India," *Language Policy* Volume 4, No 2, 2005 (I received a proof copy before numbering was applied in journal).

10. Ibid., p. 11.

11. Sohail Karmani and Alastair Pennycook, "Islam, English, and 9/11," *Journal of Language, Identity, and Education* Volume 4, Number 2, 2005, p. 158.

12. Ibid., p. 158.

13. Karmani and Pennycook, pp. 157–172.

14. Ibid., p. 161.

15. Ibid., p. 163.

16. Ibid., p. 160.

17. Ibid., p. 161.

18. Tariq Rahman, "The Muslim Response to English in South Asia: With Special Reference to Inequality, Intolerance, and Militancy in Pakistan," *Journal of Language, Identity, and Education* Volume 4, Number 2, 2005, p. 127.

19. Ibid., p. 132.

20. Vaudine England, "Defining a Malaysian Identity," *International Herald Tribune* (7 June 2005), p. 1.

21. Ibid., p. 6.

22. Ratnawati Mohd-Asraf , "English and Islam: A Clash of Civilizations?" *Journal of Language, Identity, and Education* Volume 4, Number 2, 2005, p. 111.

23. Ibid., pp. 112–113.

24. Thomas Clayton, "Language Choice In A Nation Under Transition: The Struggle Between English and French in Cambodia," *Language Policy* Volume 1, Number 1, 2002, pp. 3–25.

25. Ibid., p. 4.

26. Ibid., p. 4.

27. Ibid., pp. 5–7.

28. Ibid., p. 16.

29. Ibid., p. 21.

30. Ministry of Education, Culture, Sports, Science and Technology, Press Release, "Developing a strategic plan to cultivate 'Japanese with English Abilities'" (12 July 2002), http://www.mext.go.jp/english/. Retrieved on April 5, 2005.

31. Ibid.

32. Ibid.

33. Yuko Goto Butler and Masakazu Iino, "Current Japanese Reforms in English Language Education: The 2003 'Action Plan,'" *Language Policy* Volume 4, Number 1 (2005), p. 28.

34. Ibid., p. 28.

35. Ibid., pp. 28–29.

36. Ibid., pp. 25–26.

37. Ibid., p. 39.

38. See Joel Spring, *The American School 1642–2004 Sixth Edition* (New York: McGraw-Hill, 2005), pp. 421–428, 461–463.

39. "Defense Department Takes the Offense On Languages," *Education Week* (8 June 2005), p. 12.

40. Ibid.

41. Ibid.

42. Guangwei Hu, "English Language Education in China: Policies, Progress, and Problems," *Language Policy,* Volume 4, Number 1 (2005), p. 8.

43. Ibid., p. 16.

44. Elissa Moses, *The $100 Billion Allowance: Accessing the Global Teen Market* (New York: John Wiley & Sons, Inc. 2000), pp. 4, 10–11.
45. See Joel Spring, *Educating the Consumer-Citizen: A History of the Marriage of Schools, Advertising, and Media* (Mahwah, NJ: Lawrence Erlbaum Associates, 2003).
46. Spring, *How Educational Ideologies are Shaping Global Society* ...
47. Ibid., pp. 66–164.
48. For details on these types of progressive educational programs see Spring, *How Educational Ideologies Are Shaping Global Society* ...

Author Index

Subject Index